*New Perspectives on Property and Land
in the Middle East*

HARVARD MIDDLE EASTERN MONOGRAPHS

XXXIV

New Perspectives on Property and Land in the Middle East

EDITED BY

Roger Owen

WITH CONTRIBUTIONS BY

Martin Bunton, Huri Islamoglu, Denise Jorgens
Martha Mundy, Abdul-Karim Rafeq,
Birgit Schaebler, Amy Singer

DISTRIBUTED FOR THE
CENTER FOR MIDDLE EASTERN STUDIES
OF HARVARD UNIVERSITY BY
HARVARD UNIVERSITY PRESS
CAMBRIDGE, MASSACHUSETTS
LONDON, ENGLAND

Contents

Preface

This volume is the product of two workshops on Land and Land Records that took place at the Center for Middle Eastern Studies at Harvard in the spring of 1995 and 1996. The workshops had two distinct aims. The first was to bring together scholars who were working on primary sources connected with land and land registration to allow them to compare notes on problems connected with the documents they use. The second was to take a more general look at the state of the art as far as thinking and research about questions of landed property in the Middle East were concerned. The result is something of a collective effort with an important role being played by those who attended the workshop discussions but whose papers are not presented here. The book includes one additional paper by someone not present at the workshops, Dr. Birgit Schaebler, a visiting scholar at the Center for Middle Eastern Studies, 1997 to 1998 and 1998 to 1999.

The papers published here represent work in progress. Their aim is not only to illustrate some of the types of present-day research together with the methods and problems involved but also to suggest new avenues for future examination. I should note, too, that our original intention was to add an appendix with illustrations of some of the actual primary sources. But this turned out to be a difficult and expensive project and must wait for another day.

As far as the system of Arabic and Ottoman Turkish transliteration is concerned, consistency is confined to the individual chapter, not to the volume as a whole.

I would like to take this occasion to thank all those who helped me with the organization of the workshops and also to thank Margaret Owen for her thoughtful editing and rigorous proofreading.

June 1999   Roger Owen

Introduction

Roger Owen

Land was the major economic resource in the premodern Middle East as it was almost everywhere else in the world. It provided the most important part of the livelihood of the bulk of the population and a large share of each government's taxes. As a result, questions of ownership, land management, and control over access to the agricultural surplus—as well as the settlement of the fierce disputes that inevitably followed—occupied a central role in administration, in law, and in rural practice over the centuries. It also meant that any change in the land regime would have significant repercussions at all levels of society—from the villages, where communal access to land was deeply embedded in local social relations, to the relative positions of the aristocratic, military, and religious elite.

All this is well known but has also been much neglected by Middle Eastern historians. To speak very generally, studies of ownership and landed property have been dogged, until very recently, by three great problems. First, they have tended to be framed almost exclusively in terms of Islamic legal categories that often bear little relationship to actual practice. Second, they generally assume a simple, unilinear progress from premodern to modern (Western) forms of property and private ownership. Third, they tend to translate Arabic and Turkish terms uncritically into their supposed equivalents in a predominantly European legal vocabulary.

This volume contains an implied, and occasionally, explicit critique of such an approach. Like all good critiques it also attempts to provide an alternative based on a new interpretation of a wide variety of primary material, ranging from the official laws to the micropractices to be found in the records involving registration, disputes, and transfers at the village level. Its main focus is on the process of transformation ushered in by the Ottoman and Egyptian Land Codes of 1858, but it also contains issues relating to sixteenth-century *awqaf* (Singer) and to the administrative interventions of the colonial period (Bunton and part of Schaebler).

However, before introducing the seven studies, I would like to set out a view of land and land management that I have found useful. It has the advantage of cutting through many of the difficulties that accompany the traditional approach based on Islamic legal categories. It can also be used to highlight, but certainly not to solve, many of the particular problems posed by the introduction of new categories and new practices concerning recording and registration during the nineteenth century, when attempts by the Ottoman and Egyptian governments to impose their single claim on the land and its surplus were negotiated, contested, and amended in many different sites and by many different social actors. As the various contributors to this volume skillfully demonstrate, the sheer variety of this experience, and the fact that only a few of the sites where it took place have been properly explored, prevents the creation of a new, and more coherent, analytical approach at this particularly historical moment. For the present all we can do is to follow John Locke's example when he likened philosophical practice to that of a "humble under-gardener" clearing away the accumulated weeds, the better to see the real difficulties inherent in understanding the profusion of hidden plants now revealed before us.

My own approach is based on the observation of Tusun Aricanli and Mara Thomas that the Ottoman/Islamic system as it existed until the mid-nineteenth century was one in which two distinct groups exercised rights over the land and its produce.[1] The first is what they call a "stratum" of claimants to the agricultural surplus—that is, the persons conventionally described as tax farmers. As they also note of the Anatolian context, members of this stratum bear some superficial resemblance to Western European landlords. But, in fact, they were neither as independent of political power as was the case in the West, nor did their claims constitute anything like claims to ownership of the land itself. Furthermore, their competition for access to the surplus took place within the realms of state practice without challenging the authority of the central power to manage the land regime as it saw fit. In other words, they sought only that share of state revenue that might accrue to them as a result of their own privileged position within the state apparatus. Finally, this was not a situation in which claims to the surplus could either be institutionalized or systematically regenerated. It follows that so-called state ownership of land must be seen in practice not as ownership per se but as a monopoly over the right to distribute access to share in the surplus and, by extension, to prevent any obstacle to its proper use.

The second group contained those people (usually referred to as peasants or cultivators) who made the actual production decisions and who worked the land themselves. Unlike the members of the first stratum, some of them managed to obtain quite clearly defined property rights—for example, as a result of either their improvements to the land itself or their investment in buildings and trees. They might also establish their entitlement to pass on their usufructuary rights to their heirs or to sell or to mortgage them to others. This was a situation in which, according to Aricanli and Thomas, the usufructuary right itself could also be considered as a "major form of private property" because it was always "protected by the state."[2]

Two results would seem to follow. First, the Aricanli/Thomas schema provides us with good reason to begin our investigations not with the notion of property itself but via the twin notions of access to land and access to its surplus and thence to the many different ways in which this was organized in different Middle Eastern geographical and administrative contexts. Second, by positing the existence of a two-tier system before the modern period, it also suggests that one important method of investigating the mid-nineteenth-century process of transformation is to examine the different ways in which the two tiers of rights—the right of access to the land and the right to its surplus—collapsed into one another to create a single right to both land and surplus that over time came to be regarded as much the same as the right to individual private property.

As far as the first case is concerned, the study of what little we do know about Middle Eastern rights of access would suggest that, by the beginning of the nineteenth century, we are looking at another pair of distinct though related spheres. The first involves the more marginal areas of cultivated land where the general outlines of the local allocative mechanisms are immediately apparent. Such areas could include new lands, frontier land (which often meant the same as new land), lands with shifting patterns of cultivation as in Lower Iraq, or flooded land where field boundaries had to be reestablished on an annual basis.[3] While the exact nature of the process of allocation is generally unclear, it seems that it usually involved the division of the land among the members of the village or tribe or group on the basis of a capacity to cultivate, usually defined in terms of manpower, animals, or plows. It was subsequently redistributed at shorter or longer intervals, sometimes for reasons of equity, at others so as to be able to accommodate newcomers to the community. Schaebler also suggests that, where such systems involved the allocation of individual parcels in more than one section of the total cultivated area, this answered the needs of communal self-protection against marauders since all the cultivators would be working on one particular section of the village land at any one time.[4]

The second situation is much more complex and relates to land that had been in permanent cultivation for a much longer period of time and to rights of access to individual plots that had obtained certain propertylike characteristics such as continuity, the right of transfer, and so on, supported by custom, by regular practice or state policy, and by their congruence with certain local interpretations of Islamic law. This would be true of Lower Egypt, Mount Lebanon, and Anatolia, as well as, perhaps, the lands immediately surrounding important centers of urban administration.

Nevertheless, it is important to note that however much such rights might have hardened over time, they had to be exercised in a context of limited resources, sudden misfortunes, and the recognition that certain agricultural tasks could be undertaken only in common. It is also possible to argue that a key role in the whole process of land allocation remained with the local community, using local mechanisms to mediate the changing balance between village land and labor, particularly in terms of Mundy's "roulette of biological reproduction," which inevitably dealt different hands to different local families in terms of the numbers of births, length of working life, and death and so affected their ability to continue to cultivate their plots by maintaining a stable male labor force over time.[5] Given the fact that villages remained the defining units as far as taxation and the award of new lands were concerned, this too must have influenced both the decisions made and the role played by village opinion in the settlement of the inevitable disputes.[6]

Finally, to return to the question of the collapse of the two tiers as a result of processes set in train by both the Ottoman and Egyptian land laws, this apparently simple notion breaks down in reality into a myriad different situations and outcomes depending on a whole host of factors—some administrative, some relating to the balance between local forces, some on the nature of the land itself. By and large, it is best seen as a process of negotiation between state and society in which the general aim of the former to establish individual title to each piece of land, as well as its introduction of new practices of registration, categorization, and measurement, had to be brought into some new configuration with existing systems of land allocation and management and the social relations that they embodied. To make the matter more complicated still, this same process was interrupted by World War I and then resumed in the quite different political conditions created by the British and French mandates and the emergence of independent Turkish and Egyptian states.

The four chapters in Part One deal with different aspects of the process just described. Even given the fact that the authors approach it from their own separate perspectives, theirs was no easy task. The sources themselves are often difficult to understand, while the meaning and logic of the changing rural reality they illustrate are even more difficult to grasp and then to explain. As a result their papers must be taken largely as a first effort to delineate the field, to conceptualize the changing relationship between state and society where landed property was concerned, and to provide some indication of the wide range of possible trajectories and outcomes as these new relationships were worked out in the different parts of the Ottoman empire through the late nineteenth and early twentieth centuries.

Huri Islamoglu begins by trying to situate the transformation of rural property relations within the larger context of changing state power that took place in the Ottoman empire, as well as the rest of Europe, once policies of internal consolidation had largely replaced those of territorial expansion from the eighteenth century onward. Prior to this moment, she describes the Ottomans as governing a "distributive-accommodative" state in which definitions and classifications of property rights represented the differentiated and particularistic claims to a share of the tax revenues by different groups. In the nineteenth century, however, the administration sought to establish its own, singular, claim to such revenues to the exclusion of all other entitlements. This in turn, she argues, released rural land from a "web" of revenue claims, allowing it to be constituted as a legally recognized object and so as property to be improved by its individual owner, who was now directly responsible to the state for payment of tax.

Islamoglu then makes the important point that this change in the ordering of property relations was not undertaken, as it was in Western Europe, in the name of the sanctity of private property. Nor can it be analyzed in terms developed from European experience where such changes were conceived of as taking place within the separate sphere of the economy and so divorced from day-to-day political practice. Rather, the historian has to recognize the highly contentious and conflictual nature of the claims to ownership that were deployed at this time in the Ottoman empire and the way these, in turn, reflected the different sets of power relations that existed between the state and various social groups.

All this is amply illustrated not only in the text of the 1858 Ottoman Land Code but also, in Islamoglu's argument, in the attempt to implement it in the various different regions of the empire. For one thing, although the general aims of the code were reasonably clear, the text itself was, of necessity, highly qualified, reflecting, as it did, the problematic nature of the attempt to codify rights in a context in which the state was anxiously pursuing such potentially contradictory aims as the award of individual rights, the protection of the interests of the peasant population, and the maintenance of a legitimating idiom based on its role as the distributor of justice. For another, as her study of the process in the Yanya district (now part of present-day Albania) reveals, the inevitable tension between the text of the new code and its actual implementation led to the creation of a commission that awarded ownership to the existing estate holders but restricted in such a way as to provide their tenants with certain safeguards concerning the open-ended nature of their tenancy and the maintenance of existing rents. This she interprets as the recognition of the absolute right of property based not on the French notion of the "religion" of property rights but on a new understanding of the nature of state power as representing a system of ordering, classifying, and then organizing social relations.

Martha Mundy approaches the process of implementing the same code in what is now northern Jordan from quite the opposite direction: that is, she begins with the practice itself—deriving her categories of analysis from an interrogation of the local records—before going on to draw some general conclusions about the larger meanings involved. Here we see a very detailed example of the multidimensional process of producing a single claim to land in the context of two particular village communities. We see how it involved new categories, new terminologies, and new administrative procedures, all of which had to be brought in to some sort of relationship with local practices as understood and interpreted by those with specific local knowledge. We are shown a long process of negotiation over many years, as well as the large number of different actors from different institutions—such as the village assembly and the district council—each with new possibilities and often new skills for advancing their personal or collective interests. We see how, out of this, there emerged new practices and new understandings, all of which were open, in their turn, to fresh negotiation and contestation. The result is a model that is both comprehensive and subtle enough to be used to analyze as many other regions of the Ottoman empire as local records allow.

Mundy then places her analysis within the larger context of what she calls "political administration," where the main institutions and practices concerned with law, tax collection, security, and communal representation in these and other rural districts were recast within a new administrative order based on the general principles of individual subjecthood and tax liability that underpinned the new order of Ottoman government in its closing years. At a more general level still, what she is examining and recording is a process that she rightly calls the "making of property relations," which she goes on to characterize as one of the essential features of the modern state.

A third approach, adopted by Denise Jorgens, is to try to infer intent or purpose from the text of the nineteenth-century land laws themselves, including a comparison with the text of those laws that they replaced or that were introduced in adjacent parts of the Ottoman empire. As her close analysis of the Egyptian Land Code of 1858 shows, this was the culmination of a series of attempts to deal with a process of radical social change in the rural areas during the Muhammad Ali period when the combined impact of conscription, increased taxation, and the creation of large estates had forced many peasants off land that they and their families may have worked for many generations. The result was an explosion of claims often based, as Kenneth Cuno has noted, not on an appeal to law but on the strong belief that prior occupancy gave rights that needed no further justification.[7] This was something with which, again in Cuno's argument, neither the local courts nor an agrarian regime striving to maximize the productive use of land was able to cope.[8]

The 1858 Land Code attempted two things. First, it sought to stabilize the existing pattern of possession by making it more difficult for those claiming prior or customary right. Hence, anyone possessing *miri* land for more than five years and having paid the required taxes could not have it taken away. In other words, as Jorgens rightly points out, "no further claims would be accepted." More generally, in all cases of disputed rights, the law favored the present possessor. Second, the procedures set out in the law took away much of the responsibility for dealing with such disputes from both the local shaykhs and lower-level courts by placing it firmly in the hands of the central administration and the higher courts directly under its control. For example, only the latter now had the right to issue legal title deeds. This ensured that the consent of the state was required for all new transactions.

How this all fits into the larger context of change in the rights to land and its revenues remains a matter for argument and interpretation. I have suggested that one way of looking at it is as a process by which the separate levels of access to land and to its revenue became conflated in a single notion of individual ownership. In the Egyptian version, the state, having taken over the right of surplus collection from the old tax farmers, then seeks to regularize its access to a share of this same surplus based on the award to individual title. Others, like Islamoglu, would place more stress on the highly contested nature of this process, in which different social groups, using different idioms to express their interests and concerns, negotiate the passage toward a singular right of control over a single object—that is, land defined no longer as a system of claims but as a particular piece of ground, within the larger and more general process of the creation of the modern nation state.

The final paper in Part One, by Martin Bunton, addresses the equally intriguing question of how the new rural order established in late Ottoman times was used, understood (or deliberately misunderstood), and then amended by the British mandatory government in Palestine. Once again the mix is a complex one and full of tension. There was the attempt to provide some legitimation for the British presence by the argument that jurisdiction should be exercised in conformity with the Ottoman/Islamic laws in force at the time of the outbreak of war on 1 November 1914.[8] There was the introduction of new European assumptions about the importance of private property and its close link with economic and social development. There were the facts on the ground arising not only from particular Palestinian practice but also from the administrative necessities of colonial rule including the promises made to the League of Nations to encourage the establishment of a Jewish national home. And, finally, there was the essential tension that stood at the root of all modernist reform—whether in the late Ottoman empire or in the European empires—between the often contradictory aims of encouraging private ownership of land while also protecting the rights of sitting tenants.

It is possible to address such questions in general, as Bunton does, through an analysis of the twists and turns of colonial land policy beginning with the rejection of the Land Transfer Ordinance of 1920. They can also be addressed (often with more satisfying result) by looking at the way the tensions outlined above worked themselves out in particular instances, in this case with reference to the regulation of land rights in two so-called *çiftlik*s, former estates of the Ottoman Sultan 'Abd al-Hamid II. The comparison is instructive. While in the first case, that of the Beisan estate in northeast Palestine, the mandatory government was led to give ownership rights to the former Sultan's tenants in 1921, ten years later it gave no such rights to other tenants in the *çiftlik* villages of Sajad and Qazaza. At play in both cases was a complex mixture of considerations, some political, some economic, some focused directly on the role of the mandatory state itself. At play too were different possible interpretations of Ottoman legal categories, as well as the particular gloss that the British tended to put on such notions as "customary" or "prescriptive" practice and "state land."

The three papers in Part Two provide a more discrete analysis of three other topics that must form part of any comprehensive treatment of rights to rural land: the management of *awqaf* land, the status of non-Muslim outsiders (later "foreigners") when it came to land ownership, and the nature of what, in the colonial period, came to be designated as *musha'*, or the system of communal cultivation underpinned by the distribution and redistribution of village lands, in parts of what became southern Syria and northern Palestine and Jordan.

Amy Singer's account of the status and administration of certain imperial Ottoman *awqaf* in and around Jerusalem in the sixteenth century is particularly valuable not only for its detail but also for the way in which it challenges strongly held conventional assumptions concerning its inevitable bad management from an economic point of view. As she is able to demonstrate, administrators used many ways to maximize returns from such land—for example, by adding new land to it or by exchanging part of it for other, more remunerative, lands elsewhere. Furthermore, as these administrators were men of considerable means, they had every interest in preventing the *waqf* properties they managed from acting as a constant drain on their own resources. For all these reasons it is proper to assume that, in the sixteenth century, at least, *awqaf* land should be considered first and foremost in terms of its place within the rural economy even if, as far as the administrators were concerned, questions of personal status and of the religiously sanctioned services they provided must also have been a significant consideration. And if this was true of one century, it seems reasonable to assume that it was at least partially true of later centuries as well.

The question of "foreign" ownership of real property, both landed and urban, is addressed by Abdul-Karim Rafeq in an intensive study of the relevant Syrian court records. To do this he first has to address the question of who or what was a "foreigner," a difficult category to establish in the mid-nineteenth-century Ottoman empire but a category that was absolutely essential to create when it came to the registration of individual title under the 1858 Land Code. There were, in fact, various categories that need to be taken into consideration: non-Muslim Ottoman, on the one hand, and either subject or "protégé," of a "friendly foreign state," on the other. In the first case, proper identity was to be established by the head of the prospective purchaser's religious community; in the latter, after foreign ownership had been legalized by the law of June 1867, by the appropriate foreign consulate.

As Rafeq points out, it is not known for certain how many protégés in Syria in the 1860s had gone on to obtain foreign nationality. However, he can demonstrate not only the existence of sales of property to both Europeans and local persons with foreign nationality but also the way in which these sales were facilitated by other protégés and foreign nationals who worked for the European consulates. Another important discovery is that the overwhelming proportion of foreign purchasers of property in and around Damascus in the early 1870s were either local Christians or Jews, of whom about half had managed to obtain Austrian nationality and just over a third French. This, in turn, gave them important advantages over Ottoman citizens when it came to exemption from certain taxes and other privileges. It may also have helped them to extend their original rights—for example, the right first to rent *waqf* land and then, if they improved it, to own it outright. Nevertheless, for all the local significance of foreign nationality, as well as its ability to exacerbate local tensions, the numbers involved, as Rafeq points out, were not large. The British consulate in Damascus contained only forty-eight protected males in 1870.

In the last paper, Birgit Schaebler examines the practice of distributing access to village lands in terms of the microhistory of three adjacent districts of the Hawran in southern Syria during the nineteenth and early twentieth centuries. There, title to the bulk of a village's arable land was held in common in undivided shares, with each share entitling its holder to work plots in all of the several sections into which the land was divided for the purpose of day-to-day cultivation. Meanwhile, the shares were awarded to village members according to a variety of different criteria: for example, the number of plows or oxen or males of working age. To make matters still more complicated, some villages seem to have practiced a system (which Firestone has labeled "open-ended") in which newcomers who possessed the means to work land were given shares of their own while other villages did not. Schaebler presents historical material that provides examples of many of the possible permutations involved.[9]

However, of more immediate concern to her argument is not the actual process of distribution and redistribution as such but the way it can be seen to express, as well as to reflect, status and power relations within the community. Looked at from this perspective, the geographical setting itself is all-important. This includes the nature and quality of the land, the pattern of settlement, and the relations of its inhabitants to local centers of power. The fact that the Hawran was always something of a frontier region with a long history of conflict, population movement, and new settlement was also of the greatest significance. In such areas, local management of access to land was crucial, as was the close linkage between the methods of distributing both such access and the associated tax burden. A final factor was the presence in the highlands of the Hawran of a predominantly Druze population with a form of sociopolitical organization that combined communal solidarity with marked hierarchical features very different from that of the Sunni Muslim inhabitants of the plains. At the village level, for example, the shaykh of the ruling clan was responsible for local defense, the distribution of taxes, the decision whether to admit newcomers, and the organization of labor, in terms of which section was to be worked on any particular day. In return, he received the right to a quarter of the shares and so to a quarter of the total land.

The final part of Schaebler's analysis concerns the way this system was affected by the great changes resulting from the centralization policies of the Ottomans, the spread of market relations, and then the arrival of the French in the early 1920s. All this was productive of regular revolts as well as a change in relations between the Druze peasants and their shaykhs, notably the powerful al-Atrash clan, which, in Schaebler's words, began to "colonize" the southern parts of the Hawran highlands at the end of the nineteenth century. Much of this turmoil, as always, had its roots in a struggle over land. Particular bones of contention were the way in which the Atrash seem to have abused the system of the redistribution of shares to their own advantage and the fact that, as a result of their build-up of local power, many villagers began to lose access to village land. All this was actively resisted in a variety of ways leading to the mass revolt known as the *'ammiyya* in 1889 and 1890.

The last chapter in this story is provided by the French, who, having begun like the British in Palestine with the intention of stabilizing the distribution of village lands by giving individual title to each particular plot, ended up with a general policy of registering only shares to common land without specifying which actual pieces of land they referred to. In the Hawran, however, the widespread revolt of 1925 to 1927 seems to have put a stop to even such a limited process of intervention, and the shaykhs and villagers were left to sort out a new relationship to power and land among themselves.

The value of such "on-the-ground" research, which combines an intimate knowledge of the terrain with a thorough study of the archival resources, is enormous. Fortunately for those who engage in such work, like Schaebler and Mundy, the transforming events of the late nineteenth century are still just within historical memory, thus making them available as an additional resource. By such methods we can begin to reach an understanding both of the major forces at work and of the huge number of different ways in which they interacted with more local interest before achieving more or less the same outcome: the creation of a new land regime based on individual title to what began to be conceived of as essentially private property.

To conclude: there are two ways of summing up the information presented by the seven papers presented in this volume. One is to say, truly, that they simply scratch the surface of a vast and still largely unexplored field of inquiry. But I believe that they also provide very good reason to support the more hopeful conclusion that they constitute both a necessary critique of existing analyses and the bare bones of a much more fruitful alternative approach. Through the links they establish between the general and the particular, the attention they pay to the necessary contradictions and inconsistencies that must always accompany the introduction of new rural orders, their notion of the central role of contestation and negotiation, and, finally, their insistence on the wide range of variables that have to be taken into account, they can be said to prove the utility of an approach that could be used to examine the same types of processes and problems anywhere within the Ottoman, and former Ottoman, empire.

NOTES

1. "Sidestepping Capitalism: On the Ottoman Road to Elsewhere," *Journal of Historical Sociology* 7, no. 1 (March 1994): 25–47.

2. Ibid., 34–35.
3. For example, Kenneth M. Cuno, *The Pasha's Peasants: Land, Society, and Economy in Lower Egypt, 1740–1858* (Cambridge: Cambridge University Press, 1992), 66; Albertine Jwaideh, "Aspects of Land Tenure and Social Change in Lower Iraq during Ottoman Times," in *Land Tenure and Social Transformation in the Near East,* ed. Tarif Khalidi (Beirut: American University of Beirut Press 1984), 334–38.
4. This volume, chap. 7.
5. Martha Mundy, "The Family Inheritance and Islamic Law: A Reexamination of the Sociology of Fara'id Law," in *Islamic Law: Social and Historical Contexts,* ed. Aziz Al-Azmeh (London: Routledge 1988), 52.
6. For example, ibid., 60; Abdul-Karim Rafeq, "Land Tenure Problems and Their Social Impact in Syria around the Middle of the Nineteenth Century," in Khalidi, *Land Tenure,* 390 ff.
7. Cuno, *The Pasha's Peasants,* 189–90.
8. Ibid., 190.
9. Ya'akov Firestone, "Crop-Sharing Economics in Mandatory Palestine," pts. 1–2, *Middle Eastern Studies* 11 (1975), 3–23, 175–94.

Part One

THE TRANSFORMATION OF PROPERTY RELATIONS FOLLOWING THE 1858 LAND LAWS

· ONE ·

Property as a Contested Domain: A Reevaluation of the Ottoman Land Code of 1858

Huri Islamoglu

This chapter studies the transformation of property rights on land in the Ottoman empire in the nineteenth century. My argument is that this transformation, that signaled the rise of private property rights, took place in relation to changes in the nature of state power. Put simply, I argue that the practices of a certain type of state that developed in the nineteenth century were largely responsible for the constitution of individual ownership rights. Of these practices, I concentrate on law, more specifically on the Land Code of 1858. The larger project of which this chapter is a part also focuses on the administrative practices of registration and of surveying of property. Second, I argue that property laws, as well as the state practices of registration and recording, represented spaces in which social actors confronted each other in negotiating the definitions and orderings that these practices made possible. That is, definitions of property rights represented domains of resistance and contestation imparting to these rights their highly contingent political and historical character.

3

CONCEPTUAL PARAMETERS

Implicit in the study of the transformation of property rights in the Ottoman empire undertaken here is a critique that extends in significance beyond the Ottoman example. This critique addresses a set of arguments regarding the development of private property, relations between state and society, as well as the relation of law to state and to society. These arguments, embodied in a discourse of liberalism and traceable to the work of the political economists and jurists of the eighteenth and nineteenth centuries, formed part of the world view of European middle classes in the era of liberal capitalism.[1] They have enjoyed a renaissance since the 1980s and are recast in debates on "growth through trade," "state and market," "globalization," "privatization," and "the rule of law," in relation to developments in the different world regions, most provocatively in the former socialist areas.

Central to the liberal perspective is the assumption that state and society constitute separate domains. Private property belongs to the societal domain; it is deemed to be the central institution of the market economy, which makes possible the exchangeability of resources, including land, labor, and goods in markets. There is, however, little agreement as to the origins of private property, and a tension between the historicist and the naturalist explanations has characterized debates around property since the seventeenth century.[2] The critique undertaken here primarily addresses the historicist orientation, which posits a causality between commercial expansion and the development of private property.[3] Confronted with increased opportunities for economic gain or changes in relative prices, maximizing individuals are expected to free what constitutes the object of property from juridical and administrative obstacles that restrict its free circulation.

Both commercial expansion and the rise of private property presuppose the absence of state intervention.[4] *State* refers, in the liberal conception, to the realm of politics, of particularistic, subjective interests; it stands in opposition to what are deemed to be universal and objective relations in the sphere of exchange. The characterization of economic relations as universal and objective derives from an understanding that individuals possess a natural propensity to maximize their gains and that their individual preferences constitute the patterns of supply and demand that achieve the most efficient allocation of resources. The state, on the other hand, is assigned the task of policing the market transactions of the profit-maximizing individuals.

Finally, bifurcation of law into private and public consecrates the oppositional relation between society and state. Private law, referring to the law of contracts (with definitions of legal subjects and objects) and formulations of private property in civil codes, is perceived as a formalization of what takes place in society, or the sphere of exchange, thus making possible certainty and predictability in market transactions.[5] Public law defines the administrative rules and procedures; most important, from a liberal perspective, it defines the rules of conduct of the state and, in doing so, subjects the state to the rule of law. The latter, imbued with an objectivity and institutional insularity and sanctity, stands apart from both the domains of policing and exchange.[6]

Formalization of the property relation in private law in the nineteenth century involved its definition as being a relation between a person (the legal owner or possessor of the right of ownership) and an asset or a "thing."[7] In relation to landed property, this suggested a juridical disentanglement of the individual right from the bundle of rights that previously constituted property. It entailed the legal constitution of land as a thing, alienable, disposable. Among other things, this presupposed the obliteration of the distinction between movable (goods) and immovable (land) property: land was rendered as transactable as any other commodity.[8] Casting of the property relation in terms of a person and an asset represents an objectification of that relation; its abstraction from the web of power relations that are constitutive of it. It signaled a rupture with previous representations of property relations in terms of entitlements and obligations of persons or groups that were inseparable from their status or their relations to each other in a hierarchically ordered society.

The liberal world view was inseparable from a vocabulary of European domination over non-European areas in the latter part of the nineteenth century and in the twentieth century. This vocabulary represents the dichotomous perception of social reality, which characterized the liberal perspective, and echoes the spatial bifurcation between Europe (the West) and non-Europe (the East). Thus, European history is cast as the privileged domain of exchange of private property, of circumscribed state presence, and of the rule of law.[9] Non-European history, by contrast, describes a sphere of stunted commercial development or economic stagnation, of despotic states, and of the absence of rule of law.

The history of the Ottoman empire has long been fashioned in the image of the East. Here, state intervention in society or economy, most dramatically manifested in the form of state "ownership" of land, was understood to be a feature of Ottoman despotism and has been held responsible for limited market activity, for the inability of private property to develop, and for the consequent absence of commercial classes, of a bourgeois revolution, of a liberal constitutional state, and of the rule of law.[10]

My intention here is not to indulge in the ifs and buts of this high drama of presences and absences and produce yet another revisionist history of the Ottoman empire. Instead, I propose to go beyond the binary perception of the Eastern and Western histories by problematizing the arguments on which this bifurcation rests.

Most important, I challenge the liberal discourse in its characterization of the development of private ownership. By confining this development to the "rational" responses of maximizing individuals engaged in exchange activities and to objectification of those responses in law, the liberal perspective abstracts private property from the power relations that were (and continue to be) constitutive of it. Power relations, however, do not exist in isolation, but are part of historical contexts. The centralized states that developed in Western Eurasia during the eighteenth and nineteenth centuries formed such a context. Military and political competition among states was largely responsible for the development of these states. This chapter argues that private ownership was an ordering of property relations on land by the centralized states; it was part of these states' attempt to establish absolute control over revenues from land to meet the exigencies of interstate competition. As such, private ownership belonged to the sphere of power relations that characterized the domination of centralized states.

Individual ownership represented an abstraction of the property of the individual from the web of multiple entitlements to revenues from land and from the diverse, shared claims over land use. In concrete terms, it meant, first, the establishment of the singular and general taxation claim to the exclusion of the multiple revenue entitlements of different groups. Second, it meant the definition of the absolute ownership of the title holder to the exclusion of the former claims to land use. As will be discussed in relation to the Ottoman example, resistance on the part of groups excluded by claims of private ownership accounted for the highly fluid character of property relations in the "age of property," as the nineteenth century has been succinctly described.[11] The perception of the property relation as one embedded in confrontations among groups or individuals stands in contrast to the liberal perception of it as an outcome of cost-benefit calculations on the part of maximizing individuals, objectified in law. It points to the character of the property relation as a power relation. In this respect, this chapter concurs with the Marxist critiques of the liberal understanding of the property relation as one between a person and a thing.[12] But it departs from these critiques where they subscribe to the precept of the separation of state and society and view the development of private property as an outcome of the struggles of commercial classes waged in the society. From the Marxist perspective, though with notable exceptions, both the state and law represent superstructures that rubber-stamp the outcomes of class struggles. By contrast, this chapter argues that private property was the result of an ordering on the part of centralized states and came about through the practices of the state, including administrative rulings or law, as well as registration, cadastral surveying, and mapping. Second, the chapter seeks to establish the sites of power relations or power struggles. The latter are not mere abstractions but take place in historically specific contexts, in relation to specific issues. State practices that ordered, or defined, property relations are contexts, or sites, of the confrontations among groups or individuals over property rights. They represent power fields. This chapter emphasizes not only the power relations that constituted private ownership but also the historical contexts[13] in which these power relations were engaged. I will argue that these contexts impart to the individual struggles their particular terminologies and vocabularies and, in so doing, to a large degree shape the actions, as well as the discourses, of both the propertied and the dispossessed. They form the political arena in which all actors have a chance of participation.

This chapter focuses on administrative law[14]—law as a form of governance—and points to the constitution of private ownership rights through the categories and systems of classification of the centralized state. It challenges the liberal position that state practices hinder the development of individual ownership and that autonomy of law is a precondition for that development.

First, contrary to the liberal understanding, law here is not viewed as a simple formalization of what has already taken place in the sphere of exchange. It is argued that law is constitutive of the relations it defines—that is, by defining the actual property claims or rights of persons or groups, law enables these rights. In this respect, this chapter subscribes to E. P. Thompson's view of law as being "deeply imbricated within the very basis of productive relations which would have been inoperable without this law."[15]

Second, the analysis of this chapter takes issue with the liberal view of the law's autonomy, which confines the definition of individual ownership to the sphere of private law. In this relation, the historically problematic character of the law's autonomy and of the separation between public and private law needs to be stressed; neither autonomy nor separation can be assumed to have had their origins in Roman law, which was reintroduced in Western Europe in the seventeenth century.[16] Both the autonomy of the law and the institutional differentiation between public and private law were part of power configurations that varied from one region to another. They represented contested domains throughout Europe.[17] That this was so was most dramatically demonstrated in postrevolutionary France. There, the demarcation of the domain of private law, as comprising property law and the law of contracts, was effected through the formulations of jurists with close affinities to propertied classes.[18] These formulations, as well as the decisions of the courts regarding private property in land, were vehemently contested, and the legal constitution of private property primarily took place through administrative rulings or law and through decisions of the administrative tribunals.[19]

In the nineteenth-century Ottoman empire, a differentiation between private and public law and a drafting of a civil code was attempted. This was largely in response to pressures on the Ottoman government to emulate European legal systems to facilitate European trading within the empire. Initially, the Ottoman government was pressured by the French to adopt the French civil code; Ottoman jurists, most of whom were also high-ranking state bureaucrats, resisting that proposal, compromised by undertaking to draft a civil code premised on the precepts of Islamic jurisprudence.[20]

Known as the *Mecelle* (collection),[21] the Ottoman civil code was subject to a nineteenth-century European understanding that the *shari'a*, or Islamic law, referred to a body of private law that, under Ottoman despotic rule, was superseded by the ruler's law (*kanun*), or administrative law.[22] This understanding assumed a binary aspect, an oppositionality between the precepts of Islamic law and the *kanun*. This aspect was most vividly demonstrated in what the Europeans perceived to have been a perennial tension between the categories of *mülk* (freehold) and *miri* (state ownership in land). This chapter shows that the designation of the category of *mülk*, as a formulation of private ownership that already existed in the *shari'a*, has been misleading and that in the nineteenth century the categories of both *mülk* and *miri* had to be reconstructed for the formulation of the general category of individual ownership. A dichotomous perception of law that was an outcome of historically specific power configurations, most significantly in postrevolutionary France, was projected backward in time onto Ottoman history as part of the process of the rewriting of that history in the nineteenth century. Such rewriting was inseparable from the establishment of European domination over the Ottoman empire, and it is a tribute to the effectiveness of that domination that the assumptions on which the new history rested were internalized (or least acknowledged) by Ottoman elites and subsequently by the intelligentsias of the successor states in the former Ottoman lands.[23]

In the mental climate of European domination that emphasized a dichotomous perception of law, the *Mecelle* was expected to introduce a general formulation of private property and rules of transactions for private property, or rules of contracts. In practice, however, the *Mecelle* remained an uncompleted venture, and property law and the law of contracts, in the nineteenth-century Ottoman setting, were part of the terrain of administrative law. To the extent that injunctions of an Islamic "private law" crystallized, they were complementary to the rulings of administrative law. This, in turn, points to the specific character of the Ottoman legal discourse and the power fields that this discourse embodied. Most significantly, in the nineteenth century and since the inception of the empire, the jurists who were engaged in the interpretation and the formulation of the precepts of Islamic law were also responsible for the formulation of *kanun*, or administrative law.[24] As such, *kanun*, contrary to the popular misconceptions of it, was not really the unequivocal word of the ruler. In the nineteenth century, the figure of Ahmet Cevdet Paşa, the renowned jurist and statesmen who was responsible for the drafting of both the Land Code and the *Mecelle*, was a rather dramatic representation of the intertwined character of the discourses of administrative law and the injunctions of Islamic jurisprudence. Thus, both laws were arenas where the legal constitution of individual ownership took place. That there was a dialogue between what is purported to be the unbridgeable worlds of Islamic or private law and administrative law is shown not only in the overlapping of provisions but also by the fact that Ottoman jurists, in deliberating on lands issues, drew freely on both bodies of law.[25]

However, the understanding of law as governance departs from perceptions, evoked by Michel Foucault's work, of social reality constituted through the practices of the centralized leviathan and subject to its all-embracing gaze.[26] This chapter seeks to introduce a sense of law in which multiple actors, including the different state agencies, confronted each other to negotiate and contest and in so doing cast and recast the very terms of domination and subjugation.[27] In the case of property relations, it is possible to speak of contestation as being part of the fabric of the very rulings that defined these relations: the struggles of different groups left their imprint on law and administrative practice. Thus, the analysis attempted here points to a fluidity in property relations that are power relations among persons or groups existing in a historically specific context.[28] What is suggested here is a politics of property, of the market, with openings and possibilities for action and initiative on the part of individuals and groups. At the same time, domination is about "framing" the different power fields and about defining the terms of contestation and of resistance. It represents a context that shapes the different power fields while at the same time being shaped by them. The environment of centralized states has been such a context.

The perception that links the development of private property to the practices of the state assumes an understanding of state power radically different from the liberal perception, which reduces that power to its policing function and views its interventions as being detrimental to the development of private ownership and of market activity. State power[29] here refers to the capabilities to order, regulate, and classify social reality. The exercise of those capabilities by the groups who hold state power implies that they are able to effect the power constellations that would make possible orderings or regulations of social relations and of economic activity towards defined objectives. Individual orderings are effected through administrative practices that represent multiple power fields in which both social and legal actors (or state actors including central agencies, tax collectors, and judges) confront, cajole, and dominate or are dominated.

Giving unity to this context of multiple power fields (which comprise the state) and a pattern to different relationships of subjugation and domination are idioms of rule; they form the representations of individual states. The figure of the just ruler in the Ottoman case was such a representation.[30] The idioms of rule pose the objectives of state power and provide the categories in relation to which individual orderings are established. They refer to a discourse that naturalizes and renders normal the multiple orderings of social reality and a given pattern of domination. It is important to note that this discourse is not in any way essential; it is continually produced through rituals and routines that become part of the daily experience of persons. In the case of centralized states of the late eighteenth and nineteenth centuries, where the efficacy of bureaucratic practices became the self-definition of states, public registration of life events including births and deaths, as well as property, were rituals of this nature.

Finally, the notion of state as a context of power, in which multiple actors operate within the parameters of historically formed vocabularies, breaks with the dichotomous view of social reality that casts state and society as inhabiting separate domains. State practices were constitutive of relations of private ownership, which they ordered, classified, and defined. As such, these relations did not have an autonomous existence in a mystified sphere of the market or society outside of the orderings of the state. On the other hand, state practices are power fields in which both state and social actors confront each other and negotiate the terms of the domination and subjugation that this kind of property implied. Thus, state and society interpenetrated in ways that make it impossible to think of them as separate and opposing domains. To cast lines of demarcation between them is to suggest the existence of historically specific power configurations that lead to this demarcation.[31]

In effect, this chapter argues that the "order of the market" and "the order of property" it presupposed were outcomes of the governance practices of the centralized states and of the power fields that characterized these states. Historically, commercial environments (in agrarian contexts) had demonstrated tendencies toward a transformation of land and labor, as well as goods, into commodities freely disposable or exchangeable in markets. Such tendencies towards commodification have been associated with the development of the right to private ownership. In relation to early Islamic societies, Baber Johansen's work points to a proliferation of rulings regarding private ownership of land by Islamic jurists during periods of commercial expansion.[32]

But these developments were confined to historical moments that were not sustained; for the most part they represented discrete pockets of commercial production for domestic or external markets. That is, prior to the eighteenth and nineteenth centuries, in the context of the power relations that prevailed both globally and within different regions, exchange activity was largely that of goods. Commodification with respect to factors of production, including land and labor, was limited, and production was, to a large degree, for subsistence and for the payment of taxes. This chapter argues that "the order of the market," or capitalism as a generalized system of commodity production and exchange, belonged to a historically specific moment—to a terrain of specific power configurations. Its development has been inseparable from the ordering of social relations by centralized states that represented such a terrain. However, this should not suggest that the argument presented here assigns agency to the state or its practices in the determination of property rights to the exclusion of social groupings representing different interests, including the commercial. It simply seeks to resituate these interests in power fields that were constitutive of property rights.

What does the above conceptualization suggest from the point of view of the writing of comparative history? First, it suggests a distancing from the understanding of "great transformation" as the moment of the market, its liberation from the shackles of feudal politics or states, a moment that belonged to Europe. Instead, one could talk about the "great transformation" as one of multiple state transformations that signaled the reordering of social realities and that represented radical ruptures from what had been. These transformations and the formation of the centralized leviathans that originated in the context of interstate competition in Western Eurasia and were subsequently generalized to other world areas (through exigencies of European colonial rule as well as resistance to that rule) remain the single most important agency in the constitution of the "order of the market." On the one hand, examination of the orderings of social reality by centralized states and of the categories in which these orderings were cast may point to a history widely shared by different world regions, cutting across the East/West divide. On the other hand, the notion that constitution of private ownership, of market exchange activity, and of law as autonomous and differentiated into private and public took place in power fields in which these were negotiated, resisted, and contested, points in a direction of problematizing the histories of both European and non-European areas. It calls into question the casting of world history as one of contrasting ideal images.

TRANSFORMATION OF THE STATE

In the Ottoman empire, the transformation of the territorial state meant the dissolution of the distributive-accommodative mode of state power. The Ottoman territorial state developed during the fifteenth and sixteenth centuries in competitive struggle with other states and political entities in the Balkans and in central Europe and to the east in Persia and Anatolia. The might and the survival of the state greatly depended on its ability to have access to the ever-increasing sources of revenue urgently required to build and maintain armies. This, in the sixteenth-century environment, meant territorial expansion.

In keeping with military and political imperatives, state practices that ordered social relations partook of an distributive-accommodative logic. The technology of warfare prior to the introduction of firearms had led to reliance on cavalry armies. This was true regardless of the fact that since its inception the Ottoman state had had a highly disciplined infantry corps, the Janissaries, that won the envy of *raison d'état* states elsewhere in Europe. To raise cavalry armies, the state distributed the rights over revenues from agricultural lands to veteran soldiers, to army commanders, and to local rulers in conquered territories, in return for delivery of mounted soldiers. These groups were also entrusted with the administration of the different regions and were exempt from state taxes. The distributive nature of state power, however, extended beyond the concern for raising armies. The members of the religious establishment who were not necessarily expected to deliver soldiers were also recipients of revenue grants and of the privilege of exemption from state taxes. As such, distribution of revenue grants was as much directed toward enlisting the political allegiance to the ruler of the different groups as it was toward securing a cavalry army. It was aimed at accommodating different groups into the ruling bloc and, in doing so, sought to preempt their potential resistance to the ruler's authority. It was also a means of incorporating the different regions into the imperial system.

The pattern of exchange of revenue entitlements for political allegiance[33] reflected an understanding of state power that prevailed prior to the nineteenth century. In this context, the state was represented by the figure of the just ruler.[34] An understanding of justice, cast in terms of the ruler's ability to ensure order or freedom from social strife, provided the idiom of rule that imparted a coherence to diverse practices. It made it possible for the ruler to represent the state and differentiate himself from the members of the ruling bloc with whom he competed for entitlements to revenues.[35] At the same time, the exercise of the ruler's justice toward the groups that were part of the ruling group involved the making of provisions for individual circumstances in different areas, as well as for different types of revenue holdings, such as *vakıf* (pious endowment), *mülk* (freehold), or *tımar* (military revenue grants). These provisions, embodied in provincial regulations and state ordinances issued in response to immediate problems, represented settlements negotiated between the ruler and the members of different groups and were subject to variations over time with changes in the power positioning of the respective parties.[36]

The ruler's justice also presupposed the perpetuation of the subsistence production of peasant households that provided rural as well as urban households with foodstuffs. In fact, the ordering of property relations on land was premised on an understanding of a "moral economy" of subsistence and provisioning, propelled by a concern on the part of the central government to prevent social unrest resulting from food shortages. To ensure the continuity of food production, rules restricted the alienability or divisibility of the subsistence holdings, limited the freedom of movement of cultivators, and regulated fallow practices. Rules also sought to protect the subsistence producers from extortion by revenue holders. To this end they delineated the use rights of producers, as well as their obligations to different groups of revenue claimants, including the ruler or the central treasury, in terms of the forms in which dues were paid (in kind, in labor, or in money), the rates at which they were paid, and exemptions from payment in return for services rendered. These regulations directed toward the preservation of subsistence production were characterized by a responsiveness to individual circumstances. As such, they varied from one locality to another regarding conditions of production and political or military status of groups or individuals. They represented a series of settlements negotiated between the cultivators and the extractors of their surpluses over long periods of time. Similarly, rules that regulated actual land use represented multilayered, shared claims that were negotiated, including webs of grazing and planting rights on common lands as well as on individual plots. At the same time, these rules sought to protect food production from the onslaught of pastoralism and from being taken over by commercial crops.

Orderings of property relations were, in fact, inseparable from the differentiated and particularistic claims over revenues of the different groups, on the one hand, and from the claims of subsistence producers to land use, on the other. The title to land (*raqaba*) generally lay with the ruler (or the treasury). This did not represent a title of ownership in the modern sense but an ability on the part of the ruler, or the central government, to distribute rights to revenues from land and, in so doing, to negotiate with different groups or individuals the conditions of their allegiance. State "ownership" also served to define the boundaries of the use rights of cultivators who had heritable use rights over their plots. Not only were there limits on the divisibility and alienability of use rights, but they were also restricted in terms of the time periods for which lands could be left uncultivated or left in fallow and in terms of the cultivation of non-grain crops.

This, in turn, points to an understanding of property on land as consisting of a bundle of rights representing claims to land use, revenues, and title.[37] These claims were continuously re-negotiated and redefined. For instance, given the differentiation of rights to revenues and title on a plot of land, depending on the nature of the settlement negotiated among the parties, the rights to revenues could rest with a freeholder (*mülk*), a pious endow-ment, or with the treasury, while the title rested with the state or the treasury. This should not suggest that the claim of the state to title was an absolute one: especially in areas where there was strong resistance to the Ottoman conquest, the Ottoman ruler conceded the right to title to former ruling groups following the conquest. These groups included members of the religious estab-lishment in the Muslim region of Anatolia. On the other hand, the rights to revenues from such lands could be assigned to state officials and state regulations relating to subsistence production applied to these lands.

Representation of property rights on land as a "bundle of rights or claims" also establishes relations of distribution and extraction of tax revenues and of access to land use as power re-lations among groups or individuals. It refers to entitlements that were continually negotiated among groups and individuals. The negotiated settlements were, in turn, summed up in differ-ent rulings, whether in the form of government regulations, or-dinances of the ruler, or court decisions.

What needs to be underlined here is that the different catego-ries that defined entitlements to revenues and to land use did not correspond to an understanding of ownership. I have already discussed what state ownership stood for within the confines of this administrative universe. Similarly, *mülk* (freehold) did not signify private ownership. Instead, *mülk* was a category of enti-tlement to tax revenues that the grantee held, as was the case with revenue grants, by a *berat* or an official document of enti-tlement from the ruler. The holder of the *mülk* grant could alien-ate his right to revenues, transfer it to his heirs, and convert it into mortmain property or *vakıf*. Trees, buildings on agricul-tural holdings, and other produce were also classified as *mülk*, which, in this case, referred to an entitlement to the fruits of the land. These claims were differentiated from *miri* claims on fields. The *raqaba* (ownership) generally rested with the central treasury. The cultivators of agricultural lands had inheritable usufruct rights (*tasarruf*) on these lands, which they held by a deed issued for a fee by the local administrator *cum* revenue holder.

The transformation of the distributive-accommodative state took place in the environment of intensified military and political competition among European states beginning in the seventeenth century. Interstate competition and the requirement to maintain standing armies, which in this period came to prevail over cavalry armies, were factors in empowering the central government at the expense of the provincial power nodules. Confronted with high costs of warfare, as well as the financial burdens of an expanding bureaucracy, the centralizing state sought to increase its revenues. Earlier territorial conquests had been a primary means of augmenting the revenues that accrued to the ruler. Conquests also enabled the ruler to accommodate rival political claims through the system of revenue grants. By the eighteenth century, the Ottoman state had reached the limits of its territorial expansion both in Europe and in the East; in the nineteenth century it began losing territory in the Balkans and in Egypt.

Unable to expand outward, the central government turned inward to establish control over the revenues that had formerly accrued to the members of the ruling bloc. This was a long drawn-out process of incessant struggle between the central government and the members of the religious establishment, provincial notables, and the old-guard military establishment. One phase in this conflict had been a recasting of the system of revenue grants on the part of the central government, in terms of life-term assignments of tax farms in the eighteenth century. The practice of tax farming involved large cash advances made to the central government by the tax farmers in return for the right to collect taxes from a given region; its preponderance coincided with commercial expansion in agriculture. From the point of view of the central government, it also represented an attempt to accommodate as tax farmers those provincial elites that were not part of old distributive networks. In so doing, the central government sought to weaken the hold of old elites over land while, at the same time, increasing its share of agrarian revenues.[38] In the nineteenth century, with the crystallization of a central army and a central bureaucracy, the government undertook new orderings of property relations on land. These orderings aimed at establishing the general claim by the state over revenues to the exclusion of the entitlements of the different groups (including the ruler and his entourage) that formerly constituted the ruling bloc (including the tax farmers). At the same time, the central government sought to subject these groups to taxation, thus abolishing their privileges in the form of tax exemptions.

All this, however, entailed a change in the nature of state power that was no longer represented by the ruler and distributive practices that were accommodative of different interests and groupings. State power was no longer associated with the person of the just ruler but became "the state" writ large, represented through efficacy and the generality of its bureaucratic practices. The latter, including legal codes and land cadastres, no longer referred to negotiated settlements that were responsive to individual circumstances and that sought to accommodate the multiple claims in prescriptive, prohibitive regulations. Instead, state practices represented a pattern of domination that obliterated the particularistic claims through subjecting them to the universal, general claims of the state. As such, these practices came to constitute domains of contestation in ways the particularistic injunctions, which represented the orderings of social relations in the pre-nineteenth-century context, did not. As mentioned earlier, the particularistic injunctions were summations of negotiations that had already taken place among different parties; they represented settlements negotiated so that social order could prevail. By contrast, modern administrative rulings or codes (as well as the modern cadastre) represented continually negotiated texts; they represented sites of contestation, resistance by groups whose interests were no longer accommodated by the general formulations of the law. What in fact happened was a radical departure from the former administrative universe where the particular, and its articulation in regulations, defined the very ends of state power in terms of justice dispensation. We discuss this problem in relation to Land Code of 1858.

The pattern of state formation in the environment of interstate competition described for the Ottoman state has close parallels with states in Europe, especially in those areas where land and the agricultural economy were the primary source of surpluses coveted by the centralizing states and their internal political rivals. In the European context unlike the Ottoman one, centralizing states, confronted with limits to territorial expansion on the continent, increasingly engaged in colonial conquests. Despite this, throughout the eighteenth and the nineteenth centuries the different European states were locked in struggles with local power groups over control of land revenues.[39]

At the same time, state centralization was taking place in an environment of commercial expansion to which colonial conquests contributed significantly. In this commercial setting, individual states no longer saw generation of wealth simply in terms of extensive measures—that is, territorial conquests that enabled access to new sources of revenue—or of appropriation of resources that were controlled by rival political groups within individual territories.[40] Taxation came to be perceived in more intensive terms, those of the state's regulation of economic activity to increase productive capacity, which would result in an expansion of taxable incomes. French physiocratic convictions appear to have been an inspiration for this perception. The belief that land was the chief source of value and was an economic asset or a factor of production seems, in a number of European regions, to have stimulated attempts at cadastral mapping as the scientific basis for the improvement of the most important asset.[41] Similarly, the ordering of property relations in terms of individual rights was, more and more, grounded in the conviction that private ownership of land was essential for economic growth, in that only those who controlled the surplus production could be expected to invest in capital improvements.[42]

Michel Foucault pointed out that exigencies of interstate competition made it imperative for the individual states to develop capabilities for steering economic activity in ways that would both enhance productive capacity and subject expanding economic activity to state controls.[43] These capabilities, which Foucault referred to as techniques of government, already existed under the *raison d'état* states of the sixteenth through eighteenth centuries and in Prussia came under the rubric of *Polizeiwissenschaft*.[44] They included practices of inspection and regulation of economic and social life, especially in urban areas that witnessed population explosions during this period. But the regulatory practices of states that evolved after the eighteenth century did not simply represent an intensification or generalization of earlier governmental techniques. They represented new ways of ordering and regulating social reality (and therefore controlling it) in terms of categories that differed radically from those orderings and regulations under earlier states.

As an aspect of this rupture and the establishment of control over economic activity, Foucault pointed to the institution of the economy, through state practices, as a separate domain. In this regard, he stressed the inclusion in the "economy" of production that hitherto had belonged to the domain of the household. Expanding on Foucault's perception, it may be argued that in the nineteenth century the "economy" referred to the sphere of commodity exchange of private individuals. Formerly, market exchange was primarily confined to the exchange of goods; the inclusion of production in the sphere of market exchange implied that the primary resources, land and labor, would be constituted as economic assets, as factors of production, exchangeable and controllable. It implied the constitution of land and labor markets. Previously, under territorial states, land was perceived as territory; it was primarily a resource for the production of foodstuffs and of tax revenues. To these ends, its alienability was restricted; its use was delimited. At the same time, represented in terms of the categories of revenue grants or tax farms of the different social and political groups or in terms of subsistence and surplus producing household units, land as a resource eluded control by any one group or interest. Similarly, people or inhabitants of territories were defined in particularistic terms and with reference to family, village, town quarter, or tribe. Representations (in law and in other state practices) of land as an economic asset or as a "thing" and of inhabitants in specific locales as, for instance, population or laborers were abstractions from particular contexts and presupposed the existence of the context of the modern state, of its controlling practices, and of its ordering of social relations.

Foucault focused on the ways that compilation of statistics and registration with the police made possible the constitution of the category of population as measurable, identifiable, or tractable—that is, it became an object of taxation or conscription and an economic resource. For Foucault, the institution of the "economy" as a separate domain, in terms of the "objectification" of persons as population, was inseparable from the establishment of state control over economic activity or from the exercise of governmental power. From the perspective of this chapter, Foucault's analysis suggests, by pointing to the character of governmental practices as being constitutive of social reality, a blurring of the demarcation between state and society. In doing this, it dispenses with endless quibbling about incompatibilities or contradictions between the practices that originate in the spheres of state and society and about the nature of the state's role in the development of the market economy. Yet this analysis tends to absolutize the process of "constitution" of social reality through state practices. Thus, with relations of domination internalized or subsumed in the "objects" of domination (such as land, labor, and population), there appears to be no way of escaping or contesting governmental power. Put differently, Foucault does not problematize the processes of "constitution." Statistical practice, which was responsible for constituting objects of control and exchange, is viewed in relation to a capacity for exercising governmental power and not as a field of power where resistance to it may be located.

In the nineteenth-century Ottoman context, as was the case in most European regions, subjecting agricultural wealth, particularly land, to state regulation was central to the project of the modern state. The ordering of property relations in terms of individual ownership rights was central to such regulation. Individual ownership rights represented a dual abstraction of the property claim of the individual from the web of multiple, particularistic entitlements to land revenues and from the diverse, shared claims over land use. The dual abstraction sought to establish the total control by the central state over revenues that no longer referred to the multiple entitlements of different groups but to the singular, general taxation claim of the state. Second, it sought to achieve the absolute control by the individual owner over the income from and use of the land.

From the point of view of an administrative ordering of social reality, individual ownership signaled a differentiation between the categories of income and of taxation, of property and of taxation. The Land Code of 1858 was a representation of this differentiation in that it addressed the issues related to landed property, while taxation was controlled through a separate set of regulations. What the separation of property and taxation reveals, however, is a change in the conception of economic activity away from one primarily directed toward subsistence production and to the production of surpluses in the form of tax revenues and toward one that emphasized its productive character. It points to a recognition that agrarian surpluses were no longer expected to be exhausted by revenue claims but were expected to deliver an income to the owner. In fact, taxes were to be calculated as a proportion of income. Thus, Ottoman land surveys of the nineteenth century were called surveys of income (*temettuat defterleri*)[45] and no longer *tahrir defterleri,* which were the tax surveys of the earlier period. Given the understanding of economic activity as a productive, income-generating venture, the central state sought not only to establish its claims to total revenue but also to establish its control over the totality of the wealth produced by individual owners in the countryside. The latter concern manifests itself in the coverage of the income surveys that sought to take stock of all forms of wealth and not simply to list the taxable resources, as was the case with the earlier tax surveys. The administrative constitution of the individual ownership right was central to the process of establishing control. It took the form of creating the legal owner, the right of property, and the object of property or the land as a thing, measurable, controllable, and alienable;[46] it also entailed the separating of the object of property from its subject or the legal owner from his right of ownership.[47] Registration of title to individual holdings,[48] the recording in income surveys of these holdings, as well as the administrative rulings enabled these definitions and separations. They also represented the sites for resistance to the formulation of individual ownership.

In his study of property rights in Egypt during the nineteenth century, Tim Mitchell describes the separation of the right of ownership from its object—land—and refers to this process as one of effecting a difference between the abstract (or the code of law that defined the right of ownership) and the concrete (or land, which was constituted through regulatory practices including registration and cadastral surveys).[49] Mitchell argues that effecting a difference between the right and its object represents a way of producing, through state practices, manageable spaces; individual ownership was one such space.[50] However, Mitchell does not simply emphasize the extension of governmental power that the creation of individual ownership implied. He points to the resistance to the generalization of private ownership rights and the formation of a new class of landowners who were inseparable from the processes of the creation and the disciplining of a labor force. Cultivators who had lost their use rights over land to the new landowners and were forced to work as laborers on the land vehemently opposed the ordering of private ownership. Yet Mitchell's analysis falls short of problematizing the sites in law and administrative procedures where resistance and contestation took place and left their imprint on the very practices that subjugated the resistors. It simply points to the struggles against the patterns of domination on land, almost as if these struggles were doomed to impotence before the all-embracing ordering of property relations on the part of the state, before an exercise of unequivocal governmental power; it does not venture into the domain of politics of property.

This chapter argues that law and administrative practices were the power fields in which individual ownership was constituted. The Land Code of 1858, which was the central piece of legislation on landed property in the nineteenth century, represented one such power field. Different stakes—on the part of former claimants to revenues, groups with claims to ownership, those with use claims over the land, and the different governmental agencies—clashed or were poised in uneasy compromise. The text of the Code was highly revealing of the politics of property in the mid-nineteenth-century Ottoman empire; it carried the stamp of the struggles carried out by different groups. These were by no means mute tussles lurking beneath the thick fog of the government's implacable stare. They rendered the ordering of individual ownership rights highly fluid, continually contested and subject to qualifications, as is witnessed by the issuing of special regulations that represented modifications or specification of the general precepts of the Code in the context of regional expectations. At the same time, those moments in which the general law was particularized were also the moments when the particular defined itself in terms of the vocabularies and categories of that law.

THE LAND CODE OF 1858 AS A FIELD OF POWER

The Land Code of 1858 instituted, to use Ranajit Guha's phrase, a "rule of property" or the singular claim of ownership by the title holder.[51] However, the Code applied only to state lands over which the central government in the nineteenth century had consolidated its control and established its taxation claims to the exclusion of the revenue claims of the former ruling groups. This has led both the liberal and the Marxist observers of the nineteenth-century Ottoman empire to argue that the Code represented a reasserting of state ownership on land. This is assumed to have impeded the development of individual ownership rights on land.[52] From a legal liberal perspective, the history of land ownership in the Ottoman empire has been one of the gradual transformation of *miri* status (state ownership) into *mülk* (freehold).[53] This view assumes that the *mülk* category as it existed in the Ottoman context corresponded to individual ownership right, representing, as it were, a nodule of resistance and an alternative to state ownership.[54] The argument presented here challenges these understandings.

First, it seeks to show that the category of *mülk* as it was recast in the Ottoman context did not so much refer to absolute ownership as to a certain kind of a claim over land revenues and a claim over its fruits (see the previous section on the Transformation of the State). Second, this chapter shows that procedures of registration and issuing titles of ownership, as well as drafting lease contracts, which enabled transactions in land, were initially applicable to state lands alone.[55] Individual ownership rights were constituted primarily through these practices.[56] The title of ownership replaced the former titles to land revenues and to its use (*tasarruf*):[57] it signified the separation of the ownership claim from the former revenue and use claims, establishing it as the singular and absolute claim over land, only to be limited by the taxation claim of the state. As will be shown, the extension of these practices to *mülk* or *vakıf* lands signaled not only the institution of individual ownership rights on these lands but also their subjection to the control of the central government. Viewed from this perspective, the status of *miri* (state land) can be said to have been inseparable from a legal-administrative formation of private or individual ownership rights.

At the same time, in the nineteenth century the very meaning of *miri* seems to have undergone a change. It was no longer associated with the distributionist logic of state power, whereby the *miri* status enabled the ruler, as the custodian of the treasury, to assign revenues from state lands to different groups to obtain their political allegiance and to ensure subsistence production, thus preventing social strife. As mentioned earlier, this concern for order conjoined with an understanding of distributive justice. In the nineteenth century, the *miri* status signified the control of the central government over land revenues to the exclusion of all other groups. It also enabled the constitution of individual ownership through state practices, including transfers of state lands by means of sales contracts. Sale of lands in return for the issuance of title deeds provided the central state with an important source of income. Most significantly, the new understanding of *miri* closely linked the development of individual ownership rights to the practices of the modern state.

A central theme of this chapter is that the constitution of individual ownership rights signaled the total control of the central government over land that was the primary economic resource. Such control was made possible by the fact that individual ownership represented a separation of the revenue claim from the property claim and in so doing created the space for the establishment of sole taxation by the central government to the exclusion of the revenue claims of groups that formerly formed the ruling bloc. Central government controls were also exercised, through the performance of the procedures defining individual ownership rights, by state agencies. The text of the Code is replete with references to the competence of state agents (*memuru marifetiyle*) who were responsible for the registration of lands; they were also empowered to deny access by the title holder in the event, for instance, that he or she discontinued cultivation for three years.[58] Moreover, the public character of registration of landed property, in the presence of an official commission, may have further underlined the presence of the central government in the countryside, thus establishing this process as a central ritual of the modern state.[59]

However, the extension of state control was strongly resisted by those groups whose revenue claims were obliterated by the new property regime. This resistance, and the power struggles between the central government and the former revenue claimants, are revealed in the system of classifying landed property introduced by the Code. First, the Code departed from previous classifications of land on the basis of recipients of revenue grants—for example, the pious endowment lands (*vakıf*), lands held as freehold (*temlik*), the lands of which the revenues were allotted to military commanders (*tımar*), to bureaucrats (*ze'amet*), to palace members (*has*), or to tax farmers (*mukataa*). Lands were now to be classified on the basis of conditions of access or use as, for example, common lands (*metruke*) or uncultivated land (*mevat*). Lands were also classified as state lands (*miri*) and as freehold (*mülk*). *Vakıf* lands generally belonged to the *mülk* category. Those lands from which *vakıfs* drew an income but that were not freehold were considered *miri* and were called *mevkufe*. This separation of state, freehold, and *vakıf* lands no longer signified assignments of revenues of these lands to different groups of revenue claimants. It represented a delineation of those lands that were at the disposal of the state to transfer to individual owners from those that were not. Thus, through this separation, the central government was conceding to the resistance of the holders of *mülk* and *vakıf* to its taxation policies and its procedures of registration. The separation was also revealing of the change in the nature of the understanding of *miri* and of the change in the nature of state power.

Throughout the nineteenth century, the central government had attempted to confiscate *vakıf* and *mülk* properties and to abolish tax farming. These attempts failed, tax farming remained the prevailing mode of tax collection, while *vakıf* and *mülk* holders continued their control over the land. These groups resisted the state taxes that were imposed on them when the system of revenue grants was revoked. Yet confrontations between the central government and the former ruling groups took place within the categories and classifications of the Land Code. The fact that the precepts of the Land Code applied to state lands alone left non-state lands in an administrative limbo. That is, non-state lands were not subject to the administrative practices of registration and issuance of title deeds or to the precepts of the law of contracts, especially in relation to leases. This meant that they escaped state scrutiny and taxation. At the same time, given that previous regulations that made possible transactions in land were annulled, *vakıf* and *mülk* holders, as well as former tax farmers, increasingly had problems in exercising their control over land. Added to this were pressures from the representatives of the central government, and gradually the practices of registration, of issuing of title deeds, and of drawing up lease contracts were extended to *mülk*[60] and *vakıf* lands. In certain instances, this enabled the former revenue holders to establish their ownership claims over lands that had been their revenue grants. The discussion in the next section of this chapter on Contestations of the Code and the Special Provisions suggests that the central government was not necessarily adverse to this development. The extension of state procedures also signaled the subjection of these groups to state taxes, which in many instances they continued to resist. But the terms of resistance were established through the categories of the Code. As such, the former ruling groups could resist taxation as landowners with titles to the land but not as legitimate claimants to the revenues of the land.[61]

The institution of individual ownership rights also represented a separation of the property claim from the subsistence claim of those with rights of access to land. It involved the establishment of the ownership claim to the exclusion of the use of and income from land, whereby the title of ownership overrode the titles to land use (*tasarruf*) and the customary rights over land, including the collective grazing rights of the villagers. This was, however, a highly contentious process, and the ambiguities built into the Code's precepts, as well as its contradictory formulations, bear testimony to the resistance to the institution of exclusive ownership rights over land.

For one thing, the Code extended protection to title holders against trespassers with the aim of preventing the claims of third parties to access to land. Such claims included those of planting trees and constructing buildings.[62] Under the old regulations, the grain fields were generally classified as *miri*, while products of land such as trees and fruits, as well as buildings, were classified as *mülk* (freehold). The Code recognized the singular claim of the holder of ownership title over trees and forbade the planting of trees by outsiders on land held with title. This suggests a change in the classification of trees to *miri*. In another article, however, trees were designated as *mülk*, while being subjected to the ownership of the title holder.[63] This concession to previous practice may point to opposition to the establishment of a single category of land that did away with spaces (possibilities) in the form of multiple categories through which multiple claims could be formulated. The concession took the form of a differentiation between rights of constructing buildings and planting trees and of ownership of the soil.

The provisions on alienability and disposability of land constituted another domain of contestation. The Code made provisions for the irrevocable transfer (*ferağ*) of land either in return for payment or without expectation of payment.[64] This, however, held the threat of dispossession for cultivators who formerly had use rights over their plots and who managed to register these plots as their private property. This group was particularly vulnerable to the vicissitudes of the commercial environment in the nineteenth century. By way of protecting the property rights of cultivators, the Code restricted alienability through prohibitions on transfers in the event of indebtedness.[65] The provision was further negotiated through an acceptance of conditional transfers, which allowed for transfers of land with the condition that it would be returned on payment of debt.[66] The incorporation of such practices by the Code, in fact, represented a recognition of the credit requirements of a commercialized agrarian economy and were directed toward the protection of the lender.[67]

The Code included provisions for renting and leasing of state lands.[68] In some areas, especially the Balkans, these provisions proved to be the subject of serious clashes between former tax farmers or notables who established their ownership rights and the cultivators who no longer enjoyed inheritable usufruct rights and were reduced to the status of tenants on their subsistence plots. Deliberations on the terms of tenancy, especially on its duration, frequently resulted in the issuing of special regulations that addressed the specific power configurations between owners and tenants in different regions. The next section of this chapter is devoted to a discussion of a long-lasting conflict of this nature in Albania in the 1870s.

Lastly, the central government and its taxation claims represented a power position from which definitions of individual ownership rights were negotiated. Above all, the central government was concerned with maintaining continuity in cultivation and therefore a continuous flow of taxes. To this end, the Code restricted the absolute rights of owners through the provision that the land reverted to the state in the event of the owners' failure to cultivate it for three years.[69] Moreover, the Code did not discourage confiscation, through the stipulation that the appropriator pay the *tapu* (title) fees and cultivate the land.[70] This has been interpreted as a measure to tie the title holder to the land, to motivate him to retain possession of it.[71] It is also suggestive of the way the central government perceived individual ownership as closely related to the creation of wealth and therefore of taxable income.

The highly qualified character of the text of the Code, as well as the classification schemes it embodied, testify to the problematic task of codifying property rights in the nineteenth century. Despite resistance, the Code established the definition of individual ownership rights as the vocabulary through which struggles over access to land were articulated. That is, a vocabulary of ownership overtook that of competing claims to tax revenues and to land use. In France, the intensity of the struggle in the countryside and the intransigence of the propertied classes, especially in relation to orderings of tenancy arrangements, did not allow for the issuing of a rural code until well into the 1880s.[72] By contrast, the Ottoman government did, in fact, issue a such a code, but it did so with great deal of trepidation. For one thing, the Code was a cross between a civil code and a rural code. In step with the civil codes of the nineteenth century, it included a definition of individual ownership rights.[73]

This should not suggest that in the Ottoman empire a notion of property, as it was formulated in the context of the natural law debates of the European Enlightenment, was perceived as being the linchpin of social and political order, as was the case in postrevolutionary France.[74] Disputes over property, "alienable and sacred" in the words of the 1791 constitution dominated the French countryside until the mid-nineteenth century.[75] In the Ottoman empire, the overriding concern for order on the part of the central state, during the first half of the nineteenth century,[76] resulted in a more dispassionate view of individual ownership rights. Ottoman statesmen showed extreme sensitivity not to allow disputes over property to be translated into political conflicts and for the most part saw to it that such disputes were relegated to the administrative domain, thus becoming the subject matter for endless bureaucratic deliberations.[77]

In fact, the Ottoman view of property in the nineteenth century partook in the utilitarian consensus that linked the security of tenure, to be ensured by absolute ownership, with expectations of increased productivity.[78] The latter, from the point of view of the central state ever hankering for revenues, signaled increases in taxable wealth.[79] In this respect, the definition of individual ownership rights by the Code was part of the process whereby the Ottoman modern state sought to regulate the agricultural economy through the introduction of measures directed toward increasing productivity.[80]

In line with the reticent posture in relation to private ownership, Ottoman statesmen painstakingly endeavored to emphasize the fact that the Code represented continuity rather than a rupture with past practices. Drafters of the Code shunned all talk of a revolutionary change in property rights but were adamant in pointing to the fact that their task had been simply one of compiling and codifying old regulations and not introducing any new ones.[81]

Despite statements by representatives of the central government, the Code represented an ordering of property relations that radically altered the allocation of land as a resource. In doing that, it became a terrain in which the winners and losers confronted each other and the representatives of the central state mediated among the contenders. The exclusionary nature of absolute, individual ownership introduced by the Code threatened to undermine the subsistence claims of cultivators in the form of hereditary usufruct rights and collective grazing rights. Given that it was inseparable from the establishment of the exclusive taxation claim of the state, it also threatened to undermine the control of the former ruling classes in the countryside. The Ottoman nineteenth century was rife with struggles against the new regime of property. In some areas, these struggles predated the Land Code. In the Balkans, when the tax farmers interpreted the text of the reform edict of 1839, in which the ruler promised security of tenure, as confirming their ownership rights on land, the cultivators broke into open revolt.[82] It is interesting to note that these cultivators demanded a return to state ownership, indicating the ways state ownership colluded with an understanding of moral economy in the old order of property. Throughout the nineteenth century, the Ottoman central government was engaged in a continuous balancing act between the exigencies of a rule of justice (read absence of social strife) and a rule of property.

CONTESTATIONS OF THE CODE AND THE SPECIAL PROVISIONS

Despite the fact that the Code included provisions limiting alienability, peasant dispossession on state lands was a common occurrence during the nineteenth century.[83] This was partly an outcome of two kinds of pressure on the peasant economy. In the first, the cash requirements of peasant cultivators operating in an increasingly commercialized environment forced them to borrow money and, in the event of default in debt payment, forced them to sell their holdings for which they held a title deed, or *tapu*. In the second, the increased taxation demands of the central state also resulted in peasant indebtedness and the consequent alienation of their holdings. In fact, the relaxation of restrictions on the transfer of *tapu* lands for payment of state taxes in 1861, and later in 1869 for payment of debts to individuals, suggests a recognition by the central state of the cash requirements of the peasantry. By meeting these needs in the nineteenth-century environment of private property, the state allowed the alienability of landed property and thus removed qualifications on absolute ownership.

Yet, in Anatolia at least, peasant dispossessions did not result in an unequivocal development of the rise of a class of large landowners.[84] Even in the Balkans and parts of western Anatolia where peasant dispossessions did take place, the individual ownership rights of the dispossessor were significantly limited or qualified. To understand why, we need to explore the ways the Code was continuously contested, resisted, negotiated, and renegotiated in different contexts.

These contexts included the courts of law, the various departments of the central government that were involved in the formulation of responses to individual petitions in the form of decrees[85] and local commissions consisting of the representatives of contesting parties. In these domains, individual precepts of the Land Code were contested and resisted by different groups in the countryside; they were recast in deliberations between these groups and the representatives of the central government. Thus, decisions of courts or other deliberating bodies or decisions by central government agencies certified by the sultan (*irade*s) are extremely revealing of the actual nature of property relations on land in the nineteenth-century Ottoman empire. They describe the process whereby multiple claims were accommodated and property rights on land were reconstituted once again as a bundle. What differentiated this bundle from the earlier bundle of revenue, use, and title claims, was that the new bundle was negotiated in the terminology of the Land Code, its definitions and its classification of landed property.

I have discussed earlier the ways these definitions and classifications were contested and qualified in the text of the Code. Yet the Code embodied a new understanding of property that represented a delinking of property rights from the multiple revenue claims and erasures of multiple-use claims (inheritable use rights including sharecropping and collective grazing rights) in favor of the singular ownership right of the title holder. The new bundle of claims, which were primarily those to access to land, had as its reference point the singular right of ownership, even when multiple claims significantly curtailed that right. This was the case in the "translations" of the former inheritable use rights into life-term tenancies, discussed below. The bundle also included the singular revenue claim of the state. The latter claim, unlike the revenue claims of the ruler or the treasury in the earlier period, was no longer the subject matter of land regulations; it was dealt with in regulations for taxation. The pervasiveness of the new understanding of property, in terms of providing the categories in relation to which landed property was defined, however, was revealing of a pattern of domination that focused on the central government and its agencies.

The account by Cevdet Paşa, the renowned nineteenth-century Ottoman jurist, of a land dispute in Yanya, a district in present-day Albania, provides a vivid description of the constitution of the bundle that made up property rights in the course of the struggles of cultivators against the former tax farmers or local notables who had acquired ownership titles.[86] This account is also revealing of the continuous negotiation and renegotiation of the terms of domination by the central state represented in the categories of the Code.

In 1875, Cevdet Paşa, who was one of the principal drafters of the Code, wrote that if the general precepts of the Code and the Law of Contract[87] were to be implemented to the letter in the Balkan provinces, the population in these areas would rise up in arms. This comment was occasioned by a bitter dispute over property rights between estate holders (*ashab-ı alaka*) and cultivators of the soil in the estate of Parga in Yanya.[88] The estate holders, who had long-standing claims over revenues from the land (as tax farmers), had sought to acquire title deeds beginning in the mid-1840s.[89] The cultivators resisted what amounted to the establishment of singular and absolute ownership rights by the estate holders and the redefinition of their own use rights in terms of restricted tenancy rights.[90]

In an attempt to resolve the dispute between the *ashab* and the cultivators, Cevdet Paşa, who had briefly served in 1874 and 1875 as governor of Yanya,[91] formed a commission, consisting of representatives of the contending parties.[92] Following lengthy deliberations, the commission negotiated a settlement and submitted its recommendations for a solution to the dispute to the Office of the Imperial Registry and the Council of State.[93]

Independently of the report of the commission, Cevdet Paşa also submitted an evaluation of the situation to the Council of State. As this evaluation provides certain insights into the deliberation process I briefly summarize its contents.

First, Cevdet Paşa described in some detail the power positions of the different actors in the dispute. The *ashab* were represented by the venerable Rauf Beyefendi, the son of a deceased high-ranking Tanzimat official, whose presence appears to have inspired awe even in the eyes of Cevdet Paşa, who was himself no stranger to power circles in Istanbul. Rauf Beyefendi succeeded in getting the cultivators to recognize the ownership rights of the *ashab* to the land. This meant an acceptance on the part of the cultivators of their status as tenants. It also meant that the cultivators gave up their hereditary use rights to the land.

Cevdet Paşa noted that the commission proposed that these conditions should not be limited to cultivated fields on state lands to which the provisions of the Code applied but should also be extended to *mülk* lands on which houses were built in the town of Parga, which was part of the estate. On the grounds of those provisions of the Code that specified that the ownership of buildings followed the ownership of land, the estate holders laid claim to the ownership of Venetian houses in Parga. While conceding the possession of the houses in both the town and the countryside to those who had built or occupied them, the owners claimed they were entitled to a rent from the land on which the buildings stood.[94]

On the other hand, ownership rights of the *ashab* or title holders were significantly restricted by the fact that the cultivators were able to resist the specification of a time duration in lease contracts. Similarly, they resisted any change in the amount of rent due. Such resistances were couched in terms of a call for adherence to local customary practices. The latter, in most cases, referred to regulations that were embodied in earlier provincial codes or in the edicts by the sultan. Under these practices, leases on state lands (*miri*) that corresponded to usufruct rights generally lasted for very long periods, often spanning the lifetimes of individual tenants and their descendants.[95] When the *ashab* laid claim to the title of the land, the cultivators expected them to abide by the regulations that had prevailed earlier. This meant that holders of title to the land could not revoke a tenancy, evict a tenant, or raise the amount of rent. Nor could they, on the death of one tenant, lease the land to another. The family of the deceased tenant was expected to continue to cultivate the land as before and to pay the rent (*imro*). The only condition under which a lease contract could be revoked and the tenant be evicted was when the tenant ceased cultivation and stopped paying rent. Only in such cases, and on grounds that the present tenant was disrupting public order, could land be leased to a new tenant.

On the basis of the settlement reached by the commission, Cevdet Paşa recommended to the Council of State that a special regulation be formulated for Yanya. This amounted to compromising the generality of the formulations of the Code before the particularity of local demands. In fact, Cevdet Paşa, the pragmatist, was pointing to a need to concede to local public opinion, to "customary practice," if social peace were to be restored in this area. He spoke, of course, from the experience of his previous involvement as a high-ranking administrator elsewhere in the Balkans where resistance by cultivators on the estates to the extension of the proprietary rights of the *ashab* was rampant throughout the nineteenth century.[96] Frequent European interventions on behalf of Christian cultivators and against the estate holders, who were predominantly Muslim, had further aggravated the situation. On the other hand, Cevdet Paşa also knew that the central government could not establish order in the Balkans simply by giving in to the demands of the cultivators. The collaboration of the *ashab* with the central government was indispensable for effective Ottoman administration of the region. Hence, the central government had sought previously to enlist the allegiance of the *ashab,* in areas such as Bosnia and Niş, by issuing a special regulation that would ensure the ownership rights of the *ashab* while at the same time limiting them in such a way as to satisfy the demands of tenants.[97]

CONCLUDING REMARKS

The central theme of this chapter has been that the resistances and struggles against individual ownership were inseparable from the process of the formation of this right. The governmental practices, including law and cadastral surveying, that constituted individual ownership, were the power fields where these struggles took place. At the same time, I have tried to show that these power fields belonged to historically specific contexts. These contexts established the goals of government; inseparable from these goals were understandings of government and of power. This chapter focused on the modern state as such a context, which provided the vocabularies, idioms, and conceptual wherewithal for communication and deliberation. It represented an idiom of rule, a hegemonic language in which individuals or groups negotiated power positions. In that sense one could speak of a boundedness of the power fields and of the limits of resistance and struggle. These limits, which were defined by the hegemonic language, were by no means absolute; they were fluid and were discursively produced through the practices of the different agencies of the central state. This production involved silences on, as well as articulations of, the central themes of power; individual ownership was one such theme.

Throughout the nineteenth century, the Ottoman government vacillated in assimilating a "rule of property" to its idiom of rule. The reform edict of 1839 was, indeed, a document steeped in liberal and utilitarian ideas of the "age of property."[98] It posed the precept of security of property (*mal*), life, and honor from the vantage point of the state's interest in the prosperity of its subjects who were the primary source of taxes. The edict explicitly stated that unless security and freedom of ownership (*malik*) and possession (*tasarruf*) of both movable (*emval*) and immovable (*emlak*) property were ensured, people would not feel part of their state or country and driven by anxiety would not use their property productively. However, the constitution of 1876, a liberal document by all accounts, did not share the enthusiasm of the edict for property. It ensured the security of possessors (*mutasarrıf*) and not of owners (*malik*) as did the edict; it stated that neither movable nor immovable property that was possessed (*tasarruf*) could be taken away from its possessors except in return for payment or in the event of its being required for public interest.[99]

Despite the reticence of the 1876 constitution, private ownership was discursively constituted through the documents of the central government. The Land Code was one such document. The official correspondence between Cevdet Paşa and the various departments of the central government provide another example of the discursive constitution of private ownership. Thus, Cevdet Paşa, in his report to the Council of State regarding the Parga affair, emphasized, and thereby reestablished, the definition in the Code of an absolute right of ownership whereby the title holder had the right to do as he pleased with his property, including the right to evict tenants and lease the land to whomever he wished. In this, however, he was not motivated by an ideological commitment to a religion of private property as it was constituted by French jurists of the postrevolutionary period. His motivation appears to have lain in an understanding of state power in terms of an ability to achieve a generality and uniformity of bureaucratic practices. This understanding of state power stood in contrast to that of the old territorial state with its particularistic practices of regulation, responsive to individual circumstances. In that world, which was lost to the nineteenth century, rules had as their point of reference an idiom of distributive justice. This should not suggest that Cevdet Paşa was insensitive to the politics of property or to the competing claims or grievances of the different groups; that he was not so is revealed by his astute analyses of land disputes. Yet while admitting to the necessity of making concessions to the demands of cultivators on the land and making recommendations for the introduction of special regulations for different regions to prevent open revolt, Cevdet Paşa insisted on the generality of regulations relating to the definition of ownership rights. Special regulations represented a mere exigency, an urgent, political response; they did not pertain to the vocabulary of the domination of the nineteenth-century state.

Cevdet Paşa took care to incorporate this vocabulary in his legal opinions. For instance, he advised the Office of Imperial Registry on the necessity for extending the practices of registration of titles and drawing up lease contracts that were effective on state lands to *vakıf* and *mülk* lands. This was an argument for the consistency and generality of bureaucratic practices. In that, Cevdet Paşa was not far from an adherence to the Weberian ideal of the modern state with a concern for bureaucratic efficacy, for ensuring certainty in land transactions.[100] The vocabulary of bureaucratic efficacy was also that of domination by the central government. Thus, the extension of practices applicable to state lands to other categories of land was tantamount to erasures of the identities of groups whose interests were represented by these categories and thus to their subjugation to the imperatives of the central government, including taxation.

General and uniform categories and procedures that were the substance of state power and that represented erasures of particularistic interests were challenged and resisted. The Parga affair testified to such a challenge. The tension between the tendency to make practices universal and uniform, on the one hand, and to make them particular, on the other, lay at the heart of the drama of state formation in the nineteenth century. It inhabited the different practices; the legal definitions of property formed one such domain.

NOTES

1. Jurgen Habermas, *Legitimation Crisis* (Boston: Beacon Press, 1975). For formulations of this understanding in court decisions on property matters in British India, see Nicholas Dirks, "From Little King to Landlord: Property, Law, and the Gift under the Madras Permanent Settlement," *Comparative Studies in Society and History* 28 (1986), 307–33.

2. The naturalist argument was most forcefully stated by John Locke, who situated private property in the natural state of men. John Locke, *Two Treaties of Government,* ed. Peter Laslett (Cambridge: Cambridge University Press, 1960). Premised on natural law formulations, the naturalist argument was also espoused by the French jurists who were responsible for the drafting of the Civil Code. Donald R. Kelley and Bonnie G. Smith, "What Was Property? Legal Dimensions of the Social

Question in France (1789–1848)," *Proceedings of the American Philosophical Society* 128, no. 3 (1984), 200–30. In the nineteenth century, liberal jurists, including Sir Henry James Sumner Maine and Jeremy Bentham, were highly critical of the natural law formulations regarding private property. They saw the development of private property in the historical context of commercial expansion. For them, private law represented a formalization of that development. Sir Henry James Sumner Maine, *Ancient Law* (London: John Murrray, 1920); C. K. Ogden, ed., *Jeremy Bentham: The Theory of Legislation* (London: Routledge and Kegan Paul, 1931). Bentham referred to property as an "expectation" on the part of the individual that developed in an environment of exchange, an expectation to be realized in law.

3. The historicist perspective has recently been taken up by the new institutionalist economists, most notably Douglass C. North, *Structure and Change in Economic History* (New York: Norton, 1981), and Eric L. Jones, *The European Miracle: Environments, Economics and Geopolitics in the History of Europe and Asia* (Cambridge: Cambridge University Press, 1981). North and Jones point to the determination of private property in terms of decisions or choices made by individuals seeking to maximize their economic gains in an environment of commercial expansion. They argue that environments of commercial activity are characterized by "market failures" or impediments (such as communal property rights) to the exchange activity of individuals. Market failure implies transaction costs. Private ownership, in this context, is an institution that achieves a reduction of transaction costs and that, in doing so, generates efficiency. It is an outcome of cost-benefit analysis undertaken by maximizing individuals to reduce transaction costs. The new institutional economics presents a challenge to the notion of the "market" as representing an abstract realm of economic exchange of homogeneous goods through voluntary transactions by large numbers of autonomous, fully informed individuals with motives of profit maximization. This abstraction characterizes the formulations of neoclassical economics, as well as the Smithian liberal formulations of the post-1980s liberal renaissance. It does not allow for either "market failures" or institutions. From the orthodox

"market" perspective, private ownership is part of the process of allocation of resources through the workings of supply and demand forces in the market. Institutionalists would not object to this characterization in principle, except for the fact that they do not take for granted the self-regulating properties of the market. Put differently, they feel that the market will not automatically achieve its ends and point to the fact that it may require a little help from institutions, including private property.

4. For an institutionalist argument on state intervention as impeding economic growth, see Eric L. Jones, *Growth Recurring: Economic Change in World History* (Oxford: Clarendon; New York: Oxford University Press, 1988).

5. For this liberal perception of law as one responding to and expediting commercial expansion, see Maine, *Ancient Law*. The present-day institutionalists prefer not to get involved in private law debates. To the extent they are at all concerned with law, they refer to the administrative rulings by the state that formalize the decisions of maximizing individuals participating in the different markets. See North, *Structure and Change*, as well as his more recent work, which focuses on the state.

6. For a critical discussion of separation of powers and the rule of law, see Habermas, *Legitimation Crisis*; for a critical view of private law, see Karl Renner, *The Institutions of Private Law and Their Social Function* (London: Routledge and Kegan Paul, 1949), especially chap. 2; and for a critique from the perspective of administrative law, see Mark Neocleous, *Administering Civil Society: Towards a Theory of State Power* (Houndmills, Basingstoke, U.K.: Macmillan Press; New York: St. Martin's Press, 1996).

7. Roger Cotterell, "Power, Property and the Law of Trusts: A Partial Agenda for Critical Legal Scholarship," in *Critical Legal Studies,* ed. Peter Fitzpatrick and Alan Hunt (Oxford: Basil Blackwell, 1987). Cotterell focuses on the ways legal formulations accommodated and guaranteed the inequalities implied by private ownership, which excluded all claims to property but those of the individual owner. Cotterell argues that through the separation of the legal subjects from the assets they own, the law could allow for an equality of the legal subjects, while inequality became an attribute of the distribution of assets. This was impor-

tant in view of the fact that equality of all persons before the law was a central precept of the rule of law formulations in the nineteenth century.

8. For a discussion of these categories and systems of classifications, see Maine, *Ancient Law,* 100 ff., 295. Maine also pointed to an obliteration of the distinction between inheritance and acquisition in establishing the alienability of land, given that alienation of inherited property of the father was subject to the consent of male children while his acquired property was not. Maine wrote: "The history of property on the European Continent is the history of the subversion of the feudalized law of land by the Romanized law of movables" (283). This notion of law as generative of categories and classifications leads to endless discussion about which law has the categories and which law does not. As the law self-consciously employed by nineteenth-century jurists, including English ones, Roman law is generally assigned the privileged position of possessing them. By contrast, and typically, Islamic law does not. Leaving aside the little-studied area of the overlaps between *shari'* precepts relating to land and Roman law (it could not be otherwise as Islamic societies developed in the former Roman lands), this view misses the particularity of debates that take place in the context of different vocabularies in relation to categories and classifications constituting individual ownership. For some of these debates, see Ebulula Mardin, *Medeni Hukuk Cephesinden Ahmet Cevdet Paşa* (Istanbul: Cumhuriyet Matbaası, 1946).

9. Habermas, *Legitimation Crisis,* demonstrates that the "rule of law" embodying the principles of separation of powers (state, society, law), of the sanctity of private property, and of equality before the law, refers to a self-definition (ideology) of Western liberal societies, and as such represents an aspiration rather the actual conditions in these societies. See also Jurgen Habermas, *Between Facts and Norms: Contributions to a Discourse Theory of Law and Democracy* (Cambridge, Mass.: MIT Press, 1996).

10. For discussion of the East/West problematic in relation to the Middle East, see Talal Asad, ed., *Anthropology and the Colonial Encounter* (London: Ithaca Press, 1973); for an evaluation of the liberal as well as Marxist (Asiatic mode of production) treatments of Ottoman history, see Huri Islamoglu-Inan, "Introduc-

tion," in *The Ottoman Empire and the World Economy,* ed. Huri Islamoglu-Inan (Cambridge: Cambridge University Press, 1987). In the case of the Ottoman empire, liberal historians argued that state ownership of land was the primary obstacle to the development of individual ownership rights. See Gabriel Baer, *Studies in the Social History of Modern Egypt* (Chicago: University of Chicago Press, 1969), 62–78. In relation to Egypt, Kenneth M. Cuno, subscribing to a similar liberal reasoning, pointed to the development of private property in land in the late eighteenth century in the context of commercial expansion and the weakening of controls by the Ottoman state over the economy. According to Cuno, this process was interrupted by the rise of a strong state under Mehmet Ali and intensified state intervention in agriculture. "The Origins of Private Ownership of Land in Egypt: A Reappraisal," *International Journal of Middle East Studies* 12 (1980): 245–75.

11. E. M. Forster, *Howard's End* (New York: St. Martins Press, 1997).

12. For a discussion of property relation as a power relation, see C. B. Macpherson, "The Meaning of Property," in *Property: Mainstream and Critical Positions,* ed. C. B. Macpherson, (Oxford: Blackwell, 1978); see also Franz von Benda-Beckman, *Property in Social Continuity* (The Hague: Martinus Nijhoff, 1979), especially chap. 1.

13. In emphasizing the contexts of struggles, this chapter departs from the moral-economy arguments that tend to assume a universal vocabulary of justice against the inherent injustice of private ownership. These arguments tend to hypostatize in moral terms the resistance to private ownership. In so doing, they abstract the different struggles from their historical contexts, from the contexts in which the dispossessed have a chance of political participation and not simply satisfied by having the moral high ground. Edward P. Thompson's work, especially "The Moral Economy of English Crowd in the eighteenth Century," *Past and Present* 50 (1971), 76–109, has been the inspiration for such arguments. They are further elaborated in the work of authors whose work comes under the rubric of subaltern studies, especially in relation to India.

14. For a discussion of administrative law, in addition to Neocleous, *Administering Civil Society,* see also H. W. Arthurs, *Without the Law: Administrative Justice and Legal Pluralism in Nineteenth-Century England* (Toronto: University of Toronto Press, 1985).

15. Edward P. Thompson, *Whigs and Hunters: The Origin of the Black Act* (New York: Pantheon Books, 1975), 261. Also, on the constitution of property through the Enclosure Acts in England, see Philip Corrigan and Derek Sayer, "How the Law Rules," in *Law, State and Society,* ed. Bob Fryer et al. (London: Croom Helm, 1981), 23.

16. Perry Anderson, *Lineages of the Absolutist State* (London: New Left Review, 1976).

17. In the case of Germany during the nineteenth century, Michael John argues that the formulations of the Civil Code were relativized in special provisions well before the Code was issued in 1892. These special provisions, which embodied the demands of the different social groups, were administrative rulings that significantly modified the precepts of the Code regarding private property. In fact, these practices defined property relations in the nineteenth century. Thus, Michael John suggests that the German Civil Code was more important as a representation of legal unity as crafted through the professional commitment and the legal skills of the German jurists than it was a representation of property relations as they existed. "The Politics of Legal Unity in Germany, 1870–1896," *Historical Journal* 28, no. 2 (1985): 341–56.

18. Kelley and Smith, "What Was Property?"

19. For the centrality of administrative law in the constitution of the English working class, see Neocleous, *Administering Civil Society.* For an argument about how the "law" of the jurists was circumvented by administrative practice in France, following the 1848 revolution and widespread resistance to the understanding of absolute private ownership embodied in the Civil Code (1804) as well as in postrevolutionary constitutions, see Jacques Donzelot, *L'invention du social* (Paris: Fayard, 1984). In this relation, Donzelot pointed to a new mode of state intervention that developed in the mid-nineteenth century and that, he argued, entailed the constitution of a "civil society" (*social*) through admin-

istrative practice, including administrative law and statistics. He explained the development of this mode of intervention in terms of the need to contain the civil resistance that found its expression in the political language of natural rights that the Revolution helped to generalize. The vocabularies of administrative law and statistics were important in diffusing civil resistance while allowing for the right of social struggle within the spaces they provided. At the same time, the language of statistics was instrumental in the objectification (naturalization?) of social reality, thereby rendering it no longer a target of resistance.

20. The French government initially proposed the adoption of the French Civil Code. The Ottoman jurists, mostly notably Cevdet Paşa, also one-time grand vezir and a high-ranking bureaucrat, objected strongly on the grounds that a civil code had to do with the identity or a self-definition of a society; therefore, adoption of a foreign code would undermine that identity. He proposed the drafting of an Ottoman civil code based on the precepts of Islamic jurisprudence or *fiqh*. Mardin, *Medeni Hukuk*.

21. For a discussion of the *Mecelle*, see Robert H. Eisenman, *Islamic Law in Palestine and Israel: A History of the Survival of Tanzimat and Sharia in the British Mandate and the Jewish State* (Leiden: Brill, 1978), 19–26. For the text of the *Mecelle*, see Hilmi Ergüney, *Mecelle Külli Kaideleri* (Istanbul: Yenilik Basımevi, 1965).

22. For a discussion of a nineteenth-century European understanding of the *shari'a*, especially in relation to French North Africa, see Alan Christelow, *Muslim Law Courts and the French Colonial State in Algeria* (Princeton, N.J.: Princeton University Press, 1985).

23. Huri Islamoglu-Inan, "Law, Property and State Power in the Ottoman Empire," unpublished manuscript. For instance, the Turkish historian Ömer L. Barkan subscribed to this dichotomous perception of law and assumed that in the Ottoman empire *kanun* and *shari'a* belonged to separate domains. Writing in the "statist," Keynesian mental climate of the 1930s and 1940s, he argued that in the nineteenth century the separation of *kanun* and *shari'a* was obliterated in the Land Code. The latter, according to Barkan, represented a reassertion of the *kanun* precept of the state ownership of land but was also infiltrated by the precepts of

Islamic jurisprudence, especially in relation to the increase in the number of heirs. "Türk Toprak Hukuku Tarihinde Tanzimat ve 1274 Arazi Kanunnamesi," in *Tanzimat*, 1 (Istanbul: Maarif Matbaası. 1940), 21–42.

24. Halil Inalcik, "Islamization of Ottoman Laws on Land and Land Tax," in *Osmanistik-Turkologie-Diplomatik*, ed. Christa Fragner and Klaus Schwarz (Berlin: Klaus Schwarz Verlag, 1992).

25. Viewed from this perspective, it is not surprising that the drafters of the Code, which chronologically preceded the *Mecelle*, drew from the precepts of Islamic jurisprudence. Among the examples of this were the provisions of the Code extending the numbers of heirs from three to nine, as well as those introducing separability of multiple, overlapping claims to land use. Ahmet Cevdet Paşa, *Tezakir*, vol. 4, ed. Cavit Baysun (Ankara: Türk Tarih Kurumu Basımevi, 1986).

26. For a discussion of Foucault's work in this context, see Colin Gordon, "Governmental Rationality: An Introduction," in *The Foucault Effect: Studies in Governmentality*, ed. Graham Burchell, Colin Gordon, and Peter Miller (Chicago: University of Chicago Press; London: Harvester Wheatsheaf, 1991). Foucault himself was well aware of the problem of political closures implied in his conception of governmentality. See Michel Foucault, "The Subject and Power," in Michel Foucault, *Beyond Structuralism and Hermeneutics*, ed. Hubert L. Dreyfus and Paul Rabinow (Chicago: University of Chicago Press, 1982).

27. This should not imply, however, that law represents a negotiated settlement (at least in the context of the modern state) in the sense that once a settlement is reached among parties, the individual parties lose their distinctness and dissolve into each other. Instead, law represents multiple power fields embodying different sets of actors who retain their distinctness. As such, law is a continuous process of contestation and of deliberation. In this sense, one could speak of law as politics, of its contextuality, and of its embeddedness in any given historical context. For the argument about law representing a continuous process of contestation and of deliberation in which the individual actors do not lose distinctiveness, I am grateful to Peter Fitzpatrick, "Consolations of the Law: Community and Deliberative Politics," paper presented at the workshop on Law and Deliberative Politics, Bielefeld, 26–27

February 1999. Fitzpatrick, however, does not specify the power contexts in which deliberations take place.

28. For a discussion of the highly qualified nature of property relations in England, see David Sugarman, "Law, Economy and The State in England, 1750–1914: Some Major Issues," in *Legality, Ideology and the State*, ed. David Sugarman (London: Academic Press, 1983); for the contested character of private property, see Thompson, "The Moral Economy" and *Whigs and Hunters*.

29. The conception of the state presented here draws on the work of Philip Abrams, "Notes on the Difficulty of Studying the State," *Journal of Historical Sociology* 1, no. 1 (March 1988): 58–89. See also Philip Corrigan and Derek Sayer, *The Great Arch: English State Formation as Cultural Revolution* (Oxford: Blackwell, 1985); Timothy Mitchell, "Society, Economy and the State Effect," in *State/Culture: State-Formation after the Cultural Turn*, ed. George Steinmetz (Ithaca: Cornell University Press, 1999).

30. Historically, idioms of rule have derived from vocabularies of statecraft that get imprinted in collective memories. One could mention the legacies of Roman and Sasanid statecraft among these vocabularies. For a discussion of Sasanian vocabularies, see Halil Inalcik, "State and Ideology," in *The Middle East and the Balkans under the Ottoman Empire* (Bloomington: Indiana University Press, 1993). The *Siyasetname* (Book of government) by Nizam-ülmülk, the Persian minister to the Abbasid rulers of the tenth century, is representative of understanding of Sasanid statecraft.

31. For an excellent discussion of the historical development of the separation between state and society in the context of the emergence of civil society in eighteenth-century Europe, see Jurgen Habermas, *The Structural Transformation of the Public Sphere: An Inquiry into a Category of Bourgeois Society* (Cambridge, Mass.: MIT Press, 1989).

32. *The Islamic Law on Land Tax and Rent* (London: Croom Helm, 1988). For a recent and passionate discussion of a global order of exchange in the pre-eighteenth-century period, dominated by China and other Asian regions including India, Persia, and the Ottoman empire, see André Gunder Frank, *Re-Orient: Global Economy in the Asian Age* (Berkeley: University of California Press, 1998). Frank undertook an effective critique of the

"stagnationist" arguments that dominate the Eurocentric accounts of Asian economies by focusing on the commercial dynamics of these societies prior to the eighteenth century. Yet by extending the notion of the "market" backward in time and attempting an equivalence between the commercial economies prior to the eighteenth century and the "order of the market" in the post-eighteenth-century period, Frank's analysis tends to overlook the power relations, including the development of centralized states, that were pivotal to the development of the "order of the market." As a result, Frank cannot explain the development of capitalism as an arena of power relations, and his analysis is bogged down in an unfruitful discussion of the origins of the industrial revolution in Europe. Frank argues that the industrial revolution was responsible for the establishment of European hegemony in the post-eighteenth-century period and, writing before the recent crisis of the Asian economies, he suggests that with industrialization underway in Asia, these areas are once again vying for hegemony in the global economy.

33. Alain Guery described this exchange in terms of the notion of "gift." See "Le roi dépensier: le don, le contraint et l'origine du système financier de la monarchie française de l'ancien régime," *Annales* 39, no. 6 (November–December 1984): 1241–69; "Etat, classification sociale et compromis sous Louis XIV: la capitation de 1695," *Annales* 41, no. 5 (September–October 1986): 1041–60.

34. For Ottoman state traditions, see Halil Inalcik, "Turkish and Iranian Political Theories and Traditions in Kutadgu Bilig" and "State and Ideology under Sultan Süleyman I," in *The Middle East and the Balkans under the Ottoman Empire: Essays on Economy and Society*. For European *raison d'état* states, see Gerhard Oestreich, *Neostoicism and the Early Modern State* (Cambridge: Cambridge University Press, 1982). For a discussion of the Ottoman state in relation to the idea of the *raison d'état* state, see Frederik Meinecke, *Machiavellism: The Doctrine of Raison d'Etat and Its Place in Modern History* (London: Routledge and Kegan Paul, 1957), 85–89.

35. In the early period, the destination of revenues that accrued to the central state was specified, such as the treasury (*bayt al-mal*) and the estates of the sultan and of the members of the palace

(*has*). For a discussion of these classifications, see Huri Islamoglu-Inan, *State and Peasant in the Ottoman Empire: Agrarian Power Relations and Regional Economic Development in Ottoman Anatolia during the Sixteenth Century* (New York: Brill, 1994), chaps. 1 and 3.

36. This particularity is manifested in the issuing of special sets of regulations for different regions and for different groups, such as nomads (*yörük*) and rice cultivators (*çeltikci*), or for different categories of revenue grant holders, such as *vakıf* and *mülk*. These regulations were often attached to the tax surveys prepared for different regions, as well as for different groupings and for types of revenue entitlements. For a detailed discussion, see Islamoglu-Inan, *State and Peasant,* chap. 1; for texts and discussions of these regulations, see Ömer L. Barkan, *Osmanlı İmparatorluğunda Zirai Ekonominin tabi olduğu Kurallar,* vol. 1, *Kanunlar* (Istanbul: Burhaneddin Matbaası, 1943).

37. The idea of property as a bundle of rights derives from Maine, *Ancient Law.* Maine employs the metaphor of the bundle in describing premodern property systems. Also see the discussion in section on Conceptual Parameters.

38. For a discussion of Ottoman state power and changes in the nature of ruling elites, see Ariel Saltzman, "An Ancien Regime Revisited: 'Privatization' and Political Economy in the Eighteenth-Century Ottoman Empire," *Politics and Society* 21, no. 4 (December 1993): 393–423.

39. For the seventeenth-century origins of the tension between central government and provincial power nodules in France, see William Beik, *Absolutism and Society in Seventeenth-Century France: State Power and Provincial Aristocracy in Languedoc* (New York; Cambridge: Cambridge University Press, 1989).

40. The notion of a state's generation of wealth in terms of extensive measures would also apply to mercantilist policies.

41. Roger J. P. Kain and Elizabeth Baigent, *The Cadastral Map in the Service of the State: A History of Property Mapping* (Chicago: University of Chicago Press, 1992), 343–44.

42. Elizabeth Genovese-Fox, *The Origins of Physiocracy: Economic Revolution and Social Order in Eighteenth-Century France* (Ithaca: Cornell University Press, 1976), 113 ff.; for a description

of property as an expectation, see Bentham, *Theory of Legislation.*

43. Michel Foucault, "On Governmentality," in Burchell et al., *The Foucault Effect.*

44. Michel Foucault, "Omnes et Singulatim: Towards a Criticism, of 'Political Reason'," in *The Tanner Lectures on Human Values,* vol. 1, ed. Sterling McMurrin (Salt Lake City: University of Utah Press, 1981), 225–54; see also Keith Tribe, *Governing Economy: The Reformation of German Economic Discourse 1750–1840* (Cambridge: Cambridge University Press, 1988).

45. For a detailed discussion of *temettuat* registers, see Huri Islamoglu, "Administering Property: Law and Statistics in the Nineteenth Century Ottoman Empire" in *Constitutions of Property Rights in Comparative Perspective,* ed. Huri Islamoglu (Albany: State University of New York, 2001).

46. *Temettuat* registers introduced the *dönüm* as the unit for measuring land. This was an aerial unit and was deemed more accurate than the *çift,* the area that could be plowed by a pair of oxen, which had served as the unit of measurement prior to the nineteenth century. Ibid.

47. This separation, indeed, represented a rupture with earlier definitions of rights to revenues and to use that did not presuppose an object separate from themselves. In these definitions, land classified as immovable was not, in its juridical perception, a thing with an existence of its own, exchangeable or alienable. For instance, in the case of freehold property or in transfers of usufruct titles to individual plots, what was alienated was not land but the rights to its revenues and to its use. Land was inalienable and restrictions on alienability were restrictions on alienability of rights and therefore their accumulation in a few hands. See Islamoglu-Inan, *State and Peasant;* see also the discussion above in the section on Transformation of the State.

48. For an excellent discussion of the technique of registration in the constitution of individual ownership in nineteenth-century England, see Alain Pottage, "The Originality of Registration," *Oxford Journal of Legal Studies* 15 (1995): 385–400.

49. Tim Mitchell, "Making Space for the Nation State," in *Colonialism, Post-Colonialism and the Production of Space,* ed. D. Clay-

ton and D. Gregory (Oxford: Blackwell, forthcoming). Mitchell's analysis is, however, too categorical in assigning the creation of the right of ownership (which he designates as abstract) to the legal sphere and of the constitution of land as a "thing" (which he designates as concrete) to the sphere of administrative practices of cadastration. The constitutions of the right and its object could be part of one and the same process. The Land Code of 1858, which represented administrative law, was one such instance. At the same time, individual ownership right was also constituted through the concrete technique of registration of title. Pottage, "The Originality of Registration." Second, in emphasizing the rupture that private ownership represented in terms of the separation of the right from its object, Mitchell overlooks the ambiguity in law regarding the "thingness" of land and the argument that, in the case of private ownership, what is actually exchanged is the right and not the "thing." Alain Pottage, "The Cadastral Metaphor: Intersections of Property and Topography," in Islamoglu, *Constitutions of Property Rights.*

50. See above, n. 47.

51. Ranajit Guha, *A Rule of Property for Bengal: An Essay on the Idea of the Permanent Settlement* (Paris: Mouton, 1963).

52. For Marxist Asiatic mode of production arguments of oppositionality between state ownership and development of private property, see Shlomo Avineri, "Modernization and Arab Society," in *Israel, the Arabs and the Middle East,* ed. Irving Howe and Carl Gershman (New York: Quadrangle, 1972); Karl Wittfogel, *Oriental Despotism* (New York: Vintage Books, 1981); for liberal arguments, see above n.10.

53. For instance, see Eisenman, *Islamic Law in Palestine and Israel.* This perception that the administrative constitution of individual ownership took place on *miri* lands poses a challenge to the view that the Code represented a reasserting of the *miri* status (state ownership) over which the central government exercised control, and subsequent legislation represented a gradual transformation of *miri* status into *mülk* (freehold) status.

54. For a discussion of the *mülk* category in the context of the bifurcation of Ottoman law into Islamic private and sultanic (administrative) public law, see the section 1 on Conceptual Parameters that begins this chapter. The *Mecelle,* premised on the precepts of

Islamic *fiqh*, was to form the domain of private law. The *Mecelle* did not introduce a general formulation of either private property or contracts. Its provisions, however, suggest an obliteration of the distinction between movables (referring to all exchangeable goods, including the fruits of land) and immovables (representing land), which would indicate subjecting of goods and land to the same rules of transactions. Eisenman, *Islamic Law in Palestine and Israel.*

55. It has been argued that the notion of absolute property that the Code embodied was built on a relation between the state and individual cultivators and increasingly assumed the character of a contractual relation between the two. The idea of contractual relations also characterized the rent or lease arrangement, as well as the transfers of *tapu* (state lands). Halil Cin, *Osmanlı Toprak Düzeni ve Bu Düzenin Bozulması* (Istanbul: Boğaziçi Yayınları, 1985). For the text of the Land Code used in this study, see Ahmet Akgündüz, *Mukayeseli İslam ve Osmanlı Hukuku Külliyatı* (Diyarbakır: Dicle Universitesi Hukuk Fakultesi Yayınları, 1986), 683 ff. Hereafter I refer to the different articles by number. For a description of *ferağ* (transfer) as a contractual arrangement in which both sides had to give their consent and for the specification of conditions under which a party could be coerced or persuaded to transfer his land, see Articles 113 to 114 and 119 of the Code. The idea of contractuality that is central to the development of absolute ownership was further advanced with the issuing of *Konturato nizamnamesi* in 1868. In fact, it was in the context of the extension of rent contracts to *mülk* lands that the assimilation of *mülk* lands to the status of *tapu* lands was debated. See Cevdet Paşa, *Tezakir,* vol. 4, 141–42, for the suggestion that the *icare-i zemin* provision of the Code should be extended to *emlak-i sırfa* and the *mülk* holders should be entitled to rents from those who planted trees on their lands.

56. Marion Farouk-Sluglett and Peter Sluglett emphasized this aspect of the Code in their study of land tenure in Iraq, "The Transformation of Land Tenure and Rural Social Structure in Central and Southern Iraq, c.1870–1958," *International Journal of Middle East Studies* 15 (1983): 491–505; also on registration, see above n. 48.

57. On multiple titles submitted by estate-holders and cultivators to prove their ownership rights, see *İrade-i Defter-i Hakani-2* (MV 24225), dated 26 Cemaziyyül Ahir 1281.

58. Akgündüz, *Hukuk Külliyatı,* Article 68.

59. Cin, *Osmanlı Toprak Düzeni,* 126–29. The public character of all land transactions, including transfers, has also been viewed as a measure taken to ensure that the title holders were not coerced or persuaded into selling their property. On public registration, see Maine, *Ancient Law,* 354 ff.

60. For the subjection of *mülk* lands to the tithe, whereby rights on these lands were delinked from the privilege of tax exemption, see Ömer L. Barkan, *Türkiye'de Toprak Meselesi* (Istanbul: Gözlem Yayınları, 1980). This implied an approximation of the *mülk* category to the category of individual ownership on state lands and a standardization of legal practice regarding different categories of land. In 1874, the practices of registration and issuance of title deeds were extended to *mülk* lands. For *emlak-i sırfa* or *mülk nizamnamesi,* see Cin, *Osmanlı Toprak Düzeni,* 130. Also see above, note 55, for Cevdet Paşa on the extension of lease contracts and registration practices to *vakıf* and *mülk* lands.

61. This may partly explain the difficulties encountered, since the inception of the Turkish Republic, in the taxing of the agricultural sector. Though these difficulties are often cast in terms of reluctance of governments to alienate small to medium-sized peasant producers, the resistance to taxes on the part of large landowners, especially in western Anatolia, no doubt contributed to the government's inability to tax.

62. Akgündüz, *Hukuk Külliyatı,* Article 25 of the Land Code. This was especially important in the case of ownership of trees, which, as is discussed in the next section on Contestation of the Code and the Special Provisions was a highly contentious issue. The Code stipulated that transfer of trees could not be treated separately from that of the land (Articles 44, 28, and 25). This in fact implied a standardization of law relating to *tapu* (that is, titled lands or *miri*) and *mülk* lands (Articles 25 and 28).

63. Article 28 recognized the ownership rights of title holders over trees that they planted on *tapu* lands. But such rights were defined as *mülk* (conceding to a continuity with previous practice) while,

at the same time, being subject to the principle that trees were subject to the status of the land.

64. Article 36 stipulated that transfer could not take place without the permission of the land official (*arazi memuru*). It stated that while the person who transferred property could not go to court to demand payment, he could seize the property. This stipulation was revised in 1879 by an *irade-i seniyye* that recognized the right of the person who made the transfer to go to court. For a discussion of *ferağ* in relation to the 1858 Code, see Cin, *Osmanlı Toprak Düzeni*, 120–28. For a general discussion of *ferağ* in light of Ebu Suud's opinions, see Inalcik, "Islamization of Ottoman Laws on Land and Land Tax," 108–9.

65. Akgündüz, *Hukuk Külliyatı*, Article 115.

66. Ibid., Articles 116 and 117. Thus, *vefaen ferağ* allowed for land transfers on the condition that they were returned after the payment of debt. On the other hand, *ferağ bil istiğlal* allowed for transfer of lands to the lender on the condition that he lease to the debtor to enable the latter to pay his debt and get back his land.

67. Cin, *Osmanlı Toprak Düzeni*, 146–56.

68. Akgündüz, *Hukuk Külliyatı*, Article 23.

69. Ibid., Article 68.

70. Ibid., Article 21.

71. Cin, *Osmanlı Toprak Düzeni*, 110.

72. Serge Aberdam, *Aux origines du code rural, 1789–1900: un siècle de débat* (Paris: Institut national de la recherche agronomique, 1982).

73. For an excellent analysis of the French Civil Code, see André-Jean Arnaud, *Essai d'analyse structurale du code civil français: la règle du jeu dans la paix bourgeoise* (Paris: Librairie générale de droit et de jurisprudence 1973). The French Civil Code, which stated in Article 544 that "property is the right to enjoy and dispose of things in the most absolute ways," had met with strong resistance in the countryside. Disputations in tribunals and in the legislature had resulted in the issuing of rulings that qualified and trans-muted the definition of Article 544; throughout the nineteenth century, the French government came to rely on local usage for ordering of property relations on land. The contentious nature of property relations may explain the preponderance of policing

measures in the French countryside. For discussion of Article 544, see Kelley and Smith, "What Was Property?" Kelley and Smith point to the condition of "public interest" introduced in Article 545, which was, in fact, a restriction on the absolute right of property.

74. William Sewell, "Property, Labor and the Emergence of Socialism in France, 1789–1848," in *Consciousness and Class Experience in Nineteenth-Century Europe,* ed. John M. Merriman (New York: Holmes and Meier, 1979).

75. For a discussion of these disputes during the revolutionary period in the 1790s from the "moral economy perspective," see Edward P. Thompson et al., *La guerre du blé au XVIIIe siècle* (Montreuil: Les éditions de la passion, 1988).

76. The instance of Bulgarian revolts in the 1840s, prior to the issuance of the Code, alerted the central state to the danger of social unrest if absolute ownership rights were to be generalized. Halil İnalcık, *Tanzimat ve Bulgar Meselesi* (Ankara: Türk Tarih Kurumu Basımevi, 1943). The Greek Revolution in the 1820s, which adopted the ideals of the French Revolution, also made the Ottoman statesmen acutely aware of the threat of rebellion in the Balkans.

77. Cevdet Paşa, *Tezakir,* vol. 4, 140–47.

78. An utilitarian flavor is clearly discernible in the text of 1839 reform edict; see the following section.

79. For a physiocratic (Quesnay) version of the line of reasoning that linked private property to increased productivity, increased production of wealth, and the interests of the state in terms of increases in taxable wealth, see Genovese-Fox, *The Origins of Physiocracy,* 110–33, especially 112–14. For a discussion of the "productive principle" in relation to the definition of private property right in British India, see Dirks, "From Little King to Landlord," 316.

80. For a discussion of Ottoman state dirigism in the nineteenth century, see Donald Quataert, "Main Problems of the Economy during the Tanzimat Period," in *150. Yılında Tanzimat,* ed. Hakkı Dursun Yıldız (Ankara: Türk Tarih Kurumu, 1992), 212–13; see also, in the same volume, Tevfık Güran, "Zirai Politika ve Ziraatte Gelişmeler, 1839–1876." Central to the constitution of the agrarian economy was the collection of

large masses of data on agricultural production that ultimately, in the mid-1840s, were compiled in the form of *temettuat defterleri.* Islamoglu, "Statistical Constitution of Property Rights."

81. "Cevdet Paşa," Islam Ansiklopedisi. See also the introduction to the text of the Code penned by its drafters. Akgündüz, *Hukuk Külliyatı.*

82. İnalcık, *Tanzimat ve Bulgar Meselesi.*

83. Tevfık Güran, "Osmanlı İmparatorluğunda Zirai Kredi Politikasının Gelişmesi, 1840–1910," in *Uluslararası Mithat Paşa* Semineri: Bildiriler ve Tartışmalar (Ankara: Türk Tarih Kurumu Basımevi, 1986).

84. Şevket Pamuk, "Commodity Production for World-Markets and Relations of Production in Ottoman Agriculture, 1840–1913," in Islamoglu-Inan, *The Ottoman Empire.*

85. *İrade*s (decrees or ordinances) are among the most important documents for the history of the nineteenth-century Ottoman empire. Beginning in 1832, the Ottoman rulers issued their orders and decisions in the form of *irade*s that had the authority of laws. The *irade*s generally represent imperial decisions on specific matters and disputes and include a detailed description of the issue at hand and the imperial decision regarding it. For an excellent study of classifications of *irade*s, see Mehmet Seyitdanlıoğlu, *Tanzimat Devrinde Meclis-i Vala 1838–1868* (Ankara: Türk Tarih Kurumu Basımevı, 1994).

86. Cevdet Paşa, *Tezakir,* 140–52.

87. The *Konturato Nizamnamesi* (law of contracts) appears to have been issued about the same time as the Code. The special regulations for Bosnia dated 1859 include a reference to *Konturato Nizamnamesi;* see "Bosna *Nizamnamesi*" in *Düstur,* 3rd ed. (Istanbul, 1282 H), 1:78–84.

88. For a description of these estates or *baştinalı* çiftliks, where sharecropping arrangements prevailed, see Ahmet Cevdet Paşa, *Maruzat,* ed. Yusuf Hallaçoğlu (Istanbul: Çağrı Yayınları, 1980), 65–77.

89. For previous attempts to settle the conflict in Parga, see Cevdet Paşa, *Tezakir,* vol. 4, 140. One solution proposed was to give *miri* lands to the *ashab;* another was to parcel and sell the land of the estate (which was *miri* or state land). Neither was acceptable.

90. For a discussion by Cevdet Paşa of similar land disputes, in Bosnia-Herzegovinia, see *Maruzat*, 65–67. In a dispute at the estate of Birgursi, in Yanya, the tenants complained of mistreatment by estate holders (including charges that the *ashab* unlawfully imprisoned them). They challenged the rights of the *ashab* to the land and submitted *tapu* documents that represented their usufruct rights in support of their claims to land. The *ashab*, in turn, charged the cultivators with not paying the shares that were due to them. In support of their claims to these shares, which were equivalent of a rent, the *ashab* sought to prove that they had the ownership rights to the land. To this end, they submitted *senedat-ı* resmiyye (official documents) allegedly dating back 150 to 200 years and sought to register the land in their names. *İrade-ı Defter-i Hakani-2* (MV 24225), dated 26 Cemaziyyül Ahir 1281. It is important to note that the practice of registering lands and issuing title deeds predated the Land Code of 1858. Two *nizamname*s (regulations) relating to the issuance of title deeds appeared on 17 May 1845 and 21 May 1847. Ilber Ortaylı, *Imparatorluğun En Uzun Yüzyılı* (Istanbul: Hil Yayınları, 1983), 159.

91. *İslam Ansiklopedisi*, "Cevdet Paşa."

92. The commission was composed of nine members—one representative from each of the five quarters of the town of Parga, the *nazır* and the *müdir* of the *çiftlik* (estate), one member from the council of the province (*vilayet meclisi*), and one member from the subprovince council (*kaza meclisi*). Cevdet Paşa, *Tezakir,* 141.

93. For the correspondence between these offices and Cevdet Paşa, see *Tezakir,* 131–39.

94. This represented a recasting of the provision in the Code that buildings and trees were subject to ownership of land (Articles 35, 28; Cin, *Osmanlı Toprak Düzeni*, 111). The dispute was over ownership of houses that the tenant cultivators had built and of trees they had planted on the land of the *ashab*. The dispute also extended to the issue of the ownership of houses in the town of Parga. Using the precept of the Code that buildings were subject to ownership of land, the *ashab-i alaka* claimed ownership of the Venetian houses in the town of Parga. Cevdet Paşa, *Tezakir,* 144. In relation to houses built by tenant cultivators, the Land Code

prescribed that in the event that the tenant moved away from the land, such buildings were either to be destroyed and the building materials carried away by the tenant or the *ashab* were to pay the tenant an amount that was the equivalent of the value of the house. In Parga, such houses were well built wooden constructions, and it appears that their builders were not only reluctant to destroy them but also laid claim to the land on which the houses stood. Cevdet Paşa posed the problem rather elegantly: "it is not within the bounds of justice and fair play to tell the tenant to remove the building and leave the land to the *ashab-ı* alaka." *Tezakir,* 147.

95. See Article 23 of the Land Code, concerning the translation into proprietary rights of very long term leases or *müddet-ı medide* (*çok uzun süren*) on *miri* lands, which stated that the title holder had the right to take over his land (*ahz ve zabt*) at all times (*cemi-i zamanında*). On *icare-ı faside* or very long term leases, see Cin, *Osmanlı Toprak Düzeni,* 8396.

96. Cevdet Paşa was dispatched by the central government to settle land disputes in Bosnia with the title of Minister of Anatolia (*Anadolu sadareti payesi*) in 1280. *Maruzat,* 61, 66–67.

97. For similar settlements in Niş, see Cevdet Paşa, *Tezakir,* 142; for Bosnia, see Cevdet Paşa, *Maruzat,* 65–69; "Bosna *Nizamnamesi* (1859)," in Düstur 3.

98. For the original text of the edict, see Suna Kili and Şeref Gözübüyük, *Türk Anayasa Metinleri* (Ankara, 1957), 11–13. For a discussion of the text, see Halil Inalcik, "Sened-ı Ittifak ve Gülhane Hatt-ı Humayunu," *Belleten* 28 (1964): 616–18.

99. For the text of the 1876 constitution, see Kili and Gözübüyük, *Türk Anayasa Metinleri,* Article 21.

100. Cevdet Paşa talked about the need for certainty as an underlying concern in putting agreements to contract form (*"maksad-ı aslı muamalat-ı   nası taht-ı emniyette cereyan ettirmek"*). *Tezakir,* vol. 4, 145.

TWO

Village Authority and the Legal Order of Property (the Southern Hawran, 1876–1922)

Martha Mundy

Of the two major forms of right to agricultural property theorized by scholars of *fiqh* and central to administrative practice and law in the seventeenth and eighteenth centuries, the legal reforms of the Tanzimat developed the vocabulary of only one.[1] In constructing a single form of property in *miri* (state) land, in lieu of the dual property rights of management of revenue production and possession for cultivation, the legal language of the reforms culminating in the 1858 Land Code adopted the idioms previously employed to frame the latter form of right. The general definitions of a single usufructuary property right developed in this legislation were accompanied by new regulations of political administration, with the courts and legal scholarship being recast within this administrative order.[2] Whereas in the eighteenth century, within the (Islamic) court, the *'ulama'* provided legal commentary to administrative practice by drawing on plural sources of law (the doctrines of the schools of Islamic law [*fiqh*], administrative law [*qanun*], and custom), the nineteenth-century reforms sought to unify and to limit the corpus of the law through codification and to establish a division of labor, both substantive and hierarchical, between different types of court. Thus, one might say that whereas in the eighteenth century the *'ulama'* interpreted administrative practice in the terms of legal doctrine, in the nineteenth century Tanzimat law announced what the elaborate regulations of the different administrative institutions would endeavor to render real. The practice of political administration, notably of new forms of registration, was central to the definition of individual wealth, corresponding to individual subjecthood and tax liability to the state—the most general principle of the new order of government.[3]

In many parts of the empire, those who had earlier held rights to revenue succeeded, initially or subsequently, in being registered as the owners of the new, more powerful form of usufructuary right.[4] But this did not happen in all areas. In some, as in the Qada' 'Ajlun (Sancak Hawran, Province of Suriye), the cultivators themselves, or at least village residents, who already enjoyed usufructuary possession, obtained the new *tapu* title. Furthermore, large-scale alienation to urban capital was to remain highly circumscribed and, where it occurred, to be hotly contested.[5]

Central to the political administration of the new property right was the articulation between title and taxation. In areas such as Yanya (Province of Bosna), where the owners of the former right to manage revenue production acquired the new unified title to land, which entailed corresponding liability to tax, little had to change in the actual organization and documentation of tax collection.[6] But where, as in the Qada' 'Ajlun, the unified title was awarded to village men and women, the institutions of political administration at the level of the village itself were necessarily engaged in the definition of those granted title and in the articulation of title with tax liability.

According to the reforms (the Vilayet Laws of 1864 and 1871) the central institutions within the village were to be the elected assembly (*hay'at al-ikhtiyariyya*) and the headman (*mukhtar*).[7] The assembly would be responsible for the distribution of the burden of all taxes due from the village, for minor dispute resolution and for the good conduct of the *mukhtar*. The *mukhtar* would be responsible for the actual collection of taxes as well as for communication downward of all regulations imposed by the government and upward with all the information concerning village residents required by the administration. Janus-faced, designated by the villagers but confirmed by the administration, this administrative officer possessed limited executive power. The officers of this village administration were in principle to be elected from those eligible according to criteria of property ownership as measured by tax receipts. Higher levels of district administration, in the form of the two councils of the *qada'* (the administrative and the judicial councils) along with the city council of the district headquarters, embraced elected representatives from the district together with senior officers of the professional administration.

The two levels of administration, the village and the district councils, were central to the definition and administration of the new forms of property. The elected assembly of the village signed the declaration of the *yoklama* ("roll-call") award of title, together with the *mukhtar* (and occasionally the imam) and the *majlis al-idara* of the *qada'* that confirmed the government's acceptance of this declaration. Thus, although the law, the grid written at the center, was imposed on the locality, the entries within the grid were composed by figures elected from below to administrative bodies constituted according to the criteria of the Tanzimat legislation. Who came to occupy the new local administrative posts is thus a central question in the degree of continuity between pre- and postreform administration.

In this chapter I examine the nature of administrative personnel and their role in the administration of the new form of property in two contrasting villages of the Southern Hawran. The two villages lie close by one another, and both adjoin the district center, the town of Irbid. Yet, as we shall see, the first proves exemplary in its engagement with the institutions of law and registration, while the second proves exemplary in its avoidance of the same. We shall consider the history of such different paths, evident until today in the two villages. The small scale of the analysis requires that we take more seriously village administration than earlier scholarship has done. In the 1970s Gabriel Baer dismissed the *mukhtar* as a powerless, colorless figure; in Baer's sociology of Palestine (and the Fertile Crescent more widely) the major players were the regional strongmen and the patrilineal clans (*hama'il*).[8] Alexander Schölch, following Baer, remarked on the lack of power of the *mukhtar,* noting that the regionally prominent men who vied for posts on the regional councils in Palestine attached little value to serving as *mukhtar.*[9] But to say this is not only to read backward from the Mandate period; it is also to forget that the event of lasting importance was precisely the routinization of local authority (in the village and at the level of the district councils) and its disciplining according to the terms of the reformed legal order. The lack of color of the *mukhtar* is a historical achievement.

In tracing the story of property in these two villages, I have drawn on interviews with older residents from the two villages and on sources of the local administration (the *tapu* registers concerning the villages surviving in Jordan, the Mandate cadastral records for the villages, registers of the *shar'i* court from the early twentieth century, a few registers of the *nizami* court from the Faysali and Mandate periods, and lastly those *nufus* records of 1910 that survived the burning of the civil registry in 1970). The most complete of these sources are the *tapu* registers.

THE REGION: THE HAWRANI ECONOMY IN THE
LATE NINETEENTH CENTURY

The great plain of the Hawran lies to the south of the city of Damascus, the villages under study falling close to the southernmost extension of the plain. The Hawran was renowned for its wheat and lentils, where twenty-five-fold yields on wheat were not exceptional. In 1833 the Baron de Boislecomte wrote that average yields in Syria were twelve to one, or twice those of

France in his day.[10] The political context of the Baron's mission was Muhammad 'Ali's conquest of Syria and the Anglo-French commercial competition there. This coincided, moreover, with the beginning of a sustained increase in grain production and settlement in the Syrian plains.[11] Haim Gerber estimates that over the long haul of the nineteenth century Syria witnessed population growth of some 1 to 1.5 percent per annum, a growth permitting the extension of agriculture across the Syrian plains and a partial transformation of pastoral into agricultural land use at the same time as the population became more urbanized.[12]

In many parts of the Syrian plain (for example, around Aleppo and Hama), this commercial development may have encouraged urbanites to deepen their effective control over village producers. But we do not know this for certain since the only source seriously studied to date remains the *shar'i* court records, not the most telling registers for rural property in the second half of the nineteenth century after the reforms had come into effect. For the Hawran, the work of Linda Schilcher on consular records and Birgit Schäbler on Mandate sources reveals the tension between the attempts of Damascene grain merchants and tax financiers to gain control over production in the region and the violent revolts by which the central Hawran resisted such control.[13] Lying beyond the central Hawran, the Qada' 'Ajlun was an important source of revenue for Damascus, its tax receipts being the highest of any *qada'* in the Sancak of Hawran. Protected both by sheer distance and by the resistance of the peasants and regional leadership of the central zones of the Hawran, it remained an area of peasant right, mediated by local regional leadership, until the second half of the nineteenth century, when direct Ottoman administration was reimposed at the height of the expansion in the international grain market of Syria. However, this market was not to prove eternal: following the opening of the Suez Canal and the further hiatus in supplies from the United States during the U.S. Civil War, cheaper grain became available to Western Europe from India and North

America. And so it happened that in the Qada' 'Ajlun *tapu* registration coincided more or less with a decline in prices in the export market for Syrian grain. This fact meant that the interest of urbanites in the acquisition of title to land in this distant rural area never deepened to challenge widespread peasant right to land. Nevertheless, although the international demand for grain dropped, the high-quality wheat and lentils of the Hawran were still valued in Marseilles as well as in the cities of the Levant. In other words, the plains remained an area where, in the late nineteenth century, large farming households could act as commercial, not only as subsistence, enterprises.

THE TWO VILLAGES: HAWWARA AND BAIT RA'S

The *tapu* registration of property in both Hawwara and Bait Ra's occurred in the first years of *tapu* administration from the district headquarters of Irbid. The *tapu* and regional administrative officers carried out the roll call as required by the terms of the *tapu* regulations. The lists of these first years of intermittent registration of village property appear more variant in form than those carried out from 1882 by the special commission for the lands of Hawran headed by Ahmad al-Nayla.[14] A comparison of all the runs of first registration for the *qada'* reveals not only the slow progress but also, and more important, the unstandardized character of the representation of property holdings in the registers of these first years. One can sense the social negotiation behind the list of names in a way that is not true of the registers produced by al-Nayla's commission's swifter and more regular procedure. The reasons behind the establishment of the special commission in 1882—whether the lack of standardization in form, the slowness of the progress of registration, a tax revolt reported in parts of the Hawran in the late 1870s, or in response to the allegations of corruption lodged in 1879 by local leaders against the governor and director of finance—are not certain. What is important for our analysis here, however, is that the land of both the villages under study was first registered by the local Irbid *tapu* office in the early years before the more standardized procedures of the special commission.

Although Clause 8 of the Land Code prohibits the registration of village land in the name of the corporation of its holders or in the name of one or two holders standing for all, the code does permit the registration of individual shares in a common holding (*al-tasarruf bi-al-ishtirak*). The third village of the *qada'* to have been registered by the Irbid *tapu* office, Hawwara, adopted this form.[15] In the register the lands of Hawwara are described as three great blocks of land, divided into 46½ shares distributed among thirty-one title holders of whom one-fifth included two or more individuals. The other village with which we are concerned, Bait Ra's, like most of the other villages of the region, also registered its lands in this form. The land of Bait Ra's formed a single undivided plot, divided into thirty shares, distributed among fifteen title holdings, in nine of which more than one individual shared. This form of registration of individual property right accommodated three factors at one and the same time: the legal requirement of individual registration of title, the cultivators' need for continuity in the systems of field rotation and layout, and the institutional responsibility of the elected assembly to assign parts in the collective village tax burden to landholders.

HAWWARA

Title to land in Hawwara was awarded not by *haqq al-qarar* but at the much higher rate of *badal al-mithl,* it being noted that those registering land in Hawwara could not prove ten years' previous cultivation of the land or, what was presumably more relevant here, ten years of tax payments in their names. That Hawwara paid the higher rate does not mean that its lands had remained uncultivated during the previous ten years. We do not know whether the village had participated in the tax revolt and therefore had incomplete tax records or, more likely, whether it paid its taxes through a middleman and did not have available individual records of tax payment. But we do know that in the year just before land registration the cultivators of the village, or an important section of them, successfully contested the claim of the shaykh of the village, whom they alleged to have been imposed on them by higher authority, to "thirty ploughs of village land."[16] It stands to reason that the shaykh in question, Na'il Gharayba, had been acting as intermediary in the payment of tax since the efforts of the cultivators to claim the land by *haqq al-qarar* were not accepted.[17] Exceptionally this battle was pursued all the way up to the Council of State in Istanbul after it moved through the provincial administration.[18]

Relations to land, in terms of both production and fiscal burden, were calculated locally on the basis of an average unit of productivity. In Hawwara, as in most other villages of the plain, this was expressed in terms of notional plows, the *dunum* in the village being itself thought of in terms of units of average productivity.[16] In the November 1876 *tapu* registration of Hawwara, the distribution of the 46½ shares or *rub'a*s of land, as villagers called the unit, follows a regular pattern, all holders having 1, 1½, or 2 *rub'a*s of land, considerable holdings given that each *rub'a* comprises two plows of land. The distribution looks an extraordinarily egalitarian affair, but one should bear in mind that, given the high registry fees paid here, some village landholders undoubtedly had to borrow money to pay them.

INITIAL TRANSACTIONS

In April 1878, only eighteen months after initial registration, three holders who appear in the first half of the Hawwara list (numbers 1, 6, 9) sold their shares to Yusuf Efendi Mikha'il Efendi Tawil. It appears that this was the Yusuf Efendi Tawil who served as head of the audit in the finance department of the Sancak Hawran for a full ten years between 1876 and 1886.[19] Within a year, however, Yusuf Efendi proceeded to sell the same five shares to Na'il Gharayba. In 1882, moreover, Na'il Gharayba, jointly with his five brothers and two cousins, registered the largest compound house in the village valued at 7,000 *qurush* along with 2,000 *qurush* worth of water wells and grain pits. This registration precedes by a year the registration of other houses in Hawwara carried out by the special commission.

Shaykh Na'il Gharayba, as he appears in several Arabic documents, appears to have acted at the level of several villages, perhaps as the semiformal government agent for tax affairs of the subdistrict (*nahiya*) or at least for commercial dealings in agriculture in the plains around Hawwara.[20] He clearly had close relations with figures in the finance administration. The exchange by which he acquired a sustantial holding of land appears to have been mediated by a major official at the Sancak level of finance administration. The code stipulates a right of preemption for village residents over outsiders, and so any villager might have been able successfully to challenge the alienation of land to Yusuf Efendi, but it is unclear whether the villagers knew of it in time.[21] Perhaps legally all that Na'il Gharayba did was to exercise this right of preemption, reclaiming within a year the land that had passed to Yusuf Efendi Mikha'il Efendi.

Of the three holders who lost their land to Yusuf Efendi and thence to Na'il, one belonged to a family that was to remain in the village but progressively to lose their land, the second was a man of the neighboring village of Aydun, and the third a figure who has left no trace in records or memory. As noted, all three came among the first names on the Hawwara list. In the second major transaction of the early years in Hawwara, however, the seller, Yusuf Suwaydan, who probably belonged to the Christian family of that name in the neighboring village of al-Husn, came toward the end of the list of original shareholders, number 30 of the 31 principal holdings in Hawwara. This second major transaction, early in 1882, is known to have been conflictual: it was contested in the *nizami* court. The sale by Suwaydan to a Sabbah, a member of a group closely allied to that of Na'il, today known as Gharayba, and whose lands were to lie on the same side of the village as those of Na'il, was contested by six men whose names either fall in the second half of the original registration or do not appear as landholders in the list although they were certainly cultivators of the land in question. These men contested the sale on the grounds that the land sold belonged to their *khalit wa-sharik,* a person who holds plots intermixed with theirs and in common holdings. In the decision of early 1882 they lost the court case. Their objection to the sale was phrased in terms of a principle recognized in late *fiqh*[22] and here interpreted according to the actual arrangements of cultivation and field layout, one—unlike the principle of village coresidence or legal coownership—not recognized by the terms of preemption of the code. The *wakil* or agent for Yusuf Suwaydan in the court case was, moreover, none other than Shaykh Na'il Gharayba.

To understand what is at issue here we need to have an idea of how the entries in the register related to the actual distribution of land. The *tapu* registration concerned shares not plots inscribed on maps; for cartographic representation we must turn to the end of the system in question, the Mandate cadastre of 1933 for Hawwara. In this village, unlike most others, the 1933 cadastre captures the distribution of plots before any consolidation of holdings. The first village to be surveyed under the Mandate cadastre, Hawwara, refused any form of land consolidation.[23] Because of the growth of village population from the end of the nineteenth century and the pattern of transactions in shares, we cannot directly extrapolate backward from the 1930s to the 1880s, but we can nevertheless use the later mapping as a guide to the kind of relations referred to by the phrase *khalit wa-sharik.*

In Hawwara of the 1930s, land was first divided into two halves; the northern half was then further subdivided into a half and two quarters, and the southern into three thirds. Internally, certain of these subunits were further subdivided according to subgroups of holders whose fields always lay adjacent one to another. A holder in such a subunit would then have at least eight, and often twelve, different strips distributed within the half of the village lands to which he belonged, the overall balance being a holding uniform in quality for its size. Four points should be noted concerning the land system in the 1930s. First, the overall distribution was one of considerable complexity with, as we have noted, each holder having eight to twelve individual strips of land, the aim being to equalize qualities of land synchronously without having to redistribute plots every other year, the common mode of diachronic equalization in the hills. Second, all the village land save the village site was allocated to holders; there were no common pastures, and flocks were let on the village fields after harvest, a practice that necessitated tight collective discipline at the level of the subblocks concerning type of crop and timing of planting and harvesting. Third, the coordination of this discipline and of a classic triennial pattern of rotation occurred at the level of the subholding units. If there was regular diachronic redistribution of plots, it occurred at this level of collective holding too (among those to whom would apply the term *khalit,* we would say) and not at the level of the village as a whole except after long intervals (fifteen to thirty years). And fourth, although the major subunits of shareholding groups often comprised genealogically unrelated families, this unit of everyday coordination was important in agriculture. Yet in this competitive village economy, family identities and properties long remained distinct without genealogies being rewritten to correspond to coholding groups.

To return to the sale by Yusuf Suwaydan, we find that the legal contest concerned an alienation of right across the major subdivisions of the village, transferring rights from members of one major subblock of the village to another. If the order of names in the 1876 register corresponds to a first division into halves (which was a common practice in many of the shareholding villages of the region and which seems to have been the case in Hawwara, despite the fact that not all names can be linked to 1933 families), the men contesting the sale were thus coholders in the second block and also enjoyed rights to cultivate some or all of Yusuf Suwaydan's land, which lay in their block as well. And so they protested a violation of the principle—albeit one invisible in the form of the entries in the 1876 register—which the alienation of land to cultivators of the other half of the village represented.

The material common interest of the cultivators—expressed in their use of the terms *khalit,* one with plots interlaced or adjoining in a common block, and *sharik,* member of a sharecropping association—finds no translation in the terms of the new law where *sharik* designates only a cosharer in a single, individualized holding of property that can be bought and sold. That Na'il Gharayba acted as legal agent in this case before a judicial council on which presided the deputy *qai'mmaqam* and several regional leaders, chosen by a combination of election from below and appointment by the administration, suggests the exemplary, educative function of the *qada'* court of first instance.[24] Here, only a few years after *tapu* registration, the villagers become familiar—albeit not always successfully—with the institutions of the new legal order. That Na'il became an accomplished performer in this system surely escaped no one.

WINNERS AND LOSERS

Yet for others the encounter proved more tragic. The original family of the village, which all the traditions of the village agree was the first to settle there, owned eight shares of land at first registration, losing one to Yusuf Efendi and thence to Na'il, and a further 5½ to others over the years before the beginning of this century. By 1933 they were left with only 1½ *rub'a*s. As told by the family's most prominent figure today—a man himself virtually without land but with a law degree, a lifetime's service as lawyer to the police at a national level, a tall house that looks over the cavernous remains of the family's once imposing compound—this woeful tale turns about three themes. First, the different meaning of land among farmers in the past, which his family had especially exemplified. Second, quarreling and division within the family that led to one branch moving to the wide-open lands of the vast village of al-Ramtha just northeast of Hawwara. Third, and intimately bound up with the older understandings governing land among cultivators, the family had repeatedly given land for wives. Indeed, the only large holding of land in Hawwara registered in the name of a woman during the last quarter of the nineteenth century was the $1\frac{1}{2}$ shares that went to the wife of a brother of one of the original holders, $1\frac{1}{2}$ shares out of the two brothers' total holding of two shares. This was her marriage endowment or *mahr*. Falha al-Qallab, as the lady was called, appears the exception that proves the rule: in the plains the days of bountiful land, when land for wives entailed the recruitment of their relatives as cultivators or the promise of political protection, were rapidly drawing to a close. Falha's name, al-Qallab, is that of the great shaykhs of the semi-nomadic Bani Hasan, who controlled the large area southwest of the central village area of the *qada'*. Although no one remembers it so today, the marriage thus had all the marks of a prestigious alliance for a prominent family of the village as much engaged in herding and extensive cultivation in outlying areas, notably al-Ramtha, as in commercial farming in Hawwara. And for all we know, the alliance was perhaps also an attempt by this family to counter Na'il's preeminence on the basis of his literacy, service to the Ottoman administration, and successful commercial farming household.

In the plains, however, commercial cultivation, competition for land, and the newly imposed conceptions of land right bound up with Ottoman administration were winning the day. In a manner expressive of this order, as well as of the disorder of the original family's adjustment to the new times, Falha came in her old age to lodge in the compound of the very family, relatives of Na'il, who had so profited from the decline of the clan into which she had married. There, as a childless widow, she supported herself by gradually selling off the land registered in her name that had once formed her wedding gift.

If the original family of the village exemplifies in a somewhat tragic manner the change of order, not all other farmers fared so badly. In what comes to be the other half of the village, dubbed the Shatnawiya after the name of one of the families, farmers generally retained their land, and some, who had registered houses in 1883 but not land in 1876, also came to acquire title. Perhaps under the shock of Na'il and other commercially engaged Gharayba allies, village men learned how to deal with the new legal conditions. The local administrative order reached its highest complexity in the years just before World War I. By then, a transfer effected in the land record office—and such were not uncommon in the case of Hawwara—required an official *'ilm wa-khabar* from the village council, clearance from the fisc with regard to payment of back taxes, and, in the case of a succession, notification from the civil registry (*nufus*) and notification from the religious court of the due division of the estate. This was an impressive degree of cross-referencing, which could have appeared a daunting amount of paperwork to a villager.

Yet if, as a descendant of Na'il remarked with irony and a wave to Palestine, "We realized the way of the future: reading, writing, education, and so like the Jews, we bought the land," it was in fact not only the family of Na'il that profited from his early entrance to the Irbid municipal council. Na'il was based in the village and present in local administration and together with the Nabulsi imam recruited to the village (whose son became a clerk in the *shar'i* court in the years leading up to World War I) enabled an engagement in, and even an adept handling of, the new system by many of the denizens of this village. The village as a body came to seek the tools of the new order, securing a primary school just before the end of Ottoman rule and the first technical school of the area under the Mandate. Such sophistication marks the village today, largely composed of persons in professional employment.[25] When I first presented my research project to the head of the municipality, a man of the Shatnawiya side of the village, he remarked that it should really be "one of our own students writing this history," before proceeding politely but carefully to ascertain the source of finance for my research and where its results would go.

BAIT RA'S

The second village, Bait Ra's, presents a different history. It too abuts the *qada'* headquarters of Irbid within the social environment of the Hawran plains. Perched on a rocky hill it commands some fine fields opening out on the Irbid plain, but in other directions its lands are poor. On the north it faces a corridor of poorer terrain traversed by pastoralists during their movements between the desert and the Jordan Valley, along the line of the Wadi 'Araba.

When set beside that of Hawwara, the first *tapu* register drawn up in 1880 for Bait Ra's presents certain unusual features. Unlike Hawwara and most other villages registered in the early years, its village site property was registered (in September 1880) just before its land, and in exceptional detail: not just houses and wells but also cisterns and grain or straw storage pits were all registered as taxable property. Not only did the villagers take care to register built structures, but it seems as though they were as keen to register property below ground as above. Furthermore, the registration of agricultural land, effected November 1880, contains two anomalies. First, the *mukhtar* is given not two but four of the thirty shares of village land. A marginal note explains that the second two were in lieu of the two he had previously enjoyed tax-free as recompense for his duties as headman, not as his personal holding. The irregularity of this award is acknowledged as such, *nizamsiz,* but is stated to be in accordance with established tradition, *min qadim al-zaman.* Second, the distribution of the thirty shares in the village lands takes the following form: a list of individual holders of twenty-four of the thirty shares and then all holders but one (twenty-three of the twenty-four together), as joint holders of the remaining six shares of village land.

This latter arrangement is found in no other village register. To what did it correspond? That in the poorer lands of the village, cultivation was collectively managed for these shares of revenue assignment? Or that certain cultivators, who in fact farmed these shares, were excluded from title in this manner? A comparison of the names in the house list and those in the list of title to land offers little evidence of the latter; only two householders appear not to have title to land. It seems most likely that the settled population in this village with its very mixed quality of land was still rather limited in 1880 and hence that it drew on plowmen from outside to aid in the cultivation of the six shares. Two facts point to this. First, much of the corridor of poorer land of the headwaters of the Wadi 'Araba, traversed by flocks of pastoralists—notably the Bani Sakhr, moving between the desert and the Jordan Valley—remained sparsely inhabited much later than did the richer lands of the plains. Even in the early twentieth century the village appears to have witnessed considerable movement of families. Second, some of the older residents of the village describe how they used to go to plow lands to the east, the *mazra'a* of Izrit and the vast village of Ramtha. Thus, although the process of *tapu* registration of title encouraged the association of residence and landholding in a single village and certain clauses of the Land Code assume this link, in the open plains cultivators did take their oxen to plow in other villages.

Thus, overall, the registration presents two anomalies: the preeminence of the household of the *mukhtar* and his three brothers, and the contrast between the unusual specification of the list of village site property and the almost unfinished quality of the land registration. These anomalies are in no manner clarified by a study of the *tapu* registers of transactions in land for the forty years following 1880. Whereas in the case of Hawwara transactions appear at regular intervals in the *tapu* registers, for Bait Ra's there is little but a resounding silence. This village situated right next to the district headquarters of Irbid, where physical distance to the land registry and the civil court was not an issue, appears simply to have avoided dealing with the administrative forms of the new legal order. The absence of transactions in the registry is broken by a few sales given a legal stamp through a legal procedure in the records of the *shar'i* court, preserved from 1909. In this, a person wanting to sell appoints an agent (*wakil*) for the sale. The procedure presents some virtues to the villager: first, the scribe of the court goes himself to the village; second, no document attesting to the status and property in question need be sought from the *mukhtar;* third, legal acknowledgment of the requirement to complete the registration of the transaction with the *tapu* office is ensured by a phrase wherein the agent undertakes to complete the legal process in the land registry, thereby freeing the seller of that responsibility and putting the onus on the agent. But more than the recourse to this legal mechanism—not infrequently employed in other villages, albeit not so exclusively as in the case of Bait Ra's—what is striking about these transactions is that the total number of shares is given as thirty-six and not thirty.

Such a sliding base for calculation, following the incorporation of new cultivators or the expansion or intensification of cultivation, was not exceptional before *tapu* registration of land. But after the registration of the total shares of a village, it could no longer so move without judicial rectification involving reregistration by the *tapu* office. Rather, the base on which shares were calculated generally remained the same, and any change in right holders or land cultivated was translated, in a period of expanding population, into the subdivision of individual shares. Shares, it should now be clear, translated into a measure of property in land, albeit not in the form of a distinct plot with fixed boundaries. This said, shifts in the base are not entirely unknown although rare.[26] In the case of Hawwara, later registers sometimes give the total of 48 not 46½ shares. This slight difference does lead one to speculate whether this reflects the exclusion of the tax-free shares of the *mukhtar* at first registration and then their subsequent reappearance long after their problematic nature was forgotten, although neither government documents nor oral history allow one to prove this. But the shift from thirty to thirty-six is of quite a different order. It prompts one once again to reexamine the hypothesis that, in Bait Ra's, residents had simply been excluded from the original register.

Aside from oral history, the only source that can throw light on village population composition is the 1910 census. The population list for Bait Ra's is almost complete, unlike the list for Hawwara, which was unfortunately destroyed in the 1970 burning of the Irbid civil registry. The 1910 population register for Bait Ra's contains a total of 69 households with 455 persons and presents the following contours. The village is dominated by the vast household (thirty-four persons) of the *mukhtar;* alongside this are several other substantial households, each numbering over fifteen persons, and many small households composed of little more than a married couple and children. Furthermore, whereas most of the families who held land or houses in the 1880 *tapu* registration appear in the 1910 list, there are also a goodly number of entirely new family names. These families would appear to have settled in the village during the generation 1880 to 1910. This relatively poor village—close to a major corridor of pastoral movement, surrounded by six other villages, and immediately adjoining the regional center of Irbid, where from the early twentieth century a number of Damascene trading families that were engaged in money lending and in the local grain trade settled—seems to have had particularly fluid social composition at the time. As a poorer village, too, it gained population only after richer sites, such as Hawwara, had become saturated or resistant to the long-term establishment of new families. Given such mobility one might have expected some accompanying land transactions to have been entered in the *tapu* defters. But, as we have seen, that was not the case.

Finally, in 1921, the silence is broken in its entirety. On the order of the newly established administrative council of the Emirate of Transjordan, an entirely new land registration is undertaken at Bait Ra's. This is calculated on the base of thirty-six shares, divided into two halves, corresponding to two "teams" or *firqas*—one led by the household of the *mukhtar,* who unsuccessfully contests the order of the legislative council arguing that the first 1880 registration should obviate them from paying fees for this new registration, and the other a veritable collection (*lafa'if,* as the local term puts it) of smaller households, collectively known by the name of one small family that arrived late in the day from Palestine and from which the *mukhtar* in the early 1990s hails, an assemblage balanced against the first half dominated by the original *mukhtar*'s clan. At just about the same time—the dates in the registers do not permit one to define precisely which was the earlier event—the record of the criminal court of Irbid contains the detailed report of the public prosecutor concerning a devastating shoot-out that took place in the village between the two "teams," leaving five persons (two of one side and three of the other) and several animals dead and a larger number of both wounded.

It is scarcely surprising that even today this village is known for the poor quality of relations between its two social halves. A murderous encounter of the scale of that in 1921 is not a topic about which older villagers readily wax eloquent. In general they declare that they never heard of the village consisting of other than thirty-six shares. And it was not for the researcher to contradict them on the basis of state documentation.

What kind of a narrative might one sketch from the various rare entries in the records? The story could describe movement over the forty-year period of 1880 to 1920 in both inhabitants of the village and in cultivation rights; an attempt by the *mukhtar* to block these movements taking the form of a change in legal title (perhaps during early years by managing village tax payments as a block payment with the names of cultivators reaching the tax collector [*tehsildar*] but not the *tapu*) taking advantage of being the one figure with some literacy, as opposed to the common lack of education in the village; the continuous engagement of village men and women in pastoral production to supplement their rather poor agricultural revenue; and/or a jealous mining of the extraagricultural capital afforded by the site on which they lived. The name, Bait Ra's, is a translation of Capitolius. One of the cities of the Hellenistic Decapolis, the remains of the village were described in detail in Schumacher's travels in northern 'Ajlun during 1885.[27] It is unlikely that such an interest in classical antiquities was not already matched by a market in objects. The Ottoman law of antiquities, in which the state made law its claims in this domain, was issued in 1874. It would seem from the detail with which in 1880 villagers registered all that could be construed as property in the village, not least that underground, that they were by then experienced in the exploration and mining of the site. This is confirmed in a deposition made to the civil court on 15 December 1879 by the *qa'immaqam*. When asked how he came to know the *mukhtar* of Bait Ra's, he answered "in connection with the issue of digging up buried valuables."[28]

In weaving such a narrative I should admit to the evocative character of my own official dealings with village leadership—of a different tone to the subsequent relaxed interviews in the homes of men and women of the village. When first I went to the municipality, the fourth village I so entered, I carried my letter of introduction from the director of the Institute of Archaeology and Anthropology at Yarmouk University in Irbid where I had by then worked for almost a decade. The head of the municipality, a man of a modest family that had moved into the village after 1880 and had given its name to the second social half of the village, curtly told me to bring a letter from the minister of education before I set foot in the village for any research purpose whatsoever. Acquiescing to the inhospitable conditions, I asked whether he could nevertheless arrange a meeting in the municipality with senior men of the clans of the village. Some days later, the meeting was held in his impressive offices. There we found, together with the head, four venerable older men and a younger man the cause for whose participation was not made clear but whose demeanor during the meeting suggested a minor or part-time employee of the general information department. Whether this was true or not, I left with a sense that a less than

noble side of the state had been invited to contribute to the defense of village control over knowledge and also that, alas, the
means at the disposal of this leader of the second "team" still
did not rival those of the other side of the village, known for its
successful careers in the army and in the more distinguished
branch of military information.

A few days later, while enjoying a stroll through the village
site on a Friday morning before prayer time and in the company
of both an archaeologist from our institute who had conducted
excavations in the village and a young man from the old
mukhtar's clan (an employee of the department of antiquities
who had just shown us a series of the Roman lamps and other
small objects coming into the local antiquities market), we encountered the father of the head of the municipality and then—
while turning along a side alley, out of the way of the village men
assembling for Friday prayers in the new mosque—his visibly
excited son. We stood before a great hole, dug in preparation for
the foundations of a new house but also exposing more ancient
constructions that our archaeologist colleague described as
Mamluk above Hellenistic. Waving his arms with some alarm,
the head declared the work a shelter for when the Israelis might
again begin bombing; indeed, such shelters had commonly been
built in north Jordan at the end of the 1960s.

An anthropologist's nightmare of an encounter—just what
one should not see and in the company of just the wrong persons—turned out just the opposite. Our evident indifference to
what we saw, in an encounter doubtless rehearsed in village fan-
tasy over the last century of confrontation with scholars and
others of the state, promised an understanding complicity with
the village's ambivalence toward the legal and economic order of
administration. So we acted our parts in a microdrama where
the successor to the institution of village headship (which since
the Tanzimat reforms formed the lowest rung of the legal and
administrative order) sought to apply the legal order only as far
as it did not impinge on familial and village autonomy, while
never questioning, as in the field of security, allegiance to the

state. This strategy, if it may be so called, had proved successful as long as village contradiction and division were managed internally. Hence the head's alarmed and less than artful invocation of the interests of national defense as he faced, when least expected, representatives of the state's forms of knowledge, together with a competent representative of the same village strategy belonging to its rival side.

CONCLUSIONS

It is a commonplace of anthropological analysis that property is best understood as relations between persons. In this chapter we have analyzed property as relations between legal subjects of different kinds, not only the living individuals of classical anthropology. For example, we considered the special commission for the lands of Hawran and the village elected assembly as legal agents in these relations, quite as much as the individual men, or more rarely women, who came to possess property rights under the terms of the Land Code and in the registers of its administration. To put the matter this way is not to say that the persons whose names appear in the register do not have a life outside the grid, a life that is better analyzed in other terms, notably as patterns of production, reproduction, and exchange. At points in this brief chapter I have made reference to analyses of these systems on such terms—for example, in the village of Hawwara when explaining the order of the list of landholders of 1876. I have also sought to describe mediating terms or levels to the analysis of property, so that it not be torn between two irreconcilable insights: the letter of the law and the life of production and exchange. Social constructionism teaches us to see social relations as the realization of categories, even of formal legal categories; political economy reminds us of the irreducible dynamics of the development of production and reproduction that, over time, impose themselves even on the letter of the law. These readings can appear irreconcilable, belonging to two orders of discourse quite closed to one another. To mediate them requires something more institutional than an invocation of dialectic. It is precisely such institutional mediation that modern law brings about through the creation of the legal agents of political administration and the constantly renewed conflict between the order of the law and the life of production that is the site of politics.[27] Accordingly, the focus here has fallen on the agents of this mediation—the institutions of political administration—as legal persons in the relations that "make" property. And when we bring these agents into our vision of the field of property relations, we find that they lie at the center of the modern state. Property relations then appear as much a product of the state as of the forces of production, reproduction, and exchange that both liberal and Marxist interpretations—considering these forces analytically prior to the state—have often treated as the sole determinant of this domain.

The Ottoman reforms, the Tanzimat, were a process of internal reform of the state wherein regional administration by intermediary persons (legal persons organized as households dealing commercially in revenue, whose fields of action were simultaneously "public" and "private," judicial and policing, commercial and fiscal) was gradually replaced by an administration wherein professionals at the top were joined by figures possessing local knowledge comprising the first level of notionally elected figures of a formal, not household, administration. To fill the boxes of the new grids of "power/knowledge" in which the subjects were framed as individuals, each with his or her individual wealth and corresponding tax liability to the public fisc, figures of local knowledge, "elected" from below into formal offices defined by the center, had to be both marshaled and schooled in the terms of the law. The frontier of local, or informal, knowledge moved downwards toward the village: hence, the attention paid here to administration at this level, where private property in land was under construction.

The major sources for historians to trace the political administration of private property in the late Ottoman period are today the *tapu* defters. To make sense of them requires that one accept both analytically the political character of the construction of property and the centrality of local administration—between the letter of the law and the life of production—in that process. A register of property is not a photograph, it is a grid of the relations between the legal agents that constitute property.[30]

ACKNOWLEDGMENTS

My thanks go to Roger Owen, who hosted the two seminars on land at Harvard University in 1995 and 1996. This chapter was first presented at the LSE Anthropology Research Seminar, November 1996, and the Workshop on Property, European Science Foundation Program on Individual and Society in the Mediterranean Muslim World, Section on Norms and Oppositions, Middle East Technical University, Ankara, Turkey, December 1996. Such improvement as it has seen since then will reflect discussions with Richard Saumarez Smith, Alain Pottage, and Huri Islamoglu.

The Jordanian research on which this chapter draws was conducted jointly with Richard Saumarez Smith while I was Research Fellow at the Institute of Archaeology and Anthropology of Yarmouk University, 1989 to 1992. It was supported by grants from the Wenner Gren Foundation and the Social Science Research Council (SSRC) (New York), the Centre d'études et de recherches sur le Moyen-Orient contemporain (CERMOC) and the British Institute at Amman for Archaeology and History (BIAAH) (Amman), the British Academy (London), the Kerr Fellowship at the University of California (Los Angeles), and the Centre National de la Recherche Scientifique (CNRS) and the Ministère de la Recherche et de la Technologie (MRT). The records I consulted were kept by the Department of Lands and Surveys, the Civil Court and the Civil Registry in Irbid, and, in the case of the Islamic Court records, by the Department of Historical Documents of the University of Jordan. My general understanding has also been enriched by work in 1997 and 1999 at the Asad Library, Damascus and the Başbakanlık Arşivi, Istanbul, supported by the Council of American Overseas Research Centers (CAORC) (Washington DC). For the welcome and support of these institutions and their staff, I remain deeply grateful.

The present chapter mixes anthropological and historical conventions. Thus, village names and names of prominent individuals are given, but where painful events are recounted, I have chosen to avoid using personal names. After some hesitation I have adopted the Arabic versions of the Ottoman legal terms when these are of Arabic origin and the Ottoman Turkish transcription for terms of Turkish or Persian origin. Although unorthodox, this corresponds to the naturalization of the Ottoman administrative terms in the locality under study.

NOTES

1. Compare the analysis of Dina Khoury of an 1840 directive concerning this reform, D. Khoury, *State and Provincial Society in the Ottoman Empire: Mosul, 1540–1834* (Cambridge: Cambridge University Press, 1997), 105–7. On the duality of forms of right in the writings of Mosuli jurists, see ibid., 178–86. Parallel debates are evident in the Damascene legal material on rights from 'Abd al-Ghani al-Nabulsi to Ibn 'Abidin (late seventeenth to early nineteenth century), which I have been examining.

2. For a general discussion of the term political administration, see Mark Neocleous, *Administering Civil Society: Towards a Theory of State Power* (Houndmills, Basingstoke, U.K.: Macmillan Press; New York: St. Martin's Press, 1996).

3. Reiterated in various forms throughout the important series of programmatic declarations in the Mesa'il-i Mühimme series of the Başbakanlık Arşivi, the central relation between the power of state and the secure wealth of individuals was also pronounced in the Gülhane Rescript. In the translation of George Young, *Corps de droit ottoman* (Oxford: Clarendon Press, 1900–1906), 3:31: "Quant à l'assiette régulière et fixe des impôts, il est très important de régler cette matière, car l'Etat, qui est pour la défense de son territoire, forcé à des dépenses diverses, ne peut se procurer l'argent nécessaire pour ses armées et autres services que par les contributions levées sur ses sujets. Quoique, grâce à Dieu, ceux de notre Empire soient depuis quelques temps délivrés du fléau des monopoles, regardés mal à propos autrefois comme une source de revenus, un usage funeste subsiste encore, quoiqu'il ne puisse avoir que des conséquences désastreuses; c'est celui des concessions vénales connues sous le nom d'Iltizam. Dans ce système l'administration civile et financière d'une localité est livrée à l'arbitraire d'un seul homme, c'est-à-dire, quelquefois à la main de

fer des passions les plus violentes et les plus cupides, car si ce fermier n'est pas bon, il n'aura d'autre soin que son propre avantage. Il est donc nécessaire que désormais chaque membre de la société ottomane soit taxé pour une quotité d'impôt déterminée, en raison de sa fortune et de ses facultés, et que rien au delà ne puisse être exigé de lui."

4. It is of course a shorthand to speak of a right as "stronger": in the language of rights what is at issue is the union of more elements in the "bundle of rights" than a given kind of property comprises.

5. Compare M. Fischbach, "Al-Mukhayba Village: A Tale of Shaykhs, Efendis, Peasants, and Land in Transjordan," *Dirasat* 21, no. 1 (1994): 46–71.

6. For a discussion of Yanya, see chapter 1 by Huri Islamoglu in this volume.

7. *Ikhtiyar* bears the two senses of "chosen, elected" and "elder, aged." It seems more appropriate to emphasize the first sense in translation rather than the second, although the "Assembly of Elders" is the more common translation of the term, which I have also used in earlier publications.

8. Gabriel Baer, *Fellah and Townsman in the Middle East: Studies in Social History* (London: Frank Cass, 1982), 140. Symptomatically, Baer entitles Part 2 of this collection of essays "The Village Shaykh in Palestine," although the analysis makes clear that there was scarcely such a figure in the period under study.

9. Alexander Schölch, *Tahawwulat jadhriyya fi falastin: 1856–1882* [Arabic translation of *Palästina im Umbruch, 1856–1882: Untersuchungen zur wirtschaftlichen und sozio-politischen Entwicklung* (Stuttgart: Steiner, 1986)] (Amman: Matba'a al-jami'a al-urduniyya, 1988), 277–79.

10. Georges Douin, *La Mission du Baron de Boislecomte. L'Egypte et la Syrie en 1833* (Cairo: Imprimérie de l'Institut Français d'Archéologie Orientale du Caire pour la Société Royale de Géographie d'Egypte, 1927), 266–67.

11. See Norman Lewis, *Nomads and Settlers in Syria and Jordan, 1800–1980* (Cambridge: Cambridge University Press, 1987), for a general account. On the sociological analysis of this expansion, see the review of *Nomads and Settlers* by Martha Mundy and Seteney Shami, *Journal of Peasant Studies* 16, no. 2 (1989): 292–94.

12. Haim Gerber, *Ottoman Rule in Jerusalem: 1890–1914* (Berlin: Schwartz, 1985), 28–81 and 48, 54, and 75, in particular.

13. Linda Schatkowski Schilcher, "The Hawran Conflicts of the 1860s: A Chapter in the Rural History of Modern Syria," *International Journal of Middle East Studies* 13 (1981): 159–79; "The Grain Economy of Late Ottoman Syria and the Issue of Large-Scale Commercialization," in *Landholding and Commercial Agriculture in the Middle East,* ed. Caglar Keyder and Faruk Tabak (Albany: State University of New York Press, 1991), 173–95; "Violence in Rural Syria in the 1880s and 1890s: State Centralization, Rural Integration, and the World Market," in *Peasants and Politics in the Modern Middle East,* ed. Farhad Kazemi and John Waterbury (Miami: Florida International University Press, 1991), 50–84; Birgit Schäbler, *Aufstände im Drusenbergland: Ethnizität und Integration einer ländlichen Gesellschaft Syriens vom Osmanischen Reich bis zur staatlichen Unabhängigkeit, 1850–1949* (Gotha: Perthes, 1996).

14. For the process of *tapu* registration in this area, see Martha Mundy, "Shareholders and the State: Representing the Village in the Late Nineteenth-Century Land Registers of the Southern Hawran," in *The Syrian Land in the Eighteenth and Nineteenth Century,* ed. Thomas Philipp (Stuttgart: Steiner, 1992), 217–38, and "Qada' 'Ajlun in the Late Nineteenth Century: Interpreting a Region from the Ottoman Land Registers," *Levant* 28 (1996): 79–97.

15. This form of registering possession becomes reified as *musha'* land in the terminology of the Mandate. The term *musha'* occurs occasionally in the marginal notes of the *tapu* defters but it is not a legal classification of land under the 1858 Land Code. See chapter 7 Birgit Schaebler in this volume on the history of *musha'* land in the central Hawran. Concerning the contribution of Ya'akov Firestone, see my article, "La propriété dite *musha'* en Syrie: une note analytique à propos les travaux de Ya'akov Firestone," *Revue du Monde Musulman et de la Méditerrannée* 79–80, nos. 1–2 (1996): 267–81.

16. Başbakanlık Arşivi, Şuraya-ı Devlet, 2884/31.

17. Başbakanlık Arşivi, Suriye Gelen-Giden, vol. 350, no. 11, dated March 15, 1876.

18. The series of registers of correspondence between the central administration and the province, Başbakanlık Arşivi, Suriye Gelen Giden, vols. 349–50, has seven different entries for this dispute between October 29, 1875 and July 22, 1876. To date I have been able to find only one document of the correspondence, Şuraya-ı Devlet, 2884/31, but I hope subsequently to find others.

19. *Salname Suriye*, vols. 8–18, 1293–1303 A.H. Concerning the background of Yusuf Efendi, he presumably hailed from a family of Nazareth with links to Suf in 'Ajlun, rather than from the Tawil family of Damascus, a member of whom later appears in the *shar'i* court records in relation to agricultural finance in the area. For the latter, see Hind Abu al-Sha'r, *Irbid wa-jiwaruha (Nahiyat Bani 'Ubaid) 1850–1927* (Amman: Bank al-Amal, 1995), 389. Nazareth, like Tiberias, was a center of money lending and finance of the grain trade for this area. A local history of Nazareth (al-Qashsh) states of the family: "Dar al-Tawil. Min Suf fi Jabal 'Ajlun kunyathum fiha al-Fraihat aqdam jududihim fi al-Nasira 'Isa waabna akhhi 'Abdullah wa-Yusuf. 'Isa - As'ad - 'Isa wa-Ya'qub wa-Hanna wa-Ilyas. 'Abdullah - Musa - 'Abdullah. Yusuf - 'Isa al-mullaqab bi-al-babur wa-Salih." As the name Mikha'il does not appear in these lower generations, the identification is less certain, however; As'ad Mansur, *Ta'rikh al-Nasira: min aqdam azmaniha ila ayyamina al-hadira* (Cairo: Matba'a al-hilal, 1934), 239.

20. He is described by the family as a literate man who—according to the family—had studied in Istanbul and knew Turkish. Na'il is never described in the Ottoman Turkish registers as shaykh, where the term invariably denotes a man of some religious renown; nor does the family today claim a pedigree of religious learning. In 1884 to 1886, when he serves on the newly formed municipal council of Irbid, he is suitably termed Efendi. He serves on an Educational Commission established in 1894 and 1895 (*Salname Suriye*, vol. 27, 1312–13 A.H./1895–96 A.D., 211 and on the board of the Agricultural Credit Bank as late as 1900 (*Suriye*, no. 1785, 26 October 1316 A.H./1900 A.D.). Abu al-Sha'r (*Irbid wa-jiwaruha*, p. 216) states that in 1892 and 1893 he serves as appraiser on the Property Tax Commission in that year, but my own notes on this *Salname* (vol. 25, 1310–11 A.H. 227–28) do not include his name. Abu al-Sha'r (*Irbid wa-jiwaruha*, 211), notes on the basis of oral

history that Na'il was an employee in the *tapu*. I believe that the person in question was Ahmad al-Nayla, head of the special commission for land registration in the Hawran, not Na'il Gharayba.

21. The director of finance whose seal and signature are on the entry in the register is the same figure subsequently prosecuted alongside the governor for corruption. See Başbakanlık Arşivi, Şuraya-ı Devlet, 2273/38.

22. The basic distinction between *khalit* and *sharik* seems to be that *khalit* refers to a property that began as individual but was combined (for example, sheep in a flock) as opposed to a notionally single property or interest held jointly and shared between persons. See Edward Lane, *An Arabic-English Lexicon,* vol. 2 (London, 1865; reprint Beirut, 1968), 788–89. The phrase appears conjoined in reference to land in late *fiqh*—for example, Muhammad Ibn 'Abidin, *Al-'uqud al-durriyya fi tanqih al-fatawa al-hamidiyya,* 2d ed., vol. 2 (Cairo, Bulaq: al-Matba'a al-amira al-misriyya, 1883), 190. I have not yet found scholarly discussion of the history of the first term in law or of its association in this manner with the second.

23. Consolidation of holdings into three plots for each owner was to occur only after 1946, when a special law was passed enabling the village to be reregistered on the basis of a new survey.

24. For the composition of this judicial council as reported in the *Salname Suriye,* see Abu al-Sha'r, *Irbid wa-jiwaruha,* 239–41. For the principles of election and selection of the members of the judicial councils of the *qada'*, see the instructions concerning the election to councils and tribunals of 1875, translated in Young, *Corps de droit ottoman,* 1:45–47.

25. On Hawwara's economy today, see M. S. al-Zu'bi, "The Role of Agricultural Activity in the Household Economy: An Anthropological Case Study of Huwwara-Irbid" [in Arabic] (Master's thesis, Yarmouk University, Irbid, 1990).

26. See M. Fischbach, "State, Society, and Land in 'Ajlun (Northern TransJordan), 1850–1950" (Ph.D. diss., Georgetown University, 1992), 157–58. According to the report in the Department of Lands and Survey, Amman, cited here by Fischbach, the villagers of Jinin al-Safa' changed the base of their calculation three times in

the period. This was possible in Jinin as the villagers had entirely refused to pay the *tapu* fees to get legal title to their land and so could change the way they calculated rights and liabilities without reference to the *tapu*. See Fischbach, ibid., 96.

27. Gottlieb Schumacher, *Northern 'Ajlun: "Within the Decapolis"* (London: Watt, 1890), 154–68.

28. Başbakanlık Arşivi, Şuraya-ı Devlet, 2273/38, 14:2.

29. For two exemplary studies that study property as such a political relation, see Bernard Edelman, *Ownership of the Image: Elements for a Marxist Theory of Law* (London: Routledge and Kegan Paul, 1979), and Georgina Born, "(Im)materiality and Sociality: The Dynamics of Intellectual Property in a Computer Software Research Culture," *Social Anthropology* 14, no. 2 (June 1996): 101–16.

30. Hence, if a historian denounces this source for not being a photograph, we may assume that what he is really saying is that he would rather not know of the *political* construction of property. It is in this light that one might comprehend Kenneth Stein's characterization of the *yoklama* and *da'imi tapu* registers in nearby Palestine as "a patchwork of incomplete, inaccurate, and unfaithful representations of the true nature of landholdings and landownership in Ottoman Palestine." Kenneth W. Stein, *The Land Question in Palestine, 1917–1939* (Chapel Hill: University of North Carolina Press, 1984), 23.

THREE

A Comparative Examination of the Provisions of the Ottoman Land Code and Khedive Sa'id's Law of 1858

Denise Jorgens

This chapter examines the reforms in the landholding system of Egypt in the late Ottoman period that accompanied the introduction of the Ottoman Land Code of 1858 and of Khedive Sa'id's law of the same year. It is built around a comparison of these two land codes as well as their antecedents. The aim of this chapter is to examine why a separate land code was established for Egypt and what the relationship was among these and other pieces of nineteenth-century legislation on landholding. In other words, how closely are the Egyptian reforms of the mid-nineteenth century, as put forth in Sa'id's law of 1858, related to the Ottoman Land Code promulgated that same year?

It is clear that while both laws represent important pieces of legislation on landholding, these reforms and innovations in the nature of the Ottoman landholding system during the nineteenth century were part of an evolutionary process and did not lead to the privatization of *miri*, state-owned arable land. Instead, the Ottoman Land Code of 1858 and Sa'id's law both confirmed and verified certain tendencies toward the extension of possession rights resulting from a variety of factors over a

much longer time; and despite these innovations, state bureau-
cracies continued to support the Ottoman doctrine of state ownership of arable land. It was only among the provincial *qadis*
that there were variations in the legal status of land and some
differences in the application of the law.[1] It should be noted,
however, that in general, *muftis* did not interfere in the
landholding system. Any changes that occurred resulted from
varying interpretations of the *qanunnames* on landholding. In
sum, Egypt was clearly an important provincial region that remained very much a part of the Ottoman empire. The overall
conformity of the Egyptian landholding reforms of the nineteenth century with the basic principles of the Ottoman
landholding system can be demonstrated through a comparative
examination of the various provisions on landholding in the Ottoman Land Code and Khedive Sa'id's law of 1858.

Beginning with the Egyptian case, Khedive Sa'id's law was issued on 24 Dhu al-Hijja 1274 A.H./A.D. 5 August 1858. Sa'id's law
originally consisted of twenty-eight articles and a conclusion
and became the basis for land legislation in modern Egypt.[2] Two
specific laws were introduced in Egypt that led to Sa'id's law—
the land laws of 1847 and 1855.[3] These two laws, together with
Sa'id's law, reaffirmed traditional practices aimed at stabilizing
the land tenure system and central administrative control of the
land and the land tax revenues. In fact, throughout the Muhammad 'Ali period, rather than new legislation on land tenure,
there were various efforts to apply the basic provisions of the established Ottoman *qanuns*. This can be seen in these new codes
that dealt with issues such as peasant rights of inheritance, preemption, sale (or more accurately transfer) of state lands, and
the rent and pawning of the usufruct rights to land.[4] Central
control of land by the eighteenth century was even weaker than
during the age of the *a'yan* when the provincial notables had effective control of state revenues, but nevertheless, in examining
the peripheral provincial regions such as Egypt, the general land
tenure system introduced by the Ottomans appears to have experienced less change than previously thought.

The Ottoman Land Code was enacted on 7 Ramadhan 1274/
21 April 1858 by the Ottoman government.[5] It was intended to
achieve various economic, social, and political aims. Before the
enactment of this new legislation, the Ottoman central administration had instituted a series of reforms to reassert its claims to
land and the land tax revenues. The 1274/1858 Ottoman Land
Code codified these earlier pieces of legislation into one comprehensive law on landholding. In many ways, it also represented a
continuation of the classical Ottoman system of landholding,
which sought to maintain state ownership of arable land and at
the same time to consolidate and strengthen the rights of the actual cultivators on lands.

As in the Ottoman case, a council in Egypt was instructed to
compose a bill that would settle disputes over land and that
would nullify all previous decrees. The legislation was reviewed
extensively, and many additions and deletions were made to the
original bill. It was designed not just to settle disputes and
claims to land but to cover all issues related to landholding. In
doing so it provided that should new issues arise that were not
addressed in the bill, then, after an investigation by the local authorities, the issues would be presented to the *Majlis al-ahkam*
(the advisory council for reforms that produced Sa'id's law,[6] a
replica of the Ottoman reform council called *Meclis-i Ahkam-i
Adliyye*) to determine whether the bill contained sufficient provisions to deal with this issue. Otherwise, additional articles
would be added in an appendix to the bill. This bill and its provisions were to be observed throughout Egypt. Anyone who violated these rules was liable to punishment under the law. Once
the final legislation was approved by the Khedive, it was printed
and circulated throughout the region.

As one of the objectives of Sa'id's law was the traditional concern for maintaining central control over the land tax revenues,
the principal provisions of the law were not new, and it attempted to deal with aberrations in land tenure that persisted
despite the legislation of 1847 and 1855. As in the Ottoman
Law, Sa'id's law draws a clear distinction between *miri* (in Egypt

'*ibadiyya*) and *milk* (in Egypt, *athariyya* or *kharajiyya*) land. Under Sa'id's law all claims on land were to be settled according to the provisions of this new legislation whether these lands were taxable lands or *rizqa* (lands endowed for charitable purposes).[7] However, the land law allowed for compromise between the actual possessor of the land and the claimant in settling matters arising from previous laws. The conditions would have to be agreed on by both parties, and a judgment rendered on it by the *mudiriyya* or provincial government. Current claims on which a judgment had not been rendered were to be settled according to this new law.

It should be emphasized that all nineteenth-century legislation on landholding preserved the basic principle of state ownership of arable land. In Sa'id's law it is stated as a denial of private land ownership rights on arable land:

> State-owned taxable land is not owned by its cultivators, but rather they only have the usufruct rights to it, so long as they undertake the cultivation of it; if they leave it [uncultivated] without an excuse for a period totaling three years their rights [to possess the land] are null and void according to the principles of the noble shari'a.[8]

Anyone who possessed state-owned taxable land for five or more years and who was paying the required taxes could not have his land taken away from him. In other words, no further claims would be accepted on the land.[9]

This principle was also stated clearly in the Ottoman law: "State land, the legal ownership of which is vested in the Treasury, comprises arable fields, meadows, summer and winter pasturing grounds, woodland and the like, the enjoyment of which is granted by the government."[10] The traditional modes of alienation were permitted because pawning, renting, and selling of the usufruct rights were established customary practices. The cession of land, for example, was described in Article 9 of Sa'id's law: "the practice from ancient times was that farmers of state-owned, *kharaji* taxable land could pass on their rights to culti-vated land and transfer it to others by legal deeds."[11]

The legal principle involved was described by the sixteenth-century Ottoman jurist Abu al-Su'ud, who stated:

> [*miri* land is] not the private property of the peasant *re'aya*, who hold it in their possession on a lease (*'ariye*), farm it or otherwise cultivate it, and render *harac-i mukaseme* under the name of tithe (*'öşr*) and *harac-i muvaddaf* under the name of *çift akçasi*. So long as they continue to cultivate it and maintain it in the proper condi-tion in the manner described above, and pay the taxes (*hukuk*), no one is allowed to interfere in their possession. They may dispose of it as they wish until their death; when they die their sons shall take their place and possess the land in the same manner as de-scribed above. If no son survives, the land is given in *tapu* to a per-son other than a family member who is capable of cultivating it in return for a rent paid in advance (*ücret-i mu'accele*).[12]

The only change was that beginning with this new legislation:

> If someone transfers, surrenders or abrogates [his right of heredi-tary possession] from one to another, then this must be done by le-gal deed issued from the pertinent court of that district or by the deputies authorized to hear legal claims and to write deeds.[13]

Penalties were imposed if it were found that deeds were written in violation of these conditions. In such cases the land was re-turned to the person making the transfer.

Thus state-owned, taxable land was not inheritable as stipu-lated by the *shari'a,* nor was it mortgageable. The same was out-lined in principle in Article 8 of Sa'id's law. However, owing to considerations of "civilization, progress and livelihood and good citizenship," the usufruct rights to land could be trans-ferred from a person who died to his rightful heirs, whether male or female. In the original Ottoman law, these rights could be inherited only by a son or by two or more sons in partner-ship. This change represented an extension of inheritance rights to other members of a peasant family. So the possessors of state-owned land were able to transfer their usufruct rights to land to whomever they desired. From this, it was permitted for the possessor to mortgage land by *gharuqa* on the condition that this took place with the knowledge of the *mudiriyya* and that the responsibility would be in the name of the one who took the land according to *gharuqa*.[14] So if the mortgagor died, his heirs were entitled to pay off the mortgage and to inherit the land after the required registration was completed. If the estate reverted to the treasury, then what was paid on the mortgage became the right of the treasury. Land that reverted to the treasury would be given to whomever desired it according to the specified conditions.[15]

The stipulations regarding the Ottoman *miri* landholding system summarized above are derived originally from Islamic law and from sultanic law. Although the innovations introduced during Ottoman, or even pre-Ottoman times, did not alter the basic principles formulated by earlier Muslim legists, some new terminology and administrative arrangements were introduced. These resulted from the evolution of the Ottoman landholding system as related to changing historical conditions and needs. It was the task of the Islamic jurists such as Abu al-Su'ud and Ottoman bureaucrats to choose and legalize certain practices or principles and to respond to the requirements of historical circumstances. On the whole, state ownership of arable land remained as a basic principle of the Ottoman landholding system. It will be clear in our examination of the provisions of Sa'id's law that there was much continuity between these traditional principles of the Ottoman landholding system and the reforms introduced in nineteenth-century Egypt.

In turning back to our review of the specific provisions of the laws, we see that in both the Egyptian and the Ottoman law, there was a limitation on the period land could be held after it was either deserted or remained fallow, after which claims to land were forfeited and it was reassigned. Article 12 of Sa'id's law states that if local villagers had legally released their land either by transferring or surrendering it to an individual at a time when the land was not cultivable, and if later the villagers made claims against the land, then these claims would not be considered after five years. If the period was less than five years and if the deed was issued from the court authorized to issue such deeds, the claim would be accepted according to judicial bylaws and further claims would not be considered.[16]

According to Article 13 of Sa'id's law, each district determined the amount of land under its control that was to be cultivated. Land left fallow by the inhabitants of a district by their own free will was given to others by decree so that the land remained under cultivation and the taxes continued to be paid to the treasury. If someone who left his land and gave up his rights to it by his own choice returned demanding his land or some of it, his request would not be considered, and he would not have a legal claim to restitution.[17] This particular provision again reaffirms the principle of state ownership of arable land.

According to Article 9 of Sa'id's law, if someone transferred, surrendered, or abrogated his right of hereditary possession, this had to be done by legal deed issued from the pertinent court of that district or by the deputies authorized to hear legal claims and to write deeds. Here again we see the affirmation of state control of transactions concerning arable land. This was done after obtaining permission from the *mudiriyya*, which confirmed the title to the land. After the completion of the transfer, surrender, or abrogation of the land, certain conditions had to be written in a deed for the one receiving the land. In the Ottoman case, land was now also registered, and a court document was required for any land transactions.[18] If it became necessary for purposes of irrigation to construct dikes, canals, or dams, the state was not liable to pay for these improvements in any way other than reducing the taxes on the land. If, however, some of the land was freehold property, then the owners were to receive some form of compensation. Care was taken so that all the conditions of the legislation were met.[19]

Article 10 of Sa'id's law goes on to discuss deeds on land written before this law was passed. Deeds written by senior judges at high level courts or by prominent representatives who were licensed to conduct litigation were to be honored. Deeds that were issued by deputy judges, such as a legal deputy of a small town or small village, were not honored and were to be replaced with deeds issued from the senior judges or prominent deputies. This was the case only if five years had not passed in the period of possession of the land. A period of one full year was established from the time of the appearance of Sa'id's law, during which such deeds could be changed. If five years or more had passed from the time of taking possession of the land, then there was no need to substitute these deeds. If it was found that the seller had died or deserted the land and the deed could not be issued again, then the matter was verified by the *mudiriyya*. Beginning with the introduction of Sa'id's law, deeds could not be issued except by the higher court or by the deputies authorized to write deeds and settle claims.[20]

In fact, the Ottomans also often reviewed title deeds to reassert state control over land. In the Egyptian case, registration efforts were attempted at various times.[21] For example, Article 15 of Sa'id's law stated: "Whereas, because certain additional lands appear in the irrigated basins, it is necessary that this additional land be added to the tax lists."[22] As a result of these new registration efforts, the law gave landholders greater security of tenure and limited the ability of others to reclaim land, specifically the peasants who had lost their land. In this case, the law also followed earlier Islamic traditions that stated that in cases of disputed ownership, the presumption was always with the actual possessor of the land.[23] A number of jurists produced treatises on this subject reinforcing the point that in cases of disputed ownership, proof was required, along with two witnesses, that gave evidence of this.[24] So the issue of state control over arable land and its mode of inheritance remained paramount.

Continuing with our discussion of the question of inheritance "which was an important area outlined in Sa'id's law as well as in Ottoman legislation on landholding," Article 1 of Sa'id's law reaffirmed the fundamental principle that state-owned taxable land was not inheritable as understood in the case of *milk* lands.[25] Only *milk* lands were subject to distribution among the legal heirs, which included sons, daughters, and other relatives according to *shari'a* stipulations. If it were the case that a possessor of state-owned land died leaving heirs, none of his heirs could be given the land by means of the *shari'a* principle of inheritance. Inheritance was regulated by the state. Reference to *shari'a* law was stated at the beginning of Sa'id's law simply to reinforce state ownership over such lands.[26] As was mentioned earlier, when a deceased person had legal heirs, out of concern for their livelihood and in order not to deprive them of their usufruct rights the legal heirs had preemptive rights over others, and the land passed to them, whether they were male or female.[27] However, this was on the condition that they would be able to cultivate the land and pay the land taxes. There was no such obligation for *milk* lands. As for the deceased who left neither descendants nor relatives as legal heirs, the land reverted to the responsibility of *Bayt al-mal.*

This situation also was discussed in Article 3 of Sa'id's law, which stated "If it is found by the Egyptian government that women from among the local population are in possession of land for which they are responsible in accordance with the current rules, and if they pay the *kharaj,* land tax, then the rules of this bill will equally apply to them."[28] Similarly, Article 57 of the Ottoman law discussed the devolution of state land by inheritance. It stated that *mevqufe* land devolved in equal shares gratuitously and without payment of any price on a man's children of both sexes. If the deceased left only sons or daughters, the one or the other inherited absolutely without any fee.[29]

Article 2 of Sa'id's law expands on the provisions regarding inheritance outlined in Article 1 and goes on to discuss the joint household in relation to landholding.[30] Certain measures were taken so that land was held by a single household member but was cultivated as the common possession of a household. Land should be registered in the name of the oldest member of the family. This was done in order not to divide the family holdings. In cases where land was held jointly, the overseer of the land would be the most senior member of the household. He would represent the administration of the land for all members of the family. To preserve the rights of the other family members, whether male or female, a distribution register was made by the head of the family that specified individuals by name and their shares, indicating the rights of each of them. This was done in the presence of all family members and in the presence of the shaykhs of the district. It was then presented to the *Mahkama al-shari'a,* and a statement of approval of its content and legal certification of it was registered with the *mudiriyya.* The distribution register was kept by the senior member of the family, who was ultimately responsible for the land. If a member of the family desired to separate from the rest, he was entitled to his share of the land. However, this was allowed only after an investigation and only if there was a legitimate reason. This was to prevent a division of the remaining members of the family and the economic dissolution of the household.

If the senior member of the family should die, then the designated share of the land of the deceased would be handled according to the requirements of Article 1 discussed above.[31] The remaining shares would stay with the other possessors, who would continue to cultivate the land. The most senior among them, whom they chose as their new representative, was responsible for maintaining the agrarian family unit and for the prosperity of the family. So long as the family had a senior family member who oversaw the requirements of the cultivation of the land and cared for the household, there would be no dispersal or ruin to the family. If the senior member of the family was negligent in administering the land, the family was obligated to make a complaint against him and to request distribution of the land. Once a complaint was issued, a penalty would be imposed on the senior member of the family. If conditions became apparent to the *mudiriyya* by means of a complaint from others, then after an investigation by the *mudiriyya* a penalty would be imposed on all adult family members. After the imposition of the penalty, the shares would be divided. If the senior member of the family died before the land was divided, then it was the responsibility of the family to find a suitable representative who was agreeable to all members; with the knowledge of the *mudiriyya* the shares were divided as mentioned. If the senior member of the family or another member of the family acquired land from another source and desired to remove it from the shares of the family land, then that land would not be subject to partition. After an official investigation determined that it was outside the possession of common property, that land would be set aside for the individual family member.[32]

Under Ottoman legislation on landholding, there had traditionally been a concern for retaining land under a single peasant family to maintain the farm unit under cultivation and to preserve the revenues for the state.[33] The Ottoman *qanuns* had always held to the idea of household units and had strengthened patriarchal authority. Article 8 of the Ottoman law stated that the whole land of a village could not be granted to a community or to a person or persons selected to represent a community. Each household that held land was given a separate title deed to the land, called *tapu*.[34] The ownership of this land had to be registered to show the actual possessors of the land. Lands were either registered as held in common by all the copossessors, with each being shown as holding a proportional share; or land was registered as being possessed by the head of the family whose members were copossessors of the land. Sa'id's law also supported the maintenance of a traditional agrarian system with joint households by strengthening patriarchal authority in peasant families and by making provisions so that land remained under cultivation when it was necessary to transfer it.[35]

In the Ottoman case, rights concerning land of the original possessor who had been absent on a journey, or under duress, were maintained if he had possessed a title deed to the land without dispute for ten years.[36] If the actual cultivator had arbitrarily taken possession of and cultivated the land, the land was offered to him on payment of the *tapu* possession fee after the lapse of ten years. If he did not accept this, the land was put up for auction and awarded to the highest bidder.[37] According to Sa'id's law, the village shaykhs, for example, were required to report deserted land and to reassign it or else the provincial government would do so. Those who deserted land would lose any claim to it after five years. The period in which claims to ceded land could be raised was reduced from fifteen to five years, and land that had been seized and reassigned could not be reclaimed under any circumstances.

So both pieces of legislation contained important articles dealing with laws of prescription between private persons on state-owned land, which was referred to as that type of land that was held by those in possession of title deeds. In the Ottoman land law, Articles 20 and 78 gave the person holding land without dispute for ten years the right to claim a title deed from the government without payment of the *tapu*.[38] Both laws also reinforced the principle that in cases of disputed ownership, the presumption favors the actual possessor or cultivator of the land. The actual possessor's ownership could be disproved only with solid evidence, such as two witnesses. The actual possessor needed only to swear that the objects were his or hers.

Additionally, both pieces of legislation gave preferential treatment to the inhabitants of a locality or an adjoining village regarding new land or unclaimed land. Sa'id's law provided:

> Land that is dissolved to the authority of *Bayt al-mal* according to the regulations of Article 1 will be assigned by the *mudiriyya* to whomever desires it; however, the people of the village will be given preemptive rights over others; similarly, if some among the people of the village don't have land or if their land is not sufficient for them, they will have preemptive rights over others; otherwise, people of neighboring areas shall take priority over others.[39]

In transferring the land, a sum of 24 *qurush* per feddan was levied by the *mudiriyya* as the fee for a title deed. In the Ottoman law a fee for transfer was an old custom. It was paid to the *sipahi*. Under the new legislation it was paid to the treasury. Under the new law it was also imperative that a printed lease document be issued containing the official seal of the government. Again, the concern of the state in both pieces of nineteenth-century legislation was to establish a title deed to the land to ensure that state-owned arable land remained under cultivation.

Both the Ottoman and the Egyptian laws allowed holders of *miri* or *'ibadiyya* land to lease the land. Arable land could be leased by the state as well as by the individual in possession of state-owned land. In the Egyptian case, the possessor who acquired hereditary rights for the cultivation of land had the right to lease the inherited land to whomever he desired.[40] To control and regulate the conditions of leases, in order to protect the state's rights the provisions of this new legislation had to be followed, through the *mudiriyya*.

In the Egyptian law, there were restrictions on leases (*ijarat*); for example, a lessee (*musta'jir*) was not permitted to plant trees or build structures that would alter the *miri* character of the land into *milk* land.[41] The land lease was designed only for the cultivation of the land during the period that was specified in the terms of the lease. The terms of the lease were for one year, renewable for only two additional years. If the lease was not prepared according to the established rules, the state had the right to rent the land to another person.

It was the same with the Ottoman law, according to which state-owned land could be leased or loaned for cultivation, in which case it was called *muqata'alu* land.[42] It could not be left uncultivated, except for sound and duly established reasons; nor could trees or buildings be erected on grain fields. A property lease also had to be in writing, otherwise it was invalid and could not be enforced.[43] Again, the concern for maintaining land under cultivation, a traditional concern of the Ottoman state, found itself expressed in both of these pieces of nineteenth-century legislation on landholding.

Related to this were the provisions on partnerships. According to Article 12 of Sa'id's law, prior to the land legislation owners of estates could give their land or part of it to others by way of a partnership or for assistance in cultivation of the land.[44] In such cases the taxes on that portion of the land were recorded in the name of the partner and not of the owner of the estate. If disputes arose regarding these partnerships, they were resolved according to the provisions of Sa'id's law. The procedures put forth in all matters of dispute applied to arable land only. If the partners had planted trees or built canals or structures on the land or if the period of the partnership had been longer than five years, these cases were settled in accordance with Shari'a law.

According to both pieces of legislation, there were limitations on the use of *kharajiyya* land.[45] Article 25 of the Ottoman law provided that no one could plant vines or fruit trees on land in his possession used for the cultivation of grain and make it a vineyard or orchard without the approval of an official. But if three years had passed, the trees became the *milk* property of the person who had planted them, and they could not be removed from the land. This is nearly identical to Article 8 of Sa'id's law, which stated that a lessee was not allowed to plant trees or build buildings on leased land. A land lease was concluded only to ensure that the land remained under cultivation. *Miri* land that contained trees or structures that were not authorized was referred to the authorities, who ruled on it according to this new legislation.[46] All of this was aimed at preserving the state-owned character of the land, since land on which there were vineyards and orchards was considered freehold property. Related to this was another provision, seen in both pieces of legislation, which concerned other uses for the land. Article 12 of the Ottoman law stated that no one could dig up the land in his possession to make bricks or tiles without the approval of an official.[47] Should he do so, whether the land was state land or *mevqufe* land, he was required to pay a penalty to the treasury.

Another important issue discussed in both pieces of legislation involved cases in which a possessor of land could lose his rights to that land. According to the Ottoman law, land that had not been cultivated, either directly by the possessor or indirectly by being leased or loaned, and remained unproductive for three years consecutively, became subject to a new *tapu*—that is, its transfer to another person required payment of the *tapu* fee, whether the possessor was present or not. Exceptions were made for the following reasons: (1) the soil had to remain uncultivated for one or two years or more owing to the nature of the land; (2) land that had been flooded had to remain uncultivated for a time after the water had subsided so that it would become cultivable; or (3) the possessor had been held as a prisoner of war. If the former possessor wished to recover the land, it would be given to him on payment of its *tapu* fee.[48] If he did not claim it, it would be put up for auction and adjudged to the highest bidder.[49]

Article 69 of the Ottoman Land Code stated that lands that had been flooded for a long time were not subject to transfer to another person under *tapu*. The possessor of the land retained it under his control. If the former possessor died, his legal heirs under this law would have possession rights over the land. If there were no legal heirs, the land was given on payment of the *tapu* value to those who met the condition of possession by paying a *tapu* fee. If the water subsided, and the possessor of the land or his heirs left it unproductive for three years without a valid excuse, it then became subject to the right of *tapu* and could be transferred to another person.[50] This point was also discussed in Article 70 of the Ottoman Land Code, which stated that if land that had been abandoned and left unproductive by the possessor for two consecutive years was then transferred by him or owing to his death devolved on his heirs and was left uncultivated as before for a further one or two years, it was not subject to transfer to another person under *tapu*.[51]

Finally, according to Article 71 of the Ottoman Land Code, if a possessor of land died and the land had been uncultivated for three consecutive years without a valid excuse, the heirs could not inherit the land without a fee. But they did retain preemptive rights, and the land would be offered to them on payment of the *tapu* fee. If they refused it or if the possessor died without heirs, the land would be put up for auction and adjudged to the highest bidder.[52] These provisions in the Ottoman Land Code that concerned maintaining land under cultivation and paying land tax revenues all existed in various articles in Sa'id's law.

The object of both of these pieces of legislation was to lay down the rule that in all cases of alienation of possession rights on *miri* land, whether by way of sale, lease, or exchange, the consent of the state, which was evidenced by registration, was necessary for a transfer of the legal right of possession of land.[53] So although a man may have paid his purchase money, if the consent of the state had not been obtained, the property remained legally in the possession of the vendor; if he died, it passed to his heirs; or if he died without heirs, it reverted to the state. If, during the negotiations for the purchase of a piece of land, the vendor died, then the would-be purchaser had a right to recover from the estate of the deceased the money he had paid. We must keep in mind that *miri* land was state-owned land, and as a result the state placed conditions on its possession. State-owned land could not be sold. Instead, its possession rights were transferred under the condition that the land remained under cultivation.

In sum, a comparative examination of the various provisions on landholding in the Ottoman Land Code of 1858 and Khedive Sa'id's law is methodologically a useful approach for understanding the agrarian history of Egypt in the nineteenth century within the context of the Ottoman empire. In this examination, it has become clear that in both the Ottoman and the Egyptian cases, the purpose of the legislation on landholding was to ensure close central bureaucratic control of state-owned lands and landholding in general and to provide an agrarian revenue source for the treasury.

There are reasons that we should expect that the Egyptian land legislation would have close connections with the Ottoman law. First, we have to recall that despite the autonomous status of Egypt, the Ottoman empire had close relations with Egypt even as late as the British occupation in 1882. Also, there were large amounts of agricultural land in Egypt that were in the possession of members of the Ottoman elite who were living in Istanbul. Thus, there was a great deal of cooperation and administrative correspondence between Egypt and Istanbul, particularly when relations became normalized after the Ferman of 1 June 1841 under Muhammad 'Ali.

In both pieces of legislation, the reforms basically aimed at consolidating and extending the possession rights on land to members of peasant families who were previously excluded from inheritance. The extension of the hereditary rights of heirs to possess *miri* arable land enabled them to inherit land directly without paying a *tapu* fee. This last point is crucial because when *miri* land became vacant and subject to *tapu,* outsiders could acquire it by paying a higher *tapu* fee. Also, through nineteenth-century legislation, governments sought to consolidate the state's rights over *miri* land by demanding that certificates be issued directly from the central administration. Previously, particularly in the eighteenth century, local authorities issued title deeds on such land. The requirement that every landowner register his or her land in the government land register office and acquire an official title deed attesting to his or her rights resulted in the consolidation of the state's control over land. Also, under the new regime, individuals could hold an official title deed granting legal use of vacant state land and pasture lands at large, thus enlarging the agrarian tax base. While it is true that as far as landholding or administrative structure is concerned, Egypt differed from the countries of the Fertile Crescent or other areas of the Ottoman empire, basic issues such as the traditional status of holders of *miri* and *milk* land and the concern for maintaining stability in the land tenure system and protecting land tax revenues were the same.

The Egyptian and Ottoman land regulations of 1847, 1855, and 1858 are more closely related to each other than has previously been thought. As mentioned earlier, rather than being an innovative step toward individual land-ownership rights, the provisions of Sa'id's law regarding matters such as inheritance of state-owned arable land simply modified earlier Ottoman *qanuns* or pursued new legislation introduced in Istanbul. The main concern in both cases was to take steps to increase agricultural production and to restore state control over state-owned lands. In fact, both the Ottoman law and Sa'id's law, in addition to reasserting state control over arable land and the land tax revenues, aimed at maintaining a particular traditional agrarian system called *çift-hane*.[54] This was done by strengthening patriarchal authority in peasant families and by providing for circumstances when it was necessary to transfer land so it remained under cultivation. This concern is a guiding principle in both the Ottoman and Egyptian land codes.

The fact that Sa'id's law was issued only four months after the Ottoman law is noteworthy. Evidently, it could not be a literal application of the Ottoman law to the conditions of Egypt, since in Egypt the whole agrarian system was dependent on the Nile River's regime and irrigation, while in the core lands of the Ottoman empire dry farming was prevalent. However, the connections between the two pieces of legislation are undeniable as far as state ownership of field land, its possession, inheritance, and transfer rules were concerned.

In the case of Egypt, while much scholarly work on Egyptian rural society and economy has been done, it is only recently that we have begun to see that a revision of some of the traditional notions of economic and social change in this field has become necessary. Generally speaking, earlier studies have marked the Muhammad 'Ali period and the modernization of Egypt under the impact of the West as a watershed in Egyptian history, without suspecting parallel developments and actual connections with the reforms and the transformation that began earlier in Ottoman history.[55]

Recently, scholars using Ottoman archival materials have provided new interpretations of rural society and economy in various regions of the Ottoman empire.[56] For Egypt, Professor Kenneth Cuno has pointed out that the economy and society of Ottoman Egypt exhibited a number of "modern" features within the Ottoman system much earlier than the Muhammad

'Ali period and that these changes could not be attributed solely to the economic influence of the West.[57] It has also become clear that the traditional economic and social structures of Ottoman Egypt endured well into the nineteenth century. This can be seen in our examination above of the various pieces of legislation on landholding.

One can, of course, mention that the Egyptian laws perpetuated earlier traditions and practices, perhaps dating back to ancient Egypt and resulting from the specific requirements of irrigation agriculture. This is obvious in Sa'id's law in the provisions dealing with maintaining dikes and canals and communal responsibilities in matters such as irrigation. Most of the provisions in both codes can be traced to the eighteenth century or even to the earlier Ottoman *qanuns* of the fifteenth and sixteenth centuries. This point is even expressed in the words of those who prepared these laws.[58] In fact, the concept of state ownership of arable land that was central to both the Ottoman Land Code and Sa'id's law was not an Ottoman invention. The Ottoman landholding system generally followed earlier Islamic traditions that made conquered lands the common property of the Muslims or the Islamic state. The early Muslim jurists agreed in defining most of the arable land of the countries conquered by the Muslims as *kharaj*-paying, taxable land under state control. In Islamic fiscal administration, the meaning of the word *kharaj* was land tax, in contrast to *'ushr* (tithe) or *jizya* (poll tax).[59] The views of later jurists, for example Abu Yusuf in the ninth century, followed this principle which gave *raqaba*, eminent domain, over all conquered arable lands to the community of the conquerors, in other words, to the Islamic state as the embodiment of the *umma*, the Islamic community.[60] The classical Ottoman land system did not reach its final formulation until the sixteenth century.[61] It is significant that while Islamic law books had no specific chapter on landholding, jurists such as the Ottoman Shaykh al-Islam Abu al-Su'ud wrote independent treatises on the subject in response to the needs of the state administration. As mentioned above, in 1568, Abu al-Su'ud attempted to explain the foundations of the Ottoman landholding system in terms of traditional Islamic concepts.[62] This was done in response to an order by Sultan Suleyman. Ottoman jurists of the sixteenth century sought to make Ottoman rules and practices conform strictly to Islamic tradition by Islamicizing existing or emerging conventions of landholding and land taxation. So the concept of state ownership of arable land was not an Ottoman invention.[63] In fact, with some practical additions and modifications determined by circumstances, the Ottomans followed the Islamic principles enumerated above.

Finally, having discussed the many aspects of continuity with earlier periods, this study also attempts to show that the land legislation of the nineteenth century nevertheless did introduce certain changes, such as the requirement that every landowner register his or her land in the government land register office and receive a title deed to the property. To achieve complete registration, the state intended to survey all lands and provide title deeds to those who possessed them. By insisting on delivery of title deeds to the actual cultivators, the state sought to regain firm control over Ottoman growers and eliminate the role of the local notables. Hence, article after article of the land codes reiterated that government officials must record land transfers of whatever kind. This, of course, resulted from the fact that in Ottoman as well as Egyptian legislation, the main concern of the state was always to assert state control over land and to stabilize land tenure and make land more of a source of revenue by ensuring that it remained in the hands of those most able to cultivate it. The ultimate goal was to obtain the maximum amount of tax revenue from the state lands for the treasury.

It should be emphasized that Sa'id's law of 1858 deals only with landholding on state-owned lands. Legal prescriptions regarding other types of land, *mawat* and *waqf* lands in particular, also had important implications for nineteenth-century Egyptian agrarian history. It appears that it was the large-scale reclamation of *mawat* land in the Delta area that led to the formation of big estates with full ownership rights and appears to be mainly responsible for the profound structural change in the Egyptian landholding system as a whole.[64] The purpose of Sa'id's law was the restoration of the traditional small peasant family farm system on state-owned land, which by and large was not connected with the emergence of the freehold big farms. In both the Egyptian and the Ottoman cases, the nineteenth-century legislation on landholding was designed to ensure close central bureaucratic control of state-owned arable lands and landholding in general and to provide an agrarian revenue source for the treasury.

NOTES

1. There was some variation in the different ways in which land was controlled and exploited in various provinces of the Ottoman empire, particularly in provinces such as Egypt. In fact local conditions and traditions varied somewhat from one Ottoman province to another, even during the sixteenth century, when central authority was at its greatest. Kenneth M. Cuno, *The Pasha's Peasants: Land, Society, and Economy in Lower Egypt 1740–1858* (Cambridge: Cambridge University Press, 1992), 179–97, and "Was the Land of Ottoman Egypt and Syria *miri* or *milk?* An Examination of Juridical Differences within the Hanafi School," *Studia Islamica* 81 (1995): 121–52.

2. The original and complete text of Sa'id's law of 1858 can be found in Jirjis Hunayn, *Al-Atyan wa-al-dara'ib fi al-qutr al-Misri* (Bulaq, Egypt: al-Matba'a al-kubra al-amiriyya, 1904); and in Muhammad Kamil Mursi, *al-Milkiyya al-'aqariyya fi Misr wa-tatawwuruhu al-tarikhi min ahd al-fara'ina hatta al-an* (Cairo, n.p., 1936). An amended version of this law was published in 1875 consisting of only fifteen articles. Although the text found in Mursi contains some misprints, it is a complete text of the law. Cuno, *Pasha's Peasants*, 193.

3. The text of Egypt's first modern land law, issued on 23 Dhu al-Hijja 1263/2 December 1847, can be found in Ahmad Ahmad al-Hitta, *Tarikh al-zira'a fi Misr fi ahd Muhammad 'Ali al-kabir* ([Cairo]: Dar al-ma'arif, 1950). The law of 1263/1847 was amended by a second law of six articles issued by Sa'id in 1855.

The text of this law, dated 8 Jumada I 1271/27 January 1855, is described in detail in Ahmad Ahmad al-Hitta, *Tarikh Misr al-iqtisadi fi al-qarn al-tasi' 'ashar* ([Alexandria]: Matba'a al-Misri, 1967). As has been pointed out by Kenneth Cuno, because of an error in the conversion of the Muslim dates, these laws are sometimes identified as having been issued in 1846 and 1854. See Yacoub Artin, *La Propriété foncière en Egypte* (Cairo: Imprimerie nationale du Boulaq, 1883); 'Ali Barakat, *Tatawwur al-milkiyya al-zira'iyya fi Misr wa-atharuhu 'ala al-haraka al-siyasiyya 1813–1914* (Cairo: Dar al-thaqafa al-jadida, 1977); Gabriel Baer, *A History of Landownership in Modern Egypt, 1800–1950* (London: Oxford University Press, 1962); and Mursi, *al-Milkiyya al-'aqariyya.* See also Sultan's Ferman to Mehmed 'Ali stipulating conditions of hereditary governorship of Egypt, 1 June 1841, Great Britain, Parliamentary Papers, 1879, vol. 78, "Firmans granted by the Sultans to the Viceroys of Egypt, 1841–73," Egypt No. 4 (1879), c. 2395, 36–39. These Egyptian laws paralleled Ottoman legislation on land holding introduced in 1847, 1849 and 1855.

4. Cuno, *Pasha's Peasants,* 64–84, discusses some of these regulations. See also, for example, Domenico Gatteschi, *Real Property, Mortgage and Wakf According to Ottoman Law* (London: Wyman, 1884), 30–32. The mistaken belief that none of these rights existed before the nineteenth century can be seen in Baer, *Landownership,* 8–10, and Gabriel Baer, "The Development of Private Ownership of Land," in *Studies in the Social History of Modern Egypt* (Chicago: University of Chicago Press, 1969), 62–78. See also "Firmans Granted by the Sultans to the Viceroys of Egypt, 1841–73," Egypt no. 4 (1879), C. 2395, 36–39 in *Diplomacy in the Near and Middle East,* ed. J. C. Hurewitz (Princeton, N.J.: Van Nostrand, 1956), 121–23.

5. Translations of the Ottoman Land Code can be found in George Young, *Corps de droit ottoman* (Oxford: n.p. 1900–1906), 45–84; Stanley Fisher, *Ottoman Land Laws* (London: Oxford University Press, 1919), 1–42; F. Ongley, trans., *The Ottoman Land Code,* rev. and ann. Horace E. Miller (London: Clowes, 1892), 1–70; and R. C. Tute, *The Ottoman Land Laws with a Commentary on the Ottoman Land Code of 7th Ramadan 1274* (Jerusalem: Greek Convent Press, 1927), 1–123.

6. Text in Mursi, *al-Milkiyya al-'aqariyya*, 128–29, 146.
7. Text in ibid., 128–29; text of the Ottoman Land Code in Fisher, *Ottoman Land Laws*, compare the Article 1,1.
8. Text in Mursi, *al-Milkiyya al-'aqariyya*, 128. A complete translation of Sa'id's Law of 1858 appears in the appendices of Denise Jorgens, "A Study of the Ottoman Land Code and Khedive Said's Law of 1858" (Ph.D. diss., University of Chicago, 1995).
9. The only exception was for land that was *gharuqa*. This was a form of land mortgage with the name referring to the amount received in exchange for land.
10. Text in Fisher, *Ottoman Land Laws*, 2.
11. Text in Mursi, *al-Milkiyya al-'aqariyya*, 131–32.
12. These *fatwas* have been translated and published by Halil Inalcik, "Islamization of Ottoman Laws on Land and Land Tax," in *Osmanistik, Turkologie, Diplomatik: Festgabe an Josef Matuz*, ed. Christa Fragner and Klaus Schwarz with a foreword by Bert G. Fragner (Berlin: Schwarz, 1992), 101–16 and come from a collection preserved at the Atif Efendi Library, no. 1734; compare in Ömer Lutfi Barkan, *XV ve XVIinci Asirlarda Osmanlı İmparatorlugun da Zirai Ekonominin Hukuki ve Mali Esaslari* (Istanbul: Burhaneddin Matbaası, 1943); see also Ertugrul Düzdağ, *Şeyhülislam Ebussuud Efendi Fetvaleri* (Istanbul: Enderun Kitabevi, 1972), which contains twenty-nine *fatwas* on land and land taxation as cited by Inalcik, "Islamization of Ottoman Laws," 108; here I have provided the transliteration of the terms as they appear in the published text.
13. Text in Mursi, *al-Milkiyya al-'aqariyya*, 131–32.
14. Text in ibid., 130–31.
15. Text in ibid., 130–31.
16. Text in ibid., 137–40.
17. Text in ibid., 140–41.
18. Text in ibid., 131–37.
19. Text in ibid., 131–32.
20. Text in ibid., 128–29, 132–33.
21. Text in ibid., 135–38.
22. Text in ibid., 145–46.
23. Cuno, *Pasha's Peasants*, 194–95.
24. Ibid., 195.
25. Text in Mursi, *al-Milkiyya al-'aqariyya*, 126.

26. To give religious legitimacy to these laws, the law makers put forth the notion that all these rules were derived from Shari'a law.
27. Text in Mursi, *al-Milkiyya al-'aqariyya*, 126.
28. Text in ibid., 128.
29. Text in Tute, *Ottoman Land Laws*, Articles 56–57.
30. Text in Mursi, *al-Milkiyya al-'aqariyya*, 126–28.
31. Text in ibid., 126.
32. Text in ibid., 126–28.
33. Fisher, *Ottoman Land Laws*, 6; on this system, called *çift-hane*, see Halil Inalcik, "The Emergence of Big Farms, *Çiftliks:* State, Landlords and Tenants," in *Contributions à l'histoire économique et sociale de l'Empire ottoman*, ed. Jean-Louis Bacqué-Grammont and Paul Dumont (Louvain: Editions Peeters, 1983), 105–26; Halil Inalcik and Donald Quataert, eds., *An Economic and Social History of the Ottoman Empire, 1300–1914* (Cambridge: Cambridge University Press, 1994), chapter on the *çift-hane* system, 143–54.
34. Text in Fisher, *Ottoman Land Laws*, 6.
35. Cuno, *Pasha's Peasants*, 196–97. Concerning restrictions on the use of *miri* land, see Fisher, *Ottoman Land Laws*, Articles 68–71; see also Articles 12, 17, 21, 36, and 46. Finally, see Article 116, which prohibits the mortgaging of land. All these provisions exist in Sa'id's law. See text in Fisher, *Ottoman Land Laws*, 7, 9, 15, 17 and 24–25; cf. Inalcik and Quataert, *An Economic and Social History*, 103–31.
36. Absence refers to "a distance from place to place of three days at a moderate rate of traveling, that is to say, eighteen hours." See Mejelle Article 1664; see also Omer Hilmi, *Ithaf ul-ahlaf fi ahkam il-evkaf* (Law relating to vakf properties) (Istanbul: Matbaa-ya Amire,1889), translation by C. G. Stavrides and S. Dabdad (1895): "Dans la prescription on considère l'année lunaire et non l'année solaire." For an English translation, see Omer Hilmi, *A Treatise on the Law of Evqaf*, translated by Sir Charles Robert Tyser (Nicosia, Cyprus: Government Printing Office, 1899).
37. See also Article 78 of the Ottoman Land Code, text in Fisher, *Ottoman Land Laws*, 26; Cuno, *Pasha's Peasants*, 193–97.
38. Text in Fisher, *Ottoman Land Laws*, Articles 8, 20, 26, 78.
39. Text in Mursi, *al-Milkiyya al-'aqariyya*, 127–28.

40. Text in ibid., 131; text in Fisher, *Ottoman Land Laws,* Articles 6, 9.

41. Text in Mursi, *al-Milkiyya al-'aqariyya,* 131.

42. Inalcik and Quataert, *An Economic and Social History,* 103–19.

43. Concerning the leasing of immovable property, see Mejelle Book II.

44. Text in Mursi, *al-Milkiyya al-'aqariyya,* 126–28.

45. Text in ibid., 131; text in Fisher, *Ottoman Land Laws,* 6–14;

46. Text in Mursi, *al-Milkiyya al-'aqariyya,* 131, 134–36.

47. Text in Fisher, *Ottoman Land Laws,* 7.

48. According to Inalcik, a *tapu* is (1) an act of homage, (2) a permanent patrilineal lease of state-owned land to a peasant family head in return for his pledge to cultivate it continuously and meet all the obligations in tax or services (3) the title-deed certifying *tapu* rights. *Tapulu* refers to a state-owned farm leased to a peasant family head under the special conditions of the *tapu* system. See Inalcik and Quataert, *An Economic and Social History,* 110–14.

49. Text in Tute, *Ottoman Land Laws,* 67.

50. Text in ibid., 24; see also Article 57 of the Ottoman Land Law.

51. Text in Tute, *Ottoman Land Laws,* 24; see also Article 57 of the Ottoman Land Law.

52. Text in Fisher, *Ottoman Land Laws,* 24–25.

53. Text in ibid., 15–16; text in Mursi, *al-Milkiyya al-'aqariyya,* 132–33.

54. Inalcik, "The Emergence of Big Farms," 105–26; Inalcik and Quataert; *An Economic and Social History,* chapter on the *çift-hane* system, 143–54.

55. Both Baer and Issawi have characterized the period of the invasion of Napoleon and the regime of Muhammad 'Ali as marking the end of the premodern and the beginning of the modern period. They have also depicted the Egyptian economy as a subsistence economy with few links to the regional or world economies. We now know this was not the case.

56. See Karen Barkey, *Bandits and Bureaucrats* (Ithaca: Cornell University Press, 1994); Cuno, *Pasha's Peasants.* See also five articles by Suraiya Faroqhi: "Political Initiatives 'from the Bottom Up' in the Sixteenth- and Seventeenth-Century Ottoman Empire," in Hans Georg Majer, ed., *Osmanistische Studien zur Wirtschafts-*

und Sozialgeschichte: In Memoriam Vanco Boskov (Wiesbaden: Harrassowitz, 1986), 24–33; "Agriculture and Rural Life in the Ottoman Empire (ca. 1500–1878): A Report on Scholarly Literature Published 1970–1985," *New Perspectives on Turkey* 1 (1987): 3–34; "Political Tensions in the Anatolian Countryside around 1600: An Attempt at Interpretation," in *Turkische Miszellen: Robert Anhegger: Festschrift, Armagani, Melanges,* ed. Jean-Louis Bacqué-Grammont et al. (Istanbul: Editions Divit, 1987), 117–30; "Towns, Agriculture and the State in Sixteenth-Century Ottoman Anatolia," *Journal of the Economic and Social History of the Orient* 33 (1990): 125–56; "Political Activity among Ottoman Taxpayers and the Problem of Sultanic Legitimation (1570–1650)," *Journal of the Economic and Social History of the Orient* 35 (1992), 1–39. See also Huri Islamoglu-Inan, "State and Peasants in the Ottoman Empire: A Study of Peasant Economy in North-Central Anatolia During the Sixteenth Century," in *The Ottoman Empire and the World Economy,* ed. Huri Islamoglu-Inan (Cambridge: Cambridge University Press, 1987), 101–228, and *Osmanlı İmparatorluğunda Devlet ve Köylü* (Istanbul: Iltesim Yayınları, 1991); Caglar Keyder and Faruk Tabak, eds., *Landholding and Commercial Agriculture in the Middle East* (Albany: State University of New York, 1991); Tarif Khalidi, *Land Tenure and Social Transformation in the Middle East* (Beirut: American University of Beirut, 1984); Abdul-Karim Rafeq, "Economic Relations between Damascus and the Dependent Countryside, 1743–1771," in *The Islamic Middle East, 700–1900: Studies in Economic and Social History,* ed. A. L. Udovitch (Princeton, N.J.: Darwin Press, 1981), 653–85; Amy Singer, *Palestinian Peasants and Ottoman Officials: Rural Administration around Sixteenth-Century Jerusalem* (Cambridge: Cambridge University Press, 1994).

57. Cuno challenges this periodization in his book *Pasha's Peasants* but still places Egyptian history within the context of Arab and not Ottoman history. There is certainly more in common with other regions of the Ottoman empire than has previously been thought. Cuno also challenges Peter Gran's discovery of capitalist structures in eighteenth-century Egypt. See Peter Gran, *Islamic Roots of Capitalism: Egypt, 1760–1840* (Austin: University of Texas Press,

1979), 3–34. I would agree with Cuno that this does not represent a new development for this period.

58. Ömer Lutfi Barkan, "Türk Toprak Hukuku Tarihinde Tanzimat ve 1247 (1858) Taribli Arazi Kanunnamesi," *Tanzimat* 1 (Istanbul: Ma'arif Press, 1940), 321–421.

59. For the status of *kharaj* land and state *raqaba* on land in the early centuries of Islam, see Hossein Modarressi, *Kharaj in Islamic Law* (London: Anchor, 1983).

60. Inalcik, "Islamization of Ottoman Laws," 107; also, I am grateful to Professor Halil Inalcik for allowing me use draft materials he used for his book, Inalcik and Quataert, *An Economic and Social History.*

61. Halil Inalcik, "Land Problems in Turkish History," *Muslim World* 45 (1955): 222.

62. Inalcik, "Islamization of Ottoman Laws," 101–16; see also Halil Inalcik, "Suleyman the Lawgiver and Ottoman Law," *Archivum Ottomanicum* 1 (1969): 105–38; on Abu al-Su'ud, see "Ebüssu'ud efendi," *Islam Ansiklopedisi*, IV-2, 62–69.

63. Inalcik, "Land Problems," 222–23.

64. Inalcik and Quataert, *An Economic and Social History,* 103–54.

· FOUR ·

Demarcating the British Colonial State: Land Settlement in the Palestine Jiftlik Villages of Sajad and Qazaza

Martin Bunton

For . . ."owners" read "occupiers."
—*Corrigenda to First Report of Lewis French, 23 December 1931*[1]

INTRODUCTION

The legal records of settlement procedures[2] in the villages of Sajad and Qazaza provide new opportunities to examine the tension that can generally be said to have characterized British colonial land policies in Palestine as elsewhere: that is, the need to reconcile the creation of a market in land with the protection of the rights of cultivators.[3] On the one hand, colonial officials in Jerusalem and London commonly held that freehold rights to property constituted the essential ingredient of a thriving economy (and, for that matter, a proper political society). British colonial officials often looked like physiocrats, believing strongly in the "modernizing" ideology of a Palestine transformed by the free working of natural economic laws that encouraged above all the smooth transfer of property.[4] Such a market approach would help ensure that land in the hands of "unenterprising" owners would soon be transferred to those who would develop

121

it more intensively. Of course, in Palestine there existed the added impetus of facilitating the Jewish national home. But as the consequences of a market in land became clearer to the Palestine government, particularly in the wake of the 1929 riots, there was increasing tension between the general desire to facilitate transactions in land and the fear that individualization of rights was in fact leading to social dislocation and the growth of a landless class.[5]

Premised on the assumption that the impact of British rule on the definition of property rights in Mandate Palestine is best understood by an approach that recognizes the ad hoc character of colonial rule,[6] this chapter attempts to bring greater precision to the study of land settlement in Palestine by grounding the analysis in "small-scale," historically specific events—particularly, the process of settling claims to *jiftlik* land in Palestine from 1920 to 1932. During this period, the Palestine government twice turned its serious attention to the question of *jiftlik* land. Shortly after becoming High Commissioner in June 1920, Sir Herbert Samuel appointed a special Land Commission to ascertain the extent of the various kinds of land that were at the disposal of the government. The Land Commission looked particularly into the history of *jiftlik* lands in the area around Beisan and concluded that the occupants enjoyed "a special sort of tenancy" and that their holding of the land should be settled legally and in perpetuity. By the terms of the Ghor Mudawara Agreement, the land was in fact registered in the names of the cultivators (on *miri* tenure). The government did not seriously consider the nature of *jiftlik* land again until the early 1930s when settlement operations were specially undertaken for a number of *jiftlik* villages, including Sajad and Qazaza. But in contrast to the approach taken in Beisan the cultivators of Sajad and Qazaza were, after prolonged court proceedings, declared "tenants and merely tenants" of the Palestine government.

By examining closely the legal and administrative procedures that led to these differing outcomes (while concurrently outlining British legislative efforts to define and regulate property transactions), this chapter aims to shed some light on the dynamics of land settlement in Mandate Palestine in a way that is time and place specific.

LAND TRANSFER ORDINANCE, 1920 TO 1921

In Palestine, this tension between the desire for, and fear of, a market in land was present very early on and reflected the weight of colonial experience and anxiety with peasant dispossession. The 1920 Land Transfer Ordinance, for example, was intended primarily to promote a market in land. But it also sought to protect the status of agricultural tenants with the inclusion of provisions that, as one colonial official minuted, were "prompted by considerations similar to those that made Lord Kitchener enact the 'Five Feddan Law' in the Sudan."[7]

The rush to reestablish the land registration system in the wake of World War I and the urgent need for a land transfer ordinance can be attributed primarily to the widely held belief on the part of local administrators that the prevention of land transactions was shackling the flow of money and thus having a "serious effect on economic conditions of the country."[8] General headquarters, Cairo, described the hastened reestablishment of the registry as "a provisional measure to meet immediate needs by military administration and remove hardship from which large proportion of inhabitants are suffering. But transactions would be under strict control of administration and of limited value."[9] Accordingly, in mid-1919 the military administration drafted an ordinance to provide for land transactions in accordance with Ottoman law (that is, what they came to know as Ottoman law), on a limited scale and under official control.

The general principle behind the 1920 Land Transfer Ordinance was that all transactions, other than leases for a term of not more than three years, required an individual to obtain written consent of the administration. There were two principle reasons for requiring the consent of the administration; both emerged from previous experience in Iraq and were reinforced by concerns expressed by the Zionist Organization. First, it was hoped that this measure would facilitate land transfers by tackling the bogey of speculation that, if ignored, would "cause an excessive rise of prices and prevent development."[10] Second, it was hoped also to prevent the aggregation of large estates. Consent would be withheld, therefore, if the administration was not certain that the person purchasing the land intended to cultivate it immediately.

But consent would also technically be withheld, by the terms of Article 6 of the Land Transfer Ordinance, unless the administration was certain that the person transferring the property (or the tenant in occupation, if the property was leased) retained sufficient land for the maintenance of his family. This condition represents one of the more significant, though perhaps least surprising from a colonial point of view, departures from Ottoman law. As Goadby and Doukhan note, Ottoman law did not provide directly for the protection of agricultural tenants.[11] In its executive instructions, the Palestine government explained to the officers concerned that, while it sought to promote in every possible way the creation of a market in land and the closer settlement of the country, it was also anxious that the interests of the present tenants and occupants of the land should be properly protected.[12] It was an anxiety born from years of experience with peasant dispossession throughout the empire (consider, for example, the Punjab Land Alienation Act as well as Egypt's Law of Five Feddans), but it is also worth drawing attention to the fact that special legislation "to give greater protection to the tenant than the Common law afforded" was being considered concurrently in England.[13]

Fundamentally linked to these changes to Ottoman law was another interesting departure: the very special powers granted by Article 8 to the High Commissioner to give or withhold sanction to sales up to any extent and without giving any reason. Although Article 36 of the 1858 Land Code had contained certain limitations on the validity of a transfer made without the leave of an official, the Provisional Law of Disposal of 1913 abolished the necessity of consent.[14] The granting of such absolute powers to the High Commissioner was highly criticized by the indigenous population. To be sure, out of approximately 2,000 petitions that were presented to the administration up to May 1921 for the disposition of immovable property, only twenty-five were refused.[15] Nevertheless, Palestinian landowners demanded the removal of necessary consent to all land transactions and desired the *status quo ante bellum:* as one official enquiry noted, "the Ordinance is objected to on religious grounds. The Sharieh Law states that 'A possessor may dispose of his possession as he pleases' and the Land Transfer Ordinance is in direct contradiction to this."[16] Such protest led a Colonial Office official to minute that:

> It has always been a matter of amazement to me that the Arabs never appreciated the benefits of these restrictions towards themselves. . . . I have always suspected that the real reason for the objection is the dislike to be told that a man may or may not do what he likes with his own property.[17]

As a result, the Land Transfer Ordinance was amended in 1921.[18] The value and size restrictions were removed so the administration could no longer object to the purchase of property for speculative purposes. Also, instead of the High Commissioner, the Director of Land Registries was henceforth charged with the responsibility of assenting to any particular land transfer.

Two quite distinct policies can therefore be said to have inspired the Land Transfer Ordinance and its amendments. On the one hand, it was hurried through in the widely held belief that the inhabitants would benefit from a free market in land. On the other hand, the ordinance represented, in the words of one prominent observer, "an attempt to exercise administratively a beneficent control over all land transactions in Palestine."[19] It is an apt description of the general approach taken by British officials in their attempts to understand the land regime they in-

herited from the Ottomans. Whether or not the framers of Ottoman law intended legislators and officials to administer the law
in a "beneficent" way, it is clear that the body of Ottoman legislation provided rich material to support such a policy. For example, some British officers hoped that, if stretched far enough, the
definition of *miri* land—of which the "ultimate ownership" or
raqaba is said to reside in the state (while cultivators were
granted the *tasarruf* or usufructuary possession) and of which
almost all of the agricultural land in Palestine was comprised—
could justify extensive state management of agricultural land.
Consider, for example, the following contribution to a Colonial
Office discussion on the expropriation of land for the British
army:

> I think that in dealing with this case we must be guided by general
> considerations of the public good rather than those of strict
> law. . . . I have written this minute on the assumption that all this
> land was true private property; but as a matter of fact there is little
> such land in Palestine, most of the land is Government land over
> which the occupiers have certain rather shadowy rights by virtue
> of their occupation; this should facilitate the work of "resump-
> tion" by the authorities.[20]

This extreme view was not widely held, and the minute met
with some deserved criticism. Nonetheless, it does give a sense
of the basic confusion that existed between the British concept
of state land (or crown land/public domain) and the concept of
miri land (which, unfortunately, was often at the time, and in the
extant literature still is, translated as "state land").[21] British officials were keenly aware during this initial period that the mass
of agricultural land fell into the *miri* category and was therefore
held on something less than freehold terms.[22] As Sir Ernest
Dowson enthused in 1925, "*miri* is governed by the civil law regardless of race or creed, and thus escapes the complications of
the multiple religious jurisdictions extant in Palestine; [*miri*]
cannot be converted into *waqf* and thus can be kept in the hands
of the people; and finally . . . (at least in theory and in law) rights

over *miri* land escheat to the State if they are not productively exercised . . . caution should I think be exercised to safeguard all existing rights of the state."[23] The Palestine government did indeed take assiduous steps to protect its effective control over whatever land it could, and early on in the Mandate it called on all persons to publicly declare all lands that could be said, theoretically or legally, to have reverted to the state. A new category of land was very quickly brought into being under the British administration of Palestine, summarily called state land or public domain, and a great deal of thought and trouble was expended by the Palestine government from the outset over this new creation.[24] The confusion over the extent to which *miri* tenure could be considered as such resulted in two important pieces of legislation during this period: the Mahlul Lands Ordinance of 1920 and the Mewat Lands Ordinance of 1921.[25]

That the state should have an interest in knowing when land has become *mahlul* is clearly supported by Ottoman law. But the provisions of the 1920 Mahlul Lands Ordinance went further and required that persons who inform the government of their possession of *mahlul* land were then entitled only, at best, to sign a lease (they were no longer entitled to a grant by *tapu*). By the terms of the 1921 Mewat Lands Ordinance, rights of cultivation were similarly revoked. Not only did the person who cultivated *mewat* no longer have a legal right to a *tapu* grant; he was now considered to be doing a wrongful act. A new juridical creature was emerging: the squatter. When asked for some elaboration during an Advisory Council Meeting in October 1920, Norman Bentwich replied that

> trespass was the offence of entering on property to which the person had no right. The penalty was five days' imprisonment and a fine of P.T. 50. The position with regard to land that a person had cultivated without permission would be that he could be turned off it.[26]

In fact, it seems clear that Ottoman law had entitled a cultivator of *mewat* and *mahlul,* who reported his occupation, to a grant by *tapu*. That is to say, under Ottoman law *miri* land could not be resumed by the (Ottoman) state as against a cultivator who paid the tithe. The terms of the 1920 Mahlul Ordinance and the 1921 Mewat Ordinance, however, gave the (British) state absolute discretion as to the manner in which it would deal with it.

One of the main objectives of the 1858 Ottoman Land Code was the economic and financial one of bringing as much *mahlul* and *mewat* land under cultivation as possible in the belief that the individual was better equipped to do so than the state.[27] As soon as they were able, the British administration turned this around and, in order to free as large an area as possible to be vested in the state, the tendency emerged to define indigenous land rights as narrowly as possible. In his "Preliminary Study of Land Tenure in Palestine," Dowson went so far as to summarize the situation in the following terms:

> fundamentally there are two main classes of land in Palestine—Mulk and the Public Domain. . . . All immovable property that is not mulk or true waqf is Public Domain. In law this is divided into three categories: (a) Miri, or public domain heritably leased, (b) Metruke, or public domain devoted to public service, and (c) Mewat, or unused and idle public domain.[28]

LAND SETTLEMENT IN THE *JIFTLIK* OF BEISAN

It was worth reviewing with some care the redefinition (and invention) under British rule of "public domain" because the Palestine government's immediate attempts to define its position regarding *jiftlik* land followed closely the same pattern established for *mahlul* and *mewat* land—that is, to guard jealously whatever control over land they thought they could. Indeed, the comparison between the three categories was often made, the tendency being to ignore the legal particulars and group all of them under the rubric of state land or, in the words of the Legal Secretary, as "lands which are at the disposal of the Government."[29]

The fact that *jiftlik* was not in Ottoman law a legal category as such (none of the Sultan's personal estates could actually be shown to have been redefined as *mulk* when he assumed ownership of them, and they were therefore always held as *miri*) but rather more like a customary form of tenure did not prevent the Palestine government from immediately trying to assume ownership as landlord.

Also known as *mudawara, jiftlik*[30] was a classification that referred to lands throughout Palestine that, at various points in the early 1870s, were supposedly "turned over" to the Sultan and, after 1908, to the Ottoman treasury. It was not well understood by the Palestine government just how these lands actually came to be registered in the name of the Sultan.[31] What was clear was that the original owners and their descendants stayed on the land and continued throughout to regard themselves as *de jure* owners. The only practical difference in their situation was that beyond payment of the ordinary tithe, they owed the state an additional 10 percent—regarded by the government as rental but by the cultivators as a payment "under duress."[32]

Responsibility for initially defining the relationship between government and the cultivators of *jiftlik* land was assigned to the 1920 Land Commission. The role of the commission in this case was essentially threefold: first, it was required to report on what steps should be taken to obtain an accurate record of *jiftlik* lands and on how to make the best disposition of them in the interests of the country; second, it would report on what measures could be taken to ensure the greater productivity of the soil; and finally, it was expected to make recommendations to protect the interests of the "tenants or occupants of Government lands."[33] The Land Commission was not a legal body and therefore did not attempt to advise on the legal basis on which the cultivators claimed ownership of their land. Rather, it aimed to formulate policy, based on the directions issued it as above. In May 1921, it recommended (as a matter of policy) the "nonalienation" of *jiftlik* land, actually referring to it as "state land." But it also recommended that the tenure of the occupants of all *jiftlik* should, on account of its peculiar history, be settled in perpetuity. It suggested long leases, the precise period of which should be governed by circumstances.

This in fact was the favored mechanism by which colonial governments generally disposed of "state land." From the point of view of increasing the public good, leasing was preferable to selling because it was assumed that the extension of British rule and good government (such as increased security and the development of infrastructure) would eventually raise property values. Government wanted to be sure that it eventually received its fair share of the increased dividend.[34] In the case of Beisan, this was compromised somewhat by the suggestion that the cultivators be offered very long leases (say, ninety-nine years). Long leases were recommended for two reasons. First, it was thought that agricultural development in the Beisan area would entail the sort of expenditure that only very long leases would secure. Second, it was conceded by the commission that the "tenancy" of *jiftlik* cultivators was somewhat special in that "these cultivators did not part with their lands willingly but by force of circumstances" and were not therefore "ordinary tenants." Implicit in official discussions over the Beisan *jiftlik* from the start was the idea of a statute of limitations. Evidence to support the state's claim had indeed decayed over time, making it more difficult for the government to be certain that it could settle legal title in its favor. British officials were never altogether convinced that the process by which ownership had been transferred to the Sultan was entirely consolidated in law in the first place.[35]

At any rate, the cultivators of the Beisan *jiftlik* declined outright the idea of leases. Refusing to admit to the legality of any alleged prior transfer of ownership to the state, they demanded that they should be treated as owners of the land and not as tenants. In the end the government did in fact agree and, by the terms of the Ghor Mudawara Agreement, legally registered the cultivators of the Beisan *jiftlik* as individual owners of *miri* land.[36] The nature of this agreement is best described by the care with which the terms for the indenture were chosen:

> Now this is to witness that this Agreement has been made between the Government of Palestine and the cultivators of the land as a permanent settlement of their respective rights.[37]

Words such as "purchaser" or "purchase price" were not included. In fact, such terms were studiously avoided since the cultivators simply refused to admit that this agreement stood for a "sale and purchase" of their land.[38]

Why, given the tendency of the Palestine government until this point to guard assiduously whatever rights in land it thought it could, did it admit the Beisan cultivators' claims to *ab antiquo* rights as deserving of legal recognition? There are good reasons for attributing this change of direction to the recognition by the government of the relevance of a sort of doctrine of adverse possession: the occupiers of the land, while perhaps not having been legally registered as the true owners, nevertheless should acquire a prescriptive title to the land because they had continuously cultivated it for at least several decades. The cost of "developing" the land and the idea of a statute of limitations (as mentioned above) were certainly contributing factors. Political considerations also played an important part when deciding on the future of the Beisan *jiftlik*. Writing ten years later, Lewis French explained that "considerations of law possibly, considerations of equity and policy certainly, forbade the Government in such a wild and unsettled locality to terminate the leases of these tenants." In this context it is worth noting the concern expressed by Samuel when he made a personal visit to the area and a hostile demonstration was organized to greet him: it was in fact shortly following this reception that government proceeded with the allotment of territory along the lines of the Ghor Mudawara Agreement. No doubt the government hoped that confirming the local population in the occupancy of their lands would reap political rewards.[39]

One of the most common reasons put forth publicly by British officials in support of securing the cultivators' tenure to the land was that by settling the question of ownership the Palestine government could thereby institute cadastral survey operations immediately and so eliminate any confusion over claims to property. And this of course facilitated market exchange: "The Administration has been anxious to come to an equitable arrangement with the present cultivators of the land," Samuel wrote in 1921, "in order to facilitate the colonization of the larger parts of the lands which are now uncultivated."[40] In 1923, Samuel again noted the benefits of market transactions:

> the Baisan Land Settlement . . . has converted the customary, but uncertain, tenure of the cultivators into a new legal tenure on terms satisfactory both to them and to the Government. Portions of the land so allocated to the cultivators, which are surplus to their real requirements, are about to be sold by some of them to an American Zionist Group, and the payments that are in prospect have had a marked effect upon local politics.[41]

Similarly, the Annual Report for 1920 and 1921, for example, described the benefits of the Ghor Mudawara Agreement in the same terms, noting also that "one of the first conditions of agricultural progress is . . . the settlement of land titles."[42]

The Land Commission, while recommending leases, had not been totally averse to this measure, describing "the free flow of money" as the primary method for making large areas of land held by individuals more productive. "We are of opinion," their report had noted, "that every encouragement should be given to landowners to sell their excess areas and that there should be no restriction on sales." As for the fear that the *fallah* would alienate all his land, the Commission assured that "as he is dependent on his cultivation as his means of livelihood having no other regular method of supporting himself and his family and as he is an intelligent person and a keen agriculturalist he is not likely to part with all his lands."[43]

PROTECTION OF CULTIVATORS ORDINANCES, 1929 AND 1933

As already noted, it was recognized from the beginning in Palestine that the development of a market in land would in its train raise the question of landlessness and peasant dispossession. Colonial officials knew this from experience, and there was no reason to think that the particular circumstances of Palestine, the limited cultivable area of which was home to a rapidly growing population as well as the target of the Jewish national home, would be any different. While it is true that the framers of the 1920 Land Transfer Ordinance attempted to preempt the problem by requiring (Section 8[1]) that suitable provision be made for tenants of agricultural land when land was sold, it was soon found that this ordinance did not in practice afford the desired protection. For example, the landlord desirous of selling agricultural land could first evict his tenants and then sell the land with vacant possession. Government consent became a mere formality: tenants disappeared with monetary compensation before government officials were even informed of the transaction. Furthermore, the ordinance gave no protection in the case of an enforced sale.[44]

In 1929, Section 8[1] of the Land Transfer Ordinance was repealed, and the Protection of Cultivators Ordinance was enacted. This new ordinance essentially tried to bring the law in line with common practice and provided for the payment of compensation to the tenant in respect of termination of tenancy, disturbance, improvements, and so forth. The previous requirement that a cultivator retain a subsistence area elsewhere was dropped. Not surprisingly, the ordinance was of very little value in preventing the displacement of tenants from the soil. The chief defect of the ordinance was that there was no record of tenancies in Palestine, as there was for instance in India, and it was extremely difficult for a tenant to in fact establish a tenancy for so many years on one holding.[45]

The reason behind such amendments to the Land Transfer Ordinance was that, until this point, landlessness was not considered too grave a problem. Rather, the focus was more on creating a market in land so as, on the one hand, to ensure that land in the hands of unenterprising owners would soon enough be transferred to those who would develop it more intensively and, on the other hand, to fulfill the obligations made regarding the establishment of the Jewish national home.[46] Accordingly, throughout the 1920s, the process of the displacement of tenants and cultivators from the land went on practically unchecked. The 1929 Land Transfer (Amendment) Ordinance simply constituted legal recognition of this reality.

But within months of the promulgation of the 1929 ordinance, the so-called Wailing Wall riots of August 1929 crushed the optimistic speculation that had surrounded the belief in market transactions, and the problem of landlessness abruptly emerged into prominence.

The Shaw Commission, which was sent out to report on the disturbances of 1929, was chiefly responsible for this changing emphasis. In March 1930 it reported that the dispossession of Arab tenants, resulting from the sale to Jews of the lands they were cultivating, had reached an "acute" level. The commission furthermore concluded that there was no alternative land on which persons evicted could then settle. The result was that a landless and discontented class was being created in Palestine and would remain a constant source of discontent and a potential cause of future disturbance. In the opinion of the commission, Palestine simply could not support a larger agricultural population than it carried in 1930, unless methods of farming were radically changed. Meanwhile, they regarded it as of vital importance that, pending the results of a thorough investigation, ways should be found of checking "the present tendency towards the eviction of peasant cultivators from the land."[47]

On the recommendation of the Shaw Commission, Sir John Hope-Simpson was sent out to examine on the spot the questions of immigration, land settlement, and development. In October 1930, he summarized the situation in the following terms:

> It is the duty of the Administration, under the Mandate, to ensure that the position of the Arabs is not prejudiced by Jewish immigration. It is also its duty under the Mandate to encourage the close settlement of the Jews on the land, subject always to the former condition. It is only possible to reconcile these apparently conflicting duties by an active policy of agricultural development, having as its object close settlement on the land and intensive cultivation by both Arabs and Jews. To this end drastic action is necessary.[48]

In this regard, Hope-Simpson recommended that government undertake an Agricultural Development Scheme aimed at improving farming methods, thereby providing sufficient land for the Arab *fallahin* as well as for additional Jewish settlement. An essential element of this scheme was that until the mechanics were worked out, all disposition of land should rest with the authority in charge of development. That is, transfers should only be permitted provided they did not interfere with the development scheme. As for the Protection of Cultivators Ordinance, 1929, Hope-Simpson was particularly critical: "what is eminently required is, not compensation for disturbance, but a provision against disturbances."[49]

Hope-Simpson's main ideas were embodied in the 1930 White Paper, which contemplated three measures to combat the landless problem: first, a development scheme that, when initially discussed, was to involve a guaranteed loan of PP 2.5 million; second, an investigation into the number of "landless Arabs" (specially defined); and third, the introduction of legislation with the object of closely supervising land transfers so as to prevent increases in the dispossession of the indigenous agricultural population. In the meantime, full power was reserved to take all steps necessary to protect the tenancy of Arab cultivators throughout Palestine.[50]

The first two projects failed miserably. In the first place, British officials in Palestine soon had to take into account the rapidly changing financial conditions. Though the economic condition of Palestine was showing some signs of improvement in the early 1930s, world economic conditions remained uncertain, and as a result of financial stringency in London the development scheme was repeatedly, and indefinitely, "postponed."[51] As for the landless Arab enquiry, it was rendered ineffectual by the terms under which it proceeded.[52] Its usefulness can be partly surmised by the fact that among the number of former cultivators who were displaced from the lands they occupied because those lands were acquired by Jewish purchasers but not covered by the special definition of what constituted a "landless Arab" were individuals who obtained employment in towns. In the event of any severe economic downturn, these were the very individuals who would lose their means of livelihood and constitute a potential danger.

With the development scheme shelved, and the landless enquiry suitably emasculated, the urgent problem left facing the Palestine government was how to stop the process of displacement. In this context, the last important consequence of Sir John Hope-Simpson's report and the 1930 White Paper was the 1933 Protection of Cultivators Ordinance. The object of this ordinance was to more carefully protect tenants from eviction by requiring that "statutory tenants" who had not neglected their holdings be provided with a subsistence area if ejected. Under this ordinance, a landlord was prevented from selling tenanted land without first relocating the tenants. When this ordinance was passed, careful consideration was given to the question of whether it was necessary to protect small owners as well as tenants. This was the Rubicon that the Colonial Office, ever conscious of the obligations under the Mandate to facilitate Jewish colonization, was desperately trying to avoid crossing. It did not appear at the time to be necessary, although the High Commissioner in particular promised to watch the situation closely, and in 1933 the Colonial Office pledged that "no restriction shall be placed on owner-occupiers in disposing of their land."[53] But within two years, in the summer of 1935, the Palestine government in fact began preparing legislation that would prevent a landowner from selling his "lot viable" (the minimum area necessary for the family's subsistence).

LAND SETTLEMENT OF THE *JIFTLIK* VILLAGES OF SAJAD AND QAZAZA

The land settlement operations in the *jiftlik* villages of Sajad and Qazaza were undertaken in 1931 in accordance with the normal procedures of land settlement as provided for by the Land Settlement Ordinance of 1928. It should be noted that this ordinance was not intended to alter the substantive law of the country but was rather meant as a law of procedure.[54] It is also notable that the whole of Palestine was not simultaneously made subject to the provisions of the new ordinance: rather, they applied only to well defined "settlement areas" that were declared "whenever it appears expedient" in the *Official Gazette*.[55]

The program of land settlement adopted in Palestine was that of progressive settlement spreading fan-wise from certain centers. This was described as "the most expeditious and economical method,"[56] since it required fewer staff, less transport, and less supervision than a program of a more sporadic nature. The centers were expediently located along the coast because the greatest amount of progress at the least amount of cost could be achieved by first concentrating in the plains. Land settlement in the hill areas was thought to be more complicated: cultivation was more patchy and less continuous, and the size and shape of holdings was expected to vary much more than in the plains.

Any interruption in the program caused by taking up a particular village outside of the prescribed schedule was to be avoided because it would involve increased expenditure and unnecessary delay. In 1936, the Commissioner of Lands and Surveys proclaimed his extreme aversion to departing from the settlement program explaining: "the difficulty is that if we tackle too many areas where there are likely to be complicated disputes, we shall bite off more than we can chew. . . . I want to make it clear that we cannot settle the odd cabbage-patch."[57]

It is therefore significant that Sajad and Qazaza were not actually included in the normal progress of settlement operations for 1931 and 1932. Land settlement was (reluctantly) scheduled in the fall of 1931 by the Commissioner of Lands and Surveys in advance of the normal operations only because it was urgently required by the new Director of Development, Lewis French. At first the Commissioner of Lands and Surveys hesitated and explained that staff simply could not be spared for any settlement in advance of normal operations. He eventually agreed to take the highly unusual step of rearranging the schedule to include forthwith these *jiftlik* villages in the program of settlement, but he also expressed strong reservations. In a letter to the Chief Secretary, he recalled the "intractability" of the Beisan inhabitants during the attempts made ten years earlier to regulate the position of the government in *jiftlik* lands. He concluded by expressing the concern, somewhat prophetically as it turned out, that settlement operations in Sajad and Qazaza might "possibly bring about a situation which Government might not wish to be faced with at the present juncture."[58]

Once declared a "settlement area," the official procedures for Sajad and Qazaza proceeded along four established stages. The first stage consisted of dividing the lands of the village into "registration blocks" of convenient size and shape and preferably of equal value. This division was in fact intended to satisfy fiscal, as well as registration, purposes. The urban property tax had been promulgated in 1928, and the intention was to replace the tithe in rural areas with a block land tax as soon as possible. British officials relied at this stage on the subdivision of village areas that to a large extent already existed. As Sir Ernest Dowson observed: "the expedient of constituting blocks of land of approximately equal value is familiar to the people and has long been used by them as an equitable basis for the apportionment of *mesha'*."[59]

These block plans were prepared by survey officers in the field who roughly sketched on a map the boundaries already defined by the villagers themselves using angle irons of their own provision. In the circumstances, the survey officer really completed some of the settlement himself. There were always a number of small disputes as to exactly where the boundary was. Maurice Bennett, assistant director in the Department of Lands and Surveys, described this process to the Peel Commission:

> If you went out and saw the surveyor doing his work you might think there was a riot on, because there is a tremendous amount of shouting and argument, but really it is a fairly peaceful business and after wasting a great deal of time they decide where so-and-so's angle iron is to go in.[60]

The survey work was all recorded in field books and then sent to the head survey office, where plans were prepared that listed, against every parcel of land, the number, the area, and the reputed owner.[61]

The plans and accompanying information were then handed over to the settlement branch, who appointed a settlement officer to initiate the second stage: the process of recording claims. The settlement officer would actually proceed to the village and set up a "camp" from which he would issue notices, provide the appropriate claim forms, and entertain the villagers with coffee and cigarettes.[62] A great deal of consideration was given throughout to the necessity of securing the cooperation of the village cultivators. It was repeatedly emphasized that the success of settlement operations depended on such cooperation: "the settlement of ninety per cent of the property parcels would present little difficulty," Dowson promised in 1930, "if investigations were carried out on the spot in the presence of the villagers and other interested parties by officers who knew the language and were in touch with local customs and feeling."[63] To help secure the cooperation of the village authorities in the settlement process, village settlement committees were constituted by the settlement officer. In any matter of common interest, the villagers were represented by this committee, which was chosen from persons nominated by the inhabitants. The village settlement committee was empowered in its own name to bring and defend actions, and it was its duty to protect the interests of absentees, minors, and incapacitated persons.[64]

In the process of recording claims, the settlement officer would as a first step record all rights of ownership, mortgages, leases for a period of more than three years, rights of way, and such other interests as might be registrable. Such claims had to be made on the proper claim forms obtained on application at the camp. During this process, the settlement officer would also ascertain from claimants the grounds on which claims were based and obtain the necessary supporting documents with names of witnesses. Schedules of claims were then prepared and posted for a prescribed period of time (not less than fifteen days), during which additional claims or counterclaims might be lodged.

The settlement officer could then commence the third stage of settlement operations: the final investigation and settlement of claims. If there were conflicting claims, the settlement officer had the judicial power to decide the dispute. In doing so, he was required to "apply the Land Law in force at the date of the hearing of the action, provided he shall have regard to the equitable as well as legal rights to land."[65] If he thought that a person who had not presented a claim was in fact entitled to any right in land, he could proceed as if such person had made a claim. The final schedule of rights for each registration block was then completed and posted in the village. Appeals against the settlement officer's decision could be filed in the land court or the district court, but it appears that on the whole appeals were infrequent. There were very few reversals of settlement officers' decisions.

The fourth, and final, stage was the forwarding of the schedule of rights, with its accompanying registration block plan, to the registry office of the subdistrict in which the village was situated. The information could then be entered into a new land register, which, boasted Goadby and Doukhan, "conforms to the best modern practice."[66] It was loose leaf in form and omitted all reference to boundaries or other verbal descriptions. Rather, land was described by reference only to block and parcel numbers. The person in whose name a parcel was registered was entitled to a certificate of registration (*kushan*) on the payment of a fee. These were the established practices followed closely by the settlement officers in Sajad and Qazaza.

THE DECISION OF THE SETTLEMENT OFFICER IN SAJAD AND QAZAZA

After completing his investigations of all the claims to rights and interests in the *jiftlik* lands of Sajad and Qazaza, the settlement officer made two significant decisions concerning the legal nature of the rights enjoyed by the cultivators. On the one hand, he decided that title to the ownership of the land, which had previously been registered as *miri* land in the name of Sultan 'Abd al-Hamid, should now be vested in the name of the High Commissioner in trust for and on behalf of the government of Palestine. This was of course in sharp contrast to the final decision made in the Beisan *jiftlik*. But it was argued by the settlement officer that such registration ought to have been done by virtue of the action of the Ottoman government on 1 September 1324 A.H. (1908) in transferring to itself the properties of the Sultan, together with their revenues and income, and also by virtue of the provisions of the Palestine Order-in-Council, 1922.

However, the settlement officer went on to say that persons who had cultivated the lands of Sajad and Qazaza should be legally registered in the schedule of rights as having "heritable and assignable rights of occupancy and tenancy." In practical terms, then, the decision resulted in the cultivators being registered as having something very close to the rights granted to the Beisan cultivators. In the Ghor Mudawara Agreement, as we have seen, the land was distributed to the cultivators on *miri* tenure—that is, with the understanding that the *raqaba* or "ownership" technically remained vested in the state while the cultivators were granted the *tasarruf* or usufructuary possession.

At the time of the settlement officer's decision, observers of legal issues pertaining to land tenure were not sure what to make of this. Lewis French, for example, noted the decision in an aside, and it warranted an uncertain footnote in Goadby and Doukhan's *Land Law of Palestine,* also published shortly after the decision was made. At any rate, the settlement officer's decision did not stand for long. In a very unusual move, the attorney general quickly appealed the decision, arguing for a much more circumscribed and limited form of tenancy for the *jiftlik* cultivators. It is worth reviewing with some care the reasons behind the granting of such occupancy rights by the settlement officer, as well as the reasons that lay behind the attorney general's appeal.

Prior to reaching his decision, the settlement officer of Sajad and Qazaza discussed the matter of *jiftlik* lands thoroughly with the settlement officer of the Gaza area, where settlement of *jiftlik* lands was concurrently undertaken (in line also with Lewis French's request). Together the two settlement officers had no difficulty coming to the same conclusions regarding "heritable and assignable rights," both on matters of principle and on the exact phraseology to be used. In fact, the Gaza settlement officer drew up a similar schedule of rights for the inhabitants of the *jiftlik* villages of Muharraqa, Kawfakha, Jaladiya, and Rafah.[67]

In appreciating why the settlement officers decided in favor of recognizing "heritable and assignable rights" in *jiftlik* lands, it is important to consider several factors. On the legal side, it is significant that Article 10(3) of the Land Settlement Ordinance made it mandatory, and not merely discretionary, that the settlement officer had regard to equitable rights. It is also significant to note that an important difference existed between actions during the established procedure of land settlement and those instituted before the land courts. Actions before the land courts were voluntary and were confined to the points at issue. In contrast, the settlement officer was undertaking a settlement of all relevant facts and interests pertaining to land on a comprehensive and territorial basis. A brief perusal of the legal records makes it clear that settlement officers were widely of the opinion that the 1928 Land Settlement Ordinance gave them the fullest powers to carry out an investigation into any claims. Even if interested parties did not lodge a claim themselves, the settlement officer, if he was satisfied that they had rights, commonly proceeded, by virtue of Section 27(4), as if they had lodged a claim.

Such appears to have largely been the case for the cultivators of Sajad and Qazaza, who, in the words of the settlement officer himself, "are illiterate and ignorant of the meaning of legal terms . . . [and] unable to properly state or define their claims."[68] In defining their rights, equitable and legal, the settlement officer had to take into consideration the following interests: cultivators of the *jiftlik* had often disposed of their rights to one another; cultivators had erected buildings and planted trees on the land without the consent of the government being required; when a cultivator died, his heirs were entitled to inherit. Moreover, such interests, it was noted, had on several previous occasions given rise to disputes that settlement officers had in fact decided judicially.

It is also notable that the settlement officer had himself already gained a great deal of knowledge about *jiftlik* lands through several years of experience in Beisan where, as we have seen, registered ownership of land had in fact been transferred to the cultivators under the terms of the Ghor Mudawara Agreement. Following that agreement, settlement officers commonly assumed the other *jiftlik* properties would be handled in the same way.[69] Finally, in understanding the settlement officer's decision, it is worth drawing attention to the nature of similar interests in England at that time, with which the settlement officer would surely have been familiar. In the words of Goadby and Doukhan: "it is natural that persons familiar with the workings of the leasehold system in England should assume that the lessee has an heritable and assignable interest."[70]

When forced to defend his decision before the attorney general, the settlement officer argued that "the practical and political objections to such a bare registration in the name of the Government alone without mention of any rights of tenants or even their existence on the land (or of the existence of their houses and trees on the land) are so apparent as scarcely to need mention."[71] But if they indeed are so apparent, why then did the attorney general refuse to acknowledge hereditary and assignable rights of cultivators in *jiftlik* lands? Shortly after being informed by the director of development of the decision by the settlement officer, the attorney general on behalf of the government appealed to the land court, sitting as a court of appeal. He appealed against the registration of such tenancy rights ostensibly on the ground that there was nothing in the legislation of the country that could justify the existence of such rights. In fact, he argued, the decision of the settlement officer created a form of tenure that was legally unknown in Palestine and that was contrary to Article 23 of the Land Code.

In the event, Judges Copland and Shehadeh, sitting as a land court, allowed the appeal and decided that the settlement officer had indeed "misdirected himself" and that equitable or customary rights as claimed by the respondents were not in fact such as could be recognized by the courts, "since they have not been exercised from time immemorial."[72] The judgment, which is worth quoting at length, continued:

> Section 10(3) of the Land Settlement Ordinance, 1928, states that the Settlement Officer shall apply the Land Law in force at the date of the hearing of the action, provided that he shall have regard to equitable as well as legal rights in land. If it were not for this provision, I should have no hesitation in holding that such hereditary and assignable occupancy and tenancy rights did not exist, and that they were a form of tenure unknown to the law, as being contrary to Article 23 of the Land Code. They are certainly

not a legal right. . . . Can they be said to come within the description of equitable rights? . . .

Equitable rights arise in many ways and are of varying descriptions. The only phase of them which it is necessary to consider in the case before us is whether such a right should be recognised as regards these lands on the ground of customary user—that is to say, whether the undisputed user for a period of something over fifty years is such that the Courts should, in the course of their equitable jurisdiction, recognise this customary tenure and give effect to it. I think that there is no doubt that . . . the lands have been held by the tenants on the customary basis of hereditary and assignable occupancy and tenancy rights, without hindrance or objection, since the establishment of the *Jiftlik*, and on no other basis. But a custom, in order to obtain the force of law, or a customary right, in order to be enforced as an equitable right, must be both ancient and invariable. In this case it is undoubtedly invariable, and the point that requires determination is whether it has been exercised over such a sufficiently lengthy period, that it may be described as ancient.

Very little help is to be obtained from any Ottoman Law . . .

I think that the correct rule is that a custom with regard to a right or interest in land, in order to be clothed with the force of law, must have existed for such a period, that its origin has been lost sight of, so that it may be said to have existed *ab antiquo,* or as the English expression goes, for such a period that "the memory of man runneth not to the contrary." And that cannot be said to be the case here.

Based on this reasoning alone, the land court therefore allowed the appeal and decided that the inhabitants of Sajad and Qazaza were "tenants, and merely tenants" of the government and had not acquired any legal or equitable rights as against the government. The observations made by the settlement officer with regard to the hereditary and assignable rights of occupancy and tenancy were consequently deleted from the schedule of rights for Sajad and Qazaza.

The question that needs to be considered in greater detail here is why the attorney general's office was so uncomfortable with the settlement officer's provision of "heritable and assignable rights" and so decided to take the very unusual move of lodging an appeal against this judgment. We can dismiss the possibility that this was a purely legal matter, such as disagreement over the procedure required to clothe custom with the force of law. The government surely had the option of considering an amendment to the land code to provide for occupancy rights along the lines of the settlement officer's decision.

In determining the government's position (that of the attorney general) against the registration of such rights, there are two matters of some importance. One is a question of policy: at the beginning of the Mandate, the task of maintaining the claims of the state to ownership of land was charged, as under the Ottoman system, to the land registry. But on grounds of principle, it was gradually accepted that the registry ought properly to be regarded only as the strictly impartial recorder of rights to land and that its position was therefore compromised by the fact that it was also charged with the incompatible duty of maintaining the claims of the state.[73] So in 1927, it was decided that the attorney general should take over responsibility for the presentation and defense of such claims. Thus, in 1931, when rights and interests in the lands of Sajad and Qazaza were being settled, it was the attorney general's "job," as it were, to push for the claims of the state.

But I would submit that a more significant clue to the attorney general's appeal is the link to particular historical circumstances after 1929. It is important to bear in mind that the reason for Sajad and Qazaza being prematurely settled resulted from the urgent request of the director of development, Lewis French, whose major responsibility was, of course, the resettlement of those Arabs compendiously named "landless." We have seen that concern over an ever-increasing landless class and over the political repercussions of its continuous growth was particularly acute at this time, especially in the wake of the 1929 riots. This mounting anxiety led British administrators to become more and more fearful that the expansion of individual rights in land, if uncontrolled, could lead to an undermining of communal bonds and thus result in social dislocation. Had land settlement in Sajad and Qazaza resulted in the cultivators being secured in hereditary and assignable rights over land, there was the fear that they might be tempted to sell their holdings and so become landless, thus creating new obligations which the Development Department would have to deal with in the future.

In appealing the decision of the settlement officer, the state was not interested in securing its rights to the land to dispose of it. The government had no intention whatsoever to evict its "tenants" from the land. Rather, it was of the opinion that had the court upheld the decision of the settlement officer that the cultivators of *jiftlik* land had hereditary and assignable rights, nothing could have prevented the cultivators from assigning their rights to others and thus becoming landless. On the other hand, peasant cultivators, with rights subject to the state, were viewed as much more politically docile.

In 1921, it might have made good economic sense to British officials to provide the occupants of the Beisan land with the "necessary" security of tenure to "develop" their land. But in 1931, individualization of land tenure was no longer being encouraged as a mark of progress. The Commissioner of Lands stated it bluntly when he warned in the early 1930s that "it is unwise to give any Arab cultivators an alienable title." And this was elaborated on by the District Commissioner in Jerusalem:

> what safeguard will there be that the recipients of *jiftlik* lands un-
> der an agreement will not immediately speculate with their hold-
> ings and complicate the problem by bringing into existence absen-
> tee landlords, landless Arabs, landowners without water rights,
> etc.[74]

CONCLUSION

In addition to providing an overview of British legislative efforts to define and regulate property transactions, this chapter has concurrently sought to ground its analysis of land settlement in Palestine in particular historical contexts through a comparison of settlement operations in *jiftlik* villages in 1921 and 1931. Together, these dual approaches reveal quite clearly that the typically colonial desire to facilitate economic development through the creation of a market in land proved increasingly problematic.

In 1921, in the Beisan *jiftlik,* registered ownership of land was transferred to the cultivators under the terms of the Ghor Mudawara Agreement, which officially admitted the cultivators' *ab antiquo* rights to the land. The reasons behind this agreement lay chiefly in the broader economic and legal context, which, particularly in the early part of the Mandate, informed the colonial approach to questions of land tenure: mainly, the conviction that systematic settlement of rights to land was essential for economic and even political development.

To be sure, many British officials felt that the mechanics of this first essay in dealing with the settlement of *jiftlik* land were not very satisfactory. But it is clear that the criticisms as they were expressed in the 1920s focused on the *limits* that it placed on transactions in land. In a confidential letter, dated 21 October 1926, the Colonial Office informed High Commissioner Plumer that

> agricultural development is a matter of primary concern to the future of Palestine. It is an object which, apart altogether from any specific obligations imposed by the Mandate, the government is bound to pursue with all the means at its disposal. The Beisan settlement may have been the best obtainable in the special circumstances of the case; but its terms ought not to be regarded as a precedent for adoption elsewhere, if they do not conduce to the best interests of agricultural development . . . in respect of such areas as may ultimately be found to be available for agricultural . . . development, the Zionist Organisation might be regarded as having the first claim to consideration.[75]

In fact, the Colonial Office was particularly anxious to hear from Plumer at that point about the possibility of acquiring land in the Rafah *jiftlik* for Jewish land companies to purchase on the open market.

By the early 1930s, however, many British officials were in a very different state of mind about the virtues of the market, and the settlement processes in Sajad and Qazaza offer interesting glimpses into the evident confusion surrounding the nature of rights that the British administration was then willing to recognize in Palestine. As expectations changed, property became a controversial subject of colonial discourse, and there was much confusion over the purposes that the institution of property ought to serve. The colonial state, in its attempt to transform Palestinian society, was neither as coherent nor as single-minded as is sometimes assumed. In the early 1930s, it appears that for the settlement officer the recognition of individual property rights was still considered proper and fair. But for the attorney general, the notion of property as entailing a claim over its disposal had become politically dangerous, and he was no longer eager to secure and endorse such a claim. The idea of private land tenure was by then regarded as much as a problem as it was a solution.

The successful appeal by the attorney general also raises several interesting points about the development of land policy in Mandate Palestine. It confirms, for example, that the court system was, to some extent, a useful instrument of British land policy, and it sheds further light on the role of judges as political actors. So broad was the term "equitable rights" that it should be recognized for the extent to which it granted the courts a wide degree of discretion in the application of Ottoman law. Whenever customary practice contravened Ottoman law, the court was obviously given some flexibility in deciding which was to prevail. To understand how a choice was made, one must always provide the context in which the decision-making process took place. In the case presented here, adherence to legal rules presided over maintaining custom. But there were times when custom prevailed over law as, for example, in the preservation of customary forms of inheritance.[76] It seems fair to conclude that a great deal of discretion was given to the courts to ensure that rules relating to property rights converged with the administrative necessities of the colonial state.

ACKNOWLEDGMENT

I am particularly grateful to Roger Owen and Eugene Rogan for their assistance throughout the writing of this chapter.

NOTES

1. Palestine, Department of Development, *Supplementary Report on Agricultural Development and Land Settlement in Palestine,* by Lewis French, Director of Development (Jerusalem: Government Printer, 1932), 1.

2. It is perhaps worth repeating the same qualification that the *Survey of Palestine* provided when discussing similar material: that is, "by 'land settlement' is meant the examination of rights to land and the solution of disputes about the ownership, boundaries, category and other registrable rights in land, its cadastral survey for the purpose, and the eventual recording of the rights in Land Registries. *It must not be confused with the settlement of people on the land*" (emphasis in the original). See Palestine, *A Survey of Palestine. Prepared in December 1945 and January 1946 for the Anglo-American Commission of Inquiry,* 2 vols. (Jerusalem: Government Printer, 1946; reprinted Washington, D.C.: Institute for Palestine Studies, 1991), 234.

3. For a discussion of how this tension was evident in British attitudes toward *musha'* land in Palestine, see Roger Owen, "The Role of *Musha'* (Co-ownership) in the Politico-Legal History of Mandatory Palestine" (paper prepared for the SSRC Workshop on Law, Property, and State Power, Büyükada, 9–10 September 1992).

4. David Washbrook makes this point in reference to British officials in India, where the aim was "to facilitate economic relationships between propertied subjects . . . as part of a scheme for the transformation of Indian society under principles drawn from British Whig political and European Physiocratic economic theory. The scheme centred on promoting the commercial and economic devel-

opment of Benghal by emancipating the individual . . . to accumulate wealth and property through the market. It was stamped by a philosophy of 'possessive individualism'." "Law, State and Agrarian Society in Colonial India," *Modern Asian Studies* 15, no. 3 (1981): 652. See also Thomas Metcalf, *The New Cambridge History of India, III.* Vol. 4, *Ideologies of the Raj* (Cambridge: Cambridge University Press, 1994), 21.

5. Colonial rule in much of subtropical Africa similarly retreated during this period from legal reform of private property. For a contemporary discussion, see C. K. Meek, *Law and Authority in a Nigerian Tribe: A Study in Indirect Rule* (London: Oxford University Press, 1937). For a more recent and very helpful study, see Martin Chanock, "Paradigms, Policies, and Property: A Review of the Customary Law of Land Tenure," in *Law in Colonial Africa,* ed. Kristin Mann and Richard Roberts (London: James Currey, 1991), 61–82.

6. As Anne Philips writes, "colonialism was necessarily makeshift." *The Enigma of Colonialism: British Policy in West Africa* (London: James Currey, 1989), v.

7. Minute by Mills, 22 November 1921, Great Britain, Public Record Office, Colonial Office (CO) 733/7. Presumably he meant Egypt, not Sudan.

8. Telegram Clayton to FO, 27 June 1919, Great Britain, Public Record Office, Foreign Office (FO) 371/4171/94476/(159). Over a year later, Herbert Samuel again argued for the reopening of the land registers saying that "the resumption of land transactions is the first condition of economic revival." Letter from Samuel to FO 23 August 1920, FO 371/5139/E10569.

9. Telegram from GHQ, Cairo to WO, 12 August 1918, FO 371/4226/118896.

10. "Note on the Land Transfer Ordinance," *Official Gazette of the Government of Palestine,* 1 October 1920, p. 10. Compare this, for example, with the Iraqi Proclamation of 30 July 1919, which began: "Whereas in consequence of the loss of records of the land registry offices, to the fact that many title deed are known to be forged or false, *with a view to check speculative land transactions* and for other reasons it is expedient temporarily to restrict dealings in land" (emphasis added). FO 371/4151/127607.

11. Frederic M. Goadby and Moses J. Doukhan, *The Land Law of Palestine* (Tel Aviv: Shoshany's, 1935), 232.

12. See, for example, "Memorandum No. 17: Description of Measures Adopted in Palestine to Protect Cultivators," in Great Britain, Colonial No. 133, *Palestine Royal Commission: Memoranda Prepared by the Government of Palestine* (London: H.M.S.O., 1937).

13. For example: the Agricultural Holdings Act, 1923; the Landlord and Tenant Act, 1927. Cited in Goadby and Doukhan, *Land Law of Palestine*, 233. See also R. R. A. Walker, "English Property Legislation of 1922–1926," *Journal of Comparative Legislation and International Law* 10, no. 1 (1928): 1–13.

14. See R. C. Tute, *The Ottoman Land Laws with a Commentary on the Ottoman Land Code of 7th Ramadan 1274* (Jerusalem: Greek Convent Press, 1927), 40–42.

15. Letter from Samuel to Churchill, 14 May 1921, CO 733/3/(205).

16. "Land Settlement Commission's Report," CO 733/18/(611).

17. It was also noted in the same minute that suspicion regarding the new powers granted to the High Commissioner could only have grown stronger "when it was seen that Zionists were buying from Mr. George Sursock over 15,000 dunams of land in the Galilee District near Jezreel. The restriction clauses then become a farce . . . it would entail the removal of an Arab village from one locality to another. . . . Villages do not grow by accident—and in dealing with any land question we really act in a matter that possesses continuity from times prior to history." Minute by Mills, November 1921, CO 733/7/58411.

18. See Kenneth W. Stein, *The Land Question in Palestine, 1917–1939* (Chapel Hill: University of North Carolina Press, 1984), 47–51; and Great Britain, Cmd. 1540, *Palestine Disturbances in May 1921: Reports of the Commission of Inquiry with Correspondence in Relation Thereto. Presented to Parliament by Command of His Majesty, October 1921* [Haycraft Report], 51.

19. Sir Ernest Dowson, "The Land System in Palestine," CO 733/109/(249).

20. Minute by C. L. M. Clauson, 2 November 1924, CO 733/50/(498).

21. Haim Gerber makes the following points: "State land, in the modern sense, is land that the state wishes to keep out of individ-

ual use, such as forest land. Such a legal category did not exist in the Ottoman Empire and came into being only in the new states. *Miri* land was not state land in this sense. There was never really a question of usurpation of such land." See *The Social Origins of the Modern Middle East* (Boulder, Colo.: Renner, 1987), 68.

22. Note that by the end of the Mandate period, land in the *miri* category came to be accepted more or less as freehold.

23. Sir Ernest Dowson, "The Land System in Palestine," CO 733/109/ (249), p. 3.

24. As Goadby and Doukhan point out, "we owe the term "Public Lands" and its definition to the Palestine Order in Council, 1922, Art. 2. . . . Public Lands means all lands in Palestine which are subject to the control of the Government by virtue of Treaty [the Treaty of Peace (Turkey) Ordinance, 1925]. . . . The fundamental characteristic of Public Lands as so defined is that they are subject to the control of the Government." *Land Law of Palestine,* 60.

25. *Mahlul* land was of two kinds: land that escheats to the state through failure of heirs or *miri* land that is left uncultivated for three years. *Mewat,* or "dead land," is land that is unoccupied, is a certain distance away from any village, and which had not been left for the public good.

26. Minutes of Advisory Council Meeting, 1–5 October 1920, CO 733/1/(434).

27. For a useful review of the literature surrounding the "intentions and consequences" of the 1858 Land Code, see Eugene Rogan, "Incorporating the Periphery: The Ottoman Extension of Direct Rule over Southeastern Syria (Transjordan), 1867–1914" (Ph.D. diss., Harvard University, 1991), chap. 8; Haim Gerber, *The Social Origins of the Modern Middle East* (Boulder, Colo.: Rienner, 1987); and Halil Inalcik and Donald Quataert, eds., *An Economic and Social History of the Ottoman Empire, 1300–1914* (Cambridge: Cambridge University Press, 1994).

28. CO 733/109/204.

29. Letter from Norman Bentwich, Legal Secretary, to Major Abramson, Chairman of Land Commission, 19 August 1920, CO 733/18/(586).

30. Defined by Article 131 of the Ottoman Land Code, *jiftlik* was a term used to describe "a tract of land such as needs one yoke of oxen to work it, which is cultivated and harvested every year." But

the term could also refer to the whole outfit of a farm, including the buildings, the animals, the stock, and the land of which it was comprised. In Palestine it was a term popularly applied to the landed estates registered in the name of the Sultan. See Goadby and Doukhan, *Land Law of Palestine*, 62. In fact, not all *jiftlik* property was reregistered in the name of the Treasury in 1908, and throughout the Mandate the Palestine government was confronted with legal actions instituted on behalf of the heirs to the Sultan. See, for example, CO 733/44/389.

31. For example, Sir Herbert Samuel explained in a letter to the Colonial Office that "there was a certain measure of oppression in the means by which the ownership of the lands was transferred from the Arab cultivators to the Sultan Abdul Hamid." Samuel to Churchill, 23 July 1921, CO 733/4. Alternatively, in 1925, Sir Ernest Dowson reached the conclusion that "it seems that at one time this Sultan was keen on being a good farmer and landlord, and that the peasantry in various parts of Palestine recognising the better regime then prevailing on the Sultan's private estates applied that the land they held and cultivated on *miri* tenure should be thus 'turned over to him.'" Sir Ernest Dowson, "Preliminary Study of Land Tenure in Palestine," CO 733/109, p. 33.

32. Samuel to Churchill, 23 July 1921, CO 733/4/(510). The 10 percent of the produce paid as rental on *jiftlik* land was also regarded by some cultivators as a payment in lieu of certain privileges, such as exemption from military service. Minute by Mills, 22 November 1921, CO 733/7.

33. Letter from Norman Bentwich to Major Abramson, 19 August 1920, CO 733/18/(586).

34. See minutes in CO 733/107/407.

35. See, for example, "Land Settlement Commission's Report," 10 February 1922, CO 733/18/(624).

36. Certain provisions of the agreement provoked much criticism, particularly, those that dealt with the amount of land to be allotted to each cultivator. Nonetheless, the legality of the transfer was never seriously questioned (except maybe by the Jewish Agency). A list of lands claimed as state domain, produced by the Palestine Land Registry in 1926, described all *jiftlik* lands as "occupied by Arab cultivators of long standing and should, presumably, be treated on the same basis as, but different in detail from, the

lands affected by the Beisan Land Agreement of 1921." CO 733/170/2.

37. The actual agreement between the cultivators of the Beisan lands and the government of Palestine is set out in Palestine, Department of Development, *First Report on Agricultural Development and Land Settlement in Palestine,* by Lewis French (Jerusalem: Government Printer, 1931), app. 3B, 153–63.

38. Ibid.

39. The Peel Commission, for example, speaks of the extent to which the government needed to "placate" this "wild and unsettled locality." Great Britain, Cmd. 5479, *Palestine Royal Commission Report* [Peel Report] (London: H.M.S.O., 1939), 260.

40. Letter from Herbert Samuel to Churchill, 23 July 1921, CO 733/4/(510).

41. "Notes on the High Commissioner's Tour: October 21st to 25th, 1923," CO 733/50/(517).

42. "An Interim Report on the Civil Administration of Palestine, 12 months ending June 1921," CO 733/22/(464).

43. "Land Settlement Commission's Report," CO 733/18, p. 20.

44. See, for example, Cmd. 3530, *Report of the Commission on the Palestine Disturbances of August 1929* [Shaw Commission Report] (London: H.M.S.O., 1930); and Stein, *Land Question in Palestine.*

45. Cmd. 3686, *Palestine: Report on Immigration, Land Settlement and Development* [Hope-Simpson Report] (London: H.M.S.O., 1930).

46. It cannot be assumed that only Jews were active in the land market. The reports by Lewis French in the early 1930s, for example, make it clear that Arab buyers (and not just brokers) constituted a significant part of the market: in 1931 French refers to "a severe land hunger" due in part to "considerable buying by Arab capitalists, partly speculative and partly investment." Until archival work is actually done in the records of the land registry, the complicated dynamics of Palestine's land market can not fully be understood.

47. Shaw Commission Report, 166.

48. Hope-Simpson Report, 142.

49. Ibid., 36.

50. For example, paragraph 12 of "The MacDonald Letter," 13 February 1931: "what [the 1930 White Paper] does contemplate is

such temporary control of land disposition and transfers as may be necessary." A copy of the letter can be found in Walter Laqueur, ed., *The Israel-Arab Reader: A Documentary History of the Middle East Conflict* (Harmondsworth, U.K.: Penguin Books, 1969).

51. The necessary funds were found though to appoint Lewis French as Director of Development. The author of two reports on the prospects of agricultural development, French con- firmed for the Colonial Office in the following terms the fears expressed by the Shaw Commission: "it is perhaps not irrelevant to speculate at long range as to whether the Arab effendi will eventually sell his lands at a profit to the Jews, and leave Arab cultivators or tenants to become serfs of the Jews (if they care to employ them on the land), or merely hewers of wood or drawers of water in the towns. If this consummation is desirable, an hypothesis which the existing (comparatively small) scheme to relieve Arabs refutes, then restrictive legislative need not be any further considered." French, *First Report on Agricultural Development*, 56.

52. To absolve Jewish responsibility for the creation of a landless class, the Jewish Agency worked hard at ensuring that the investigation define the group in narrow terms. As Stein puts it, "The number of claims submitted was neither representative nor reflective of the number of Arabs displaced . . . nor was the final tally of 899 demonstrative of anything except a Jewish Agency political victory." *Land Question in Palestine*, 157.

53. "Memorandum by the Secretary of State for the Colonies," 1 February 1933, CO 733/234.

54. See, for example, "Observations on Land Settlement," by the Commissioner of Lands, January 1932, CO 733/208.

55. Section 3(1), Land Settlement Ordinance 1928. In Robert Harry Drayton, ed., *The Laws of Palestine* (London: Waterlow, 1934), 854.

56. Minute by Commissioner of Lands, 19 July 1932, Israel State Archives (ISA), RG 22, Land Registration and Land Settlement, Box 3558, LS 8 (1).

57. Letter from Abramson to Lees, 17 February 1936, ISA, RG 22, Box 3568, LS 8 (11).

58. Ibid.

59. Sir Ernest Dowson, "The Land System in Palestine," CO 733/109/ 269, p. 21. See also Great Britain, Colonial No. 134, Palestine Royal Commission, *Minutes of Evidence Heard by the Royal Commission at Public Sessions* (London: H.M.S.O. 1937). *Musha'* was widely criticized throughout the Mandate yet was increasingly relied on in taxation reform. The importance of the *musha'* system to the fiscal survey in the 1930s would suggest another factor contributing to what Roger Owen has referred to as the "official ambiguity towards *musha'*." Owen, "The Role of *Musha'*."

60. Palestine Royal Commission, *Minutes of Evidence*, 20.

61. That is, the name of the one who says "this is my land." See ibid.

62. Letter from Director of Lands, 11 December 1922, stating the importance of budgetary provision "for coffee and cigarettes for the many local people who come into my tent." ISA, RG 22, Box 3542, G 41/9.

63. Sir Ernest Dowson, "Report on the Progress of Land Reforms in Palestine, 1923–1930," CO 733/221, p. 22–23.

64. Section 15(1), Land Settlement Ordinance 1928. In Drayton, *Laws of Palestine*, 859; Goadby and Doukhan, *Land Law of Palestine*, 274.

65. Section 10(3), Land Settlement Ordinance 1928. In Drayton, *Laws of Palestine*, 857.

66. Goadby and Doukhan, *Land Law of Palestine*, 282.

67. Letter from Commissioner of Lands and Surveys to District Commissioner, Southern District, 27 November 1936 ISA, RG 22, Box 3776, LS 1 (10).

68. I. N. Camp, Settlement Officer (Ramle Settlement Area), "Memorandum on Decisions by Settlement Officer, Sajad and Qazaza *Jiftlik*," 15 March 1932, ISA RG 22, Box 3776, LS 1 (10), p. 1.

69. One list of "state domains" provided by the Lands Department marked all *jiftlik* properties with an asterisk, explaining that: "those villages marked x are occupied by Arab cultivators of long standing and should presumably be treated on the same basis as, but different in detail from, the lands affected by the Beisan Land Agreement of 19.11.21." CO 733/116.

70. Goadby and Doukhan, *Land Law of Palestine*, 184.

71. Camp, "Memorandum on Decisions by Settlement Officer," p. 8.

72. Settlement Appeal, No.18/32, ISA, RG 22, Box 3776, LS 1 (10).

73. For a discussion of this conflict of interest, see Dowson, "Preliminary Study of Land Tenure in Palestine," 64.
74. Letter from District Commissioner, Jerusalem District, to Chief Secretary, 26 February 1936, ISA RG 22, Box 3568, LS / 8 (14).
75. Confidential letter from Colonial Office to Plumer, 21 October 1926, CO 733/116.
76. Consider the explanation provided by R. C. Tute, a land court judge, which is quoted in full: "Ancient and invariable customs exist which the statute law has not been able to break. Thus in some villages there is a custom which forbids women from taking a share by inheritance in the common lands. In other villages, and among some of the Bedouin tribes, a women who marries out of her community foregoes her interest in the communal or tribal land. It is clear that these customs originally arose for the purpose of preventing one tribe or village from obtaining a pretext for interfering with the lands of another.

    "When such a custom exists, it lies at the root of practically all the rights to land enjoyed in the area which it affects. It cannot be set aside without throwing all these rights into confusion, and creating a swarm of claimants whose operations must plunge the community into endless litigation. Under these circumstances a great increase of violent crime may be anticipated. . . .

    "It follows from these considerations that the enforcement of a Statutory scheme of inheritance is a legal as well as practical impossibility in the areas for which these ancient customs obtain. It is for this reason that the Courts have held that such customs are valid when shown to be ancient and invariable, in site of the fact that they run counter to Statute Law." Tute, *Ottoman Land Laws*, 56–57.

Part Two

CONCEPTS AND CATEGORIES
OF LAND

FIVE

A Note on Land and Identity: From Ze'amet to Waqf[1]

Amy Singer

Awqaf, pious endowments, are multifaceted institutions. Initially, a *waqf* is established according to procedures and conditions required by Islamic law.[2] Subsequent to its founding, a pious endowment functions within restrictions and according to mechanisms provided by Islamic law as well. At the same time, it operates within multiple relationships among its component properties, personnel and beneficiaries, and exists in intersecting contexts of local politics, economics, and culture. In the case of Ottoman sultanic *awqaf,* the additional interests of an imperial founder or Istanbul-based manager may continue to affect the workings of the institution after its establishment. Thus, the legal definitions of property relations that originally organized a *waqf* are only one part of its structure and operation.

Numerous assumptions and truisms about the nature of *awqaf* have long circulated among scholars of the Islamic Middle East. The endowments have been held up as paradigms of beneficent action. At the same time, they have been blamed for the absence of various economic relations and attitudes associated with private possession and the market in private property, since a *waqf,* in theory, removed property from the realm of normal market transactions.

On its founding, the ownership of property endowed to a *waqf* was, in theory, transferred to God, while its use or revenues funded the activities of the endowment. In practice, endowed properties became neither wholly inaccessible nor frozen in their endowed state. Nor were they necessarily doomed to deteriorate or change their use at some pace different from that of nonendowed properties of the same type or in their vicinity.[3] Altogether, procedures that have sometimes been deemed to be irregularities in handling *waqf* properties appear more and more to be an integral part of *waqf* existence. Ultimately, the mechanics and use of devices like *istibdal* (exchange), *hikr* (ground rent) and *ijaratayn* (double rent) provide new insights into the meaning of property, generally, as well as some clues about the real dynamics between *awqaf* and their endowed properties.[4]

Imperial Ottoman *awqaf* were a special category for many reasons. They were often much larger than other endowments. Managers appointed to them perforce had no immediate family connection to the *waqf*, and so their interests were somewhat different than those of people who managed large endowments made by private individuals. Moreover, the imperial *awqaf* seemed to epitomize the unique status of *awqaf* as property owners, being neither a private proprietor nor a public institution, though they possessed aspects of both. For this reason, perhaps, the management and fortunes of endowed properties fall short of normal expectations for the maintenance of private property, while perhaps comparing favorably with the government institutions of the same size and purpose.[5]

In the case of the Ottoman empire, scholars studying endowments are fortunate to be able to examine not only the foundation deeds, extant for earlier periods of Islamic history, but also extensive records of *waqf* management. Judicial protocols and records of imperial orders contribute additional information and perspective to the histories of individual *awqaf* and hence to the overall picture. From among the details of these records come indications and clues that are gradually altering the broader understanding of the functioning, impact and meaning of *awqaf*.[6]

One small example from the annals of an Ottoman imperial endowment demonstrates the changing status of property in the Ottoman empire and the dynamic careers of endowed properties. It reveals that the condition of being endowed was a more fluid state, less permanent and, as a result, less of a trap or snare than often assumed. At the same time, the case provides some insight into the connections that evolved between people and properties affiliated to a *waqf*.

Hurrem Sultan, wife of Sultan Süleyman I, established an endowment in Jerusalem during the 1550s with properties whose title she received as a gift from him. These properties belonged to Süleyman as sultan; the gift transaction was recorded in a series of deeds describing the various villages, farmlands, mills, and other properties transferred.[7] No prior connection is known to have existed between Hurrem and these villages. She had not visited Jerusalem and been thus inspired to endow the mosque, *'imaret* (public kitchen), caravanserai and rooms, nor did she see the city before her death in 1558. Hurrem's connection to Jerusalem was a spiritual and emotional one, and her decision to establish the *waqf* was conceived in this mood. Some additional political motivation may have existed, since beneficent acts were part of the legitimating strategy of the Ottomans generally, and particularly of Süleyman as he emphasized his position as leader of Muslims, protector of the places holy to Islam, the just and devout ruler.[8]

Once endowed, the properties were, in theory, a permanent part of the *waqf*. The connection to the *waqf* also became an integral part of the identity of the properties, and villagers from the *waqf* villages who came before the Jerusalem qadi were recorded with the name of the village and its connection to the *waqf*.[9] Some of the village revenues only belonged to the *waqf* in part, yielding their remaining revenues to other, older *awqaf* or to another revenue claimant. The revenues of Bayt Lahm and Bayt Jala were divided among the *awqaf* of the Haramayn al-

Sharafayn in Mecca and Medina and the *waqf* of the *'imaret*. The revenues of 'Isawiyya, meanwhile, were divided between the *ze'amet* (revenue grant) of Turgud, yet another *waqf*, and three individual *mulk* holders.[10]

Affiliation to a *waqf* sometimes conferred special status on the people whose village lands had been endowed. They might enjoy certain tax exemptions and protection from visits by officials, particularly if the *waqf* was an imperial endowment or part of the vast properties donated to support the holy cities of Islam.[11] As a result of this status, peasants in *waqf* villages may also have enjoyed greater access to or a more ready hearing from imperial officials who investigated complaints of abuse or impropriety in rural administration.[12] Whatever the condition, the attachment adhered to the property and not to the people and so ended if the property was transferred out of the endowment.

In practice, properties were traded in and out of endowments for a variety of reasons. During the period of its founding from 1550 to 1557 several alterations were made to the endowed properties of the Jerusalem *waqf*.[13] Soap factories and mills located in the province of Trablus yielded revenues unreliably, as well as requiring continual repairs. They were thus exchanged for revenues from twenty villages in the districts of Jerusalem and Gaza.[14]

An additional exchange was made at roughly the same time, whereby the village of Jericho was removed from the endowment and replaced by properties in the Gaza district.[15] The difficulties of organizing transport to Jerusalem for the grain produced in Jericho seem to have prompted this latter change. These examples emphasize how financial and logistical considerations motivated some decisions about endowment properties. Over the longer term as well, properties could be exchanged if they were no longer producing sufficiently on behalf of a *waqf*.

However, another issue is important here. The examples given above demonstrate that property exchanges did not take place only in long-standing *awqaf*, nor are they evidence solely of corrupt or incompetent management. Rather, the exchanges underline the extent to which a *waqf* was (among other things) an institution to be managed along sound financial lines if its duration was to be ensured. While the purpose of the *waqf* carried a measure of sanctity, the security of this purpose was dependent on economic decisions. Thus the sanctity that adhered to institutions such as mosques, tombs, schools and public kitchens, and to the commitment to maintain them in perpetuity, did not necessarily extend to the properties endowed to support them.

After an initial endowment was set up, properties were exchanged in and out of it, and outright additions were made to the original assets of the *waqf*. The large endowments of Mecca and Medina (the Haramayn al-Sharifayn) continually received supplemental contributions, since they supported institutions and residents in the holiest sites of Islam and the pilgrims who made their way there. Expenditures on regular repairs and operations outstripped the capacities of the initial endowments. In a similar fashion, contributions augmented the endowments supporting the principal mosques in Jerusalem and Hebron, as well as tombs of certain holy persons.[16]

By adding to existing endowments such as these, a person also contributed to the holiest endeavors or places in the Islamic world.[17] Participation in an established and prominent endowment may have been preferable for those who were not wealthy enough to endow an entire institution, even a very small one. Or they may have followed a family tradition, contributing to an endowment made by another family member. This could have been either for the sake of the family or in remembrance of a particular individual.

Süleyman added properties to the Jerusalem endowment in 967 A.H./1560 A.D., two years after the death of Hurrem Sultan, presumably to strengthen the *waqf* and to honor her memory. All were located at some remove from Jerusalem, in the province of Sham (Damascus). They included the village of Hara, two farms (*mezra'as*) in the Sayda (Sidon) district, and a farm in the Iqlim Tuffah district.[18] These properties had no apparent prior connection to the *waqf,* so one assumes they were selected for their revenue yields and availability. A subsequent exchange in the endowed properties occurred around the time that one 'Abd el-Kerim was appointed as manager (*mütevelli*) of Hurrem's *'imaret,* but no later than 17 Muharrem 972 /25 August 1564.[19] Properties in the district of Sayda worth 21,520 *akçe*s were removed from the *waqf* and added to the holdings of the imperial domain.[20] In their place, properties yielding 12,132 *akçe*s, which had comprised the *ze'amet* of Turgud (previously the manager and now deceased) were endowed to the *waqf.* These included the villages of Shafa 'Amru, Dhib and Kuwaykat in the district of 'Akka, and 'Isawiyya and Jadira in the district of Jerusalem.[21]

Turgud had been the manager of the *waqf* during the years 965 to 970, and possibly until his death sometime between 970 and the first mention of 'Abd el-Kerim. He already possessed a *ze'amet* in the province of Damascus at the time of his first appointment as manager, though this lasted only for a few months in 963.[22] During his second, extended tenure in this post, revenue records show that he was very successful on behalf of the *waqf,* increasing revenue yields by 50 percent from the villages acquired in place of the soap factories.[23]

As with other properties previously acquired for the *waqf* by exchange, those included in the *ze'amet* of Turgud had the advantage of being somewhat closer to Jerusalem than the ones in the Sayda district. Yet this may not be the only reason for their inclusion in the *waqf.* While all the details of this particular transaction are not available, the general outline as understood raises several questions about the connection established between the manager and the *waqf,* about the meaning of possession of a *ze'amet,* and about government policies for maintaining or increasing support for imperial *awqaf.*

Whether the initiative for the exchange was taken by Turgud before his death or by 'Abd el-Kerim on his accession to the post of manager, the exchange itself seems to reflect an identification of Turgud with the *waqf.* He served a relatively long and successful tenure as manager during the early period of its operations, though he was not involved in the original constructions and repairs made during the years of its founding. In comparison, his immediate predecessor, Bayram *çavuş,* spent large sums of his own money to complete construction of a double bath (*çift hamam*) built in Jerusalem as part of the assets of the endowment.[24]

The managers of the sultanic *awqaf* had no family connections to the founders of these endowments, as was often the case with managers of *awqaf* established by wealthy individuals. Men like Turgud received salaries and benefited from their positions through their control of subordinate appointments and the transfer of surplus revenues. However, they also incurred expenses directly connected with the functioning of the *waqf,* as the example of Bayram demonstrates. Yet Turgud did not live only on his salary as manager, as he continued to hold the *ze'amet* and enjoy its revenues. Apparently, the manager of such a *waqf* needed to be a person of means, possessing sufficient income in addition to his salary as manager to cover short-term deficits or expenditures for the *waqf.*

There seems to be no connection between the *ze'amet* properties and the *waqf* other than the person of Turgud himself and his tenure as manager. Even without knowing where the initiative lay for transferring these specific properties to the *waqf,* the personal connection remains striking. Possibly, the *ze'amet* properties were added to the *waqf* as a tribute to Turgud and a gesture acknowledging his contribution to the thriving endowment. Turgud first served as manager briefly before Hurrem died. He was manager when Süleyman made his addition to the *waqf* in late Şevval 967/mid-July 1560 and died only a few years later, while Süleyman was still alive. (Curiously, some of the *ze'amet* properties seem to have replaced ones added by Süleyman only a few years earlier.)[25] Perhaps Turgud had been in contact directly with Hurrem or Süleyman about the *waqf.*

The mechanics of the transaction are unclear. The *ze'amet* properties, which belonged to the large imperial holdings and not the sultan's private treasury, could not have been endowed

by Turgud himself without specific authorization to do so, authorization like the *mülkname*s given to Hurrem by Süleyman
for the properties originally endowed to the *waqf*.[26] The contest
for proprietary rights over imperial lands by Ottoman officials
had inspired imperial actions since the earlier days of the Ottoman empire.[27] The *'imaret* case, however, is an interesting twist
since the transfer is not one that removes property for private
benefit but rather to an imperial endowment.

Finally, the decision to add the *ze'amet* properties may have
been entirely coincidental to Turgud's connection to the *waqf*,
though this seems unlikely. At the very least, the *ze'amet* was noticed as potentially available because of Turgud's death and his
connection to the *waqf*. Yet it may simply have been the easiest
way of locating appropriate and available revenues to add to the
endowment. An enormous amount of property in the districts
around Jerusalem was endowed for the large number of *awqaf*
in Jerusalem, Hebron, and other local shrines, most of them dating from pre-Ottoman times. At the time of its founding, the
'imaret took over many properties that had been parts of *timar*s
and other revenue grants. Hence nearby additions would have
been more difficult to acquire. The *ze'amet* combined holdings
in the Jerusalem district and a little farther away in the district of
'Akka.

One element, however, might be taken to indicate that there
was a measure of personal identification involved in this particular transaction. The *ze'amet* properties of Turgud were worth
significantly less on paper, at least at the outset, than those removed from the endowment in the exchange. This suggests
some other calculation besides a purely fiscal one may have
guided this transaction. On the other hand, the exchange may
have occurred because the properties removed in reality yielded
very little.

As late as a defter written in 992/1584–1585, the original
identity of the *ze'amet* properties was preserved in their listing
as a group under the heading "'an mahsul ze'amet-i merhum

Turgud Ağa ki beh vakıf ilhak şude."[28] Eventually, this connection faded as well, and by the time the register of 1006/1597–1598 was made, the properties belonging to the *waqf* were listed by administrative district, with no indication at all that they had ever been part of other revenue units, much less whose.[29]

In and of itself, the exchange discussed here was a minor transaction. However, it intersected other local and imperial trends, confirming movements already noted while suggesting further directions to be examined. As such, it opens a small window onto decision making with regard to endowment properties and the manner in which a single endowment might influence identities. The focal connection between an institution and the properties endowed to sustain it is usually the fiscal relationship. However, the examples discussed here demonstrate that other affiliations to a *waqf,* such as a connection established through the person of the manager, could also create an identification between institution and property.

The exchange also seems to have been part of a larger trend in the movement of property between categories of beneficiaries in the Ottoman empire at this time. Here, *ze'amet* properties were transferred to a *waqf,* while the previously endowed properties were made part of the imperial domain. This constituted a net loss of revenues available in the large category of revenue grants or military-salary holdings, of which the *ze'amet* was a part. The trend has already been noted, and has been understood to reflect the shift underway from the *tımar*-based soldier-administrators to the standing Janissary and other salaried forces as the main military corps of the empire.[30]

Awqaf have been over-endowed with permanency in past understandings. While the beneficent purpose or institution supported was intended to endure, the revenue-producing properties yielded revenues to sustain this purpose, and if not, then they were to be traded for something more useful. These properties, as much as they belonged to a *waqf,* belonged to their local ecology and economy. Their productivity and use, therefore, depended on and derived from the influences of local weather, security, urban development, crisis, and a host of other factors, far more than they were affected by the fact of belonging to the *waqf*.

ACKNOWLEDGMENTS

This research was supported in part by the Basic Research Foundation administered by the Israel Academy of Sciences and Humanities. I would like also to thank the Directorate of the Topkapı Palace Museum Archives and Ülkü Altındağ for enabling me to carry out this research.

NOTES

1. All transliterations follow the *International Journal of Middle East Studies* style from Arabic or Ottoman Turkish.
2. For the basic outline see W. Heffening, "Waqf," in *Shorter Encyclopedia of Islam* (Leiden: Brill, 1961), 624–28.
3. A detailed comparison of the fates of properties of different status, some of which belong to endowments, would be a useful place to begin either to give substance to the charges against *waqf*, or to belie long-held beliefs.
4. Gabriel Baer, "Hikr," in *The Encyclopedia of Islam, New Edition. Supplement* 1 (Leiden: Brill, 1982), 368–70; Heffening, "Waqf"; Bahaeddin Yediyıldız, "Vakıf," in *İslam Ansiklopedisi* 19: 158.
5. Marcus discusses the mix of quasi-private and quasi-public considerations that shaped the particular nature of management of *waqf* properties. See Abraham Marcus, *The Middle East on the Eve of Modernity* (New York: Columbia University Press, 1989), 305–13.
6. The many recent publications about *awqaf* focus more and more on details of *waqf* management that afford a more variegated and complex understanding of individual *awqaf* themselves and of their role and effect on the local and regional contexts that fostered them. A few examples include Randi Deguilhem, ed., *Le Waqf dans l'espace islamique: outil de pouvoir socio-politique* (Damascus: Institut français de Damas, 1995); Faruk Bilici, ed., *Le*

Waqf dans le monde musulman contemporain (XIXe–XXe siècles) (Istanbul: Institut français d'études anatoliennes, 1994); and the special issue of the *Journal of the Economic and Social History of the Orient* 38 (1995) entitled "Waqfs and Other Institutions of Religious/Philanthropic Endowment in Comparative Perspective."

7. Topkapı Sarayı Arşivi (TSA) E-7816/1–11 and TSA E-7702. See also Amy Singer, "The Mülknames of Hurrem Sultan's Waqf in Jerusalem," *Muqarnas* 14 (1997): 96–102, for the significance of these documents as records not only of the transaction but also of the relationship between Süleyman and Hurrem.

8. On the image of Süleyman and how it evolved during his time, see Cornell Fleischer, "The Lawgiver as Messiah: The Making of the Imperial Image in the Reign of Süleyman," in *Soliman le magnifique et son temps,* ed. Gilles Veinstein (Paris: La Documentation française, 1992), 159–77; Halil Inalcik, "Sultan Sülayman: The Man and the Statesman," in ibid., 89–103; Colin Imber, "The Ottoman Dynastic Myth," *Turcica* 19 (1987): 7–27; and Gülru Necipoğlu, "The Süleymaniye Complex in Istanbul: An Interpretation," *Muqarnas* 3 (1985): 92–117.

9. For example, "Muhammad b. al-Mallah, Musa b. Musa . . . all leaders of the people of Jib whose tithe is part of the *waqf* ['imaret-i 'amire] . . ." (Jerusalem Sijill, vol. 35#120, p. 21, 8 Zilhicce 964/2 October 1557).

10. See Tapu Tahrir Defter #516, p. 38, from 967/1560, and Amy Singer, *Palestinian Peasants and Ottoman Officials* (Cambridge: Cambridge University Press, 1994), 83.

11. See Halil Inalcik, "Adaletnameler," *Belgeler* 2, no. 3–4 (1965): 82–84, for a discussion of *serbest* villages and the different categories among them. Imperial *awqaf* villages enjoyed the most extensive protections and guarantees from normal administrative officials.

12. This is only a speculative suggestion, based in part on my impressions from reading in the Jerusalem Sijills but more so from the frequency of complaints filed by villagers from the *'imaret waqf* in Jerusalem as they appear in the *mühimme* registers found in Istanbul. Heyd's collection of these gives some sense of how often affairs concerning these villages drew imperial attention. See Uriel

Heyd, *Ottoman Documents on Palestine 1552–1615* (Oxford: Clarendon Press, 1960).

13. There are two versions of the endowment deed for this *waqf*. The first was drawn up in Turkish in 1552 and contains only a few of the properties that appear in the later Arabic deed dated 1557. It appears that the second deed was drawn up after the terms of the *waqf* and the bulk of the properties endowed to it had finally been collected. The Turkish deed was published by S. H. Stephan, "An Endowment Deed of Khasseki Sultan, Dated 24th May 1552," *Quarterly of the Department of Antiquities in Palestine* 10 (1944): 170–94. The Arabic text is found in the Türk ve İslam Eserleri Müzesi in Istanbul, document #2192.

14. This exchange is recorded in the *mülkname* TSA E-7816/8 and the register TSA D-4576.

15. Jericho is recorded as given to Hurrem in a *mülkname* of 963/1556 (TSA E-7816/8) but does not appear in the *waqfiyya* issued for the *'imaret* in 964/1557. Two copies of this *waqfiyya* exist: an original preserved in the Türk ve İslam Eserleri Müzesi, document #2192, and a transcription made from the Jerusalem Sijill, vol. 280, pp. 18–27, and published in Kamil Jamil al-'Asali, *Watha'iq Maqdisiyya Tarikhiyya* (Amman: Matba'a al-Tawfiq, 1983), 127–42.

16. Suraiya Faroqhi, *Pilgrims and Sultans: The Hajj under the Ottomans 1517–1683* (London: I. B. Tauris, 1994), 74–84.

17. See also R. D. McChesney, *Waqf in Central Asia: Four Hundred Years in the History of a Muslim Shrine, 1480–1889* (Princeton: Princeton University Press, 1991), for a *waqf* which continually received contributions to its endowment.

18. These additions date from Evahir Şevval 967/25 July–4 August 1560. They are recorded in the *mülkname*s TSA E-7816/10 and E-7816/11. The text of the *waqfiyya* may be found in al-'Asali, *Watha'iq*, 147–50.

19. Mühimme defteri #6, 59, p. 29.

20. These appear to be, at least in part, the additions Süleyman made in the district of Sayda, as listed in the *mülkname*s and *waqfiyya* cited above (see note 15).

21. Mühimme defteri #33, 315, p. 158, 4 Şevval 985. This *mühimme* entry also includes the farmland (*mezra'a*) of Marfuqa, and the plot of land (*kita'-i 'arz*) called al-Qaqar as part of the *ze'amet*

properties, though they do not appear in the *muhasebe* registers, e.g., TSA D-3528/1.

22. Mühimme defteri #2, 134, p. 15, says that Turgud *subaşi*, who held a *ze'amet* in Sham, was appointed *mütevelli* of the *waqf*. This is apparently for his first, briefer term (20 Rebiülevval 963/2 February 1556). He is also listed as Turgud *ağa* in other sources that place him as manager of the *waqf*: TSA D-1511 relating to the summer of 1556 and then the later appointment reflected in TSA D-961 and TSA D-5262, which show him there from 1 Ramazan 965 to the end of Zilhicce 968 (17 July 1558–10 September 1561).

23. The figures are given village by village, comparing yields from 964 under Bayram *çavuş* and 965 under Turgud, in TSA D-4576.

24. The investments of Bayram are discussed in TSA D-4576, dated 12 Rebiülevvel–15 Cemaziyelahir 963 (25 January–25 April 1556).

25. Süleyman's were the only properties belonging to the *waqf* from the district of Sayda, so it seems they must have made up part of the exchange.

26. On the procedure for obtaining a *temlik*, see Halil Inalcik and Donald Quataert, eds., *An Economic and Social History of the Ottoman Empire, 1300–1914* (Cambridge: Cambridge University Press, 1994), 121–22. Conceivably this documentation exists but has not yet become available.

27. See Inalcik and Quataert, *An Economic and Social History,* 124; Baber Johansen, *The Islamic Law on Land Tax and Rent* (London: Croom Helm, 1988), 81–82; and Kenneth M. Cuno, *The Pasha's Peasants: Land, Society, and Economy in Lower Egypt, 1740–1858* (Cambridge: Cambridge University Press, 1992), 21–24.

28. TSA D-3528/1, p. 4b.

29. TSA D-3642/23, p. 2a ('Isawiyya), p. 6a (Kuwaykat, Dhib, Shafa 'Amru).

30. On this trend, see further Singer, *Palestinian Peasants,* 61; Amnon Cohen and Bernard Lewis, *Population and Revenue in the Towns of Palestine in the Sixteenth Century* (Princeton: Princeton University Press, 1978), 44–45; and Inalcik and Quataert, *An Economic and Social History,* 23

SIX

Ownership of Real Property by Foreigners in Syria, 1869 to 1873

Abdul-Karim Rafeq

NEW REGULATIONS FOR PROPERTY REGISTRATION

The traditional method for property registration in the Islamic *shar'i* courts in Syria, prior to the implementation of the Land Law of 1274 A.H./A.D. 1858, required the seller of property to present a *hujja* (document) issued to him by the court establishing his ownership of the property. If he had acquired the property through sale, the *hujja* would be known as a sale document (*hujjat al-tabayu'*). The *hujja* usually mentioned the type of the property (whether residential, commercial, or agricultural), its size measured by the *qirat* (of twenty-four *qirat*s), its location, the date of its purchase, the name of its former owner, the name of the court that issued the *hujja*, as well as the name and the *madhhab* (school of law) of the presiding judge who authorized the sale. If the owner of the property had acquired it by inheritance, witnesses had to come forward and establish in the court the owner's right of inheritance. A *hujja*, known as *hujjat al-ikhbariyya* (document of notification), would be issued by the judge on the day the inherited property was sold, establishing the owner's right to inherit it. If no sale or inheritance *hujja* was available, the seller of the property had to bring witnesses to the court to establish his continued usufruct of the property over a number of years and to show that no other person had contested his right to its usufruct.

After the promulgation of the Land Law on 7 Ramadan 1274/ 21 April 1858, *tapu* laws, initially intended to organize the granting of title deeds (*sened tapu*) for state land, were issued on 8 Jumada II 1275/13 January 1859 and on 7 Sha'ban 1276/29 February 1860. The *tapu* laws, which in fact were applied to transfers of all kinds of real property, required the transferor of property to produce in court a certificate of notification (*'ilm wa-khabar*) that bore the seals of the local *imam* (leader in prayer) and of the *mukhtar* (headman of a quarter or village) or the seal of the *kumisyun* (commission) of the locality where the property was located, whether it was a quarter or a village, thereby establishing the seller's ownership of the property. The *'ilm wa-khabar* also gave the location of the property and its boundaries.

While the *tapu* regulations applied to freehold landed property (*milk*), a special law concerning title deeds for property standing on *waqf* (religious endowment) or *miri* (state) land, such as plantations and buildings, was issued on 28 Rajab 1291/ 10 September 1874. In accordance with this law, property on *waqf* or *miri* land had to be registered, like real *milk* property, in the Defter-Khane, and title deeds had to be issued establishing its ownership.[1] In fact, this law simply endorsed existing regulations approved by Islamic law and practice.

According to Islamic law, the lessee of *waqf* or *miri* agricultural land was entitled by virtue of a special clause in the lease contract, known as the right of *mugharasa* or *munasaba* (plantation), to become the owner of one-third to three-fourths of what he planted or built on the land. The remaining portion went to the *waqf* or the *miri*. Another clause in the same lease contract gave the lessee the right of *musaqat*—that is, irrigating and caring for the remaining portion of the plantations that did not belong to him. The *musaqat* usually entitled the lessee to 999 shares out of 1,000 shares of the produce of this portion leaving one share for the *waqf* or the *miri*.[2] In practice, however, the *mugharasa* and the *musaqat* clauses affected mostly *waqf* agricultural land because *miri* land was mostly given to Timariots (feudal troops) or to tax farmers. The usufruct (*mashadd maska*) of the land itself, whether it had plantations or buildings (referred to as *qarar*) or not (in this case it was known as *sallikh*) could be transferred (*farigha*) from one person to another, not necessarily from the lessor to the lessee or from the seller of the plantations to their buyer, for a sum of money known as *'iwad* (compensation).[3]

While these new laws about the registration of landed *milk* property were being formulated and implemented, another issue regarding the abuse of Ottoman land laws by foreign nationals and their local protégés was already causing concern for the Ottoman authorities. The identity of the buyer of property, according to the Ottoman authorities, had to be ascertained. A case in point is the order issued by the governor of Jerusalem on 2 Jumada II 1275/7 January 1859 to the judge of Gaza instructing him to check the identity of a non-Muslim buyer of property. If the buyer was a Rumi Christian (Greek Orthodox), the order says, then his identity had to be checked by the head of his religious community. The property on sale also had to be checked and cleared of any impediment to its sale. Once these prerequisites had been satisfied, a *hujja* would be issued legalizing the sale.[4]

In a series of laws issued in the 1860s, the Ottoman authorities tried to regulate access to real property by non-Muslim Ottomans and by foreign nationals and their local protégés. A law dated 23 Safar 1280/9 August 1864 dealing with Protégés des consulats, and another dated 6 Shawwal 1285/20 January 1869 defining Ottoman nationality were circulated by the Ottomans to foreign embassies.[5] A third law promulgated on 7 Safar 1284/10 June 1867 gave foreigners the right to own real property in the Ottoman empire.[6]

In the court records of Damascus and to a lesser extent in those of Aleppo and Hamah, a new formula was adopted from 1282/1865–1866 onward in which the identity of the non-Muslim Ottoman buyer of real property was ascertained. The buyer had to be a subject of the illustrious Ottoman empire ("min ra'aya al-dawla al-'aliyya al-'Uthmaniyya") and not a subject of a foreign state albeit a friendly one ("laysa min ra'aya al-duwal al-mutahabba") or a protégé of a friendly country ("laysa min hamaya al-duwal al-mutahabba"). There was no need to establish the identity of a Muslim Ottoman buyer because it was taken for granted that he was an Ottoman subject.

The local authority that was to establish the identity of a non-Muslim Ottoman buyer was the patriarchate to which he belonged if he was Christian or the head of the Jewish community if he was Jewish. A certificate of notification *('ilm wa-khabar)* would then be issued to the buyer by the appropriate religious community attesting to his being an Ottoman national and a member of that community. The certificate, referred to in the court registers as *sanad* (legal instrument), carried the seal of the buyer, which was endorsed and legalized by the seal of the religious authority. The standard wording for this document of identification is found in the following example: "min ra'aya al-dawla al-'Uthmaniyya bi-mujib sanad 'ilm wa-khabar al-makhtum bi-khitmihi musaddaq 'alayhi wa-makhtum min batrakkhanat (al-Rum al-Urthudhuks) bi-Dimashq." If the buyer of property was a non-Muslim woman represented in the court by a Muslim deputy, the woman's Ottoman nationality had to be established, as in the case of a male non-Muslim buyer, by an *'ilm wa-khabar* from the head of her religious community.[7] The *'ilm wa-khabar* was usually put in a special bag *(kis)* and kept in the court.

The name of the patriarchate to which the buyer belonged was not always given in the court records, especially in those of Aleppo and Hamah. Reference was merely made to the *'ilm wa-khabar* emanating from "his patriarchate." In cases where the name of the patriarchate occurred, a differentiation was made between the Greek Orthodox (Rum), the Greek Catholics, the Latin (Roman Catholics), the Syriacs (Suryan), the Orthodox Armenians (Gregorians or Old Armenians), as well as the Catholic Armenians, and the Maronites.[8] The official accreditation given to the *'ilm wa-khabar* given by the Catholic patriarchates in official sale documents emanating from Muslim *shar'i* courts indicates the recognition extended by the Ottoman authorities at the time to these Catholic communities that had split from the mother churches about a century and a half previously. They were first recognized only in the 1830s by Muhammad 'Ali when he was governor of Syria (1831–1840) and then by the Ottoman empire, which was at the time seeking European support against Egyptian rule in Syria.

The seller of property, irrespective of his religious affiliation, did not need an *'ilm wa-khabar* to establish his identity. He had, however, to present to the court an *'ilm wa-khabar* establishing his ownership of the property on sale. This type of *'ilm wa-khabar* was issued by the *kumisyun* of the quarter or the village where the property was located.[9] A dispatch from the English consul in Aleppo, Richard Austin, dated 21 November 1870 mentions that the commission in charge of financial accounting in the villages (*kumisyun al-muhasibat al-qaraya*) was established in 1280/1863. The consul does not indicate whether the *kumisyun* in the village was only for the purpose of financial accounting (*muhasibat*) or whether it had other functions. He mentions, however, that a special commission (*kumisyun makhsus*) was established especially to look into the illegal dealings of the Jewish protégé of his consulate, Yaakub Stambouly, with a number of villagers whose liabilities to him had become greater than the value of their whole village.[10] However that may be, the type of *kumisyun* mentioned in the *shar'i* court records specifically dealt with establishing the seller's ownership of the property on sale. The *'ilm wa-khabar* issued by the *kumisyun* in this regard was preserved in the court.[11] When the office of *mukhtar* (village headman) was established by the law of the vilayets in 1864,[12] the *mukhtar* and the elders (*ikhtiyariyya*) of the village were authorized to issue the *'ilm wa-khabar,* apparently where no *kumisyun* existed.[13] In the town too, the *mukhtar* was likewise entitled to issue the *'ilm wa-khabar.*[14] The *kumisyun,* however, was more frequently cited in the court records than the *mukhtar* in issuing the *'ilm wa-khabar* concerning the property on sale. Occasionally, the body that issued the *'ilm wa-khabar,* especially in villages, was not indicated. A general statement in the court register, on such occasions, said that an *'ilm wa-khabar* carrying the seal of the village or coming from the village was received in the court.

Where the Damascus court records used the term *kumisyun,* in almost all cases in the Aleppo court records, the *majlis al-amlak* (council of title deeds), occasionally rendered *da'ira al-amlak* (office of title-deeds), appeared as the body that issued the *'ilm wa-khabar.* The *'ilm wa-khabar* issued by the Aleppo *majlis* or *da'ira al-amlak* provided information to the court about the property on sale and the number of its registration in the register (*daftar*) of title deeds and the name of its owner or owners.

Another difference between the Damascus and the Aleppo court records in matters relating to the establishment of the identity of a local non-Muslim buyer of property, or a foreign buyer, was that the Damascus records almost always mentioned the *'ilm wa-khabar* as being issued by the buyer's patriarchate, his *hakham bashi* (chief rabbi), or his consulate, depending on his religious affiliation or nationality. The Aleppo records very rarely provided such a detailed *'ilm wa-khabar.* They simply mentioned the religious community of the local buyer and the nationality of the foreign buyer without further proof or documentation.[15] The Hamah court records, like those of Aleppo, did not mention the *'ilm wa-khabar* when referring to the identity of a non-Muslim buyer of property. Could it be that the main reason for the stricter controls over ascertaining the identity of the buyer of property, as reflected in the court records of Damascus and Gaza, for example, was to prevent outsiders from illegally engaging in the real estate market throughout the Vilayet of Syria where non-Muslims were buying property?

OWNERSHIP OF REAL PROPERTY BY FOREIGNERS

The regulations regarding establishment of the Ottoman identity of non-Muslim buyers of real property, which apparently were intended to prevent foreigners from buying property illegally, did not preclude the latter from doing so. To regularize the situation, however, the Ottoman government issued a law on 7 Safar 1284/10 June 1867 giving foreigners the right to possess real property in the Ottoman empire with the exception of the Hijaz.

In justification of the law of 7 Safar 1284/10 June 1867, its preamble stated that it had been enacted by an imperial irade

in order to secure the extension of wealth and prosperity[16] in the Ottoman empire, and to remove difficulties, abuses, and doubts of all kind that arise by reason of foreign subjects becoming possessors of property (*emlak*), and to place this important matter under a firm law, and to complete fnancial and civil security.[17]

The Protocol (in Turkish *mazbata*) to the law, which had to be signed by the foreign governments who accepted the law, assured these governments that the law in no way interfered with the immunities provided to foreigners by virtue of the treaties with their governments; these would continue to apply to foreign owners and to their immovable property.[18]

Fu'ad Pasha, the foreign minister of the Ottoman empire who drafted the law, was in confidential communication with the French and the British ambassadors in Istanbul to assess their reaction to the law. Both ambassadors especially objected to clauses in the original draft of the Protocol to the law that made foreigners personally liable to the jurisdiction of local tribunals, in certain cases, without the presence and concurrence of their consuls.[19] The ambassadors were also instructed by their governments to endeavor to induce the Porte to render the Protocol, promulgated with the law, more conformable to the Capitulations. Fu'ad Pasha told the British ambassador that it required the exercise of the whole of his influence to extract the consent of his colleagues to what to many of them seemed to be a dangerous innovation. In his letter to London, the British ambassador, Sir Henry Elliot, confessed that the arguments brought forward by the Turkish government in favor of the necessity of new rules to apply to a totally new state of things appeared to him so strong that he was at a loss to refute them satisfactorily.

The Capitulations, Elliot went on to say, were represented as having been made under conditions entirely different from those of the time, when the privileges, orginally secured by them to a limited number of English and French merchants of prominent positions, were extended to every Italian, Greek, or Persian smuggler and adventurer. This inconvenience would be felt in a much greater degree if the new law were to have the effects hoped for by its advocates and dreaded by its opponents—of encouraging the establishment of foreigners throughout the empire.

The first paragraphs of the Protocol contained, according to the British ambassador, nothing exceptionable, dealing as they did with cases where foreigners could acquire property within reach of their consuls, where their habitations were declared inviolable, and the limitation of their inviolability to their dwelling houses and their dependents appeared likewise unobjectionable.

The difficulties began with the sixth paragraph, which dealt with cases at more than nine hours distance from a consular agent, where, in accusations of certain crimes of the first magnitude (including arson, armed robbery, rebellion, and counterfeiting), the police, by direction of the local authorities, were to be empowered to enter the houses of foreigners. In the view of the British ambassador, this unquestionably appeared an infringement of the privileges hitherto enjoyed by foreigners. But without some provisions such as those proposed by the Protocol, foreigners settling in districts where they were not answerable to Turkish authorities would be free from any control whatsoever.

One clause in the Protocol to which both the British and the French ambassadors took exception gave foreigners in all localities the right of dispensing with the presence of their consuls at the trial of their causes before the local tribunals. The proposal to permit individuals "in all localities," according to the British ambassador, to dispense with the privileges they were entitled to under the Capitulations appeared to him altogether objectionable and inadmissible.[20]

The French, however, saw in the law a great encouragement to the introduction of foreign capital into Turkey, to the continuation of railroads and ordinary roads, and to the prosperity of agriculture, commerce, and manufacture.[21] Eventually, the British, the French, and the Austrians were the first to sign the Protocol and accept the law.[22]

The French ambassador in Istanbul, Bourée, who signed the Protocol on 9 June 1868, exactly a year after it was issued, during which a thorough study had been made of its contents, emphasized that the Protocol did not infringe on the Capitulations but rather supplemented them. Ending his circular from Therapia on 17 August 1868, Bourée responded to the critics of the law saying:

> Il y a dans ces critiques un manque de logique dont les habitants de l'Orient auront fait justice facilement. Ils reconnaitront que si la Porte a mis certaines conditions au droit de propriété accordé aux étrangères, ces conditions étaient dans la nature des choses, et que l'effet le plus immédiat de la nouvelle Loi sera de mettre fin aux abus et aux injustices résultant de l'usage de prête-nom en matière immobilière et de substituer le fait vrai à la fiction dangéreuse, qui l'expérience en fait foi, laissait nos nationaux propriétaires d'immeubles dans l'impossibilité de se défendre personnellement, soit contre ces taxations arbitraires, soit en justice contre les contestations qui mettaient leurs droits en péril.[23]

Apart from the Protocol, the Law itself was made up of five articles. Article 1 stated that foreign subjects were allowed, with the same title as Ottoman subjects and without any other conditions, to enjoy the right to possess immovable property, urban or rural, anywhere within the empire, except the province of the Hijaz, on submitting to the laws and regulations that governed Ottoman subjects themselves in this regard. This provision did not apply to Ottoman subjects by birth who had changed their nationality, who would be regulated in this matter by a special law. The other four articles dealt with the right of a foreign subject to dispose of his property in accordance with Ottoman laws.

The special law relating to persons excluded from Article 1 of the law of 7 Safar 1284/10 June 1867 was issued on 25 Rabi' II 1300/5 March 1883. It stated that persons who were originally Ottoman subjects and changed their nationality before the promulgation of the law on Ottoman nationality of 6 Shawwal 1285/20 January 1869,[24] as also those who changed their nationality after the promulgation of this law, in accordance with its provisions, would enjoy all rights conferred by the law of 7 Safar 1284/10 June 1867, which conceded to foreign subjects the right to possess immovable property, provided always that the state of which they assumed the nationality had adhered to the Protocol annexed to the law. The special law was important for the local protégés who assumed foreign nationality. The protégés constituted the majority of the foreign nationals who benefited from the law of 7 Safar 1284/10 June 1867 and bought real property, as the court records indicate.

The application of the law of 7 Safar 1284/10 June 1867 raised another issue about Ottoman women married to foreign nationals who had children carrying their father's names and nationality before the promulgation of the law. If these women owned property but died before the law was approved by the countries of their foreign husbands, would these foreign children inherit their property? Article 110 of the Land Law of 1274/1858 denied the children this privilege. A *tezkere* (memorandum) dated 24 Rabi' II 1290/21 June 1873 was sent by the grand vezirate to the Ottoman foreign ministry regarding this matter. It stated that if the woman died before the country of her husband had signed the law of 7 Safar 1284/10 June 1867 the foreign husband and his children could not inherit the property. The law of 7 Safar 1284/10 June 1867 was communicated to the *shar'i* courts in Damascus and presumably to other courts in Syria one and a half years after its promulgation. The clerk in *mahkamat al-bab* (*al-mahkama al-nuriyya*), the seat of the chief Ottoman Hanafi judge in Damascus, notified the district courts in the city and in the rural regions of the law in two memoranda. The first memorandum, dated 24 Ramadan 1285/8 January 1869,[25] named England, France, Austria, Belgium, Sweden, and Norway as the countries that had accepted the Protocol and the law and whose natives accordingly could buy real property. The memorandum advised the judges to demand from the foreign buyer a certificate of notification (*'ilm wa-khabar*) from the consul of his country stating that he was a national of that country. The foreign buyer was also asked to state in writing at the end of the sale document that he would abide by all the regulations applicable to Muslim buyers in accordance with Islamic *shari'a*.

The second memorandum, issued by the chief Ottoman Hanafi judge in Damascus to the district courts on 3 Jumada I 1286/11 August 1869, adds the names of Prussia, the Netherlands, and Denmark to the list of countries that had accepted the law of 7 Safar 1284/10 June 1867.[26] An order dated 1 Rajab 1289/4 September 1872 sent to the *shar'i* court in Hamah listed the countries that had accepted the law of 7 Safar 1284/10 June 1867. Prussia is replaced by Germany (after its unification in 1870), Spain is added to the list, but the Netherlands is omitted.[27]

Two groups of people benefited from the law of 7 Safar 1284/ 10 June 1867: foreign citizens and local protégés who acquired foreign nationality. Damascus surpassed Aleppo in the number of protégés and foreign nationals who were active in the real estate market, but Aleppo was far ahead in the number of European citizens who bought real property. Traditionally, Aleppo had a larger European community owing to its importance in local, regional, and long-distance trade in which foreigners participated. The presence of European citizens in Damascus was more recent and was largely due to the opening up of Syria to European influence under the Egyptian rule of Muhammad 'Ali (1831–1840).

In the early 1860s, Ottoman subjects becoming protégés and foreign nationals had become a matter of great concern for the Ottoman authorities. In 1863, the Ottoman government issued regulations, in concert with the foreign missions, limiting the number of Ottoman protégés in the service of each consulate, as well as the extent and length of their protection. According to these regulations, no Ottoman subject could be nominated vice-consul or consular agent of a foreign power. But the regulations, like those pertaining to naturalization, were neither fully nor strictly implemented.

In a note communicated to the foreign powers on 8 May 1858, the Sublime Porte denounced the existing Ottoman nationality regulations and promised to issue a new law. In 1860, the Ottoman government ordered those who renounced their Ottoman nationality to sell their belongings and leave the country. In 1862 and 1863, however, Russia and the Ottoman government reached agreement on the procedures to be followed in ascertaining the credentials of Ottoman subjects with Russian nationality. By the law of nationality issued on 6 Shawwal 1285/ 20 January 1869, the Ottoman government ordered that every change of nationality had to be authorized by it. International objections were voiced against the law stating that it should have been formulated in concert with the foreign powers.[28] It is not known how many protégés in Syria had acquired their foreign nationality before and after 1869. Several of them, however, were mentioned in 1869 as buying real property in their capacity as foreign nationals. Samples from the court records of Damascus, Aleppo, and Hamah give details about the acquisition by foreign citizens and foreign nationals of local origin of real property in implementation of the law of 7 Safar 1284/

10 June 1867. Table 6.1 shows the foreign citizens who bought real property in Damascus, in the years 1870 and 1872.

Signor William Wright, son of Signor William Wright, and Signor James Scott, son of Khawaja Hazikus, both English citizens ("min ra'aya dawlat Inkilterra al-fakhima"), according to the Damascus court records, bought in equal shares in two separate transactions on the same day (6 October 1870), a piece of land with a complex of buildings on it, in the village of 'Ayn al-Sha'ra, in Iqlim al-Ballan (in Mount Hermon), which was under the jurisdiction of Damascus. The seller was a Christian from the same village, Ya'qub, son of Yusuf Mirshaq, and the price was 10 French gold liras for each of the two shares. The complex consisted of a courtyard, two open spaces, and five rooms on the upper floor. 'Ayn al-Sha'ra was considered a summer resort and was traditionally inhabited by Christians and Druzes. The reason the two Englishmen bought property there may have been to enjoy the fruit and the cool weather of 'Ayn al-Sha'ra and possibly to keep an eye on the two communities there, which were occasionally at loggerheads with each other. The Druzes at the time were under the protection of the English. In both sale transactions, the seller, Ya'qub Mirshaq, was identified in court by Nasif Mishaqa, who was the son of Mikha'il Mishaqa, a physician and chronicler who had English nationality and was employed by the British chancellery in Damascus at the time. Nasif was vice-consul of the United States of America in Damascus in 1870.[29]

In the other sale transaction, Anthony Renay and his three cobuyers were represented in court by John Barker, son of Charles Barker. The Barker family was well established in Aleppo, where a number of its members were appointed English consuls. The two houses bought by the four partners in this case were located in the Christian quarter of Damascus, near the Misk public bath. The houses shared one common entrance. The price paid for the houses was 2,040 English gold liras or 234,600 piasters, which is tremendous compared to the majority of the other houses put up for sale in Damascus during the

Table 6.1. Investment by European Citizens in Real Property in Damascus, 1870 and 1872

Name	Nationality	Type of Property	Size	Location	Seller	Price (gold liras)	Price (piasters)	Date
William Wright	English	Piece of land with buildings	12/24 *qirats*	'Ayn al-Sha'ra	Ya'qub Mirshaq	10 French	910[a]	6 October 1870[b]
James Scott	English	Same (second half of the above)	12/24 *qirats*	Same	Same	10 French	910	6 October 1870[c]
Anthony Renay, Samuel Hor, Nathaniel Bridges, Tchor Mot	English (apparently)	2 houses	Whole in equal shares	Damascus (Christian quarter)	Yusuf Warde	2,040 English	234, 600	18 October 1872[d]

[a]To unify the prices of the different gold liras, their equivalence in piasters is given. I have used the table of prices for gold liras that was accredited in the courts in Damascus in 1287/1871, and I have eliminated the fractions of the piaster in the value of liras. Thus the French gold lira is rated at 91 piasters, the English gold lira at 115 piasters, and the Mejidiyya gold lira at 105 piasters; see LCR, Damascus, vol. 627, p. 2, 25 Dhu al-Qa'da 1287/16 February 1871. In everyday business, outside the official pricing of the gold liras, however, the French gold lira was priced at 100 piasters in a sales act in 1871; see LCR, Damascus, vol. 618, p. 214, 23 Jumada I 1288/10 August 1871.

[b]LCR, Damascus, vol. 615, p. 77, 10 Rajab 1287/6 October 1870.

[c]Ibid.

[d]Ibid., vol. 631, pp. 157–58, 15 Sha'ban 1289/18 October 1872.

same period. The price apparently indicates spaciousness, good structure, good location, and also affordability by the buyers.

Of the local protégés in Damascus, who had foreign nationality and engaged in buying real property, some were Christian and some were Jewish. Among the Christians is found one Khawaja (title for a Christian notable at the time) Jurji Nahhas, a Damascene Catholic who carried Austrian nationality. His investment in the real estate market is shown in Table 6.2. By these purchases, Khawaja Jurji, son of Khawaja Ibrahim Nahhas, consolidated his real property in the Christian quarter of Bab Tuma and on the western outskirts of the city, in the villages of Hameh and Judayda, in the fertile valley of the Barada River (Wadi Barada), which attracted the rich and powerful among the Damascene notables. Summer residences, referred to as palaces, were built in the villages along Wadi Barada by Muslims, Christians, and Jews alike. The Algerian hero of the war of independence against the French in the 1830s, Amir 'Abd al-Qadir al-Jaza'iri, who chose to live in exile in Damascus, built a palace in the village of Dummar in Wadi Barada. Likewise, the Damascene Jew Sham'aya had a palace there that was known after him as Qasr Sham'aya.

The bulk of Nahhas's property in the villages of Hameh and Judayda consisted of plantations in thirty pieces of land and of the usufruct (*mashadd maska*) of these lands on which the plantations stood. Nahhas bought this property in two sale contracts, within a month of each other, on 10 August 1869 and 9 September 1869. In the first sale contract, Nahhas bought plantations in twenty-two pieces of land. The borders of the lands given in the sale contract indicate that Nahhas did not own property adjoining them before. In the second sale contract, where Nahhas bought plantations in nine pieces of land, the new acquisitions were bounded on more than one side by the lands he had acquired earlier, indicating that Nahhas was consolidating his property in these villages.

The seller in both contracts was Hasan Agha, son of 'Abd al-Qadir Afandi Chelebi al-Baghdadi, who seems to have been a

Table 6.2. Nahhas Investment in Real Property in Damascus, 1869 to 1873

Name	Nationality	Type of Property	Size	Location	Seller	Price (gold liras)	Price (piasters)	Date
Jurji Nahhas (first contract)	Austrian	Plantations (*ghiras*)	12 pieces of land (*qita' aradi*)	Judayda and Hameh	Hasan Baghdadi	200 English	23,000	10 August 1869[a]
		Same	12 *qirats* of 7 lands	Judayda and Hameh				
		Same	6 *qirats* of 1 land	Judayda				
		Plantations and *ahwash* usufruct of all these lands	2 lands	Judayda		100 English (*'iwad*)	11, 500	
Jurji Nahhas (second contract)	Austrian	Plantations	4 lands	Hameh	Hasan Baghdadi	40 English	4,600	9 September 1869[b]
		Same	2 lands	Hameh				
		Same	Garden (*bustan*)	Hameh				

Table 6.2. Continued

Name	Nationality	Type of Property	Size	Location	Seller	Price (gold liras)	Price (piasters)	Date
		Same	Jungle of willows (*ghayda*)	Hameh				
		Same usufruct of all these lands	1 land	Hameh		20 English	2,300	
Jurji Nahhas (third contract)	Austrian	House	Whole	Bab Tuma	Family of Jurjus Mudawwar	250 English	22,750	24 July 1869[c]
Jurji Nahhas (fourth contract)	Austrian	Plantations, *qima*, and *daff*[d]	Whole	Near Bab Tuma	Family of Jurjus Mudawwar	250 English	22,750	24 July 1869[e]
Jurji Nahhas (fifth contract)	Austrian	House	4 *qirats*	Midan (Damascus)	Elias Tawil	60 French	5,4604	May 1871[f]

Table 6.2. Continued

Name	Nationality	Type of Property	Size	Location	Seller	Price (gold liras)	Price (piasters)	Date
Jurji Nahhas (sixth contract)	Austrian	Plantations and a *hawsh*	4 lands	Hameh	Fatima al-Za'im and daughter	20 French	1,8202	5 December 1872[g]
Jurji Nahhas and Mikha'il Muqahhat (in equal shares)	Austrian French	2 shops, 2 coffee houses, *daff*	Whole	Marja/Bahsa	Yuhanna al-Himsi	Nahhas share 300 French (of 600 total)	27,300	6 December 1873[h]

[a] LCR, Damascus, vol. 597, pp. 149–51, 2 Jumada I 1286/10 August 1869.

[b] Ibid., p. 120, 2 Jumada II 1286/9 September 1869.

[c] Ibid., vol. 621, p. 50, 24 Rabi' II 1287/24 July 1870.

[d] The *qima* of a garden is described in this context as including, among other things, a *hawsh* (used as living quarters for peasants and animals), an earth fence, and a variety of roots of certain plants used for fodder and fertilizers. The *daff* is a long piece of land bordering a waterway and carries plantations.

[e] LCR, Damascus, vol. 621, pp. 39–41, 24 Rabi' II 1287/24 July 1870.

[f] Ibid., vol. 618, p. 208, 11 Safar 1288/2 May 1871.

[g] Ibid., vol. 634, p. 30, 24 Shawwal 1289/25 December 1872.

[h] Ibid., vol. 649, p. 32, 15 Shawwal 1290/6 December 1873.

notable of Baghdadi origin. Baghdadis figured in Damascus at the time engaging mainly in long-distance trade. The property that Baghdadi sold to Nahhas on 10 August 1869 was bought by him on 9 Muharram 1285/2 May 1868, according to the *hujja*s he produced in court establishing his ownership of the property. The second batch of property, which Baghdadi sold to Nahhas on 9 September 1869, was bought by him in two separate *hujja*s, the first dated (?) Safar 1285/24 May–21 June 1868, and the second dated 15 Rabi' II 1285/5 August 1868. Thus Baghdadi, who had bought this property in three *hujja*s within a period of three months (2 May–5 August 1868), had kept it for about a year and then sold it to Nahhas in two sale contracts within one month of each other (10 August-9 September 1869).

The price of the real property, mostly plantations, and the compensation (*'iwad*) for the transfer of the usufruct of the lands on which these plantations stood, which Nahhas paid to Baghdadi, amounted to a total sum of 41,400 piasters. This amounts to 34.07 percent of the total sum (121,480 piasters) invested by Nahhas in buying real property in the period between 1869 and 1873, according to the Damascus court records. It is not known from the *hujja*s that Baghdadi presented to the court how much he had paid for the plantations and the *'iwad* when he acquired them. What is known, however, is that Nahhas paid the price to Baghdadi in the court in the presence of the judge and in full view of the court ("qabdan shar'iyyan bi-al-hadra wa-al-mushahada al-shar'iyya"). This indicates that Baghdadi was not selling his property to Nahhas to redeem debts he owed to him. Rather, it shows the availability of cash and the consideration of real estate by absentee landowners as a commodity suitable for investment. This does not seem to have been the case with the sixth sale contract in Table 6.2, in which Nahhas bought plantations and a *hawsh* (a village building that houses peasants and animals) in four lands in Hameh from a local woman, Fatima al-Za'im, and her daughter Rahma, for 20 French gold liras (equal to 1,820 piasters). Payment here to Fatima and her daughter was acknowledged (*bi-al-i'tiraf*) in the court to have been made to them, at another place and time, which suggests that Fatima and her daughter were redeeming a debt they owed to Nahhas. The four lands that carry the plantations bought by Nahhas were bounded on more than one side by property already owned by him. With this sale the total amount of money that Nahhas had invested in buying property in the villages of Hameh and Judayda rose to 43,220 piasters, which accounts for 35.57 percent of the total money that Nahhas had invested in buying real estate. The money he invested in buying residential property in Damascus, the most expensive of which was in the Christian quarter of Bab Tuma and in Marja in the center of Damascus, amounts to 78,260 piasters, which equals 64.42 percent of the grand total he expended.

Some of the other Damascene Christians of foreign nationality who had bought property in the period between 1869 and 1873 are included in Table 6.3. The total amount of money invested by the five local Damascenes of foreign nationality in seven sale contracts of real estate constitutes 52.58 percent of the total amount invested by Nahhas. The five foreign nationals invested 40,367 piasters (63.19 percent of the total) in buying property in the countryside compared to 23,513 piasters (36.81 percent) invested in Damascus, which shows, in comparison with Nahhas, that small investors could not afford to invest much money in the countryside for fear of losing it.

The village of Sahnaya, where Lutfi bought property, was and still is inhabited by Christians and Druzes. The village of 'Ayn al-Tina, on the other hand, was predominantly Christian until the nineteenth century, when its inhabitants and the inhabitants of the neighboring village of Jaba'din converted to Islam. Both villages, however, still speak their old Aramaic language, like the neighboring Christian village of Ma'lula. Likewise, the Muslim inhabitants of 'Ayn al-Tina still speak Aramaic.

None of the five foreign nationals in Table 6.3 shared Austrian nationality with Nahhas. Three of them were French, one was English, and one was Spanish. The French nationals head the list in the amount of their investment in real estate, which ac-

Table 6.3. Investment by Damascus Christians of Foreign Nationality in Real Property, 1869 to 1872

Name	Nationality	Type of Property	Size	Location	Seller	Price (gold liras)	Price (piasters)	Date
Ni'me Lutfi	French	Plantations	18 *qirats* of 2 lands and vineyard	Sahnaya	Fatima and children		3,000	22 October 1869[a]
		Usufruct of 2 lands and several other lands					3,000 (*'iwad*)	
Ni'me Lutfi	French	Plantations	Whole	Sahnaya	Hamed 'Aql		252	21 February 1870[b]
Mikha'il Mishaqa	English	Shops	Whole	Bab Tuma	Mahmud and Muhammad Halabi	38 French	3,458	30 August 1869[c]
Mikha'il Mishaqa	English	House	Whole	Bab Tuma	Hajj Jawad Rida	121 Mejidiyya	12,705	14 February 1870[d]

Table 6.3. Continued

Name	Nationality	Type of Property	Size	Location	Seller	Price (gold liras)	Price (piasters)	Date
Hanna Himsi	French	House	Whole	Midan (Damascus)	Muhammad Agha Darkal	70 Mejidiyya	7,350	14 February 1872[e]
Antun Shamat	Spanish	Khan (caravanserai)	Whole	'Ayn al-Tina	Antun Shalhub		10,000	7 December 1872[f]
Ibrahim Adham	French	2 *abwash* and cattle	Whole	Dalhaniyya (Biqa')	Mansur Tannus	265 French	24,115	24 December 1872[g]

[a]LCR, Damascus, vol. 613, pp. 207–8, 16 Rajab 1286/22 October 1869.
[b]Ibid., vol. 597, p. 155, 20 Dhu al-Qa'da 1286/21 February 1870.
[c]Ibid., vol. 610, p. 85, 22 Jumada I 1286/30 August 1869.
[d]Ibid., vol. 614, p. 52, 13 Dhu al-Qa'da 1286/14 February 1870.
[e]Ibid., vol. 639, pp. 39–40, 4 Dhu al-Hijja 1288/14 February 1872.
[f]Ibid., vol. 631, p. 207, 6 Shawwal 1289/7 December 1872.
[g]Ibid., p. 210, 23 Shawwal 1289/24 December 1872.

counts for 59.05 percent of the total. The English Mishaqa invested 25.30 percent, and the Spanish Shamat 15.65 percent. The sellers who sold their property to the five Christian foreign nationals were composed of Muslims and Christians. The Muslims' sales account for 46.60 percent of the total and the Christians' sales for 53.50 percent. In the case of Nahhas, 35.58 percent of the value of the total property he bought came from Muslims and 64.42 percent came from Christians. The higher value of the property sold to Nahhas by Christians is to be explained by the fact that this property was mostly residential and commercial and located in Damascus, whereas the property sold to him by Muslims was mostly agricultural and located in villages.

Damascene Jews of foreign nationality were also active in buying real property in implementation of the law of 7 Safar 1284/10 June 1867. Several Jewish families, such as the Hararis, the Farhis, and the Sham'aya Angelas, were heavily involved in buying real property by virtue of this law. Other Jewish individuals also figured in this activity to the extent that the Jews surpassed the Christians in numbers and in the amount of money they invested as foreign nationals in real property.

Several members of the Harari family, who acquired English nationality, invested a great deal of money buying real property in Damascus and its countryside. Their purchases, according to the Damascus court records, are shown in Table 6.4. The money invested by the four Hararis—Yusuf, son of Harun Harari, 'Azra, son of Yusuf Harari, Raphael, son of Daoud Harari, and 'Abdullah, son of Ishaq Harari—in buying real property in six sale contracts amounts to 30,192 piasters. They bought property in a number of villages on the outskirts of Damascus, including two villages in Wadi Barada, Dummar and Ashrafiyya, which are close to the villages where Nahhas had bought most of his property at about the same time. But while Nahhas had concentrated all his rural purchases in the two villages of Hameh and Judayda and had bought property from a single Damascene seller, Hasan Baghdadi, the Hararis bought property

Table 6.4. Investment by Damascus Jews of Foreign Nationality in Real Property: The Hararis

Name	Nationality	Type of Property	Size	Location	Seller	Price (gold liras)	Price (piasters)	Date
Yusuf of Harun Harari	English	Canal leading to home	12 *qirats*	Kharab quarter	3 Muslims and a Christian	375 French	3,412.5	3 November 1869[a]
'Azra, son of Yusuf Harari	English	House	Whole	Dummar	Sayyid Muhammad Chelebi al-Habal	100 Mejidiyya	10,500	8 February 1869[b]
Raphael, son of Daoud Harari	English	Plantations	2 lands	Kafr Batna	Hajj Hasan Makkawi	105 French	9,555	24 July 1871[c]
		House	Upper floor	Ashra-fiyya	Hajj Yusuf Za'im		400	23 December 1872[d]
		Plantations	4 lands	Tall	Hajj Ahmad Talfiti	30 French	2,730	16 July 1873[e]
'Abdullah, son of Ishaq Harari	English	Plantations	1 land	Ashra-fiyya	Shaykh Mahmud Salha	39.5 French	3,594	30 June 1872[f]

[a]LCR, Damascus, vol. 597, p. 99, 28 Rajab 1286/3 November 1869.
[b]Ibid., vol. 600, p. 129, 25 Shawwal 1285/8 February 1869.
[c]Ibid., vol. 627, p. 223, 6 Jumada I 1288/24 July 1871.
[d]Ibid., vol. 634, p. 229, 22 Shawwal 1289/23 December 1872.
[e]Ibid., vol. 643, p. 19, 20 Jumada I 1290/16 July 1873.
[f]Ibid., vol. 628, p. 75, 13 Rabi' II 1289/20 June 1872.

in a number of villages scattered around Damascus from persons living in these villages. Raphael Harari, for example, in three separate contracts, bought property in three villages: Kafar Batna to the east of Damascus, Ashrafiyya in Wadi Barada to the west of Damascus, and Tall to the north of Damascus.

Unlike Nahhas, who paid Hasan Baghdadi in cash in the court, the sellers of property to the Hararis acknowledged in the court that they had received the price of their property from the buyer, implying that this had been done at an earlier date outside the court. The phrase used in the court records for such acknowledgment is "qabdan shar'iyyan bi'l-i'tiraf al-shar'i." This sort of payment appears in the majority of the sale transactions, suggesting that these buyers with foreign nationality were acquiring property in return for debts owed to them by villagers. In one of his sale contracts, dated 6 Jumada I 1288/24 July 1871, Raphael Harari, for example, bought from Hajj Hasan Makkawi plantations in two lands in the village of Kafar Batna. Hajj Hasan owed two debts to Raphael totaling 14,947 piasters. The price of the plantations amounted to 9,555 piasters, which was deducted from the debts owed to Raphael by way of settlement of accounts (*muqasasa*). This left Makkawi still indebted to Raphael for 5,392 piasters. The two debts owed to Harari were contracted by Makkawi in two *kombialat* documents dated 1 Safar 1287/3 May 1870 and 1 Jumada I 1287/1 July 1870.

While the Hararis were of English nationality, the Farhis, who outdid them in the amount of money they invested in real property, were Austrian. The Farhis who bought property in the period between 1869 and 1871, according to the Damascus court records, are the following: Salamun, son of Yusuf Farhi, Yusuf, son of Ma'ir Farhi, Ma'ir, son of de Ma'ir Farhi, and Ma'ir, son of Raphael Farhi (see Table 6.5). All the investments of the Farhis were in agricultural property outside Damascus. The four Farhis invested in five sale contracts a total of 60,786 piasters, compared to 30,192 piasters invested by the four Hararis. Biqqin and Zabadani, where the Farhis bought most of their ag-

Table 6.5. Investment by Damascus Jews of Foreign Nationality in Real Property: The Farhis

Name	Nationality	Type of Property	Size	Location	Seller	Price (gold liras)	Price (piasters)	Date
Salamun, son of Yusuf Farhi	Austrian	*qima* of 2 gardens	18 *qirats* of 1 garden and 11 *qirats* of another	Outside Damascus[a]	Sayyid Muhammad Chelebi al-Habal	330 Mejidiyya	34,650	28 May1869[b]
Yusuf, son of Ma'ir Farhi	Austrian	Plantations	6 lands	Biqqin village (Suq Wadi Barada)	Shihada, son of Hasan and family		9,000	21 December 1869[c]
		Usufruct of the 6 lands and of 8 other lands in the same village					2,651	
Ma'ir, son of Ma'ir de Farhi	Austrian	Plantations	9 *qirats* of a garden and a field	Biqqin village	'Ali Mahmud and 2 Muslims from Madaya village (near Biqqin)		800	4 March 1870[d]

Table 6.5. Continued

Name	Nationality	Type of Property	Size	Location	Seller	Price (gold liras)	Price (piasters)	Date
Ma'ir, son of Raphael Farhi	Austrian	Plantations	Whole	Zabadani village (near Biqqin)	Shaykh ʿAli Hamdan	35 French	3,185	22 March 1871[e]
		Flour mill and bayka for animals	8 qirats	Zabadani	Shaykh ʿAli Hamdan	100 Mejidiyya	10,500	22 March 1871[f]

[a]The first garden is located in the Qinya and Hammuriyya region in the southern outskirts of Damascus, the second between Bab Srija and the nearby village of Mezze.
[b]LCR, Damascus, vol. 603, pp. 6–7, 16 Safar 1286/28 May 1869.
[d]Ibid., vol. 613, pp. 22–24, 6 Ramadan 1285/21 December 1869.
[d]Ibid., vol. 621, pp. 61–62, 1 Dhu al-Hijja 1286/4 March 1870.
[e]Ibid., vol. 623, p. 44, end Dhu al-Hijja 1286/12 March 1871.
[f]Ibid., p. 45, end Dhu al-Hijja 1286/12 March 1871.

ricultural property, were major summer resorts, then as now, for Damascenes and are close to the villages of Wadi Barada. The sellers were either inhabitants of the same villages or of nearby villages, such as Biqqin and Madaya, which are next to each other. No cash payments were made by the buyers to the sellers in court. In two sales contracts on the same day (30 March 1871), Ma'ir Farhi bought property from Shaykh 'Ali Hamdan of Zabadani worth 13,685 piasters. A settlement of accounts (*muqasasa*) took place on this occasion between Ma'ir Farhi and Shaykh 'Ali Hamdan whereby the price of the property was used to defray debts that Shaykh 'Ali owed to Ma'ir. The amount of the debts and their dates are not given in the court records. The property that Shaykh 'Ali sold to Ma'ir Farhi was partly inherited by him from his father and partly established by him (*min insha'ihi*). Other cases in the court records indicate that Ma'ir Farhi offered credit to villagers. In one case dated 12 Jumada I 1290/8 July 1873, for example, a number of villagers from Duma were indebted to Ma'ir Farhi for 124 French gold liras (equal to 11,284 piasters).[30] In an earlier case, dated 17 Jumada II 1273/12 February 1857, the same Ma'ir Farhi, in partnership with Yusuf, son of Menahim Farhi, bought from Hajj Mahmud al-Kayyal two-thirds of a *bayka* (building used to store and sell grain and also to house animals) in the Shaghur quarter, outside the southern walls of Damascus, for the sum of 2,700 piasters. Neither Farhi was mentioned in the court records at that time as a holder of foreign nationality.[31]

Although the four Farhi Jews who were active in the real estate market in the region of Damascus had Austrian nationality, other Farhis had French nationality according to French dispatches from Damascus. Salamun, son of Ishaq Farhi, for example, had French nationality, according to the French consul in Damascus, in a letter he addressed to the governor of Syria dated 15 January 1875. In this letter, the consul complained to the governor on behalf of Salamun against a villager from Aftaris who had not paid Salamun a debt of 15, 000 piasters.[32]

Other Damascene Jews from different families also bought

real property as holders of foreign nationality in the period between 1869 and 1873. Some are included in Table 6.6. The amount of money expended by the six Damascene Jews of foreign nationality mentioned in Table 6.6 in nine sale contracts amounts to 124,289 piasters. Of this amount, Yusuf al-Bushi of French nationality[33] invested in a single sale contract 88,270 piasters (71.01 percent of the total), buying a house and a garden in the Damascus quarter of Mi'dhanat al-Shahm, close to the Jewish quarter and the Kharab Shi'i quarter. Sham'aya Angela ranks a low second after al-Bushi in the amount of money he invested in two sale contracts in Damascus worth 18,973 piasters (15.16 percent of the total).

Buyers of foreign nationality usually acted individually in buying real property. The exceptions in Table 6.6 are Daoud 'Atiyya and Shihadeh Saqqal, who jointly bought real property in four sale contracts in the village of Hadidat al-Turkman to the east of Damascus for a total amount of 12,510 piasters. The four sale contracts took place within a period of eleven days, between 13 and 24 December 1872. They involved buying houses and plantations from peasants in Hadidat al-Turkman. December was the season when the financial resources of the peasants dried up and they usually failed to meet their financial obligations. Selling property to pay off debts was a common practice.

The amount of 124,289 piasters invested by the six Jews in buying property breaks down into 109,868 piasters (88.39 percent) for residential and commercial property in Damascus and 14,421 (11.61 percent) for property in the countryside. Most of the houses that the Jews bought in Damascus were located in or near the predominantly Jewish and Christian quarters in the city. Business relations crossed the barriers between the religious communities: all the sellers to the Jews were Muslims, most of whom held the dignified religious titles of hajj, shaykh, and sayyid.

A close examination of the religious affiliation and foreign nationality of the buyers of real property in the Damascus region as revealed in the court records sheds light on the amount of

Table 6.6. Investment by Damascus Jews of Foreign Nationality in Real Property

Name	Nationality	Type of Property	Size	Location	Seller	Price (gold liras)	Price (piasters)	Date
Daoud 'Atiyya	French	House and planta-tions	Whole	Hadidat al-Turkman village[a]	Hajj Mahmud Rasul	21 French	1,911	17 Decem-ber 1872[b]
Daoud 'Atiyya and Shihadeh Saqqal	French	House and planta-tions	Whole	Hadidat al-Turkman	Shaykh Hasan Jayrudi	22 French	2,002	13 Decem-ber 1872[c]
		House and planta-tions	Whole	Same	Hajj Mahmud al-Mitlawi	38 French	3,458	23 Decem-ber 1872[d]
		House and planta-tions	Whole	Same	Husayn Hajj 'Ali		2,500	23 Decem-ber 1872[e]
		House and planta-tions	Whole	Same	Muhammad Zayn	50 French	4,550	24 Decem-ber 1872[f]
Sham'aya Angela	Austrian	Shop	Whole	Khan al-Jadid (in Kharab quarter)	5 children of Muhammad Drayliyya and mother	50 French	4,550	24 June 1873[g]

Table 6.6. Continued

Name	Nationality	Type of Property	Size	Location	Seller	Price (gold liras)	Price (piasters)	Date
		House	Whole	Zuqaq al-Buwari (next to Khan al-Jadid)	Sayyid ʻAli Nizam	158.5 French	14, 423	3 November 1873[h]
Yusuf al-Bushi	French	House and garden	Whole	Miʾdhanat al-Shahm	6 of the Muslim Midani family	970 French	88, 270	30 August 1873[i]
Signor Musa Iliyya	French	House	3 *qirats*	Qaymariyya (Damascus)	Sayyid Salim Mutlawi	25 Mejidiyya	2.625	14 January 1873[j]

[a] Also known as Hadithat al-Turkman.
[b] LCR, Damascus, vol. 634, p. 78, 16 Shawwal 1289/17 December 1872.
[c] Ibid., vol. 639, pp. 76–77, 12 Shawwal 1289/13 December 1872.
[d] Ibid., vol. 634, p. 64, 22 Shawwal 1289/23 December 1872.
[e] Ibid., p. 65, 22 Shawwal 1289/23 December 1872.
[f] Ibid., vol. 639, p. 74, 23 Shawwal 1289/24 December 1872.
[g] Ibid., 27 Rabiʻ II 1290/24 June 1873.
[h] Ibid., vol. 643, pp. 113–114, 12 Ramadan 1290/3 November 1873.
[i] Ibid., vol. 644, pp. 55–58, 6 Rajab 1290/30 August 1873.
[j] Ibid., vol. 639, p. 16, 15 Dhu al-Qaʻda 1289/14 January 1873.

money each group expended in buying property as well as the location of the property, as shown in Table 6.7.

The local Jews of foreign nationality outnumber the Christians of foreign nationality and the European citizens who bought real property in and around Damascus. Also, while all the foreign citizens were English and the majority of the Christian buyers had French nationality, the Jews had more varied nationalities. Six Jews were Austrian (42.86 percent of total) compared to four who were English and four French (28.57 percent for each group). The average investment per person in each group was 39,403 piasters per foreign citizen, 30,893 piasters per Christian, and 15,376 piasters per Jew. Among the Christians, Nahhas stands out as the most important single buyer, investing 121,480 piasters in buying real property, which equals 65.53 percent of the total investment of Christians. The Jewish buyers, on the other hand, had a more balanced investment per person. They ranked second, after the foreign citizens, in buying real property (37.11 percent for foreign citizens, 33.79 percent for Jews, and 29.10 percent for Christians). The reason for the higher percentage of the investment of the Jewish buyers is partly their larger numbers and also their greater financial capacity to buy more expensive houses in Damascus. The lower average of investment per person among the Jews is explained by their buying more rural property than either the Christians or the foreign citizens.

Table 6.8 shows that more money (72.15 percent of total) was invested in urban than in rural real property. This applies to all groups. It is significant, however, that the Jews of foreign nationality invested more money (47.38 percent of total) in buying real property in the countryside than either the Christians (39.7 percent) or the foreign citizens (00.77 percent). This indicates more financial relations between the Jews and villagers, especially in matters of loans and credit. The Jews bought rural real property mostly from villagers, whereas the main buyer of rural real property among the Christians, Jurji Nahhas, bought the

Table 6.7. Religious Affiliation, Foreign Nationality, and Amount of Investment by Buyers of Real Property in Damascus

| | Number of Buyers | | | | | Amount of Investment (piasters) | |
	Total Number	Austrian	English	French	Spanish	Total Amount	Average Amount per Person
Foreign Citizens	6		6			236,420	39,403
Christians (foreign)	6	1	1	3	1	185,360	30,893
Jews (foreign)	14	6	4	4		215,267	15,376
Total	26	7	11	7	1	637,047	24,501

Table 6.8.   Investment in Urban and Rural Property in Syria by
             Foreign Citizens and Nationals

	Total (piasters)	Urban Property		Rural Property	
		Amount (piasters)	Percent	Amount (piasters)	Percent
Foreign citizens	236,420	234,600	99.23	1,820	0.77
Christians (foreign)	185,360	111,773	60.3	73,587	39.7
Jews (foreign)	215,267	113,290	52.62	101,987	47.38
Total	637,047	459,663	72.15	177,394	27.85

bulk of his rural property from an urban person, Hasan
Baghdadi.

The amount of money invested by local persons of foreign nationality buying real property breaks down according to nationality as shown in Table 6.9. Local buyers of Austrian nationality
headed the list of foreign nationals in the amount of money they
invested (50.23 percent) in buying real property. French nationals ranked second (35.7 percent) and English nationals were a
low third (11.57 percent). Among the Christians, those of Austrian nationality came at the top in investment (65.54 percent),
followed by French nationals (20.35 percent), and then by English (8.72 percent) and Spanish nationals (5.39 percent). Among
the Jews, those with French nationality headed the list in investment in real property (48.92 percent), followed by those of Austrian nationality (37.05 percent). Jews of English nationality
ranked a low third (14.03 percent). Overall, however, the Jews
of foreign nationality invested more money in buying real property (215,267 piasters—that is, 53.73 percent of the total) than
the Christians (185,360 piasters, which equals 46.27 percent).
Also, the Jews, as already stated, invested more money buying

Table 6.9. Nationality and Investment by Foreign Nationals in Syria

	Austrian		English		French		Spanish		Total Amount (piasters)
	Amount (piasters)	Percent	Amount (piasters)	Percent	Amount (piasters)	Percent	Amount (piasters)	Percent	
Christians	121,480	65.54	16,163	8.72	37,717	20.35	10,000	5.93	185,360
Jews	79,759	37.05	30,192	14.03	105,316	48.92			215,267
Total	201,239	50.23	46,355	11.57	143,033	35.7	10,000	2.5	400,627

rural real property (47.38 percent) than did the Christians (39.4 percent).

Table 6.10 shows the kind of gold liras that the foreign nationals used in their sale transactions. The total number of liras used in all the sale transactions was 6,243 liras, of which 3,097 liras were French (49.61 percent), 2,400 liras were English (38.44 percent), and 746 liras were Mejidiyya (11.95 percent). Buyers of Austrian nationality used 45.96 percent of the French liras, whereas the French nationals used 44.11 percent of French liras. The large percentage of the English liras (85.00 percent) used by English nationals equaled in fact the price paid by four English citizens for the price of two houses in Damascus, which cost 2,040 English gold liras. The other English citizens used French gold liras. The Ottoman Mejidiyya gold lira was the least used, accounting for only 11.95 percent of all the liras used in buying real property. Austrian nationals used more Mejidiyya liras (57.64 percent) than did the English (29.63 percent), and the English used more Mejidiyya liras than did the French (12.73 percent). The greater use of French liras seems to have been due largely to their lower official rate (91 piasters per French lira) compared to the English lira (115 piasters) and the Mejidiyya lira (105 piasters). The greater circulation of French liras in the real estate market could be an indicator of growing French financial activity in the region at the time. The French, it is to be recalled, were heavily involved in promoting their commercial interests in the region in competition with the English by investing in transportation, such as their financing of the Beirut-Damascus road inaugurated in 1863 and the Suez Canal undertaken by Ferdinand De Lesseps and opened in 1869. Also, imported French Jacquard looms were widely used in Syria at the time.

In contrast to Damascus, Aleppo had traditionally more foreign citizens, some of whom belonged to long-established families, such as Picciotto and Poche. The law of 7 Safar 1284/10 June 1867 gave them legal justification to buy real property and register it in their names. Variations occur between the court re-

Table 6.10. Foreign Nationals and Gold Liras in Syria

Nationals	French Gold Liras		English Gold Liras		Mejidiyya Gold Liras	
	Number	Percent	Number	Percent	Number	Percent
Austrian	1,423.5	45.96	360	15	430	57.64
English	307.5	9.93	2,040	85	221	29.63
French	1,366	44.11			95	12.73
Total	3,097	100	2,400	100	746	100

cords of Aleppo and those of Damascus in matters relating to the registration of property. The Aleppo records were in general more precise than those of Damascus in the legal terminology they used in regard to the nationality of the foreign buyer. When a foreign citizen bought real property, the Aleppo records usually stated his nationality and referred to the Ottoman laws and agreements giving him the right to buy such property. An example of this is the selling of property in 1872 to Khawaja Brunel François, son of Antoine Brunel, a citizen of France who had the right to buy land in the Ottoman empire, in accordance with the established agreements, with his own money and for himself ("ba'a min naqil hadha al-kitab al-khawaja Brunel François walad Antoine Brunel min tib'at dawlat Faransa al-fakhima alladhi lahu salahiyya li-shira' al-aradi bi-al-mamalik al-mahrusa hasab al-'uhud al-mu'assassa wa-huwa ishtara 'ala mujib al-'uhud bi-malihi li-nafsihi").[34]

The Aleppo court records do not, however, always include the notification document ('ilm wa-khabar), which gives the nationality of the buyer and merely mention the nationality of the foreign buyer without further proof. The required proof of a person's nationality in the Damascus records, as in those of Gaza as early as 1859, seems to have been necessitated by the fact that more foreigners, among them Jews, were attempting to buy real property in Palestine, which was part of the province of Damascus at the time, long before the issuing of the law of 7 Safar 1284/10 June 1867.

Table 6.11 shows the Aleppo court records of certain sale contracts by foreigners in the period between 1869 and 1873. The Poche brothers, Frederick, Albert, and Rudolph, children of Yusuf Poche, bought in three sale contracts on the same day, 24 Ramadan 1287/18 December 1870, six houses and other property in the village of Bashkoy in a region located on the main road leading to Alexandretta from Aleppo, in the Qada' of Jabal Sam'an, which was part of the province of Aleppo. The houses contained wells for storing hay, water wells, stables, and living rooms. All the houses were close to the threshing ground, indi-

Table 6.11. Investment by Foreign Citizens in Real Property in Aleppo

Name	Nationality	Type of Property	Size	Location	Seller	Price (gold liras)	Price (piasters)	Date
Frederick, Albert, and Rudolph, children of Yusuf Poche, in equal shares	Austrian	2 houses and cave for storage	Whole	Bashoy village (Jabal Sam'an)	'Abd al-Qadir Abi-'Aqd		2,000	18 December 1870[a]
		2 houses	20 *sahm*	Bashkoy	Muhammad al-Luk and 2 family members		2,000	18 December 1870[c]
		2 houses and 45 fig trees		Bashkoy	Bakir al-Jaghl and 2 partners		2,000	18 December 1870[c]
Brunel François	French	House	Whole	Mahallat Jub Asad Allah	Hajj 'Abd al-Rahman 'Adas and grandson		10,000	2 October 1872[d]
Musa, son of Ilyahu di Picciotto	Austrian	Fodder shop	Whole	Suq Khan al-Tutun	Hajj 'Abdullah al-Turk	20 Mejidiyya	2,100	31 March 1872[e]

[a] LCR, Aleppo, vol. 301, p. 305, 24 Ramadan 1287/18 December 1870 (Appendix 29).
[b] Ibid., p. 306, 24 Ramadan 1287/18 December, 1870.
[c] Ibid.
[d] Ibid., vol. 302, p. 135, 29 Rajab 1289/2 October 1872.
[e] Ibid., p. 32, 21 Muharram 1289/31 March 1872.

cating that the Poche brothers were investing money in agriculture. The houses were bought from Bashkoy villagers whose ownership of the houses was established in the court through a document of *'ilm wa-khabar* carrying the seals of the *mukhtar*s and the *ikhtiyariyya* (elders) of the villages adjoining Bashkoy. The document states that the sale contract was valid and that the sellers' ownership of the property they sold was genuine ("ba'da an warada 'ilm wa-khabar makhtum bi-akhtam mukhtarin wa-ikhtiyariyyat al-qura al-mujawira li-al-qarya al-madhkura bi-anna al-mabi' al-mazbur sahih jari fi milkiyyat al-bayi'in al-marqumin").[35]

The Italian family of Marcopoli, whose members were traditionally appointed Italian consuls in Aleppo, was related to the Poche family. Like the Poches, the Marcopolis engaged in buying real property. Maria, wife of Fingino Marcopoli, was the daughter of Yusuf Poche. Fingino, his wife, and four children bought a *bayka*, used for stocking foreign and Aleppo goods, according to the court records, in Mahallat al-Jallum al-Kubra in Aleppo on 23 Dhu al-Hijja 1262/12 December 1846 for the price of 12,500 piasters. Fingino registered the *bayka* at the time in the name of Ahmad Agha Qana'a, by way of cover-up (*muwada'a*), apparently because as a foreigner Fingino was not allowed to own real property in 1846. After Fingino died and the owership of the *bayka* was challenged by the Qana'a family, Fingino's heirs brought a case before the *shar'i* court in Aleppo on 14 Rabi' II 1291/31 May 1874 claiming the *bayka* for themselves and using as proof for its ownership their continued use of it as actual owners since the time it was bought in the name of Ahmad Qana'a. The ownership of the *bayka* by Fingino's heirs was established in 1874, after the law of 7 Safar 1284/10 June 1867 had been implemented.[36]

Khawaja Musa, son of Khawaja Ilyahu di Picciotto, was consul of Austria in Aleppo when he bought, on 31 March 1872, a shop used for selling fodder in Suq Khan al-Tutun in Aleppo. Musa apparently remained Austrian consul for some time. In 1300/1883, for example, he was still Austrian consul in

Aleppo.[37] Of Italian Jewish origin, the Picciotto family, whose members first came to Aleppo as merchants, had a long history in Aleppo. An early Picciotto, Raphael, became Austrian consul in Aleppo in 1784.[38] In the middle of the nineteenth century, the Picciottos in Aleppo were still described as Faranj (Faranja).[39] The Picciottos monopolized the office of Austrian consul in Aleppo and occasionally acted also as consuls for Denmark. Ilyahu di Picciotto, for example, was nominated consul of Austria and Denmark in Aleppo.[40] In July 1872, Daniel di Picciotto was mentioned as vice-consul royal of Denmark. In November of that year, his titles were quoted as "vice consul de Denmark, gérant le vice consulat d'Autriche-Hongrie à Alep."[41] Another Picciotto member, Hillel di Picciotto, was vice consul of the United States of America and Belgium in Aleppo at the time.

According to the Aleppo court records, a member of the Picciotto family called Ilyun, who was son of Hillel (who was son of Ilyahu di Picciotto, a Jew of Austrian nationality), appointed in the court in Aleppo on 23 Sha'ban 1292/24 September 1875 the English consul in Alexandretta, Amid Frank Wig, as his deputy. The deputy had authority to transfer (*farigha*) Ilyun's right of usufruct (*tasarruf*), apparently the *mashadd maska*, for the cultivation and plantation of fifty pieces of *miri* land in the villages of Ashkar Beyli and Aktchoy in the region of Alexandretta, in the Qada' of Bilan, which was part of the province of Aleppo. The documents (*awraq al-qujanat*) that Ilyahu held for each piece of land, indicating its location and borders, were given to the deputy, who was authorized to transfer the usufruct of the lands to any interested party ("bi-faragh al-aradi al-mazbura li-man yarghab bi-istifraghiha") for a compensation ('*iwad*). The superintendant of the fifty *miri* lands, referred to as *sahib al-ard*, who probably was either the *ustadh* or the *subashi* but not the owner, was present in court, and he witnessed the appointment of the consul as deputy for Ilyahu in accordance with *nizam al-aradi*, apparently a reference to the Land Law of 1274/1858.[42]

Among the rare cases of foreigners selling real property to local people is the case of the brothers Baberto (Roberto?) and Fingino, the children of Francis Dikwan, described in the court records as Latin of English nationality, who sold a house in ruins they owned in Aleppo to a Syriac Christian woman of Ottoman nationality. The house was located in Mahallat Jubb Asad Allah, next to a house jointly owned by the two sellers and the woman buyer. It sold for 1,500 new piasters. The sale contract was authorized after an *'ilm wa-khabar* from the *mukhtar*, and the local elders had been received in the court stating that the house was owned by the two sellers.[43]

Foreign citizens in Aleppo were involved in a special type of sale contract known as *bay' bi-al-wafa'* (sale of property with the right of redemption),[44] according to which the buyer gave the seller the right to redeem his property on paying back the price he received for it after an agreed time. Under this arrangement, the buyer had the right to use the property during that time. Very often this sort of sale ended being final when the seller failed to redeem his property. A clause in this type of sale contract gives the buyer the right to dispose of the property should the seller fail to honor his commitment.

Khawaja Binyamin Filkruz (Villecroze), son of Louis Villecroze, a French merchant living with his family in Aleppo,[45] bought on 5 Rabi' I 1287/14 June 1871 from Sayyid Ahmad 'Abd al-Baqi a house and a press for sesame oil in Mahallat al-Qasila in Aleppo for 206.75 Mejidiyya gold liras. The sale, described as *bay' bi-al-wafa'*, gave the seller the right to redeem his property after eleven years beginning on 1 Rabi' II 1287/1 July 1870 if he paid back the same amount of money. If he failed to do so, the sale contract gave the buyer power of attorney to sell the property for the same amount of money.[46] Four years later, the same Binyamin Filkruz, acting through an Aleppine Greek Orthodox deputy, Khawaja Na'um Mitri, bought on 29 Safar 1291/17 April 1874 from Hajj Mustafa Ma'sarani two houses attached to each other in Mahallat al-Mughazila in Aleppo for the sum of 260 Muscovy (Russian) gold liras.[47] The seller was to redeem his property after two and one half years from the date of sale. If he failed to do so, the buyer had power of attorney to sell the houses. The sale contract mentioned that the *majlis al-da'awa* (council of litigation) had issued an *'ilm wa-khabar* acknowledging the mortgage (*rahina*). The use of this term in the document reveals the true nature of *bay' bi-al-wafa'* that was basically a mortgage under another name.[48]

Apparently a brother of Binyamin Villecroze, Khawaja Dezire, son of Louis Villecroze, a French citizen and medical doctor for the French consul in Aleppo, bought through a deputy, Khawaja Mantura, son of Hanna Popolani[49] of Austrian nationality, on 15 Dhu al-Hijja 1287/8 March 1871 from Hajj Ibrahim Agha a house in Mahallat Oghlik and a shop for weaving outside Bab al-Nasr in Aleppo for a sum of 250 Mejidiyya gold liras. The sale was *bay' bi-al-wafa'*, to be redeemed within a year from the date of sale, failing which the buyer had the right to sell the property.[50]

According to Joseph Schacht, the sale of real property with the right of redeeming it (*bay' bi-al-wafa'*) aimed at avoiding the irrevocable alienation of land but is not admissible in strict Islamic law either as a sale or as a pledge. This type of sale was the result of the symbiosis of customary law with *shar'ia* law to provide greater flexibility in the law of contracts. Although the security provided to the buyer by the seller was tight in such cases, the buyer very often ended up in purchasing the "mortgaged" property.[51]

Binyamin and Isidore Villecroze, Aron Alataras, and Guillaume Vigoureuse, French merchants in Aleppo, were quoted on the rate of exchange of the various currencies in the city.[52] In a plea to the French consul in Aleppo, Guillaume Vigoureuse declared that he had four wells for stocking hay in the village of Tall Nissibin to which he referred as "my village" (*day'ati*). A villager from the village of Hreitan, Muhammad ibn Raznum, filled the wells with hay and refused to vacate them. Vigoureuse asked that Muhammad pay him the rent of the four wells for four years, a total of twenty liras. He referred in his plea to his partner, Sayyid 'Uthman Daqqaq, who had been beaten by Raznum, and to insecurity in the region that resulted in brigands stealing his wheat stored in a well.[53]

The Aleppines who adopted foreign nationality and bought real property figure much less than their Damascene counterparts in the court records. The cases shown in Table 6.12 of Aleppines buying real property in Aleppo occur in the court records of Aleppo in the period between 1870 and 1875. The three Aleppines with foreign nationality, Ghurra daughter of Jurji Qasir, 'Azra son of Ibrahim Nahmad al-Yahudi, and 'Azra son of Rubin Kabay al-Yahudi, who had bought real property in the period between 1870 and 1874, constitute about 17 percent of the number of Damascenes with foreign nationality who bought similar property in a similar four-year period between 1869 and 1873. Most of the real property bought by foreign nationals in Damascus was agricultural and rural whereas in Aleppo it was mostly residential and urban. All the property purchased in Aleppo was paid for in new piasters, whereas in Damascus it was paid for mostly in European gold liras. The residential property bought by foreign nationals of local origin in both Aleppo and Damascus was located mostly in the quarters with which the buyers had religious affiliation. The only woman buyer of foreign nationality in either Damascus or Aleppo was Ghurra, daughter of Jurji Qasir, wife of Khawaja Yusuf Conti, and mother of Felix Conti who acted as deputy for his mother in the sale contract. Ghurra, whose name was Arabic, was Latin by rite, and apparently acquired French nationality through marriage ("min ta'ifat al-Latin wa-min tib'at dawlat al-Faransa al-fakhima").

The *shar'i* court of Hamah was notified on 1 Rajab 1289/4 September 1872 of the names of the countries that had accepted the law of 7 Safar 1284.[54] This was probably not the first time that the court of Hamah was notified about this law because the Damascus courts were notified about the law in 1869. Also, the French consul in Hamah and Hims, Khawaja Faddul, son of

Table 6.12. Investment by Aleppo Citizens of Foreign Nationality in Real Property

Name	Nationality	Type of Property	Size	Location	Seller	Price (new piasters)	Date
Ghurra, daughter of Jurji Qasir	French	House	Whole	Mahallat al-Jallum al-Kubra	Mahmud Agha Sabbagh and wife	25,250	5 June 1870[a]
ʿAzra, son of Ibrahim Nahmad al-Yahudi	Austrian	House	Whole	Mahallat Bahsita	Salamun Sweika al-Yahudi	22,500	20 January 1873[b]
ʿAzra son of Rubin Kabay al-Yahudi	English	House	Whole	Mahallat ʿAbd al-Hayy (Abi ʿAjjur)	Naʿum and Ilyas Azraq	15,000	13 August 1874[c]

[a]LCR, Aleppo, vol. 301, p. 98, 5 Rabiʿ I 1287/5 June 1870.
[b]Ibid., vol. 302, p. 181, 21 Dhu al-Qaʿda 1289/20 January 1873.
[c]Ibid., vol. 304, p. 347, 29 Jumada II 1291/13 August 1874.

Antun Bambino,[55] was mentioned in a number of cases in the Hamah court records as buying real property, offering credit to villagers, and acting as guarantor to local persons long before that date. In a case dated 9 Rabi' II 1281/11 September 1864, three years before the law of 7 Safar 1284/10 June 1867 was promulgated and five years before its contents were communicated to the courts of Damascus, Faddul Bambino bought shares of one-half and one-fourth of whole vineyards from Muslim owners in the villages of Wattan and Marana in the Qada' of Hisn al-Akrad that was dependent on Hims. The total price Faddul paid for these properties was 2,500 piasters. Shortly afterwards, Faddul bought half a vineyard in the village of Qanaqiya for the price of 600 piasters.[56] In both cases, the sellers of the property stated in the sale contracts that the sale was final (*batt*) and legally binding (*lazim*), being neither revocable by redemption (*bay' bi-al-wafa'*) nor made under coercion (*ikrah*).

The fact that Faddul was mentioned in the two sale contracts concluded in 1864, and in other court documents at the time, as French consul, suggests that he was a French national, in which case his buying real property was illegal because it was done before the enactment of the law of 7 Safar 1284/10 June 1867. It could be, however, that Faddul did not have French nationality even though he was the consul of France and that he was buying property in his capacity as an Ottoman national of local origin. Faddul's sales contracts and those of his family and other Frenchmen were later on challenged, however, by the native sellers and were considered illegal in a case brought before the court of Hamah on 21 Rajab 1288/6 October 1871. The case was in implementation of a notification (*i'lam*) addressed to the *mutasarrif* of Hamah in accordance with a provincial order dated 2 Rabi' II 1288/ 21 June 1871 issued by the office of the council of provincial administration (*da'irat majlis idarat al-wilaya*) regarding the real property sold to Faddul and other French persons. Faddul Bambino, his daughter and wife, and a number of French notables—namely, Achille Bonweil (Bonneville?), Oge Biro, and Victor Burle—were asked by the *majlis al-dawla* (council of property registration), which dealt with the *tapu*, to undertake a review of their sale contracts and to exchange their unofficial documents of ownership with official documents in accordance with the new *tapu* regulations ("tabdil al-sukuk al-shar'iyya allati fi aydihim al-ghayr rasmiyya bi-hujaj shar'iyya wifqan li-al-nizam").

The property owned by Faddul Bambino, his family, and the other French persons consisted of plantations and arable lands in four villages in the region of Hims, which was within the jurisdiction of the *liwa* of Hamah. The four villages were Umm Sharshuh, Bigata, Suwayda, and Jiblaya. The court ruled that Faddul and associates relinquish certain properties to the sellers because of illegalities in their registration and retain other properties whose registration was valid. The issuing of the new *tapu* documents to the French nationals conforms to the law of 7 Safar 1284/10 June 1867.[57]

The four villages referred to in this case in the Hamah court records could have been the same four villages referred to in a dispatch by the French consul in Damascus dated 8 August 1872. This states that French nationals had bought half of the land and the plantations in four villages in the Hamah region and had reached agreement with the peasants for the exploitation of the land.[58]

The opposition of the peasants to Faddul Bambino and his French associates and the intervention of both the French consul in Damascus and the French ambassador in Istanbul on their behalf are described in detail. The dispatch says that only one French proprietor, Monsieur Chevalier, who owned property near Ba'albak, was not opposed by peasants.[59] Another Frenchman, Monsieur Deschamps, who bought property in the region of Ba'albak, was harassed by the peasants working the land, and his brother was attacked and suffered injuries as well.[60]

Twenty-five Christian and Nusayri persons from the Qada' of Safita, which fell within the sancak of Tripoli, sent a petition to the governor of Damascus on 1 Rajab 1286/17 October 1869, in their capacity as Ottoman subjects, accusing vice-consul Faddul Bambino of laying claim for three years to their lands in the Qada' of Hisn and the Nahiya of Hazzur. Whenever they tried to reclaim the produce of their lands, the associates of Bambino would tell them that the lands had become the property of France.[61]

Faddul Bambino was described by the French consul in Damascus in his dispatch dated 8 August 1872 as "un des plus grandes propriétaires non-rayas de la Syrie."[62] Born in Syria, Faddul was employed by the French as consular agent in Tripoli and then in Hamah in 1840. His services to the French were highly appreciated. During the socioeconomic riots in Damascus in 1860, Faddul defended the French consulate in Damascus and those taking refuge in it, which earned him the praise of Amir 'Abd al-Qadir al-Jaza'iri who himself defended the Christians. The French consul in Damascus described Faddul in 1863: "C'est un auxiliaire fort précieux pour le consulat de Damas."[63] To promote the standing of Faddul Bambino before the local authorities, he was elevated on 16 March 1853 to the rank of French vice-consul in the agency of Hims and Hamah and became answerable to the French consul in Damascus.[64] The French consulate in Damascus at the time was responsible for 53 French individuals who included 27 adult men (over 15 years of age), 17 women, and 9 children (under 15).[65]

Faddul Bambino, like other European nationals, usually acted through a deputy in matters of real property and debts.[66] He also had a *turjuman* (dragoman), who was accredited by the Ottoman authorities because Faddul was French vice-consul. On 3 October 1877, for example, the French consul in Damascus notified the governor of Syria that Khawaja Qaysar Abu Shanab was nominated in place of Khawaja Jurji 'Abbud as *turjuman* for the French vice-consul in Hamah.[67]

Faddul Bambino extended his real estate activity to Hamah itself. In one case he bought a house in Hamah for the enormous price of 16,000 piasters, 15,000 of which were deducted for a debt that the seller owed to Faddul. The rest of the money was paid to the seller.[68] Faddul was also mentioned in a dispute over the sale of cotton, which indicates the wide range of his economic activity.[69] He died in early 1879, while still French vice-consul in Hims and Hamah. His deputy, Monsieur Robert Bambino, dragoman, was nominated interim vice-consul by the French consul in Damascus pending the appointment of a successor. The consul notified the Ottoman authorities of this appointment.[70] Until a few months before his death, Faddul Bambino was still struggling, with the help of the French consul in Damascus, to regain possession of his property.[71]

The Hamah court records also mention Khawaja Musa Iskandar Wisi, Russian consul in Hims, as partner with a Muslim villager in the ownership of a mare. The consul appealed to the court of Hamah about the mare that was stolen.[72] No information is given about his dealings in real property.

POLITICAL IMPLICATIONS OF THE OWNERSHIP AND RENTAL OF REAL PROPERTY BY FOREIGN NATIONALS

The number of foreigners who bought real property in Syria as revealed in the court records of Damascus, Aleppo, and Hamah during the period of 1869 to 1873 was not great by any standard. Yet an important decision was taken by the Ottoman government when it gave foreigners the right to own real property in the Ottoman empire. The decision had political and economic repercussions in the empire at large.

The declared aim of the law of 7 Safar 1284/10 June 1867, as expounded in the Protocol attached to it, was to better control the access of foreigners to real property and to eliminate abuses in the real estate system. This does not seem to have been fully achieved. Abuses increased because the protégés who had become foreign nationals had it uppermost in their minds to secure foreign support in promoting and protecting their interests through exploitative financial dealings. Local Christians and

Jews, before and after the law of 7 Safar 1284/10 June 1867, were not prevented from buying and selling real property. When buying real property they had to establish their Ottoman identity through a document of notification (*'ilm wa-khabar*) from their relevant religious authorities to prove to the court that they were neither foreign nationals nor protégés of friendly countries.[73]

Becoming a protégé of a friendly country gave the protected person several privileges, including exemption from the payment of certain taxes. In 1852, the *farda*, a capitation tax imposed by the Ottomans on male adults, changed into a property tax, estimated with reference to rent, and became known as the *vergu* (rendered in Arabic *werko*),[74] was waived for foreign nationals. In a letter to the governor of Syria, the French consul in Damascus reminded him of the law he had issued exempting French nationals who owned property from paying the *vergu* tax unless they volunteered to pay it. The consul urged the governor to instruct the *qa'immaqam* of Ba'albak not to take this tax from the French owners of real property in his district.[75]

According to the memoir of the Aleppine Syriac Catholic school teacher Na'um Bakhkhash, each consul in the city of Aleppo had between fifteen and fifty protected persons. The Grand Vezier issued orders in April 1847 to the governor of Aleppo instructing him to allow every consul to have two dragomans, two guards (*qawwas*), and six servants (*khadam*). All other protégés should pay *farda* and *kharaj* (tax on land).[76] Five months later, in August 1847, an order from Sultan 'Abd al-Majid arrived in Aleppo, according to Bakhkhash, exempting the protégés from the payment of *farda* and *kharaj*, reimbursing them for what they had already paid of these taxes, and asking the governor of Aleppo to send his assistant the *kahiya* (*ketkhuda*) to the consuls to apologize to them for taking the taxes and to seek their good will ("wa-yursil al-basha al-kikhiya yasir askusa [excuse] li-al-qanasil wa-yasta'tif bi-khatirihim").[77]

The British consul in Damascus complained in 1870 about the exploitative dealings of the protégés and the local persons who had acquired British nationality. In a letter to the British ambassador in Constantinople, Sir Henry Elliot, dated 21 November 1870, the British consul in Damascus, Richard Austin, wrote:

> The European subject or protégé, instead of engaging in honest commerce, was encouraged to seek inordinate and usurious profits by sales to the government and by loans to the villagers. In such cases he of course relied entirely upon the protection of a foreign power on account of the sums to be expended in seeing native functionaries before repayment could be expected. Thus the consuls became as it were huissiers or bailiffs, whose principal duty was to collect the bad debts of those who had foreign passports.

The consul continues:

> Damascus contains a total of 48 adult males protected by H.B.M. Consulate, and of these the three principal are Messrs Daud Harari, Ishak Toby and Yaakub Stambouly. All are Jews who were admitted to, or whose fathers acquired, a foreign nationality, given with the benevolent object of saving them from Moslem cruelty and oppression in days gone by. These protégés have extended what was granted for the preservation of their lives, liberties and property, to transactions which rest entirely for success upon British protection.

The consul gives the example of the village of 'Arneh, on the eastern skirt of Mount Hermon, which owed Stambouly 106,000 piasters. The sum was originally 42,000 piasters. According to the consul, Stambouly had been allowing bills signed by the ignorant peasantry of the province to accumulate simple and compound interest, until the liabilities of the villagers had become greater than the value of the whole village. The consul then writes that he had not yet passed through a single settlement where Stambouly's debtors did not complain loudly of his proceedings. As well as 'Arneh, Stambouly had dealings in Azra

(Azra'), Zabadani, and Majdal Shams, a stronghold of the Druzes. In the words of the consul:

> Some villages have been partly depopulated by his exactions, and the injury done to the Druzes by thus driving them from the anti-Lebanon to the Hawran may presently be severly visited upon the Ottoman authorities. This British protégé is compelled every year in his quality of shubasi (farmer of revenue) to summon the village shaykhs and peasants, to imprison them and leave them lying in jail till he can squeeze from them as much as possible, and to injure them by quartering Hawali or policemen upon them, who plunder whatever they can.

After relating scandals committed by the protégés, the consul suggests to the ambassador that he inform the protégés that the consulate "will not assist them to recover debts from the Ottoman government, or from the villagers of the province, and that it will not abet them in imprisoning or in detaining the latter."[78]

According to the court records of Damascus, Daoud Harari's son, Raphael, an English national,[79] bought real property in three villages, Kafar Batna, Ashrafiyya, and Tall, in three separate contracts, worth a total of 12,685 piasters. The sum equals 42 percent of the total money invested by the Hararis in buying real property in the period between 1869 and 1873. Ya'qub Stambouly was reported in the court records of Damascus as lending a sum of 62,104.3 piasters to Mustafa Bey Hawasili, the chief of the paramilitary troops (*zabtiyya*) who wrought havoc in the Christian quarter of Damascus during the 1860 riots, for which he was held responsible and executed by the Ottomans.[80]

The French consul in Damascus also complained to his superiors of his involvement in the financial scandals of his protégés. On 15 January 1877, he submitted to the governor of Syria a petition by Khawaja Salamun Ishaq Farhi, a French national, in which he sought his intervention in the redemption of a debt of 15,000 piasters owed to him by Salim Dris from the village of Aftaris.[81] A month later, another petition was submitted to the French consul in Damascus from French national Hayim Levi

Bushi seeking his intervention in the recovery of the sum of 27 French gold liras that Bakir Agha Haram Aghasi owed him according to a legal document. Hayim requested the referral of his case to the commercial court in Damascus.[82]

Before foreigners were granted the right to own real property in the Ottoman empire in 1867, they were able to rent real property either on their own or in partnership with local people. A case in point is the rental partnership between Anistinaz, daughter of Shmuel Rudolph and wife of Johann Wetzstein, the Prussian consul in Damascus, and Musa Afandi, son of Sayyid Muhammad Abu al-Su'ud al-Muradi, a Damascene notable. Sayyid Sa'id Kilani Zadeh, acting as deputy for the partners, rented for them in equal shares five *qirat*s of all the lands of the village of Sakka in the Marj, to the east of Damascus, on the borders of the Ghuta (the green belt around Damascus). The partners also acquired the *mashadd maska* (right of usufruct) of these lands. The lands of Sakka were *waqf* to the Tiruzi mosque in Damascus. The lease period was for nine years, beginning on 16 Dhu al-Hijja 1274/28 July 1858. Because of the length of the lease, which exceeds the three-year limit (*'aqd*) authorized by the Hanafi *madhhab*, the official *madhhab* of the state, the lease contract had to be approved by the accommodating Shafi'i judge, whose ruling would then be endorsed and executed by the Hanafi judge. The yearly rent of the lands was 32 piasters. The lessees were entitled by the clause of *mugharasa* or *munasaba* to plant plantations in the land and to own as freehold all that they planted ("wa-mahma yaghrusu min dhalika yakun milkan talqan lahuma"). The clause, contrary to the established practice, was to the full advantage of the lessees. Usually lessees of *waqf* land owned from one-third to three-fourths of what they planted or built on *waqf* rented land.[83] Since foreigners were not entitled to own real property before the law of 7 Safar 1284/10 June 1867, it seems that the ownership of the plantations on the land jointly rented by Anistinaz and Musa Afandi al-Muradi was registered in the name of the latter who as a Muslim was entitled to own real property.

The law of 7 Safar 1284/10 June 1867 did not interfere with the right of foreigners to rent real property. After the promulgation of this law, however, those foreigners who rented *waqf* land became entitled by virtue of this law to own as real property part or all of the plantations and buildings they planted or built on the land. They also were entitled to care for the portion of the plantations and buildings belonging to the *waqf* by virtue of the clause of *musaqat* that allowed them to acquire 999 out of 1,000 shares of the produce of the portion of land belonging to the *waqf*. A common practice before the law of 7 Safar 1284/10 June 1867 from which foreigners profited had been to rent *waqf* property, spend money on maintenance and reconstruction on the property, and make the *raqaba* (guardianship) of the *waqf* indebted to the lessee for all the sums of money he spent on this work. The lessee thus kept the lease of the *waqf* property for many years, paying the rent from the accumulating debt the *waqf* owed him.

In Aleppo, for example, Marianah, daughter of Daoud Hess, *min ta'ifat al-afranj* (from the European community), and mother of Edward Barker, English consul in Swaydiyya (near Antioch) and later in Aleppo, rented on 1 Muharram 1242/5 August 1826 by way of *musaqat* all the trees in the *kuttab* garden, outside Bab al-Faraj in Aleppo, which was *waqf* land endowed by Hajj Musa al-Amiri. Marianah was to receive 99 shares out of 100 shares of the produce of the trees; the remaining share would go to the *waqf*. She was also allowed to plant trees in the empty spaces in the garden, and these were to belong to the *waqf*. After the *musaqat* was contracted along these terms, Marianah rented the remaining empty spaces in the garden, which were suitable for growing vegetables. She also rented the *hawsh* in the garden, which was made up of two floors. The rent for one year was 200 piasters, which Marianah paid in advance to the *mutawalli* (administrator) of the *waqf*.[84]

The lease contract was renewed apparently every year at the same rate of rent.[85] The format of the lease deviates from the normal rental procedure where the *musaqat* forms an integral clause in the lease contract. Here, the lease of the *musaqat* and the lease of the empty spaces for the growing of vegetables were separate. The important thing, however, is that Marianah was not allowed to own any part of the trees she planted in the garden, which were to belong to the *waqf*. These terms are unlike those of the lease contract of Anistinaz and Musa al-Muradi in the village of Sakka, which allowed them to own as freehold all that they planted on the *waqf* land that they rented. Marianah was compensated for this apparent limitation by her continued lease of the *waqf* property and the accumulation of debt on the *raqaba* of the *waqf*. As proof of this, Marianah transferred to her son Edward Barker, English consul in Swaydiyya, on 21 Ramadan 1266/31 July 1850, the amount of 79,422 piasters, which the *kuttab* garden of the *waqf* owed her ("raqbatan lahu 'ala al-amakin al-madhkura"), apparently for construction work and other expenses incurred at the *waqf* property.[86] If the rent of the *waqf* was 200 piasters per year, then Marianah and her son Edward Barker could rent the *waqf* property for 379 years to redeem the debt. Marianah, however, continued to rent the *waqf* in her name, as a document dated 1 Muharram 1273/1 September 1856 indicates.[87] The name of her son, Edward Barker, replaced hers as lessee of the *waqf* in the lease contract dated 1 Muharram 1287/3 April 1870.[88] Edward Barker had by then become English consul in Aleppo.

Marianah's long lease of the *kuttab* garden in Aleppo profiting from the debt owed her by the *waqf* was paralleled by the lease of a *waqf* caravanserai (*khan*) in Aleppo by English merchants. These merchants rented the *khan* for decades until it became known after them in a document from the 1830s as Bayt al-Inkliz and later on as Khan al-Inkliz. Khan al-Inkliz, called in the lease documents Khan Altaf, was located in Mahallat al-Jallum al-Kubra. It was a *waqf* founded by Mu'itab (rendered Mutab) Ahmad Pasha and his wife Humayun Khatun at an unknown date. It consisted of eleven rooms (*oda*s) on the ground and upper floors, a courtyard, three *bayka*s, and a *qaysariyya* (workshops) for artisanal use. The structure of the *khan* underwent periodical reconstruction work executed and paid for by the English merchants with the approval of the administrator of the *waqf* and at its expense.

A series of lease documents written in Arabic and preserved in the Public Record Office in London shows that Khan Altaf was rented by English citizens from at least 1147/1735 up to at least 1298/1881, which is as far as these documents go. On 1 Ramadan 1147/25 January 1735, the administrator of the *waqf* leased the *khan* to Khawaja Clark, son of Clark from the English community of *musta'minin* (foreigners granted *aman* or security) in Aleppo. The lease period was for seven years and eight months ending at the end of Rabi' II 1155/3 July 1742. The rent for the whole period amounted to 812 2/3 piasters and was paid in advance, the yearly rate being 106 piasters. On 1 Muharram 1155/8 March 1742, a new lease contract was issued to Khawaja Werne and his partner Khawaja Baker, son of Baker from the English community of *musta'minin* in Aleppo. The lease was for two years ending on 8 Dhu al-Hijja 1156/23 January 1744, at an annual rent of 106 piasters. Nearly a hundred years later, on 17 Rabi' II 1253/21 July 1837, the administrator and the superintendent of the Khan Altaf acknowledged to the then lessees, William Barker and his mother, Marianah Hess, that the *waqf* owed them 40,000 piasters by way of *raqaba,* which is in effect accumulated debt on the *waqf* for money the lessees had spent on repairs, reconstruction work, and other maintenance costs over a period of many years. The *khan* was referred to in this document as Bayt al-Inkliz.

In a later document, dated 12 Sha'ban 1269/21 May 1853, the same *waqf khan* owed Edward, son of John Barker, and his mother Marianah Hess, who rented the *khan* for 352 piasters a year, a sum of 14,157 piasters for repairs according to a document dated 15 Rabi' II 1241/28 November 1825, in addition to another sum of 40,000 piasters for other repairs mentioned in the document dated 27 Rabi' II 1253/31 July 1837. Other repairs in the same *khan* cost an additional 21,000 piasters during the period up to the drafting of the lease contract on 12 Sha'ban 1269/21 May 1853. The grand total for repairs that the Khan Altaf owed to Edward Barker and his mother Marianah Hess up to 1853 thus amounted to 75,157 piasters. The lessees gave up 1,000 piasters as a contribution to the *waqf* which left the total debt owed them at 74,157 piasters. The rent of the *khan* being 352 piasters a year, the lessees could thus keep the *khan* in their rent for 210 years to redeem the debt.

In a document dated 15 Rabi' II 1281/17 September 1864, the same Khan Altaf was mentioned as being indebted to its lessee Edward John Barker, the English consul (his mother Marianah was not mentioned), for the sum of 143.5 Mejidiyya gold liras (15,067 piasters) for repairs done during the period between 1 Muharram 1278/9 July 1861 and the end of Rabi' I 1281/2 September 1864. The earlier debts were still standing. Further debts owed by the *khan* to Consul Edward Barker for repairs were indicated in three other documents in the years 1287/1870, 1295/1878, and 1298/1881.[89] A uniform statement appears at the end of each of the documents dated between 1281 and 1298/ 1864 and 1881 that mentions that should the lessee (Consul Edward Barker) decide to give up the rental of the *khan,* the debt the *waqf* owed him would be considered a contribution to the *waqf.* On the other hand, should the administrator of the *waqf* evict the lessee from the *khan,* he would be obliged to pay the lessee what the *khan* owed him in full. If the lessee decided to sublet the *khan,* he had the right to do so. Such statements could only encourage the English consul to keep renting the *khan.* According to the available documents, 150 years had already elapsed since the *khan* had been first rented out to English individuals in 1735. If the English had bought the *khan* after foreigners had been allowed to own real property in 1867, they would not have been better off than they were renting it along the terms described. Since the *khan* was *waqf,* they could, however, have bought only the structure, not the land, and they would have been liable to the payment of taxes from which the *waqf* was exempted. By becoming owners of the *khan* (that is, its structure), they would themselves have paid for repairs and maintenance in the *khan*.

The rental by foreign nationals of *waqf* agricultural property especially had political implications in a politically tense region. This was particularly the case when the lessees of *waqf* land were foreign Christians and Jews, who were able by virtue of the terms of the lease contract to own property, such as trees or buildings, on the land and to claim it long after their lease contract had expired and they no longer cultivated the land. The lease contract of *waqf* land usually included the traditional clause of *mugharasa* or *munasaba* (that is, plantation), which allowed the lessee to own as freehold part or all of what he planted on the land. He was also allowed to own part or all of what he built on the rented land in th same way as a local Muslim was entitled to when renting *waqf* land. Foreign nationals also had an advantage over the local Muslims in that they still enjoyed the legal immunities provided to them by virtue of the treaties between their countries and the Ottoman state.

Despite the establishment by the Ottoman state of European-style courts in the second half of the nineteenth century, the *shari'a* courts still had jurisdiction over the rental of *waqf* land well into the early years of the French Mandate. The court never asked questions about the motives of the foreign nationals for renting small or large tracts of *waqf* land, whether the lease included whole villages or not, or whether the rental contract had the clause allowing the lessee to own property on the land. The court also never questioned the foreign lessee about whether he knew the land he was renting or whether he had ever set foot in the province where the land was located. The main concern of the court was to check the power of attorney given by the absentee foreign national to the local agent deputizing for him who was usually of the same religion as the foreign national.

The French mandatory power, by contrast, was reluctant to meddle in the affairs of the *shari'a* court and the rental of *waqf* land for fear of alienating Muslim public opinion and antagonizing the influential foreign lessees. When litigation arose between foreign nationals, in their capacity as lessees of *waqf* land and owners of property standing on it, and the administrator or supervisor of the *waqf,* or when peasants working the land challenged the ownership of the absentee foreign nationals, the French administration usually referred the case to the appropriate court to avoid pressure from either side. The court usually ruled in favor of the *waqf* beneficiaries, whether those were charitable establishments (such as mosques, convents, schools, or hospitals) or were handicapped and sick people (such as the lepers, who had whole villages assigned to them as *waqf* for their upkeep). The rationale of the court in issuing its judgment was that the foreign nationals were absentee owners who did not live on or off the land and that the peasants who worked the land and lived on it for many years were entitled, together with the beneficiaries of the *waqf,* to the revenue of the land.

Charitable *waqf* property also suffered from abuse by local notables who usurped its revenue in their capacity as administrators or supervisors of the *waqf.* Deprived of their revenue, many charitable establishments fell into ruin and eventually disappeared. Very often a street was named after the mosque that was built in it. The name continued, but the mosque did not. The Damascene Hanbali scholar, Shakyh 'Abd al-Qadir Badran, writing in the first half of the twentieth century, visited many sites in Damascus and its environs where charitable establishments had once stood. Fittingly, he entitled the book in which he related his findings, *Munadamat al-atlal wa-musamarat al-khayal* (Speaking to the ruins and chatting with phantoms).[90] This situation was not particular to Damascus and applied to other regions in geographical Syria (*Bilad al-Sham*).

Waqf property that had traditionally played a major role in financing basic religious, educational, and humanitarian services thus fell into disuse throughout Syria. Government intervention and the removal of *waqf* from the control of the *shari'a* court and the traditional administrators and supervisors to the control of the ministry of *awqaf* also did not help in promoting the essential societal functions and benefits of the *waqf*. Administrative routine and corruption limited the benefits of the *waqf*. In 1949, the first military government in Syria dissolved the family *waqf* (*waqf ahli* or *dhurri*), which was obstructing urban planning. The charitable *waqf* (*waqf khayri*), however, remained under the control of the ministry of *awqaf*, but it no longer performs its full social programs as in the past. The nationalization by the socialist governments of large agricultural properties in the late 1950s and 1960s ended the private ownership of properties standing on *waqf* as well as *miri* (state) land.

NOTES

1. For these laws, see Stanley Fisher, *Ottoman Land Laws* (London: Oxford University Press, 1919), 43–57, 63–68.
2. For examples of *mugharasa* and the *musaqat,* see Abdul-Karim Rafeq, "City and Countryside in a Traditional Setting: The Case of Damascus in the First Quarter of the Eighteenth Century," in *The Syrian Land in the Eighteenth and Nineteenth Century,* Berliner Islamstudien, vol. 5, ed. Thomas Philipp (Stuttgart: Steiner, 1992), 312–23.
3. For more information on the ownership of plantations on *waqf* land and on the transfer of the *mashadd maska,* see Rafeq, "City and Countryside," 295–332.
4. See Abdul-Karim Rafeq, "Ghazza, dirasa 'umraniyya wa-ijtima'iyya wa-iqtisadiyya min khilal al-watha'iq al-shar'iyya, 1273–1277 A.H./1857–1861 A.D.," in *Buhuth fi-al-tarikh al-ijtima'i wa-al-iqtisadi li-bilad al-Sham fi-al-'asr al-hadith* (Damascus, n.p., 1985), 1–95, especially 41.
5. For these two laws, see George Young, *Corps de droit ottoman* (Oxford: Clarendon Press, 1900–1906), 2:226–29, 238–40.
6. For the text of this law in English translation, see Fisher, *Ottoman Land Laws,* 57–59; F. Ongley, trans., *The Ottoman Land Code,* rev. and ann. by Horace E. Miller (London: Clowes, 1892), 168–71. The Turkish version and an Arabic translation are given in *Min al-dustur al-jadid,* trans. Niqula al-Naqqash (Beirut: al-Aba' al-

yasu'iyyin, 1873), 167–71. An Arabic translation by Nawfal Ni'mat Allah Nawfal, revised by Khalil al-Khuri appears in *al-Dustur* 1 (Beirut, 1301 A.H.): 68–69.

7. See, for example, Law Court Records (LCR), Damascus, vol. 576, p. 17.

8. For examples, see LCR, Damascus, vol. 563, pp. 4, 17, 80, 93, 95, 224; vol. 576, pp. 15, 17, 28; vol. 586, pp. 3–4, 9, 31, 63.

9. See, for example, LCR, Damascus, vol. 576, pp. 15, 17, 28, 46.

10. Public Record Office, London, Foreign Office (FO), 78/2259, p. 64.

11. See, for example, LCR, Damascus, vol. 576, p. 15, cases dated 28 Sha'ban 1282/26 January 1866, p. 17, 7 Ramadan 1282/24 January 1866.

12. Gabriel Baer, *Fellah and Townsman in the Middle East: Studies in Social History* (London: Frank Cass, 1982), 109 ff.

13. See, for example, LCR, Damascus, vol. 634, p. 64, 22 Shawwal 1289/23 December 1872.

14. See, for example, ibid., vol. 631, p. 98, 13 Dhu al-Qa'da 1288/24 January 1872.

15. For examples from the Aleppo court records, see LCR, Aleppo, vol. 298, p. 224, 12 Rajab 1284/9 November 1867, p. 225, 29 Rajab 1284/26 November 1867, p. 315, 16 Dhu al-Hijja 1284/9 April 1868, p. 316, 17 Safar 1285/9 June 1868; vol. 300, p. 150, 10 Ramadan 1285/25 December 1868; vol. 301, p. 33, 3 Rabi' I 1287/3 June 1870, p. 89, 6 Jumada I 1287/4 August 1870, p. 171, 16 Dhu al-Hijja 1287/9 March 1871, p. 173, 9 Muharram 1288/ 31 March 1871, p. 177, 15 Dhu al-Hijja 1287/8 March 1871, p. 227, 25 Rabi' II 1288/14 July 1871; vol. 302, p. 26, 17 Muharram 1289/27 March 1872, p. 32, 21 Muharram 1289/31 March 1872, p. 135, 29 Rajab 1289/2 October 1872. For examples from the Damascus court records, see citations from these records in other footnotes.

16. Fisher, *Ottoman Land Laws*, 57, renders the word more accurately as "property"; Ongley, *Ottoman Land Code*, 168, renders the first part of the preamble as follows: "In order to extend the riches and the prosperity of the Imperial Domain."

17. For sources referring to the text of the law in different languages, see Fisher, *Ottoman Land Laws*, 57–59, and Ongley, *Ottoman Land Code*, 168–17; FO 78/2115, Constantinople, 18 June 1867;

Min al-dustur al-jadid, 167–69; and al-Dustur, 1: 68–71, together with the Protocol.

18. For the text of the Protocol in French, see FO 78/2115, attached to dispatch from Constantinople, 21 June 1867.

19. FO 78/2115, no. 142 Confidential, Constantinople, 10 April 1867.

20. Ibid., no. 60, Constantinople, 13 December 1867.

21. Ibid., no. 187, Paris, 20 December 1867.

22. Ibid., no. 641, Paris, 16 July 1868; Constantinople, 2 November 1868.

23. Ministère des affaires étrangères, Nantes (MAEN), Fonds: Damas-Consulat, vol. 25, Therapia, 17 August 1868 (preceded by the French text of the imperial decree of 7 Safar 1284 and the Protocol with commentary). A printed text of the 17 août 1868 circular by the French ambassador in Constantinople appears in Damas-Consulat, vol. 66.

24. For the text of the law, see Young, *Corps de droit ottoman*, 2:226–29.

25. See text in LCR, Damascus, vol. 601, p. 1.

26. See text in ibid., vol. 602, p. 2.

27. LCR, Hamah, vol. 61, p. 328, end Rajab 1289/3 October 1872.

28. For these regulations, see Young, *Corps de droit ottoman*, 2:223–29

29. For the Mishaqa family, see Mikhayil Mishaqa, *Murder, Mayhem, Pillage and Plunder: The History of Lebanon in the Eighteenth and Nineteenth Centuries*, trans. Wheeler M. Thackston, Jr. (Albany: State University of New York Press, 1988), 1 ff, 255, 261, 270; see also LCR, Damascus, vol. 610, p. 85, 22 Jumada I 1286/30 August 1869; vol. 614, p. 52, 13 Dhu al-Qa'da 1286/14 February 1870.

30. LCR, Damascus, vol. 643, p. 117, 12 Jumada I 1290/8 July 1873.

31. Ibid., vol. 487, p. 250, 17 Jumada II 1273/12 February 1857.

32. MAEN, Damas-Consulat, vol. 30 (correspondence with the authorities, November 1873-December 1880), Arabic letter no. 162, 15 January 1875.

33. Another Jew from the Bushi family, Hayim Levi Bushi, had French nationality. Hayim asked the French consul in Damascus to inter-

vene on his behalf with the governor of the province of Syria about a debt of 27 French gold liras that Bashir Agha Haram Aghasi owed him. See ibid., 25 February 1875.

34. LCR, Aleppo, vol. 302, p. 135, 29 Rajab 1289/2 October 1872.
35. Ibid., vol. 301, p. 306, 24 Ramadan 1287/18 December 1870.
36. Ibid., vol. 304, p. 232, 14 Rabi' II 1291/31 May 1874.
37. Ibid., vol. 328, p. 88, 17 Shawwal 1300/21 August 1883.
38. Abraham Marcus, *The Middle East on the Eve of Modernity: Aleppo in the Eighteenth Century* (New York: Columbia University Press, 1989), 46.
39. Na'um Bakhkhash, *Akhbar Halab,* ed. Yusuf Qushaqji (Aleppo, 1985–1992), 2:428.
40. Ibid., 1:39. 195; 2:29, 356, 428.
41. MAEN, Alep-Consulat (Aleppo), vol. 27 (1871–72), two letters addressed by David di Picciotto to the French consul in Aleppo, dated 31 July 1872 and 6 November 1872.
42. LCR, Aleppo, vol. 304, p. 511, 23 Sha'ban 1292/24 September 1875.
43. Ibid., vol. 302, p. 26, 17 Muharram 1289/27 March 1872.
44. Joseph Schacht, *An Introduction to Islamic Law* (Oxford: Clarendon Press, 1964), 78.
45. Bakhkhash, *Akhbar Halab,* 3:236.
46. LCR, Aleppo, vol. 301, p. 95, 25 Rabi' II 1287/25 July 1870.
47. A Muscovy gold lira was equal to about 100 piasters in Damascus at the time.
48. LCR, Aleppo, vol. 304, p. 155, 29 Safar 1287/31 May 1870.
49. Bakhkhash, *Akhbar Halab,* 2:42. For the Popolani family in Aleppo, see ibid., 1: 30, 106, 173, 210.
50. LCR, Aleppo, vol. 301, p. 177, 15 Dhu al-Hijja 1287/8 March 1871.
51. Schacht, *Introduction to Islamic Law,* 78.
52. MAEN, Alep-consulat, vol. 28 (1873), 30 September 1873, 31 March 1874.
53. Ibid., Letter by Vigoureuse to French consul in Aleppo, 26 October 1870.
54. LCR, Hamah, vol. 61, p. 327, 1 Rajab 1289/4 September 1872.
55. The name, Jan (Jean) occasionally preceded his name, and Bambino was very often written Banbino.

56. LCR, Hamah, vol. 60, pp. 40–41, 9 Rabi' II 1281/11 September 1864; see also p. 64, 23 Jumada I 1281/24 October 1864.

57. For details about this case, see LCR, Hamah, vol. 61, pp. 260–61, 21 Rajab 1288/6 October 1871.

58. Ministère des affaires étrangères, Paris, Correspondance commerciale, vol. 5, 5 August 1872, quoted by Abdul-Karim Rafeq, "The Impact of Europe on a Traditional Economy: The Case of Damascus, 1840–1870," in *Economie et sociétés dans l'Empire ottoman (fin du XVIIIe–début du XXe Siècle)*, ed. Jean-Louis Bacqué-Grammont and Paul Dumont (Paris: CNRS, 1983), 411–32, at 432.

59. MAEN, Damas-Consulat, vol. 65 (1851–1913), Damascus, 8 August 1872.

60. Ibid., 25 May 1873, 30 May 1873.

61. Ibid., 8 August 1872.

62. Ibid., vol. 72 (1827–1896) ("Surat al-'ard mahdar al-muqaddam min ahali qada' Safita al-tabi' li-sanjaq Tarablus ila dawlat-lu afandim wali wilayat Suriyya fi ghurrat Rajab 1286/7 October 1869.")

63. Ibid., vol. 65, Damascus, 21 August 1863.

64. Ibid., 14 November (1872 ?).

65. Ibid., "Etat numérqiue des Français domiciliés dans l'arrondissement consulaire de Damas au moi de novembre 1872."

66. See, for example, LCR, Hamah, vol. 59, pp. 16, 340, 353.

67. MAEN, Damas-Consulat, vol. 29, letter in Arabic sent by French consul in Damascus to the governor of the province of Syria dated 3 October 1877.

68. LCR, Hamah, vol. 59, p. 186. The presumed date of the case is 28 Safar 1280/14 August 1863. The case is incomplete in the Hamah register and has no date. Faddul was challenged by the deputy of the seller about the sale. The names of witnesses are given at the end.

69. Ibid, p. 16, 19 Jumada I 1280/1 November 1863.

70. MAEN, Damas-Consulat, vol. 30, order of 8 March 1879.

71. Ibid., Damas-Consulat, 27 August 1878.

72. LCR, Hamah, vol. 63, p. 185, 29 Rajab 1287/25 October 1870.

73. See for examples, LCR, Damascus, vol. 563, p. 4, 11 Sha'ban 1281/9 January 1865; see also pp. 17, 80, 93, 95, 224.

74. See Abdul-Karim Rafeq, "The Impact of Europe," 430.

75. MAEN, Damas-Consulat, vol. 30, Damascus, 7 November 1877.
76. Bakhkhash, *Akhbar Halab*, 2:51, 56.
77. Ibid., 2:66.
78. FO 78/2259, Damascus, 21 November 1870.
79. See above p. 15.
80. See Abdul-Karim Rafeq, "New Light on the 1860 riots in Ottoman Damascus," *Die Welt des Islams* 28 (1988): 412–30, at 426.
81. MAEN, Damas-Consulat, vol. 30, Damascus, 15 January 1875.
82. Ibid., 25 February 1875.
83. See the text of the lease contract in Ingeburg Huhn, *Der Orientalist Johann Gottfried Wetzstain als Preusischer Konsul in Damaskus (1849–1861)* (Berlin: Klaus Schwartz, 1989), 258. I failed to locate the copy of this lease contract in the Damascus court records probably because of the irregularity of a foreign woman owning plantations on *waqf* land by virtue of the *mugharasa* clause, even though *waqf* was in partnership with a Muradi Damascene notable.
84. FO 861/37, Aleppo, Arabic document dated 1 Muharram 1242/5 August 1826.
85 See, for example, ibid., 1 Muharram 1248/31 May 1832, 1 Muharram 1265/27 November 1848.
86. Ibid., 21 Ramadan 1266/31 July 1850.
87. Ibid., 1 Muharram 1273/1 September 1856.
88. Ibid., 1 Muharram 1287/3 April 1870.
89. All the documents dealing with the lease of Khan Altaf by the English are given in FO 861/35, Aleppo.
90. 'Abd al-Qadir Badran, *Munadamat al-atlal wa-musamarat al-khayal* (Damascus: al-Maktab al-Islami, 1960), 53, 145.

SEVEN

Practicing Musha': Common Lands and the Common Good in Southern Syria under the Ottomans and the French

Birgit Schaebler

INTRODUCTION

Musha' is probably still the most puzzling and controversial form of land tenure found in the Middle East. Neither its origins nor its real spread and importance seem to have been sufficiently explained. *Musha'* was identified by the officials of the Mandate powers and described in a number of works written during Mandate times. Of these, a few take up the task of describing diligently and faithfully what had actually been found. Others jump from a very restricted data base to daring generalizations that are heavily influenced by the European experience.[1] This point is important: while agricultural societies all over the world do share certain universal features, like the peasant household at the core of society, it should not be assumed that all agricultural societies necessarily follow the same path of development as the European ones.[2]

Scholarship on *musha'* so far has concentrated on establishing the main basic features of this complicated system, on the compatibility of *musha'* with Islamic law, and, from an anthropological perspective, on placing it "as a variation of systems between

241

geography and institution."[3] This contribution to the discussion of *musha'* will concentrate on the microhistory of a specific area and on the practice of *musha'*—that is, the ways in which common lands were redistributed. It will also link this practice with general notions of the common good that were operating within the communities in Southern Syria. The common good does not, of course, mean here the Western traditions of the common good starting with Cicero. Neither does it mean what has been termed the great and the little tradition of Islam.[4] It is rather the aim of this chapter to find out how the communal organization of land is related to political notions of a common good.

This chapter also seeks to locate *musha'* within the microhistory of a certain space. Like every other sociopolitical practice, *musha'* is continuously contested between different forces bargaining for different ends. In our case, we even have a peasant war erupting out of the practice of *musha'*. It is this connection with status, politics, and power that we shall uncover. Other problems with regard to *musha'*, generally still unanswered, are the impact of the Ottoman Land Code of 1858 and of French colonial land regulations, and the question of its compatibility with large landholdings.

In *musha'* villages, and maybe in preindustrial agricultural societies in general, land is more than a mere means of production. Every aspect of land tenure is intricately connected with the sociopolitical life of the community. Most conflicts seem to arise over access to land or rather the abuse of perceived rights to the land. Land issues in the Middle East are complicated because of the vast variety of forms of landholding. "Al-ard btifriq bi-l-shibr" (land differs from one foot of ground to the next) is an old saying for which the area under investigation in this chapter provides ample proof. We will look at the microhistory of three adjacent landscapes, inhabited by two different communities: the northern, mountainous part of the Hawran highlands, inhabited by Druze settlers since the early eighteenth century; the southern part of the Hawran highlands, consisting of a wide fertile plain and settled by later Druze immigrants, after 1860; and, to a somewhat lesser degree, the adjoining stretch of the huge Hawran plain to the west of the highlands, inhabited by Sunni Muslims. There is also a partly autochthonous Christian population living in these areas, mainly in the Druze highlands, which is highly adapted to Druze society, donning the same dress and in whose villages the same forms of land tenure are reproduced.

The latter phenomenon hints at an important point. Ethnicity, so often willfully overlooked by social historians, does play an important role: at least in the frontier regions of the Ottoman empire it was the local, communal customs that determined the way land was accessed, worked, and handed on to the next generation, "below" or "beyond" Ottoman law. Even more, the amount of taxes levied by the state and the degree of privileges and exemptions granted by the state were a function of the relative strength and bargaining power of a given community. It is hardly astonishing, therefore, that the practice of *musha'* varied and depended on the inner workings of society and its general notions of a common good.

MUSHA': THE TERM AND THE STATE OF THE ART

Early attempts to explain the *musha'* system focused on lifestyle. It was either assumed that the origins of the system go back to the process of settlement of nomads or that, rather, a *sens paysan* was indispensable to the development of such a system, attributing it to the sedentary peasant.[5] Later studies avoided issues of lifestyle in regard to the origin of *musha'* in favor of an examination of the specifics of collective land acquisition.[6] Other explanations yet center on the hypothesis of a very old state regulation,[7] on the Ottoman system of tax collection,[8] or more pragmatically, on how the system is well adapted to the practical necessities of rain-fed cultivation in combination with livestock breeding on the frontier to the steppe.[9] Geographers have been preoccupied with the peculiar field form accompanying *musha'*: long striped fields, with the strips up to several kilometers long but often only a few meters wide.

Recently, a more systematic analysis has been put forward by Firestone, who summarizes in the last of a series of articles the state of the art on *musha'* and places this form of land tenure squarely in the context of Islamic law. This somewhat legalistic and economistic approach provoked criticism from an anthropological perspective: Mundy swiftly took up Firestone's last contribution and suggested that *musha'* should be viewed more as a "variation of systems between geography and institution" than as a fixed legal and economic category.[10]

To begin with, even the term *musha'* itself is controversial. It is usually taken to mean common land, land held in shares. In practicing *musha'*, the single most important element is the periodic redistribution of lots. In the Hawran, the expression *al-ard musha'* is first reported in a newspaper article of 1910. In a series of articles, the Damascene newspaper *al-Muqtabas* covered the southern Syrian countryside and its integration (or rather the lack thereof) into the state and the reforms of the Young Turk era. The particular article sought to further the cause of the Hawranis of the plain in connection with their problems with their neighbors, the Druzes of the highlands, and was penned by Khalil Rif'at "al-Hawrani."[11] The sentence in question reads:

> The land of the villages of the Hawran is held in common [*musha'*] in the hands of its inhabitants and every house [extended household] holds a share because the land of the village is distributed among the houses. And in the Hawran there is no village belonging to a single man, with very few exceptions.[12]

Here *musha'* is obviously used to designate "common, undivided" land, in the same way Firestone reports its usage in Palestine with regard to a house not yet divided up among heirs.[13] It is most remarkable that in the minute account of the Hawran village of Busra in Le Play's *Les Ouvriers de l'Orient* of 1877, based on local fieldwork carried out in 1857, the same expression seems to have been used. The French sentence in question reads: "La propriété de ce territoire est indivise, et chacun en cultive une étendue proportionnée au nombre de paires de boeufs qu'il possède; aussi la paire de boeufs ou Fedhlan est-elle l'unité généralement employée pour apprécier la richesse de paysans."[14] A French report of 1936 speaks of the "système de 'moush'a' (propriété commune)" for the Hawran plain.[15]

In the highlands, however, which also featured the common lands, the term *musha'* is used to designate the old communal grazing land of the village, often even termed "*al-musha' al-qadim.*" Even village elders, traditionally most concerned with the village lands, are not aware of the term *musha'* designating a system as it came to do during Mandate times. A local thesis in agricultural planning and administration, dealing with the history of agriculture in the Hawran highlands, defines the term as follows:

> The lands of the [Druze] mountain came in two forms: (1) the *musha'* lands (*aradi al-musha'*), representing grazing grounds and forest, which the inhabitants were not allowed to use for agriculture and only for grazing; (2) the lands under the plow (*ard al-falaha*).[16]

The periodic redistribution of these lands under the plow is designated in this text as *i'adat tawzi' al-ard*. Neither does the earliest description found thus far of such a redistribution, in Burckhardt's 1810 to 1812 account of the highlands, mention the word *musha'*, although he diligently collected all kinds of agricultural terms in Arabic.

All this seems to suggest that in the plain, *musha'* was used in the general sense of an undivided unit described above and that one answer to the question of a Mandate official, asking to whom the land of a Hawran plain village belonged, was most probably *al-ard musha'*. From there the term made its way as "*musha'* system" into the literature. In the Hawran highlands, however, the answer must have been different since here we find a form of "manorial *musha'*" and the term *musha'* was used quite distinctly (communal grazing lands).

Before turning to the three landscapes that are the focus of this chapter, I want to offer an overview of what I see as the basic characteristics of this form of land tenure. What I would like to introduce, in keeping with the theme of this book, is the notion that the phenomenon of *musha'* should be thought of more in terms of access to land than in terms of land itself. Starting with this condition in mind, the most basic trait of *musha'* is that the bulk of a village's arable land was held in common, in shares, in most areas called *sahm*s. The cultivated land was divided into several sections, each of which was fairly homogeneous with regard to soil type, terrain, access from the village, and other advantages. Each share was entitled to an, ideally, equal portion of the common cultivated land as a whole and a portion of each section. These shares, which gave access to land, were periodically redistributed.

The number of shares was determined in several different ways. The criteria in use were either based on what I define as the principle of "productive capital" of the community (the number of plows, plow animals, or males capable of plowing), the principle of "human capital" of the community (the number of males of any age in a given village), or, as in the area I studied, the number of clan heads (clans). The first method can be called the *faddan* method, and the second the *dhukur* method. The case I studied stands out in that it features an especially unequal way of determining shares: the shaykh of the village, the chief of the most powerful clan, held the right to a quarter of the shares—that is, access to a quarter of the village lands and its surplus.

Martha Mundy, concentrating on the microsystems of village production, has this finding to add: in the idiom in which *musha'* land is conceived, she maintains, the male or the team of oxen corresponds with different forms of labor and organization of work in the fields. In areas where cultivation was geared toward the subsistence of the village but where cattle were raised for the market, the unit of production was formed of a man and his wife (a bachelor counted only half), and the fields could be worked with a mule or horse as well as with a pair of oxen. In contrast, in areas where wheat was grown for the market, the unit of production was thought of in terms of oxen teams—the capital, to which human labor could also be attached by means of contract.[17]

The number of shares in a given village could be open or fixed. Villages that practiced open-share distributions admitted additions (that is, newcomers) to the shares determined under the locally accepted principle (plows, males able to plow, males regardless of age, males of high standing). The shares gave access to nonspecific, changing pieces of land or to fixed, stabilized pieces of land, to that new lots might be added, depending on the availability of fresh land that could be made arable. Village communities that had fixed the number of shares only redistributed the established number of shares. The fixation of the number of shares did not, however, automatically entail their attachment to fixed lots of land. It is important here, again, to note the dual aspect of shares giving access to land and the lots of land themselves.

Both forms of distribution had to come to terms with population growth. If the lots of land had not been stabilized, they could be reapportioned. If they had been stabilized, they could not be reapportioned. Thus tiny little portions of land, 1/10 or even 1/100 of an original plot, came into being. As we shall see, the question of stabilization of plots also entailed aspects of power and, simply, greed.

It is at this juncture, also, that the state comes into play, with its choice either to register the land or to register the shares. Mundy, working on the microhistory of land registration by the Ottoman Defterkhane, found that wherever land was registered in shares, the number of shares was fixed. Fixation of the number of shares, therefore, she argues, has to be seen as a result of registration and not a stage in the process of the dissolution of the whole *musha'* system.

This chapter shows that the practice of *musha'* went on even after Ottoman registration, thus giving the next land-registering authority, the French Mandate, its own nut to crack. Unlike the British land offices, those of the French Mandate seemed to learn in the process that it was more advisable to register each villager's share in the common lands as a fraction of the total, without attaching the title to any specific piece of land. They registered the share, the right to access to the land, but not the land itself, on the grounds that *musha'* was deeply rooted in the social life of the village communities.

In the following I undertake to place the practice of *musha'* into its sociopolitical setting. The logic of *musha'*, I argue, is to be found in the sociopolitical rather than in the economic or legal sphere. *Musha'* is not to be seen as a fixed category but as a practice that both expresses and reflects status and power relations and the notion of a common good within a community.

THE SOURCES AND THE SETTING

Sources

The sources most commonly used for the analysis of land tenure and agricultural life in the Middle East are Ottoman court records. But, as Cemal Kafadar reminded participants in a conference on law and its application in the Ottoman empire, there are various important rural and non-Sunni communities that, for some reason or other, used their own procedures of conflict resolution and communal administration and were therefore not represented in the *shari'a* courts. As for the nineteenth century, the *sened tapu* (title deed) registers of the Defterkhane, housed in the Tapu ve Kadastro Genel Müdürlüğü in Ankara, are still closed to scholars.[18] These communities, then, do not appear in the court records and other Ottoman legal sources. Nor did they, as rural people, write up their own chronicles.

For long stretches of time, therefore, the only rich sources historians have at their disposal are oral traditions and European travel and consular reports and later the archives of the mandatory powers. European sources tend to come under heavy criticism for their "Western bias" and their tinted information, flawed by the feeling of superiority and hostility toward the Ottoman empire. It has to be taken into consideration, however, that there are huge differences between travel reports of the first half of the nineteenth century and earlier and those of later times. While many of the early travelers undoubtedly saw themselves as "scientific travelers," trying to give honest descriptions of what they saw, in the tradition of Volney's claim for an enlightened "classe questionneuse par excellence," most of the later travel reports, having become a literary genre, display the triumphant sense of European superiority and reflect more on the personality of the writer than on his observations.[19]

An example for the first kind of traveler is John Lewis Burckhardt (1748–1817), a Swiss who had studied Arabic in Cambridge. He is considered one of the most reliable representatives of early ethnographic description. He visited the Hawran twice, in 1810 and in 1811, and dedicated a separate chapter of his book to its inhabitants, providing us with valuable information about social and political conditions in the area.[20] Burckhardt's description of the Hawran, including its early description of the practice of *musha'*, was deemed worthy of being translated into Arabic by a local historian of the Druze highlands. Burckhardt's findings and analysis, therefore, have become part of the historical knowledge of the region and have permeated all local accounts of the *'ammiyya*, the peasant revolt of 1889 and 1890. Given the extraordinary collective memory of this tribal society, however, where the clans jealously preserved their history through oral tradition, songs, and poetry, it can be surmised that Burckhardt's account must have sounded familiar and reliable. Otherwise he would not have been translated by a "son of the Jabal," who himself collected oral traditions and wrote the first account of the question of land and the peasant revolt based on local sources.

Setting

Since the settlement situation is important for the issue of the common lands and the practice of *musha'*, it is dealt with here in some detail. Gaulanitis (Golan), Trachonitis (al-Laja' and al-Safa), and Auranitis (Hawran) are the names given by the Romans to the basaltic landscape stretching eastward from the sea of Galilee to the Syrian desert and bordering on the Ghuta oasis of Damascus. The Hawran landscape in stricter terms is made up of the plain (the Nuqra), the Laja', and the highlands. Both the plain, a broad treeless plateau, and the highlands are of a Miocene lava cover that has been deeply weathered and provides excellent soil for wheat cultivation. Where the lava cover comes from younger (Pleistocene) discharges, however, the weathering process is not nearly so advanced.[21] There remain two extensive bizarre lava landscapes composed of this material, al-Laja' and al-Safa. The Laja', which joins the highlands in the northwest and forms a part of them, contains in its midst prehistoric heaps of rubble and cracked lava slate canyons with floors composed of fertile older lava soil that serve ideally as hidden grazing areas. The name Laja', which means "refuge" or "asylum," is thus quite fitting.

French archeologists, seeking to reconstruct the ancient agricultural landscape, have elaborated an interesting picture of the area between the first century B.C. and the seventh century A.D. Its geography very obviously determined its settlement. The issue of water naturally decided where a settlement would be located: villages were founded near springs or where a large collective cistern could be built to collect rainwater. Because the ground of the highlands was covered with large and small blocks of stones ("large blocks could measure 60 × 60 × 60 centimeters and weighed up to 400 kilograms"),[22] cultivating the land required first that the stones be cleared, either by piling them around the large stone blocks or layering them in long walls. Fields measured 30 meters wide (or less) and 500 meters long (or longer), which suggests the cultivation of grain.[23] The area around the villages was reserved for gardens and fruit orchards.

Nearly all of the villages of the highlands, and many of the adjoining plain, are located today on the ruins of an ancient predecessor. Following a golden age early in the Ottoman era, the Hawran went through a period of depopulation. The highlands, for example, had 12,038 inhabitants in seventy-two villages in 1596, while the population in 1805 amounted, in a generous estimation, to only 4,200 people in twenty-one villages.[24] We can only speculate as to the causes of depopulation: several extremely dry years in a row, locusts, the plague or cholera, and the extreme weakness of the Ottoman central administration. Travel reports allow us to trace the revival of settlement: one such example is Qanawat in the north of the highlands, which in 1596 had been populated by twelve Muslim and fifteen Christian households, 85 people altogether, some of whom were Beduin who had become sedentary. Seetzen, an early traveler passing through the village in 1805, failed to mention a single inhabitant. In 1812, Burckhardt found two Druze families growing tobacco; in 1816 five to six families were living among the ruins; 300 inhabitants were reported in 1821, the majority Druze, with a few Christian families. In 1922, according to a French count, Qanawat had 600 inhabitants, exclusively Druze. The southern plain of the highlands was all but deserted until around 1860. This is how the area presented itself to the eyes of newcomers:

> From Keres to Ayun . . . the ground is covered with walls, which probably once enclosed orchards and well cultivated fields. At Ayun are about four hundred houses without any inhabitants. On its west side are two walled-in springs, from whence the name is derived. . . . From Oerman we proceeded one hour and a quarter, to the town and castle called Szalkhat: the intermediate country is full of ruined walls. . . . The town which occupies the south and west foot of the castle hill, is now uninhabited; but fifteen years since a few Druse and Christian families were established here, as

well as at Oerman: the latter retired to Khabeb, where I afterwards saw them, and where they are still called Szalkhalie. The
town contains upwards of eight hundred houses.[25]

THE PRACTICE OF *MUSHA'*: THE REDISTRIBUTION
OF COMMON LANDS IN THE DRUZE HIGHLANDS

The taxes which all classes of Fellahs in the Haouran pay, may be
classed under four heads: the Miri; the expense of feeding soldiers
on the march; the tribute to the Arabs; and extraordinary expenses. The Miri is levied upon the Fedhan; thus if a village pay
twelve purses to the Miri, and there are thirty pair of oxen in it,
the master of each pair pays a thirtieth. Every village being rated
for the Miri in the land-tax book of the Pasha, at a fixed sum, that
sum is levied as long as the village is at all inhabited, however few
may be its inhabitants.

In the spring of every year, or, if no strangers have arrived and
settled, in every second or third spring, the ground of the village is
measured by long cords, when every Fellah occupies as much of it
as he pleases, there being always more than sufficient; the amount
of his tax is then fixed by the Sheikh, at the ratio which his number of fedhans bears to the whole of the number of fedhans cultivated that year. Whether the oxen be strong or weak, or whether
the quantity of seed sown or of land cultivated by the owner of the
oxen be more or less, is not taken into consideration; the Fellah is
supposed to keep strong cattle and plough as much land as possible. The boundaries of the respective fields are marked by large
stones (hudud).[26]

This is Burckhardt's description of *musha'*. Two connections
are evoked by this early description of land distribution: taxation and new settlement. Burckhardt's description of land redistribution does not mention where exactly in the Hawran he witnessed it or who described it to him. There is much, however,
that suggests that he is talking of the northern part of the Jabal
Hawran, settled by Druzes and Christians. First, he spent a lot
more time and effort in studying the Druzes, whose chief shaykh
he befriended, than studying the Hawranis in the plain. Second,

the big stones that he mentions as being used as boundaries for the fields are to be found much more in the mountain than in the plain. And third, the context in which he places his narrative of redistribution also focuses on the Druzes and the Christians. It is therefore of interest to note that periodic redistribution is still known in the southern part of the highlands today but is not remembered and known any more in the north. The most impressive living history source I met, Shaykh Hani Abu Fakhr, whose year of birth is given as 1883 and whose knowledge of events in his area goes back reliably as far as 1860, does not know of any land redistribution in the northern part of the Jabal.[27]

This indicates that the practice of redistribution must have been abandoned between 1810 and around 1860, the year in which the frontier of settlement in the north was reached, by means of great waves of immigration of Druzes after the violent events in Mount Lebanon. Land redistribution then seems to have been discontinued, which means that the plots of land must have been stabilized. Given the geographical conditions of the antique, delimited fields, stabilization as soon as stable settlement was reached does make sense. This confirms a pattern found in other areas as well: in Palestine it has also been established that the mountainous areas that had been settled longer tended toward individual usage (individuated plots), while the plains that were settled later tended toward collective or shareholding usage.[28]

The case of the highlands obviously supports the theory that associates the *musha'* system with the new settlement of farmland. The periodic land redistribution accompanying settlement activity beginning around 1860 in the south of the Druze highlands remains vivid in the collective memory of its inhabitants. Immigrants came in most cases as clans, but also as families, led by their clan or family head. Houses and land, both of which existed in abundance, were distributed among them when they arrived. The land in the village was partitioned into four (in special cases five) stretches of land (*wajahat*). The shaykh, with help from the village elders, separated these areas with ropes into long strips. The measuring standards were the *marasa* and *dira'*.[29] According to the capacity of a family to work, meaning the number of oxen teams, work horses, or mules,[30] the shaykh then distributed *sahms* giving access to land from each section to the male heads of family. The distribution proceeded by lottery: each participant turned in a stone, piece of wood, or the like, and at each section a lot was drawn by a neutral party. The holders of the *sahm*s, then, held rights to access land in all four or five corners of the village.[31] It can be assumed that in the beginning the distribution of land followed the open-ended model: all the different descriptions in the south give as an explanation for the distribution "the coming and going of the people." But there were political reasons as well: Bouron's 1927 description of the redistribution of land, based also on stories passed by word of mouth, mentions distribution taking place according to the relative importance of families,[32] implying the presence of new forces at play. The Atrash shaykhs, manorial lords, used the redistribution to drive out peasants that had fallen into disgrace, replacing them with loyal followers.[33] Redistribution clearly took on an arbitrary character, so much so that it would be one of the most important motives for the peasant revolt of 1889 and 1890.

Hamad Qarqut, born in 1906 in Dhibbin, offers an exceptionally clear report of what he learned from his father—namely, that a redistribution had taken place in Dhibbin around 1885 ("four years before the *'ammiyya*"), which had been a great event. Village land was divided into four sections. In each quarter, eighteen long strips (there were eighteen big clans in the village, so the *dhukur* principle in this case applied to clan heads) were marked off by ropes, making a total of seventy-two portions (*sahms*). Each clan, by the drawing of lots, received a *sahm* entitling it to land, in each portion. After World War I, another big land redistribution took place, "because the people wanted it,"[34] and again the division was made into seventy-two portions or *sahm*s.[35] Between these years, the number of shares became fixed, and the plots stabilized. The events that caused the transition from "open-ended" to "fixed-share" redistribution are, as we shall see, political: the peasant revolt of 1889 and 1890 and the *sened tapu* registration in 1894 and 1895.

In 1936, still under the auspices of the French Mandate but with an urban nationalist as governor, the people of al-Suwayda', capital of the highlands of the Hawran, decided to distribute their "old *musha'* land" (*al-musha' al-qadim*), which was located on a mesa east of the city, stretching out to the villages of Sala, Kafr, and Shahba. It was called Dhahr al-Jabal (the back of the mountain) and had hitherto been used as grazing land. This decision sparked off four years of negotiations, debates, and political struggle. The leading family of al-Suwayda' and the Jabal, the Atrash, demanded that the land be distributed solely among the landowning families of al-Suwayda' in proportion to their ownership of arable land and therefore claimed one-eighth of the old *musha'* for themselves. The landless inhabitants of al-Suwayda' and families in political rivalry to the Atrash demanded that the land be distributed according to number of males. The inhabitants of the neighboring villages also demanded a share of the land. Finally, a compromise was reached with the help of the French officials, who exerted a little pressure on the Atrash clan. The Atrash received an eighth of the land. The old *musha'* land was divided into thirteen parcels (*tubna*s), and for every *tubna* an expert, a land elder, from one of the big families, was named. There were, again, thirteen leading, first-rank clans in al-Suwayda'. Each *tubna* was then divided into 270 shares. The number of shares was further determined by rating every male of the village, regardless of his age, with one share (*sahm*), and every *faddan* of property owned with two shares (*sahm*s). The sum of those shares was then distributed among all male inhabitants of al-Suwayda'. Thus land holding was counted double, but landless males could also obtain land. The inhabitants of the neighboring villages were excluded. In the words of one contemporary observer, "The distribution took a long time and was carried out in stages, since it was difficult to find all those who had a right to a share."[36] It was on these lands that the first *bustan*s of fruit trees were planted, which remain to the present day an important source of income in the Jabal.[37]

What we find here, in 1936, is a combination of the old *faddan* and *dhukur* methods—principles of productive capital (land) and human capital (males) combined. It was not really open-ended, since it restricted the distribution to the inhabitants of al-Suwayda' and excluded claimants. But neither was it a fixed-share distribution, since it was the first of its kind on this particular stretch of land, and the shares were established in an open combination of principles.

What this historically late case of land redistribution does clearly demonstrate is the connection between sociopolitical power relations within the village community, on the one hand, and the politics of the surrounding state, on the other. Whether the *faddan* or the *dhukur* method, whether open-ended or fixed-share distribution, it was all a function of the power relations between peasants, shaykhs, and the state. Before we return to this question in greater historical detail, a few clarifications with regard to local conditions are called for.

Jadhar[38]

The increasing stabilization of settlement generated a further phenomenon: the permanent use of plots of land around the village for the planting of fruit trees and grape vines, both of which require attention over a longer period of time. Burckhardt, in 1810 to 1812, underlining the lack of security and stability in the settlement, noticed the absence of fruit gardens and orchards, and quoted a peasant in explanation:

> Shall we sow for strangers? was the answer of a Fellah, to whom I once spoke on the subject, and who by the word strangers meant both the succeeding inhabitants, and the Arabs who visit the Haouran in the spring and summer.[39]

Seetzen reports several times on the Hawranis' awareness that their land was *miri* rather than *mulk* land. They seemed to have raved repeatedly to him about the absolute "paradise" in 'Ajlun, where all the land "is said to be *milk,* inheritable property," "full of fruit and other trees."[40]

Sometime in the second half of the nineteenth century—whether due to Ottoman encouragement or to local initiative remains unclear—plots of land were taken out of the village lands and established as the *jadhar* in a ring around the village. This area was then devoted to fruit orchards, the size of which varied according to the area of land under cultivation. In Dhibbin the ratio between *jadhar* and farm land was said to be approximately 3:100.[41] The *jadhar* was no longer included in the redistribution of land. It remained as property of the various families and was important for the *mahr.*

Faddan

Faddan was the name given to a team of oxen and consequently also to a measure of land, including untilled fields, which a peasant and his family could cultivate with a pair of oxen from sowing time to harvest. A man owning two teams of oxen thus held two *faddan*s of land.[42] Ideally, the soil of all of the *faddan*s in a village would be of equal quality due to the careful selection of the plots that formed them.

The *faddan* had no definite size, however, and its area could vary according to the ability of the peasant and his oxen teams to work, as well as how close a relationship he enjoyed with the shaykh. The number of *faddan*s in a village depended on the number of settlers, with the size of the individual *faddan*s depending on the peasants' productivity. Of fundamental importance as well was the geographical location and make-up of the soil. In the highlands these key concerns were always involved in the question of how much of the land was *wa'r*—that is, how much ground was covered or mixed with stones, rendering it unfit for agricultural uses. With increasing settlement and decreasing availability of land, the amount of land a village had at its disposal as well as the size of the individual *faddan*s came to depend on the power of the shaykh and the village as a whole along with the individual *faddan* "holders."[43] The *faddan* was therefore not a metric measurement or, strictly speaking, even a standard indication of surface area; it was rather a social unit of measurement testifying to the productive strength or wealth of a village or individual.[44] Burckhardt offers a vivid description:

> If it is asked, whether such a one has piastres (illou gheroush), a common mode of speaking, the answer is "A great deal; he has six pair of oxen going (Kethiar bi-mashi sette fedhadhin)."[45]

The result was that the area represented by a *faddan* was different in every village.[46] The standard measurement accepted by all villages, insofar as such was even necessary, was most probably the *mudd* of seed.[47] The *faddan* could be expressed in different ways:

According to area: in *dunum* (919.3 square meters = 40 *dira'*, equaling 1,000 square meters)[48]

According to output: in *mudd* (in the highlands 20 kilograms, in the plain 14 kilograms)[49]

According to seed: in *mudd*

According to ideal shares: in *sahm*

According to subunits: in 24 *qirat* (the 1/24; 24 *qirat* = 100 percent)

When asked what a *faddan* is today, older peasants in the less spacious north answer mostly in *mudd*, whereas those in the spacious south answer in *dunum*. The number of *dunum* given for the *faddan*, however, differs from village to village. Because the *dunum* was brought in by the Ottomans to standardize the measurement system, the variation in the number of *dunums* per *faddan* substantiates the claim made above that the size of the *faddan* differs from village to village and is more of a social than a metric expression. It must again be pointed out that, in the local way of thinking, the value of the *faddan* is not a function of its metric accuracy. Rather, it says something about the organization of labor and is further expressive of the strength of villages in men and plows and the wealth of individuals. For the plain's village of Busra, Le Play established for the year 1857 that a peasant owning one *faddan* cultivated approximately seven hectares.[50]

Over time, as settlement activity was stabilized, the inheritance of rights to access and to usufruct in *sahm*s became established on the village level. The *sahm* was an ideal portion of the village lands, similar to a share. Because the *sahm*s gave rights to access in different portions of the village land and because they became smaller and more spread apart with each inheritance (an arbitrary matter among the Druzes, in accord with the will of the testator),[51] the fragmentation of holdings characteristic in such circumstances finally reached the point that "one of the *sahm*s included 20 pieces (*qit'a*) of land in very different places and the land of such a piece did not exceed 10 meters, while its length was 100 meters."[52]

This fragmentation was also found in the plain. It is remarkable that even today the old people in the villages give the village lands in *faddan* in the highlands and in *rub'a* (quarter) in the plain and are able to rattle off the amount of *faddan/rub'a* of each and every family—usually until they are stopped by one of their adult children.

COMMON LANDS

The oppressions of the government on one side, and those of the Bedouins on the other, have reduced the Fellah of the Haouran to a state little better than that of the wandering Arab. Few individuals either among the Druses or Christians die in the same village in which they were born. Families are continually moving from one place to another; in the first year of their new settlement the Sheikh acts with moderation towards them; but his vexations becoming in a few years insupportable, they flee to some other place, where they have heard that their brethren are better treated, but they soon find that the same system prevails over the whole country. . . . This continued wandering is one of the principle reasons why no village in the Haouran has either orchards, or fruit-trees, or gardens for the growth of vegetables.[53]

To understand the question of the common lands, it is important to grasp the sociopolitical conditions of power of which they formed the base. The political system that the people of the Hawran had established in close cultural contact with the Beduin tribes then dominating the area was a tribal one. This is true for both the Sunni plains people and the Druzes of the highlands. Both groups featured more or less powerful clans, village shaykhs, and a *shaykh al-mashayikh* (paramount shaykh). But the political system of the Druzes was much more nuanced, marked, and hierarchical and featured a much higher degree of inner dynamics. The Druzes, unlike the Sunni Muslims of the plain, also had the common bond of their faith at their disposal, which both set them apart and melded them together in times of outward threat and pressure.

Shaykhs and Peasants

The Druzes had a system that they called the *mashyakha* system. The fundamental principle on which this society was based was a patrilinear kinship group, the clan, which in turn was made up of family households. The *mashyakha* designates a type of chief's honorary position, his paramount chieftaincy, as well as the power of his clan in terms of the number of villages over which the clan wields control by providing the village shaykh, his chiefdom. While at the beginning of the nineteenth century there existed three chiefdoms, *mashyakhat,* their number rose to ten at the end of the 1850s, and in 1924 there were fifteen reported chiefdoms in the highlands. These chiefdoms were ranked in a hierarchical order of nobility. The chief of the most noble clan held the position of *primus inter pares* and was designated as *shaykh al-mashayikh* (shaykh of shaykhs, paramount shaykh).

Within this system, there was always a tension between the territorial principle, the village, and the kinship principle, the clan. While the ruling clan of a village did everything to enhance and augment its power, the defense of a village, for example, was organized under a village banner (*bayraq*) and not the banner of its first clan. All male inhabitants therefore shared in this responsibility for the common good. The village *bayraq* was usually carried by the sons of a poor clan, without rank, who thereby lost many of its male members in battle but amassed a wealth of the symbolic capital of honor.

The village shaykh, along with the other important representatives of the clan, was the master of his village and represented it in external affairs. It was his responsibility to set the *miri* (the tithe for the *miri* land) in the village, which was determined according to the number of *faddan*s in the village and which he turned over to the *shaykh al-mashayikh*, who acted as a tax farmer.[54]

Similarly, until the 1970s he determined the agricultural division of labor in the village. The peasants assembled themselves in his *madafa* (guesthouse), where it was decided which corner of the village lands was to be worked the following day. He also controlled "the selection of harvest guards, control of pasturage, and the agricultural cycle."[55] This was because, even though the cultivation of the single plots of land was carried out individually, there was group responsibility for working a certain strip of land. The reasons for such a "field agreement" lie in the cultivation techniques (most of the plots of lands, and specifically the long strip fields, could be reached only by passing through neighboring plots; for grazing purposes, a fallow that was closed off made the most sense). But the most important reason probably was security: up until the 1890s, if not beyond, peasants carried weapons to their work in the fields in both the plain and the highlands. As long as everyone worked in the same corner of the village land, the village community was constantly defensible.

The shaykh had the right to request from the peasants of the village a kind of socage labor on his land, measured in days, which in the highlands was called *sukhra*. The shaykh was also the chief military leader of the village, who led its men into battle. In the name of the village, he allowed or denied the Beduin the use of the village's grazing land or watering holes and decided if and where a new settler might settle. He collected tribute for a variety of permissions and services, which in the highlands were called *al-qud* for the use of grazing land, *al-qulat* for water, and *al-qusra* for the protection that he provided to new settlers.

He was also responsible for the maintenance of the *madafa*, which was the center of political power in the village, and only the shaykh had the right to have an official *madafa*. The shaykhs seem to have complained frequently about their high expenditures; all the early reports dwell on the high costs of maintaining a *madafa*. This justified the shaykhs' right to exempt up to eight, ten, or twelve pairs of oxen from his taxes and for the same reason to collect up to ten *ghararas* of grain from the village.[56] The amount of service and payment required by the shaykh varied from village to village. Burckhardt's good Druze friend, Shibli al-Hamdan, who was, after all, a candidate for the position of *shaykh al-mashayikh* of the Druze highlands, was in 1812 allowed six *faddans* tax-free and received two to three *ghararas* of grain a year from his village, 'Ara.[57] His Sunni colleague, the shaykh of Busra, was in 1857 allowed to cultivate all of his nine *faddans* tax-free by his villagers, who also consented to pay his share of the *khuwa* (protection money) to the Beduin.[58] The Druzes at that time no longer paid any *khuwa* and even requested it from some plains villages under their "protection."

The *qahwaji*, who prepared the coffee in the shaykh's *madafa*, was also paid by the village; wedding presents were given to the shaykh out of the gifts given to the groom; and the shaykh also received fees paid by the Beduin and new arrivals. In addition, the shaykh kept a portion of the *miri* he collected from the village.[59]

At the beginning of the nineteenth century, when the area was not so densely settled, the power of a shaykh was limited; a family that disagreed with the shaykh's requirements would simply move to another village with a more moderate shaykh. Burckhardt himself witnessed a quarrel between a village shaykh and a Christian farmer over a tax issue. The *fallah* was supposed to pay the same taxes for the ensuing year as he had in the one preceding, although he now had one fewer pair of oxen. The *fallah* threatened not to "sow even a single grain"[60] and began making preparations for departure. The dispute was settled peaceably and the peasant stayed. On the other hand, the shaykh did have the power, presumably in consultation with his supporters among the elders, to expel an unwanted peasant from the village. This power was strongly curtailed, however, at least in times of low settlement, by the village's own interest in having as many males with oxen teams as possible working the land, so that the taxes, levied on the whole village collectively, would be borne by as many individuals as possible.

By far the most important right of the Druze shaykh, however, was his right to a quarter of the village lands. While the Hawran shaykhs shared the other rights and privileges, this right was unique to the Druze shaykhs. Thus, the higher rank of the Druze shaykh within his community and the higher degree of social differentiation in the Druze *mashyakha* system was expressed, to borrow Martha Mundy's expression, through the idiom of land.

The shaykhs thus had both privileged rights of access to the common lands and to the surplus of the peasants—that is, the members of the village community. The shaykh's role was, ideally, to identify with and oversee the common good of the village. Assisted by a council of elders, he was entrusted with the guardianship of the common good of the community. There are many accounts of how the community indeed elected another family member for this task, if a new shaykh (usually the oldest son of the former shaykh) did not live up to village expectations. As we shall see, the struggle for the common good, expressed in (the expropriation of) the shaykhs' lands could also be very violent.

Who tilled the shaykhs' lands? And how large were the shaykhs' landholdings? At the beginning of the century this land was tilled by *harratin* (hired native laborers) in the plain and *falatiyya* (the landless) in the highlands, in addition to the villagers' socage labor.[61] The shaykhs, notably the Druze shaykhs, belonged to what was called the elite (*al-khassa*) while the peasants, members of smaller clans, belonged to the *'amma* (the common people). The lowest stratum of the *'amma* was the *falatiyya* in the highlands.[62] They could either work as day laborers or enter into a work contract. The type of work contract that achieved currency in the Jabal Druze (as in most of the areas on the edge of the steppe in Bilad al-Sham) was the *muraba'a* contract. The *murabi'* had only his labor power to offer and was provided with oxen, plows, and seed. "A labourer who has one Fedhan, or two oxen, under his charge, usually receives at the time of sowing one Gharara of corn. After the harvest he takes one-third of the produce of the field; but among the Druses only one fourth. The master pays to the government the tax called Miri, and the labourer pays ten piaster annually," wrote Burckhardt in 1810 to 1812.[63] In the middle of the century "the quarter" is also reported for the plain, and in 1936 a difference in remuneration between Druze highlands and Sunni plain was again in existence.[64] The contracts seemed to vary according to supply and demand or the power of the group.

The *murabi'* lived with his farmer or shaykh, sleeping on a kind of bench running along the wall in the stables and barn, still visible today. Unless he had land of his own and was still forced to work as a *murabi'* because it did not amount to enough to make a living, he was part of the household of the farmer with whom he lived. At the beginning of the nineteenth century, Seetzen mentions Shi'ites (Mutawalis) from the Jabal al-

Amil offering their services as seasonal workers in the plains.[65] With increased settlement, it was often poor peasants from the plains or the highlands themselves or the odd sons from large families with only small property who worked as *murabi'un* for the shaykhs or rich peasants. Often, these sharecroppers worked for years without remuneration, thus "earning" a daughter of the household. This system remained intact well into the 1950s, until the poor and landless peasants left in large waves of emigration and headed overseas.[66]

As to the size of the landholdings, prior to the uprising, Atrash lands measured between 1,000 and 3,650 hectares— truly large holdings. In the cramped north, the Amir of Shahba held about 2,500 hectares—likewise a stately property, like that of the al-Halabi in al-Sawara al-Kabira with 1,667 hectares. Here we have for the first time figures pertaining to the question of the development of large landholdings in the second half of the nineteenth century. The map of the shaykhs' lands shows the situation after the '*ammiyya*, in the 1920s; it is also valid for the late 1890s, however, because by then the settlement boundaries of the highlands had already been reached. If rapid population growth in the highlands also meant that holdings were quickly broken up among many heirs, the first generation of "manorial lords" were immensely wealthy by Hawrani standards.[67]

Ottomans

Throughout the second half of the nineteenth century, most determinedly in the 1880s and 1890s, the modernizing and centralizing Ottoman state sought to tighten its grip over these frontier areas and abolish the special status of the Hawran with regard to regulated taxation, land registration, and recruitment into the army, from all of which the whole of the Hawran had been hitherto exempted. Indispensable for all these measures was a population count. Of all these demands, recruitment was regarded as the most unacceptable, and head count and land registration were widely believed to be nothing more than preparatory steps for conscription. Several times the inhabitants of the plain and the highlands made common cause against the government's decision to introduce the new order of things, abandoned their fields, buried their grain, and took refuge in the Laja'.[68] Both the plain and the highlands saw Ottoman enforcement campaigns, but it was the highlands that were subjected to several punitive campaigns, for which the villages of the plain had to provision the troops.[69] The areas that resisted most violently were the highlands, the Laja', and the neighboring villages in the plain. In 1892, for example, violent opposition to cadastre and *tapu* was reported in Dar'a and Busra al-Hariri, while in Qunaytira land had already been registered for several years.[70] Resistance decreased with increasing distance from the Laja', and the highlands. After the Druze revolt of 1896 had been brutally repressed and dozens of shaykhs and families had been sent into exile, the cadastre was expanded and the first head count was conducted.[71] In the summer of 1897, the villagers of the Hawran staged a dramatic mass exodus into the Laja' and the Safa, fleeing the state's decision to finally introduce conscription and the regulated *'ushr* (tithe). Since this exodus took place at harvest time and caused a stir in Damascus, the government in the end reversed its decision. As late as 1910, Hawranis complained about the fact that their cattle were being counted for taxation, whereas the herds of the Druzes were not—which meant that the Druzes still paid a lump sum tribute for them instead of a regulated tax. Due to geographical and societal conditions, it proved more feasible for the state to penetrate the wide plain than the highlands, and it also sought to play one off against the other. These Ottoman policies of the Tanzimat era changed power relations in the countryside, not only between population groups but also within these groups:

> The peasantry [of the highlands], while apparently possessing an abundance of the simple necessities of life as raised by themselves from the produce of their fields and flocks, presented by their independent bearing, healthy and contented appearance, and the self-respect shown by the care in their clean homespun but dura-

ble apparel, a marked contrast with the denizens of the squalid and poverty-stricken villages of the plains.[72]

So stated vice consul Jago in his report in 1880. What were the reasons behind these differences? The right to surplus in the plain lay with the urban tax farmers. Either the land of the Hawran plain was sold to urban "agroentrepreneurs" (even the Christian wife of the Prussian consul was allowed to buy and colonize two whole villages together with a Muslim compagnon),[73] or the tithes were farmed out to a ring of speculators. Tax farming, which should have been done away with by the new land law, was still widely in use. The main financial goals of the Tanzimat reformers had involved shifting the tax burden from the land to urban wealth, supplanting indirect with direct tax collection by salaried agents of the state, replacing the excise taxes (which were levied mainly on households and land plots regardless of ability to pay), and abolishing many of the historic exemptions that had been granted over the centuries.[74] But tax farming, not direct collection, remained the norm throughout the empire.[75] The state was not consistent in its policies towards rural producers and tax farmers, shifting support back and forth to both of these groups. It was, of course, the cultivators who paid for these seesaw policies. So, ironically, as we shall see, the peasants under control of the state (which was supposed, after all, to protect them) were a lot worse off than the peasants of the highlands. These, however, would also be affected by the seesaw policies of the state.

In the highlands the phenomenon of urban tax farmers did not exist. But life was also easier here with respect to taxes. An especially detailed French report from 1890 offers a good illustration of conditions. Taxation in the various *qada*s of the Hawran varied according to the extent to which they had been integrated into the Ottoman system:

Anciently, the Hawran as a whole paid to the State, under the name of a personal tax, a fixed and unique tribute. The only exception were the inhabitants of the plain, who were in addition obliged to provide the Mecca pilgrimage caravan with a certain amount of wheat, barley, fire wood and charcoal, and who also had to transport these provisions to Muzayrib, located along the route of the caravan. . . . Nowadays the fiscal regime varies from district to district, i.e., according to the degree of authority that the state holds there.[76]

The highlands had retained the privilege of paying a fixed annual tribute. This sum amounted to 307,000 piasters in 1890, consisting in theory of the following: *wirku* (property tax) and *'ushr* (tithe), flat rate: 230,000 piasters; exemption from military service for the Druzes, flat rate: 50,000 piasters; exemption from military service for the Christians, flat rate: 12,000 piasters; estimated sheep and goat tax, flat rate: 15,000 piasters.

The Druzes subtracted from this tribute the allocations made to their *shaykh al-mashayikh* as the *qa'immaqam* and to the *mudirs* and their horsemen, which added up to half of the total. Thus the Druzes paid much lower taxes than they would have had to pay following the customary method for calculating annual estimates (according to quality, quantity, and price). In the highlands every village just paid a fixed flat rate. It is no wonder that the shaykhs were keen to retain their tax privilege.

Nor did the chiefs of the Laja' have much cause for complaint: they paid 13,000 piasters a year. According to Guillois, they received 17,000 piasters a month from the state treasury to prevent them from mounting raids in the plains and in exchange for accompanying caravans from Muzayrib to Mecca and back in defense against the Beduin of the steppe. Other districts paid taxes per head of livestock—namely, 10 piasters per camel, 3.50 piasters per sheep, and 3.50 piasters per sheep. They also paid *wirku, 'ushr,* pasture taxes, and the *badal* for being exempted from military service. All peasants of the Hawran were treated like the Christians in this respect and were not conscripted in exchange for payment of the *badal al-'askari* (military substitution fee). Only the Laja' was exempted from this tribute. Tax rates were also not fixed in a uniform manner: in the plain, in the districts of Dar'a, Busra, and Shaykh Sa'd, the *'ushr* was calculated for a specified number of *mudd* of wheat, which varied by the year. In 'Ajlun, in contrast, it was calculated according to land area and amounted to 180,000 piasters a year. Qunaytira paid 300,000 piasters, and al-Salt 10,000 Turkish pounds. All in all, tax receipts from Hawran amounted to 70,000–75,000 Turkish pounds.[77]

The Druze shaykhs energetically defended the privilege of paying a tribute instead of a calculated tax, which they themselves collected and from which they derived profit. The peasants tended to side with them, although there are indications that they were aware of the benefit of greater stability and property that came along with registration. Given the chronic financial misery of the *sancak,* however, especially following the Russian-Ottoman War, the Ottoman officials could often go years without being paid their salaries. They survived off bribery and extortion. This is part of the explanation for the often noted persistent indebtedness of the "miserable peasants of the plain":[78] they sustained the state treasury, its officials, the urban tax farmer, and the village shaykh, and they had to pay the *khuwa* to the Beduin or, in some cases, to the Druzes.[79] The Druze peasants, in contrast, had to sustain only their own shaykhs, in addition to paying the state's taxes. Since Ottoman functionaries had not yet been allowed to penetrate the social landscape of the highlands, Druze peasants were spared their exactions. It is indicative of this favorable situation that secondary families from the highlands (not even the first rank ones) acted as money lenders to villagers from the plain.[80] It is all the more puzzling, then, why Druze villagers from the south of the highlands in the end rebelled against their shaykhs and preferred to be ruled and taxed by Ottoman officials instead of their shaykhs.

COMMON LANDS AND THE STRUGGLE FOR THE COMMON GOOD: THE *'AMMIYYA* IN THE DRUZE HIGHLANDS

The Atrash were a new type of shaykh. They were a combination of *Gutsherren,* manorial rural entrepreneurs, and feudal overlords. Isma'il al-Atrash colonized the southern part of the highlands by putting his eight sons in the best villages. The smaller ones were colonized from Salkhad. The settlers who rendered these lands fit for cultivation were either refugees from Lebanon, or they were canvassed by the Atrash from their old homelands. To the question of where the settlers came from, the answer in the south is always the same: "The shaykh brought the people."[81]

The new style of settlement conducted by the Atrash in the south, their accumulation of great wealth, and the support they received from the state naturally had far-reaching consequences for internal social conditions in the highlands, in particular the relations between shaykhs and their dependent villages. In their capacity as Ottoman administrative officials, as *qa'immaqam*s and *mudir*s of villages, the Atrash shaykhs disposed over an armed entourage.

In the north the organizing principle of settlement had been the clan. This, along with the not inconsiderable factor of limited land, had given rise to a small number of large clans. In the newly settled south, in contrast, a large number of small clans found themselves living under an Atrash shaykh, who served as their tax and tribute collector, and as the beneficiary of feudal labor services. In the north, where family relations ameliorated this relationship and the tightness of the thickly populated landscape did not allow the large landholdings of the south, the income differential between peasant and shaykh was also smaller.[82] In the south, the huge manors of the Atrash built of black basalt, now ruins, testify to their wealth and power at the time.

Here a process of "feudalization" had undermined the old tribal system: with Ottoman assistance there was now a shaykh who (as *mudir,* as Ottoman official) had an armed entourage at his disposal, which he could deploy against his own village. The new relationship between shaykh and dependent peasant came to expression in typically "feudal" privileges: in the context of the *'ammiyya* we hear that only the shaykhs were allowed to wear the red shoes from Aleppo, *sarmayat al-halabiyya*.[83] There are reports concerning the habits some shaykhs had of keeping Christian mistresses (although the report by the French Consul of the *jus primae noctis* derive from knowledge of the feudal past of his own country).[84] It is also manifest that the shaykhs, in the recession of the 1880s, attempted to wring their diminishing profits from the villagers—through tributes up to one-third of the harvest and more corvée services.

If, in the initial stages of settlement in the south, the shaykh with his armed entourage guaranteed the security of newcomers and was thus unquestioningly followed, this situation naturally changed as conditions became more stable. Oral history in the highlands records this: "At the beginning Shaykh Sa'id al-Atrash defended the village with his men. He oversaw the construction of the old cistern and brought settlers."[85] But after only a few years the new families, enjoying high grain prices, low taxes, and ample land, had established themselves economically, even though they had to pass on as much as one-fourth of their yield of newly cultivated land to the shaykh.[86] Having become respectable villagers, they wanted to be recognized and treated as such. Some, it is recounted, even wanted their own *madafa*. The shaykhs were not perceived as fulfilling their role as guardians of the common good any more. This would have direct consequences on their share of the common lands.

The all round dissatisfaction with the neofeudal conditions was so great that it also moved the defenders of morality, the religious shaykhs, to take a position. A local historian of the highlands quotes a document (*hurm*) that was composed in one of their assemblies in al-Suwayda'. It forbids the secular shaykhs and their horsemen, "on pain of excommunication," to wield weapons against "the sons of their own kind" (*abna' al-jins*). Moreover, it forbids the sale of water and pasture to either sedentary peasants or Beduin, "since water and pasture are given by God." And it prohibits the shaykhs from taking young animals (sheep and goats) in tribute, especially from herds that pastured on the *ard al-musha'*, the communal grazing lands.[87] This means that some of the religious shaykhs fashioned legitimation for the disaffected from divine law. The position of the religious shaykhs is important here. Due to the separation of the spheres among the Druzes, they were responsible for only the spiritual good and survival of the group. Worldly and political matters did not belong in their sphere and could cost individual shaykhs their good reputation. Their interference thus indicates that the common good of the community was at stake. The old, patriarchal, life-furthering relationship that had tied the men to their shaykh had given way to an overlord and quasi-serf relationship[88] that violated the notion of the common good that had been binding in the highlands. Villagers (shareholders) and landless sharecroppers of four villages in the south began to organize. They met in an old council site called Majdal al-Shur and drafted the following document:[89]

Praise to God

The reason for this document lies in the defamations, the greed, and the infringements we have suffered at the hands of our shaykhs, who suppressed us and drove us out from our places and from the whole area, without our provoking it. Their aim was to split our ranks.

For thirty years we have with great effort built up the villages and inhabited them, and we have always obeyed our shaykhs and tried to please them.

We have paid to the treasury of the state the *miri* taxes; we have cared for the general order and the defense of the honor in all events.

We have given ourselves and our souls cheaply, and we have spilled our blood for defending the honor of our shaykhs.

And therefore we have made up our minds, and we are unanimous, we, who have put our names and our seals to this document, to bring to a standstill their infringements on us and to care for our weal and to see to it that justice is done and order is just. And indeed, if there happens an infringement on us, like expulsion, or if our honor and our houses are threatened, then we rise up with one hand on one bridle, and none of us will stay behind. God and the nabi Shu'ayb are to witness this speech. And he who does not extend support to his people in the four villages, who are united by this document, shall be expelled from God and his prophets, and he shall not find grace on the day of judgment and it shall be upon him a curse so big as the distance between earth and heaven, and no path will ever lead him into heaven. His wife will be of more worthiness than he is in all events. Whoever goes astray from the path of his people merits to suffer all these disgraces.

15 Sha'ban 1306/16 April 1889

According to the oral tradition of the *'ammiyya* in the highlands, among all those who signed the document, there were two who could have written it: a Druze who immigrated after 1860 to the highlands and worked as a *murabi'* for an Atrash shaykh or a Christian from Lebanon who could read and write and lived in 'Urman.[90] Of the eighty-one signatories, twenty-four possessed seals and thus were from aspiring second-rank clans or even noble clans from the north; the rest were unknown, individual names belonging to the *murabi'un*.

The Majdal al-Shur compact offers as reasons for the mutual assistance pact precisely what we have identified as "feudalization": the signatories express their opposition to the feudal privileges of the shaykhs. The first and most important issue seems to have been concern over being driven off the land, and the shaykhs' goal to cause the villagers to fight among themselves, another clear violation of the notion of the common good. Villagers being driven off the land appeared also to the French consul as a primary cause of the *'ammiyya*. Together with other abuses of power, the consul pointed out, the Atrash, toward whom the discontent was directed, had ordered redistribution of land entirely at their own discretion, naturally bestowing the best located and most fertile parcels on "their [own] creatures." Land redistribution was actually an old custom, against which no one had any objection until the Atrash abused the practice. They were constantly ordering redistribution, with those who had the misfortune of having displeased them finding themselves banished to the far corners of the territory (which also had the effect of rousing the peasants against each other). Moreover, each redistribution went along with lavish tributes being given to the shaykhs.[91] This contemporary description corresponds to the stories related by Hamad Qarqut. At the beginning land redistribution had taken place "for the sake of justice" and on account of the steady stream of new immigrants. Later, however, the shaykhs started reserving the best lands for themselves and their supporters, using redistribution to drive off those who had fallen from favor.[92]

This was all the more intolerable as it was known that conditions were different where the Ottoman Land Law of 1858 was in force, and every cultivator who had entered his name in the registry and paid the corresponding *tapu* tax had his rights of usufruct confirmed, which he could sell, lease, and bequeath.[93] This relative security offered a positive contrast to the conditions of insecurity in the south of the highlands, where usufruct depended on maintaining good relations with the shaykh.

The Majdal Shur compact does not mention any concrete demands as to the shaykhs' lands. But the *diwan* of a local poet (and member of the Atrash clan) who devoted some verses to the *'ammiyya,* has the following to say:

> And it was decided that we leave our land, so we went and left everything behind;
> And their first demand was: a quarter of the shaykh's land! And our shaykhs would be have-nothings!
> And their second demand: we have a right to the *qusra!* And our shaykhs have become unimportant!

And their third demand was all these privileges and they denounced their shaykhs as tyrants.[94]

The *qusra,* to which the rebels laid claim, was precisely the defense tribute collected by the shaykh. Actually, the villagers did not want to be defended by him but rather to defend themselves along with him but at the point in the uprising signaled in the *diwan,* they obviously had begun wanting to get rid of their shaykhs altogether.

Both sides dispatched delegations to Damascus to persuade the provincial government of the justice of their cause. The French consul, impressed by the developments, wrote as follows in June 1889:

> This is perhaps the first time that something of this sort has taken place, for previously the Druze, though they are often at odds among themselves, have taken care to keep the Turks out of their internal disputes; their cardinal rule was also to avoid the interference of the governor in their internal affairs.[95]

According not only to this report but also to the petition of the *avam* (the common people in Ottoman terms) that is to be found in the Ottoman archives, the peasant delegation explained that they had had enough of the capriciousness and demands of their shaykhs and wanted them replaced by Ottoman officials. This was a revolutionary demand: for the first time some Druzes were prepared to renounce solidarity with their shaykhs and to invite Ottoman officials to register the lands and to collect taxes.[96]

The provincial government let it be known that it would require proof of this willingness.[97] It called for an end to the conflict and the shaykhs, under the leadership of the *qa'immaqam,* Ibrahim al-Atrash, quickly declared in a petition that from now on the lands would be registered, the traditional rights (of the shaykhs) annulled, and the taxes would be properly collected. The internal administration would be reformed, and the common people protected against encroachments.[98] Clashes between Atrash shaykhs and peasants soon ensued. The shaykhs had to relinquish their discretion over land redistribution, leaving it to the free disposal of the villagers.[99] By the end of the summer the Atrash shaykhs in Malah and 'Urman had to give up half of their traditional quarter of the village lands to the rebels. The shaykh of al-Qurayya, Mustafa al-Atrash, gave back what he had appropriated in previous years, and the same thing happened in Imtan.[100] In assemblies the shaykhs were called on to cease treating the peasants as a cheap labor force working for them on the land. Instead, the rebels demanded that they be regarded as coproprietors who would give up a portion of the harvest to the shaykhs in the form of tribute, from which the shaykhs would then pay the taxes due the empire. This is how the French consul understood the reports he received from his Druze informant.[101] Remarkably, the description by the Austrian consul is nearly equivalent:

> The eagerness to strike that has appeared in our time in Europe has found its way to the Hawran mountains, a ten-hour ride by horseback from Damascus. A large part of the Druze cultivators there, in an assembly held recently, have resolved on the repeal of the privileges granted to their shaykhs, expressing the desire to be regarded and treated, not as has previously been the case, as day laborers for the shaykhs, but as coproprietors of the lands they cultivate.[102]

The villagers obviously wanted to be regarded as shareholders, as "real" members of the village community. They demanded a decrease or the end of socage labor (*sukhra*), which had obviously been used excessively. There appeared to be also a demand for the end of the arbitrary redistribution—that is, of stabilization of the plots of land and permanent right of access to them. The call for *tamlik* (property making) also appears in the stories told in the highlands as one of the motivations for the uprising—that is, the expropriation of half of the shaykhs' rights to land and redistribution among the landless.[103] The demands of the rebels do not seem to have been clear and consistent, and the compact does not offer any concrete proposals about land.

In another assembly, in addition to the single clear demand—
that villagers no longer be driven from the land—another demand appears that the shaykhs should not collect more than
one-quarter of the harvest for their manorial tribute, meaning
the tax due to the state would not be included in this sum.[104]
Oppenheim, who visited the region, also reports in 1893 that a
central issue of the *'ammiyya* was "to refuse giving up the traditional third of the harvest to the Shaykhs."[105] The issue for the
clans possessing *sahm*s in land was to have their holding recognized and to put an end to the redistribution, thus stabilizing the
plots. The exorbitant socage labor should also be decreased or
abolished and the payment of tributes should be regulated. For
the *murabi'un,* who had been installed instead of villagers fallen
from grace, in contrast, here was a chance to obtain *sahm*s and
become members of the community. Obviously, the Atrash, who
had forfeited their authority, were to be replaced by shaykhs
who were able to create consensus among the villagers and act
as guardians of the common good again.[106]

The Atrash shaykhs agreed to the demands of the rebels, on
the condition that the latter cease to challenge the authority of
their chiefs by calling for their replacement by Ottoman
officials.[107] The peasants now really did organize themselves in
an *'ammiyya,* in a movement of the common people, as is suggested by the term. The French consul described them, drawing
on French history, as an *assemblée nationale:*

> This assembly replaced the former assemblies of the shaykhs and
> made sovereign decisions in regard to all of the concerns of the na-
> tion: in particular it arrogated to itself the power to select shaykhs
> and to do so from among members both of the noble families
> [*khassa*] and of the (common) people [*al-'amma*].[108]

This meant that the *'ammiyya* villages withdrew themselves
from the authority of the traditional Atrash shaykhs, dealt
among themselves with the daily business of the village, and
submitted their affairs to their own committees, elders' councils,
and so forth. The appropriated eighth of the shaykhs' lands

were distributed among the *falatiyya*, the landless. A verse from the local *diwan* also reports on these revolutionary events, naming completely unknown men without any rank.[109]

In the French consul's assessment of the situation, while the "social revolution" had not yet been achieved and the "feudal lords" were not yet defeated, popular demands had "progressed too far for a countermovement to be feared. The Turks have only to fold their arms and let events follow their due course until the day when the influence of the shaykhs has completely disappeared and the people, deprived of leadership and tied to the soil as proprietors, will not have any chance to resist the orders of the governor in Damascus."[110]

Ottoman troops had indeed seized the opportunity to penetrate farther than ever before into the highlands. Mamduh Pasha, the *mutasarrif* of Hawran with the rank of a brigadier general, undertook to restore law and order.[111] After heavy clashes with the rebellious Druzes, who had driven out their Atrash shaykhs to Damascus, the Ottomans brought back these shaykhs into the highlands and into their former positions.[112] The *'ammiyya* thus failed in this respect. But it put a halt to the arbitrary redistribution of the common lands. Half of the shaykhs' rights to land was appropriated. According to French statistics of the 1920s, the Atrash shaykhs held only one-eighth of the village lands in the south, as opposed to the traditional shaykhly quarter of the land in the north, where the *'ammiyya* had not extended.[113] Only the Atrash of 'Ara were excepted from the expropriation of rights because the local shaykh (who is also the poet), as an anti-Ottoman, had been favorably disposed toward the movement at the beginning and had kept his men out of the fighting. The Atrash branch of al-Suwayda' also failed to give up the quarter of the lands. In Dhibbin the Atrash shaykh used all kinds of tricks to get the expropriated rights to the quarter of the lands back.[114] This situation is reflected in the map of shaykhs' lands.

The practice of *musha'*, the redistribution of land, continued until the Mandate era. No oral account in the southern part of the highlands mentioned a complete halt to land redistribution. This means that they went on despite Ottoman *tapu* registration. The first registration was carried out in the rebellious south in 1894. In the appendix of his book, Hanna reproduces a *sened tapu* document, dated 2 Tishrin 1312, for Ibrahim al-Jarmakhani of the village of 'Urman.[115] This was one of the four rebel villages of the south, and Ibrahim al-Jarmakhani was one of the rebel leaders. The local *diwan* mentions the stabilization of land (that is, plots) for the year of 1895, when people started to build stone walls around their land.[116] Consular reports speak of land registration in 1896, after the Druzes had been badly punished by an Ottoman campaign, so it can be assumed that the cadastre took until then. A report of 1896 mentions the mocking answers given to the land officials in Druze villages, an old subversive device with which peasants had countered registration for centuries.[117]

COMMON LANDS UNDER THE FRENCH

When the French took over their Mandate in the 1920s, they conducted a survey of the highlands and the plain. Much like the Ottomans before them, they assembled the village elders and asked them a catalogue of standardized questions. This survey is housed in the Nantes archive. It clearly shows that the way land tenure was expressed, and probably organized, was the same as before the Ottoman *tapu* registration. A typical survey sheet would start with the name of the *nahiya* (subdistrict) and the village, list the main families and clans, the *chefs du village,* the *chefs religieux,* the important notables, and the number of inhabitants (according to faith), houses, prayer houses, shops (if any), warriors, and animals (horses, camels, mules, donkeys, sheep, and oxen). Then followed the land, in number of *faddans,* and land distribution (*répartition des terres*). A typical entry here would assign one-quarter to the shaykh (or one-eighth to the Atrash if it was an *'ammiyya* village), and the rest to the inhabitants. Or if the village was inhabited only by one clan, the names of the brothers would be given and how many *faddan*s they held. This was followed by a list of water wells and their location, antique ruins, grazing lands, and water and steam mills. The survey thus gives a rather faithful depiction of the political, social, and economic conditions of each village and the highlands as a whole in 1922 and served as the basis for the two maps in the appendix.[118]

But what were French policies with regard to *musha'*? Since so little work has been done on French land policies, it seems necessary (and also fruitful) to place the story of the common lands and the practice of *musha'* in a somewhat wider context. The reorganization of land tenure was "one of the first preoccupations of the high commissariat's services."[119] The grand architects of French land policies were Edouard Achard, the agricultural advisor to the High Commissioner, and M. C. Duraffourd, chief of the Survey Office and of Land Amelioration in Syria and Lebanon, a private concession and not a government department. Achard laid out his ideas and vision of Syrian agriculture in an unpublished, internal paper entitled "Notes agricoles sur la Syrie," dated 24 January 1924, and several published articles. The major goal emerging from these writings is undoubtedly the introduction of small proprietors of land, similar to those in France:

> La constitution de la petite propriété dont les effets sur l'amélioration des cultures et l'accroissement des rendements est indéniable doit être, en effet, le but vers lequel doit tendre la politique agraire.[120]

This required the dissolution of the great latifundia, the stabilization of the plots, and finally the dismemberment of the common lands. The order to be followed would logically be first the division of the "collective property" of the village community, next the partition of lands held in common by a single family, and then the dismemberment of the state domains, with the latifundia being the very last to be taken care of in this manner. This whole process would have to be underpinned by the cadastral survey, which would provide the titles so bitterly needed for the creation of the class of peasant smallholders, which was the ultimate goal of all these policies.

Achard thus joined the club of critical Mandate officials who unanimously indulged in long jeremiads against "the tenure so inimicable to good farming."[121] In 1925 he condemned the principle of "collective ownership" and the redistribution of lots on the grounds that a system of this kind hardly encouraged the peasant to intensify agricultural production and reduce its costs.[122] This attitude led to decree 171 of 10 March 1926, "Démembrement du Mouchaa":

> Considérant que la tenure en commun de la terre annihile les efforts individuels et nuit au développement de l'agriculture, stipule que les propriétés indivises seront démembrées et partagées entre les occupants, soit en conformité de l'accord intervenu entre les co-propriétaires intéressés, soit d'office, le partage et le lotissement étant effectués par la commission de délimitation et de recensement qui est instituée dans chaque Caza. Ces opérations sont exemptes de droits de succession et de partage.

This decree abolished the common lands *de jure* but was not widely enforced by the mandatary. It was amended by decree 1590 of 28 November 1929, which rendered the procedure compulsory if a majority of the villagers demanded it.[123] Land was to be (1) delimited, (2) identified, immobilized, and registered in the cadastre, and (3) legally inscribed into the land title register, *le livre foncier,* founded with decrees 186, 187, 188, and 189 of 15 March 1926. But the works of the cadastre went slowly, especially where *musha'* villages were concerned. Due to French meticulousness, there are a number of very detailed reports on *musha'* villages to be found in the Nantes archive—albeit not of the Hawran and its highlands but mostly of the Homs *qada'.* The following observations can be made: cases are reported where one member of the village community maintains that his lot is independently divided from the common lands of the *musha'* village, whereas the other villagers strictly deny this and maintain that his lot is still *musha'*.[124] *Musha'* was also reported from the Lattakia region and the Hama *qada'*. Here, in the village of Srehine, the nonirrigated *ba'l* lands were reportedly held "sous le forme 'Mouchaa' et sont soumises à un partage périodique entre les ayants-droits." The lands irrigated by three norias with water from the Orontes River, however, were partitioned into three farms (*zoors* in the French report) in divided, independent lots, which legally were *mulk,* by their owners.[125] For the *musha'* village of Helfaya (1,000 inhabitants) twelve clans were reported as holding the 47 faddans of the village. "Malgré titres de propriété indiquant parcelles divises," the report reads, "partage périodique entre les ayants-droits" made it still a *musha'* village. The same was true for Kafr Toum, Hama *qada'*:

> L'ensemble de terres du village est possedé suivant plusieurs titres de propriété [fixed shares], ces titres indiquent la division et paraissent s'appliquer chacun à un lieu dit [stabilized plots], bien que la situation de fait soit Mouchaa [i.e., redistributions took place].[126]

In 1935, Duraffourd penned a study in which he discussed the pros and cons of the common lands and the practice of *musha'*. The periodic redistribution of the lands, which characterized this form of land tenure, wrote the *régisseur du cadastre,* constituted a breach of the free exercise of the right to property. The social and economic repercussions of this breach were nefarious, since the shareholders enjoyed their holdings only for a limited time, which made it impossible for them to embark on any soil improvement or tree plantation and put them at a disadvantage when it came to loans from the agricultural bank.[127] To this problem, he went on, had to be added another one: that of the subdivision of the lands, which ended in excessive parceling and unreasonable dispersion. The disadvantages here lay in the loss of land for tillage, given the long and narrow stripes of field, and the loss of seed, dung, time, and money, given the dispersion of the plots. All in all this meant a loss of about 30 percent in efficiency: 10 percent due to time lost in moving about between the different strips, 10 percent due to loss of land, and 10 percent due to excessive seeding. Moreover, all cultivators were forced to follow the same rhythm of labor and sow the same kind of seed in the four or five corners of the common lands where they held plots. Therefore, Duraffourd prescribed the dismemberment of the plots of the common lands. This operation would consist in determining the rights of shareholders and then in the casting of lots, which was to be combined with a regrouping of the plots of each group of shareholders or each family. This would allow the preservation of the family or group character that was associated with working the common lands; the ties of interest that existed between the members of a family would be safeguarded and might even be strengthened and reconstituted due to the allotment of property in only one or two lots. This in turn would strengthen the family, destined to take the place of the community, which itself had succeeded the "primitive collective," the tribe or clan. Such an evolution thus would not disrupt the customs and traditions but would conform with them. It would protect the social cell on which society was based: the family. In one single operation the agrarian problem and the problem of the land would be solved.

It is quite extraordinary how Duraffourd's attitude to the common lands and the practice of *musha'* came to differ from that of his colleagues. In Transjordan, settlement of title was invariably accompanied by a division of the common lands into individual holdings. In Syria, the Survey Office under Duraffourd registered title to *musha'* quotas or lots, not to individual holdings, unless these already existed or unless there was a marked demand for it.[128] Especially after having found in the village surveys that the practice of *musha'* had gone on even when property titles had been granted by the Ottoman defterkhane, Duraffourd considered that "the practice of *musha'* [obviously] had a real basis in the social life of the country and should not be abolished."[129] His Bureau du cadastre, therefore, when establishing title to land in a *musha'* village, followed the practice of registering each villager's share in the common lands as a fraction of the total, without attaching the title to any specific piece of land. Rather than disregard the old practice that stood in the way of building up strictly individual private property, he tried to instrumentalize it for the creation of, eventually, small family farms. In effect, the old practice of *musha'* itself seemed to offer a remedy for the excessive parcellation of land and unreasonable dispersion if the state encouraged families to put their lots together and did not enforce individual registration.

In fact, there are a few reports in the Nantes archive of cultivators demanding "the government to intervene and distribute *musha'* lands among the shareholders so that everyone knew exactly which lot belonged to him."[130] But this kind of work progressed only slowly. In 1938, for example, 95 villages were delimited, among them a number of *musha'* villages, which amounted to 125,000 hectares and 44,262 individual properties. In 1939, 126 villages with 203,513 hectares and 31,686 individual properties were delimited.[131] But in all the reports and the maps accompanying them at times one region is conspicuously absent, and that is the Hawran. What place did the Hawran take in French land policies?

The question of the Hawran brings us back to politics. Nowhere in Syria did resistance against the French start earlier, and nowhere did it gain more momentum than in the south of Syria. In 1920, shortly after French troops had entered Damascus, a French officer was shot at a train station in the Hawran plain by a Hawrani villager, in the first political assassination attempt of the Mashriq. At that point in time, the Druzes, who had been courted by the first High Commissioner, Gouraud, helped the French put down the Hawran revolt. Most of the Hawran, in turn, remained neutral in the Druze revolt of 1925, which spread over wide parts of Syria. Like the Ottomans before them, the French clearly saw that it was in their interest to keep the two groups and regions apart. "There is no question of trying to reconcile them. We would not gain anything thereby," said one of their reports.[132]

While the French were careful not to interfere too much with
the village structures of the Hawran plain, including the practice
of *musha'*, the policies of a French captain in the highlands provoked the Druzes to rebel. These policies included the question
of land. The "notorious Carbillet," as he went down in the history of the Mandate, is generally seen as the proximate cause of
the Great Revolt of 1925. But he was, in fact, only a true embodiment of the contradictions of French Mandate policies.
Carbillet was an officer full of impatient energy, who had been
the only person to declare himself willing to serve in the Jabal
Druze and had even given up his pleasant post in Beirut to take
the assignment.[133] Carbillet had the burning ambition to use the
potential he saw in the Druze highlanders to make "his Jabal"
into a model colony. The kind of colonial modernization associated with such a project naturally interfered profoundly with the
tribal power structure of the Jabal society. Carbillet saw himself
as the representative of the people against their despotic
shaykhs. He had, as he put it later, "defended sixty thousand
Druze against twenty chiefs."[134] It was the Atrash shaykhs
whom he took on primarily and whose leading clan members
carried on a constant campaign against him in favor of an indigenous governor from their own ranks. Carbillet had used a political deadlock situation among the indigenous elite to become
governor himself, contrary to Franco-Druze stipulations. In
public speeches he referred to the *'ammiyya* against the Atrash
and praised the shaykhs who had taken an active role in it.

He supported peasants (he spoke of "le parti des agri-
culteurs")[135] in land distribution disputes with their shaykhs and
encouraged the planting of vines on newly claimed land (which
is to say, land that had been cleared of rocks).[136] In many villages
of the highlands, *musha'* had not been practiced for more than
twenty years. But the custom was still alive in the sense that villagers, or rather shaykhs, could demand a redistribution of lots,
which then had to take place. All kinds of conflicts between families, which had actually nothing to do with the land itself, could
provoke such a demand. Carbillet obviously sought to use these

occasions to strengthen the position of the peasants. In one of his reports he recounted the "partition of lands" in the village of Tira. All the notables of the village had demanded a new redistribution. The shaykhs of three leading families held half of the lands, the villagers (smaller families without any rank) held the other half. A commission of eight experts (two experts for each of the four quarters of the lands) had been set up, and a date had been set when the operation had to be finished. Carbillet inspected the location and ratified the partition. It was remarkable, he wrote, that in his presence the population elected several individuals for the commission that had not been proposed by the shaykhs. The peasants also demanded that lands where vines had been grown should not be redistributed, which he endorsed. It was to be noted, he wrote in the report, that the shaykhs often demanded new distributions only to get at the plots of peasants who had planted them with vines and had thus added value to them.[137] Now and then the reports also mention that dissatisfied parties dragged shaykhs before the tribunals to get land back.[138] Carbillet also encouraged the planting of fruit trees, another measure to have plots stabilized and exempt from redistribution. When collecting oral history in the highlands, I was often told that "the French were with the small people," especially when it came to land.

Carbillet would probably have gone to pains to apply Law 171 of 1926, which in fact prohibited *musha'*, but he was successfully ousted by the Atrash shaykhs of the highlands, who in the summer of 1925 unleashed their revolt against the Mandate. When the revolt was finally put down in 1927, the French were careful not to interfere with internal matters again. French rural policies of the 1930s and 1940s were exclusively geared toward the elite. In fact, Mandate policies followed a pattern all too familiar nowadays: reminiscent of many modern development projects, money and resources went into big irrigation projects, which were often not only inefficient but downright counterproductive. The history of the storage dam of Shahba is the story of such a failed development project.[139] With regard to *musha'*, the authorities encouraged the village communities to consider the last repartition as the final one or to proceed to a definitive, final one. Until 1931, most of the 118 village communities of the highlands had come to an understanding in this matter anyway. It was only in three villages that no agreement could be reached between shaykhs and peasants or between shaykhs themselves.[140] But it is indicative of the successful cooperation between the Druze elite and the Mandate authorities, seen in other fields as well, that the detailed reports on village lands, so painstakingly drawn up in other Syrian regions, were never even attempted in the Hawran, either plain or highlands. Indeed, when in 1936 the National Bloc came to power in Damascus and for a very short and troubled interval sent an urban nationalist as governor to the highlands, his office looked into the matter of the three villages and ordered that the Bureau du cadastre conduct a survey. The file is revealing. It states that indeed the *reconnaissance foncière* had been carried out by the *chef des travaux du cadastre* of Damascus, seconded by an inspector specializing in collective lands. Detailed reports of three villages—namely, Shahba, al-Suwayda', and al-Qurayya—had been established. Since "certain questions, however, necessitated a supplementary inquiry, especially with regard to the partition of lands," the reports cited above had been laid aside "until further information could be obtained."[141] I made an extensive search of all registers of the Bureau du cadastre, as well as many other files relating to both land and the Hawran. Neither these reports nor any other survey of the highlands after the initial survey of 1922 were found. All three of the above-mentioned villages (the three villages that had not come to an internal agreement on their common lands) were politically sensitive: al-Suwayda' was the capital of the Jabal and under Atrash dominance; al-Qurayya was the village of Sultan al-Atrash, the leader of the Great Revolt; and Shahba was the seat of the second most important clan of the highlands, the 'Amir family. Up until the land reforms in 1958 and 1963, the lands of the Hawran were not touched on again by any state authority.

CONCLUSION

The common lands and the practice of *musha'*, which have been the focus of this chapter, are certainly better documented in the Hawran highlands than in any other *musha'* practicing region as yet studied. Not only do we find the earliest description ever of the practice of *musha'*, we also find a regular peasant war erupting out of this practice or, rather, its abuse.

This is what *musha'*, according to my own findings, most notably represents: a custom or practice that is at the very base of the village community. *Musha'* is obviously not a function of economic progress, and its logic has to be sought in a realm other than economics. Land in *musha'* communities clearly is more than a means of production. It is rather the very expression of the community. A village is expressed in a given number of *faddan*s. In the Great Revolt, for example, the rebels in hiding demanded from the village communities provisions and ammunition. The ammunition was levied on the village per *faddan*.[142] This way of demanding tribute obviously followed the Ottoman model of taxation. Still, it expresses the village community in *faddan*s. An individual cultivator is also expressed in the number of *faddan*s he can work and, at the same time, the number of oxen teams he uses to work this land. To ensure that every original cultivator of the community receives the utmost justice in terms of the community's lands, open-ended redistribution is practiced. The earliest mention of this practice, Burckhardt's 1810 to 1812 description, puts it also clearly in the context of scarce population, abundance in land, an unstable settlement situation, and taxation. All this seems to suggest that *musha'* was a practice with a twofold mission. Externally, the mission was to establish and stabilize the village community in the face of government's demands for taxes that were levied on the community and in the face of outward dangers like Beduin encroachments, so common in frontier areas (the areas where *musha'* was almost exclusively found). Of equal importance, however, was its internal mission, the power this practice gave to assert adherence to the village (the territorial and communal principle), thereby counterbalancing the tendentiously disruptive force of adherence to the clan (the kinship principle). The practice of *musha'* (the periodical redistribution of lands) also has to be seen as a ritual in which the village community asserted itself through its council of elders and performed an act of judicial and political administration. This, and having the males of the community all work in one corner of the lands fully armed, meant security for the village. Practical agricultural necessities strongly suggested sowing the same crops in the four or five corners of the village lands. *Musha'* therefore also has a strong disciplining function. Clearly, the individual had to submit to the interest of the community. These issues thus tie into what has been termed the "common good" in Western political thought. There are no clear statements as to this common good, comparable to Aquinas's famous definition, to be expected in our case here. Nevertheless, the village community was a body politic, governed by firmly held notions of what was good, expedient and just. Given the strong tendencies to division and factionalism that are inherent in tribal clan structures, the practice of the common lands may even have been designed to forge the village community above petty clan interests, even if the shares to the village lands were held clanwise. All rain-fed frontier areas featured definite tribal traits in the sociopolitical organization of the rural population, and these were the areas where *musha'* prevailed.

To be entitled to a share of the common lands, however tiny this share might be, validated a person as a real member of the community. A *sahm*, therefore, was also something like a membership card, like the coveted Harvard card (or any other university card), for example, which establishes a person as a member of the community with rights of access to the libraries and faculty club. The landless in this sense were not only poor, but they were also not real members of the village community, a fact that emerges from the *'ammiyya*, when shareholders fought to be recognized as coproprietors of the common lands and real members of the community, and the landless fought for a share of these rights. This also helps to explain why emigrants from *musha'* villages in this century clung so determinedly to their *sahm*s, even if these gave them access to no more than tiny pieces of land. To give up the *sahm* would mean to give up membership in the village community. In times when tilling the land was no longer a means of earning a living, membership was still important.

But before this discussion is termed too romantic, it should be pointed out again that the notion of the common lands and common good serves to curb the ambitions of the individual member of the village community. In fact, this is what the notion of the common good is all about: the French sources unveil clearly the pressure brought against individuals who wished to break away from the custom. Social envy is to be seen as an important constituent in these tightly knit communities. But again, this tight social structure hints back to a not so distant past, when it was needed for the survival and success of these communities. The old maxim of *himayat al-ard,* the protection of, or rather, the clinging to the land, so utterly politicized (and discredited) by the Arab-Israeli conflict, had a real base.[143] Up until this very day, people strongly disapprove of individuals selling their land in the villages of the Hawran. Contemporary village descriptions during my fieldwork were often accompanied by the very critical remark that people of a given village had either recently or even some time ago sold land to people from other villages. This was considered as bad, amoral, and weakening the community and thus also refers back to the disciplining function of *musha'.*

While the rationale behind *musha'* is not primarily economic, a cost-benefit factor seems to be involved. The fact that the practice of *musha'* was abandoned in the northern, rugged part of the highlands within fifty years suggests that it is abandoned once stability of settlement is reached, when villagers intimately know the lands and community is established, and when the costs (time and effort) compare unfavorably with the results. It seems to be upheld, at least as a possibility to be demanded, when the costs of redistribution are smaller than the expected benefits, which in the course of time seem to take on more mundane and even pure power traits, such as settling disputes or simply robbing others of the fruits of their labor. One aspect of *musha'* surely is the reproduction of power vested in the village shaykh and elders who carry out this practice in the name of the common good of the village. It is also indicative of the strength of these notions that abuse is not tolerated endlessly and that the reconstitution of the common good is again expressed in the idiom of the common lands: to curb the ambitions of the shaykhs, their share of access to the village lands was cut back by half in the *'ammiyya*.

It is important to note that all this coexisted with Ottoman law. The practice of *musha'* even continued after Ottoman land registration. While this registration seemed to help stabilize the plots, expressed in the villagers' building walls around their fields, *musha'* continued to exist in theory. The practice of *musha'*, a new redistribution, could still be demanded, and the last recorded redistribution of village lands took place in 1925. Distributions of the old communal grazing lands, called *musha'* in the highlands, were carried out until recently. We don't seem to know anything about Ottoman perceptions of this practice. But we do know French perceptions of *musha'*, and here it is indeed important that Duraffourd, in charge of registration, gave *musha'* the credit of being deeply rooted in the social structure of the villages that followed this custom and tried to instrumentalize it for the ultimate goal of French colonial land policies: the creation of the small landholding family.

To sum up, the question that poses itself now is the following: is the story of *musha'* in the Hawran highlands typical, exceptional or only exceptionally well documented? Due to their turbulent history, the case of the highlands is certainly exceptionally well documented. Rural landlords living within the community and acting as tax farmers, like the shaykhs in the highlands, certainly did occur only rarely. For all we know, this kind of manorial *musha'* then seems to have been the exception, not the rule. The Hawran plain did know *musha'* in its general and more equalized form: shaykhs did not have more rights to access to the common lands than the other villagers. Land thus expresses the more stratified tribal structure of Druze social organization. But the Druzes, immigrating from Lebanon, where *musha'* was not recorded, did not seem to bring the custom with them. Rather, it seems that it was practiced by the people who already lived in the region and was adapted by the Druzes to their specific society. This argument, however, has to remain speculative, since we simply do not know enough about the historicity of *musha'*. But what can be deduced from the case of the Druze highlands and its specific form of common lands is, again, that we are dealing here with a sociopolitical practice designed to express and enforce community and foster the common good. This applies all the more to cases that were even more community oriented in that they did not grant their elite an extra share of their common lands, as was the case in the villages of the Hawran plain.

But the question is also raised as to what kind of sources we should study. Clearly, cadasters and registers alone do not tell us much about what *musha'* is all about, whereas oral history narrative sources, and also the political analyses of the powers legislating the common lands, taken together, can paint a colorful picture of this custom—which, again, should be viewed not so much as a category of land but as a sociopolitical practice contested by different forces and adapting over time. This view also explains the longevity of the practice: it faded away only when superseded by more differentiated forms of political organization, conflict resolution, and identity construction in rural communities, as with the beginnings of parties, unions, and, later on, rural associations in the 1930s and 1940s.

ACKNOWLEDGMENTS

The field research for this chapter was undertaken in 1990, 1991, 1992, 1993, and 1996 and generously funded by the German Research Association through the Graduiertenkolleg on the Modern Middle East at the Universities of Erlangen-Nuremberg and Bamberg. Many people have discussed the problem of *musha'* and the common lands with me. Among them, I wish to thank first of all the men and women of the villages of the Hawran, plain and highlands, who so generously hosted me in their *madafas* and shared their time and memories with me. I also wish to express my gratitude to my mother, Erika Schäbler, whose presence in a critical phase of my fieldwork allowed me to conquer patriarchal territory so freely and respectably and whose interest in all things rural may well have inspired mine. I benefited from discussions with Abdallah Hanna, Wolf-Dietrich Huetteroth, Martha Mundy, Abdul-Karim Rafeq, and Eugen Wirth. The chapter was written during my visiting fellowship at the Center for Middle Eastern Studies at Harvard in the spring of 1998. I wish to thank the director of the center, Roger Owen, for including it in the present volume.

NOTES

1. Probably the most faithful account is André Latron, *La vie rurale en Syrie et au Liban* (Beirut: Institut français de Damas, 1936); more ideologically tinted by the European model of development is Jacques Weulersse, *Paysans de Syrie et du Proche Orient* (Paris: Gallimard, 1946); other studies include Paul Klat, "Musha' Holdings and Land Fragmentation in Syria," *Middle East Economic Papers* (1957): 12–33; and "The Origins of Land Ownership in Syria," *Middle East Economic Papers* (1958): 51–66.

2. This position was taken most explicitly and in a much wider framework by Tosun Aricanli and Mara Thomas, "Sidestepping Capitalism: On the Ottoman Road to Elsewhere," *Journal of Historical Sociology* 7, no. 1 (1994): 25–48. On the emphasis of the universality of peasant society as opposed to an imperial tradition (of "free" peasants), see Halil Berktay, "Three Empires and the Societies They Governed: Iran, India and the Ottoman

Empire," in *New Approaches to State and Peasant in Ottoman History*, ed. Halil Berktay and Suraiya Faroqhi (London: Cass, 1992).

3. Ya'akov Firestone, "The Land-Equalizing Musha'-Village: A Reassessment," in *Ottoman Palestine 1800–1914: Studies in Economic and Social History*, ed. Gad G. Gilbar (Leiden: Brill, 1990), and Martha Mundy, "La propriété dite musha' en Syrie: une note analytique à propos les travaux de Ya'akov Firestone," *Revue du Monde Musulman et de la Méditerrannée* 79–80, nos. 1–2 (1996): 267–81. Earlier works of these authors on this subject include Ya'akov Firestone, "Crop-Sharing Economics in Mandatory Palestine," *Middle Eastern Studies* 11, no. 1 (1975): 3–23 (pt. 1) and no. 2 (1975): 175–194 (pt. 2); "Production and Trade in an Islamic Context: *Sharika* Contracts in the Transitional Economy of Northern Samaria, 1853–1943," *International Journal of Middle East Studies* 6 (1975): 185–209, 308–324; Martha Mundy, "Shareholders and the State: Representing the Village in the Late Nineteenth-Century Land Registers of the Southern Hawran," in *The Syrian Land in the Eighteenth and Nineteenth Centuries*, ed. Thomas Philipp (Stuttgart: Franz Steiner, 1992), 217–38; "Village Land and Individual Title: Musha' and Ottoman Land Registration in the 'Ajlun District," in *Village, Steppe and State: The Social Origins of Modern Jordan*, ed. Eugene Rogan and Tariq Tell (London: British Academic Press, 1994), 58–79; "Qada' 'Ajlun in the Late Nineteenth Century: Interpreting a Region from the Ottoman Land Registers," *Levant* 28 (1996): 79–97.

4. On the common good in the Western tradition, see Peter N. Miller, *Defining the Common Good* (Cambridge: Cambridge University Press, 1994), introduction. On a more general use of the notion, which experiences a revival in the thought of the communitarians, see Amitai Etzioni, *Rights and the Common Good: The Communitarian Perspective* (New York: St. Martin's Press, 1995). On the great and little tradition in Islam, see Talal Asad, *The Idea of an Anthropology of Islam*, Occasional Papers Series (Washington, D.C.: Center for Contemporary Arab Studies, Georgetown University, 1986).

5. Latron, *La vie rurale*, 184; Weulersse, *Paysans*, 108.

6. Wolf-Dieter Hütteroth, "Die Bedeutung kollektiver und individueller Landnahme für die Ausbildung von Streifen- und Blockfluren im Nahen Osten," in *Geographische Zeitschrift: Beitraege zur Genese der Siedlungs- und Agrarlandschaft in Europa* (Wiesbaden: Steiner, 1968), 85–93.

7. Wirth believes that in light of the research findings, it is most probable that the *musha'* system established itself in Egypt and the Levant countries during the reign of the Mamlukes, perhaps in the late thirteenth century Eugen Wirth, *Syrien: Eine geographische Landeskunde* (Darmstadt: Wissenschaftliche Buchges, 1971), 228.

8. See, for example, Mundy, "Shareholders," 231; Roger Owen, *The Middle East in the World Economy* (London: Methuen, 1981), 258

9. Norman Lewis, *Nomads and Settlers in Syria and Jordan, 1800–1980* (Cambridge: Cambridge University Press, 1987), 63, 221. For a more recent picture, see Owen, *Middle East,* 256–59.

10. Firestone, "Reassessment"; and Mundy, "La propriété dite musha'."

11. On the specific discourse of *al-Muqtabas* at this time, and its greater implications, see Birgit Schäbler, "Von 'wilden Barbaren' zur 'Blüte der Zivilisation': Zur Transformation eines Konzeptes und zur Neubewertung des frühen arabischen Nationalismus" (From "wild barbarians" to the "avant-garde of civilization": the transformation of a concept and a reappraisal of early Arab nationalism), in *Aneignung und Selbstbehauptung Antworten auf die europäische Expansion,* ed. Dietmar Rothermund (Munich: Oldenbourg, 1999).

12. *Al-Muqtabas,* no. 509, 27 October 1910: "ard al-qura fi Hawran musha' bi-yad ahliha fa-li-kull dar hissa li'anna ard al-qariya maqsuma 'ala-al-dur fa-laysa fi Hawran qarya li-rajul wahid tu'add milkan siwa"; also quoted in Mundy, "La propriété dite *musha',*" n. 1.

13. Firestone, "Reassessment," 103.

14. F. Le Play, *Les Ouvriers de l'Orient,* vol. 2 of *Les Ouvriers européens* (Tours: Mame, 1877), 307. The minuteness of the whole account strongly suggests that it is a literal translation from oral Arabic.

15. Eliyahou Epstein, "Le Hauran et ses habitants," *L'Asie française* 343 (September-October 1936): 247.

16. Mu'dad Hamad Qarqut, "Awda' 'ala al-tarikh al-iqtisadi wa-al-ijtima'i li-muhafazat al-Suwayda' wa-al-wada'a al-zira'i al-rahin" (thesis submitted for diploma in agricultural planning and administration, under the supervision of Dr. 'Abd Allah Hanna, Damascus University, 1988), p. 7. Unfortunately, this thesis also mixes local observations with sweeping generalizations on feudalism and other topics, taken from the literature. It may well be that this definition of *musha'* is influenced by European accounts. It is true, however, that none of the village elders I interviewed used the term *musha'* to describe the form of land tenure of their villages.

17. Mundy, "La propriété dite musha'," 281.

18. "Law and its Application in the Ottoman Empire," workshop of the Islamic Legal Studies Program, Harvard Law School, 17–19 April 1998. Martha Mundy probably has worked most on *sened tapu* registers, but she found them in land offices on the spot.

19. On an early scientific traveler see Birgit Schäbler, "Ulrich Jasper Seetzen (1767–1811): Jeveraner Patriot, aufgeklärter Kosmopolit und Orientreisender" (Ulrich Jasper Seetzen (1767–1811): Frisian patriot, enlightened cosmopolitan and traveler to the East), in *Ulrich Jasper Seetzen (1767–1811): Leben und Werk, Die arabischen Länder und die Nahostforschung im napoleonischen Zeitalter. Vorträge des Kolloquiums vom 23. und 24. September in der Forschungs- und Landesbibliothek Gotha, Schloss Friedenstein* (Gotha: Forschungs- und Landesbibliothek, 1995).

20. John Lewis Burckhardt, *Travels in Syria and the Holy Land* (New York: AMS Press, 1983), 97–100. Burckhardt spoke excellent Arabic, translated *Robinson Crusoe* into Arabic in Damascus, and was known and respected as Shaykh Ibrahim. After eight years of residency in the Near East, he died of an infectious disease. His travels were financed by the Association for Promoting the Discovery of the Interior Parts of Africa. See Dale F. Eickelman, *The Middle East: An Anthropological Approach* (Eaglewood Cliffs, N.J.: Prentice-Hall, 1981), 29 ff.

21. Wirth, *Syrien*, 409.

22. Pierre Gentelle, "Eléments pour une histoire des paysages et du peuplement du Djebel Hauran septentrional," in *Hauran I. Recherches archéologiques sur la Syrie du Sud à l'époque hellénistique et romaine*, ed. Jean-Marie Dentzer, 2 vols. (Paris: Geuthner, 1985–86), 1:35.

23. François Villeneuve, "L'économie rurale et la vie des campagnes dans le Hauran antique," in Dentzer, *Hauran I*, 1:80.

24. Calculated according to Hütteroth/Abdulfattah; Ulrich Jasper Seetzen, *Reisen durch Syrien, Palästina, Phönicien, die Transjordan-Länder, Arabia Petraea und Unter-Ägypten*, ed. F. Kruse (Berlin: n.p., 1854–59), 94.

25. Burckhardt, *Travels*, 97–100.

26. Ibid., 299f.

27. I was able to verify the stories he told about the Jabal events of 1860, and all the names, events, and places, in contemporary consular reports.

28. Haim Gerber, *Ottoman Rule in Jerusalem, 1890–1914* (Berlin: Schwartz, 1985), 208f.; Mundy, "Qada' 'Ajlun in the Late Nineteenth Century," 84.

29. *Dira'* (lower arm) is comparable to the ell, which according to Wehr's dictionary is 0.68 meter in Syria and was used as such in the highlands and the plain. The *marasa* (rope) is made up of a certain number of *dira'*s; it varies, however, from village to village. In 'Ara a *marasa* is 18 to 20 meters, and in Imtan in the southern highlands it is 32 meters, according to the inhabitants.

30. Bouron states that in 1927 a team of oxen were of equal status to a work horse (*qudaysh*) and to a mule (*bakhil*). Narcisse Bouron, *Les Druzes* (Paris: Berger-Levrault, 1930), 334.

31. Discussions with older peasants.

32. Bouron, *Les Druzes*, 334.

33. For a detailed description see Qarqut, "Awda'," 9ff.

34. Oral history: several interviews with Hamad Qarqut and his son Mu'dad, summer 1993.

35. In 1947 the first consolidation of farmland took place in Dhibbin: during the redistribution, the land was only divided into two sections with 36 *sahm*s. Oral history: interviews with Hamad Qarqut.

36. Source: Jadallah 'Izz al-Din al-Halabi, agrarian engineer with a university diploma, 28 September 1993, interview and correspondence. He was involved in the matter.
37. In the early 1980s, a similar operation was undertaken in the village of al-Kafr, but there the land was distributed solely among landless inhabitants.
38. This term probably stems from *jidhr* (root); what is meant is deep-rooted plants such as trees and vines; the verb *jadhara* means "to set root."
39. Burckhardt, *Travels*, 299.
40. Seetzen, *Reisen*, 94, 123.
41. Oral history: Hamad Qarqut. During the redistribution in 1885, the *jadhar*, which ran in a ring around the village, was not included. Thus the *jadhar* had become established by 1885.
42. Burckhardt, *Travels*, 461.
43. Qarqut, "Awda'," 9 ff.; also Bouron, *Les Druzes*, 334. Latron mentions that he had heard that in Jabal Hawran the *dunum* of the shaykh is larger than the *dunum* of the peasant. Latron, *La vie rurale*, 26.
44. For a good description and analysis, see Latron, *La vie rurale*, 11 ff.
45. Burckhardt, *Travels*, 295.
46. A clear distinction must be made between this *faddan* and another unit with the same name. This other *faddan* is found mostly in Egypt and, probably due to the larger amount of research on Egypt, is cited in some handbooks as being the only *faddan*, which can lead to confusion. The *faddan* used here is derived from the amount of work a peasant can perform with his team of oxen on one day and is given by Walther Hinz, *Islamische Masse und Gewichte* (Leiden: Brill, 1970), as being 5,306 2/3 square meters or 4,200.833 square meters in the nineteenth century.
47. Latron, *La vie rurale*, 16; Bouron, *Les Druzes*, 334f. Especially in the less spacious north of the Jabal, the *faddan* was (and is) expressed in terms of *mudd*; in the broad plains to the south with their much larger *faddan*, it is given in *dunum*s. Interviews with old peasants.
48. According to Latron the *dunum* was the official Ottoman unit of measurement for area. The metric system was introduced by the Ottomans in 1869 but was repealed in later years by various de-

crees. Evidently the traditional and the metric system existed simultaneously until well into the Mandate period. Latron, *La vie rurale*, 27 ff.

49. The *mudd* is comparable to a bushel and is actually a cubic measurement. The *mudd* of wheat traditionally made up 20 liters or 20 kilograms in the highlands; the *mudd* of barley was 14.5 kilograms. Bouron, *Les Druzes*, 334. Le Play gives for the year 1857 the mudd of the plain (Busra) as 14 litres. Le Play, *Les ouvriers de l'Orient*, 389.

50. Le Play, *Les ouvriers de l'Orient*, 393.

51. Druze inheritance practices do not follow conventional Islamic rules. The testator is completely free to do what he likes in his will, which in earlier times was made orally in the presence of the village shaykh or the chair (*ra'is*) of the religious *majlis*. However, the Druze did apply the following principle: "Alli warrathu bayyak, ilak wa li-khayyak" (What is left by your father is for you and your brother). The inheritance of *sahms* generally followed the principle of equality, even if the deceased failed to leave a will.

52. Salama 'Ubayd, *Al-thawra al-Suriyya al-kubra* (Beirut: Matbi' dar al-ghad, 1971), 110.

53. Burckhardt, *Travels*, 299.

54. Burckhardt, *Travels*, scattered indications; Salah Mazhar, "Al-thawra al-'ammiyya," unpublished manuscript, al-Suwayda", 1972, 7; 'Abd Allah Hanna, *Al-'ammiyya wa-al-intifadat al-fallahiyya (1850–1918) fi Jabal Hawran* (Damascus: Al-ahali li-al tiba'a wa-l-nashr wa-al-tawzi', 1990), 124; Sa'id al-Sughghayyir, *Banu Ma'ruf fi-al-tarikh* (al-Qurayya, Syria: Zayn al-din, n.d.), 402.

55. See the village study of Raymond Hinnebusch in his *Party and Peasant in Syria: Rural Politics and Social Change under the Ba'th* (Cairo: American University, 1979), 90f.

56. Burckhardt, *Travels*, 301. A *gharara* is a measurement based on surface area, not on weight. One gharara in 1812 in the Hawran is given by Burckhardt as 80 *mudd*, the *mudd* being equivalent to $4\frac{1}{2}$ *rotola*s, or $6\frac{1}{2}$ pounds.

57. Ibid.

58. Le Play, *Les ouvriers de l'Orient*, 323, 324.

59. See the detailed "income statistics" in ibid., 356.

60. Burckhardt, *Travels,* 306.
61. Ibid., 297; Le Play, *Les ouvriers de l'Orient,* 377.
62. *Falatiyya* comes from the word *faltan,* which means something like "hillbilly." For this information, I am indebted to 'Abd Allah Hanna.
63. Burckhardt, *Travels,* 297.
64. Le Play, *Les ouvriers de l'Orient,* 377; Epstein, "Le Hauran" 247.
65. Seetzen, *Reisen,* 61.
66. Discussion with Salman al-Khatib, born in 1900 in the Muslim village of Smad, bordering the highlands. He worked his way as a *murabi'* from the Druze highlands to Palestine and is now, with 300 dunums (30 hectares), *akbar fallah* (richest peasant) in his village. Interview on 23 August 1993; Burckhardt, *Travels,* 297 f.; Le Play, *Les ouvriers de l'Orient,* 378f. For more on the *muraba'a* contract, see also Latron, *La vie rurale,* 85.
67. See appended maps showing shaykhs' lands. Concerning the calculations, the hectare values are taken from the Office of Agriculture and Land Reform in al-Suwayda". They are not 100 percent accurate because surface conditions in the Jabal make measuring very difficult and not all land was measured. The *faddan* values originate from the French inquiry of 1922. Sample inquiries in villages in all four parts of the Jabal show that the oldest peasants of the village confirmed the *faddan* values given in the French inquiry, with only a few minor exceptions. For calculating the *dunums,* I relied on the assertions made by the officials in the Office of Agriculture and Land Reform, who also collected their data on the size and boundaries of the village land orally from the meetings of the village elders. I have assumed that the standardization of measures was made using the *dunum.* The *dunum* was established as being 919.30 square meters by the French Mandate power (Ordinance 186/87, 15 March 1926) and was later rounded off to 1,000 square meters. The hectare value divided by the *faddan* value yields the *dunum* value. This, in my opinion, is how the hectare value was originally derived in areas that had not been measured. My calculation of the *dunum* value was, with minor exceptions, in agreement with the data gathered in the sample inquiries. It must again be pointed out that, in the local way of thinking, the value of the *faddan* is not a function of its metric ac-

curacy. Rather, it says something about the organization of labor and is further expressive of the strength of individual villages in men and plows. The overall surface of the Jabal in the 1940s was, according to French measurements, 330,100 hectares, 180,000 of which were rain-tilled. These numbers also coincide with my calculations. Ministère des affaires étrangères, Nantes (MAEN) Beyrouth 2381; village descriptions; also National Archives and Record Administration, Records of the Department of State, College Park, Md., USA, 84/3247/7; letter from surveyor's office, al-Suwayda' 26 October 1987, giving the official hectare numbers of surveyed villages by that date, and handwritten list courtesy of the Office of Agriculture and Land Reform, giving the hectare numbers of all villages surveyed to date (September 1993). The two maps have to be read in conjunction; since not all of the land received enough rainfall to be tilled, the rest was used for raising cattle. The information about the cattle was also taken from the French survey of 1922. For a detailed account see Birgit Schäbler, *Aufstände im Drusenbergland: Ethnizität und Integration einer ländlichen Gesellschaft Syriens vom Osmanischen Reich bis zur staatlichen Unabhängigkeit* (Gotha: Perthes, 1996).

68. MAEN, Beyrouth, Constantinople, Guillois to Montebello, 2 March 1889; Barré de Lancyr to Hanotaux, 19, 21 July 1897, 16 September 1897.

69. For the Hawran plain see for example: MAEN, Beyrouth, Constantinople, Guys to Mouy, 17 December 1877; the punitive campaigns against the highlands were conducted in 1881, most brutally in 1896, and again in 1910. See Schäbler, *Aufstände im Drusenbergland* and "State(s) Power and the Druzes," in *The Syrian Land: Processes on Integration and Fragmentation in Bilad al-Sham from the Eighteenth to the Twentieth Century,* ed. Thomas Philipp and Birgit Schaebler (Stuttgart: Steiner, 1998).

70. MAEN, Constantinople, Guillois to Cambon, 11 July 1892.

71. MAEN, Constantinople, Guillois to Hanotaux, 27 November 1896; Politisches Archiv des Auswärtigen Amtes, Bonn, AA Türkei R 14024, Schroeder to Hohenlohe-Schillingsfürst, 19 February 1896.

72. Public Record Office, FO 195/1264, "Report of a Journey Made by Vice-Consul Jago of Damascus during May and June, 1879."

For another report of the miserable indebtedness of the plains, in contrast to the Jabal, see MAEN, Beyrouth, Constantinople, Correspondance, Giullois to Ribot, 25 April 1890.

73. Ingeborg Huhn, *Der Orientalist Johann Gottfried Wetzstein als preussischer Konsul in Damascus (1849–1861)* (Berlin: Schwarz, 1989); Linda Schilcher, "The Grain Economy of Late Ottoman Syria," in *Landholding and Commercial Agriculture in the Middle East,* ed. Caglar Keyder and Faruk Tabak (Albany: State University of New York Press, 1991), 195.

74. Stanford Shaw, "The Nineteenth-Century Ottoman Tax Reforms and Revenue System," *International Journal of Middle East Studies* 6 (1975): 421.

75. *An Economic and Social History of the Ottoman Empire 1300–1914,* ed. Halil Inalcik and Donald Quataert (Cambridge: Cambridge University Press, 1994), 2:855.

76. Ministère des affaires étrangères, Paris (MAEP), Correspondance politique des consuls, Giullois to Ribot, 25 April 1890.

77. Ibid.

78. Cf. the description of the process in MAEN, Constantinople, Correspondance, Giullois to Ribot, 25 April 1890.

79. The border villages between the highlands and the plains often called on the neighboring Druzes for protection against the Beduin; the shaykh in question then raised tribute (*khuwa*) or otherwise incorporated the village into his sphere of influence. At the end of 1878, for example, the shaykh of Salim, Muhammad Abu 'Assaf accepted such a call for help from the village of Izra' on the western edge of Laja'. He moved with his entourage into the village, took up residence there, and was confirmed in his new status as shaykh of Izra' by the district governor (*mutasarrif*). For Midhat Pasha, then governor (*wali*) of Damascus, this village was much too near the capital city of the *sancak* of Hawran, Shaykh Sa'd, and he ordered Abu 'Assaf to return to the highlands.

80. MAEN, Beyrouth 551, "L'affaire Oumm Waled"; French Mandate officials got themselves entangled in a debt affair that reached back to the end of the Ottoman empire. The detailed accounts (a succession of officers emphatically took the side of their respectice clienteles) reveal the money-lending pattern.

81. Several conversations in southern villages.

82. On this argument see Ridwan Muhammad Ridwan, "Al-haraka al-'ammiyya," in Hanna, *Al-'ammiyya*, 373–94, esp. 383 ff.

83. Hanna, *Al-'ammiyya*, 191 ff.

84. MAEP, CCP, Giullois to Ribot, 25 April 1890; stories of this sort in oral history interviews.

85. Conversation with Hamad Qarqut from Dhibbin.

86. Conversations in Imtan and Dhibbin.

87. Mazhar, "Al-thawra," 17; also quoted in Hanna, *Al-'ammiyya*, 186.

88. Hanna Batatu, *The Old Social Classes and the Revolutionary Movements of Iraq* (Princeton, N.J.: Princeton University Press, 1978), 469.

89. Salah Mazhar, "Al-thawra al-'ammiyya," unpublished manuscript, al-Suwayda', 1972, 18f; Haytham al-'Awdat, *Intifadat al-'ammiyya al-fallahiyya fi Jabal al-'Arab* (Damascus: al-Awdat, 1976), 55f; 'Abd Allah Hanna, *Al-'ammiyya wa-al-intifadat al-fallahiyya* (1850–1918) *fi Jabal Hawran* (Damascus: al-Ahali li-al-tiba'a wa-al-nashr wa-al-tawzi', 1990), 194.

90. Hanna, *Al-'ammiyya*, 194.

91. MAEN, Beyrouth, Constantinople, Correspondance, Giullois to Montebello, 14 March 1889.

92. Conversations with Hamad Qarqut; these views are also set out in his son's dissertation: Mu'dad Qarqut, "Awda'," 10.

93. Articles 3, 9, 36, 54–55, of the Ottoman Land Law of 21 April 1858/7 Ramadan 1274.

94. Mazhar, "Al-thawra," 29, who also offers the explanation for the verse that I have adopted.

95. MAEN, Constantinople, Correspondance, Giullois to Imbert, 29 June 1889.

96. Başbakanlık Arşivi, İrade, Meclis-i Masus, 4607, Petition of the *avam* (Ottoman term for *'amma*, common people).

97. MAEN, Constantinople, Correspondance, Giullois to Imbert, 29 June 1889.

98. Başbakanlık, İrade, Meclis-i Mahsus, 4607, Report of the *qa'immaqam* Ibrahim al-Atrash and the *mudir*, 30 September 1889/4 Safar 1307.

99. MAEN, Constantinople, Correspondance, Guillois to Montebello, 8 August 1889.

100. MAEN, Constantinople, Correspondance, Guillois to Montebello, 18 September 1889; letter of Father Jules Kersanté to Guillois from Najran, 19 August 1889.

101. MAEN, Constantinople, Correspondance, Guillois to Montebello, 26 November 1889.

102. Quoted from Juergen Brandt, "Die Politik des französischen Imperialismus in Syrien und Libanon vom Ende des 1. Weltkriegs bis zum Vorabend des grossen Volksbefreiungskrieges" (Diss. A, Leipzig, 1966), 112.

103. Cf. Hanna, *Al-'ammiyya*, 203.

104. MAEN, Constantinople, Correspondance, Guillois to Montebello, 7 May 1890.

105. Max Freiherr von Oppenheim, *Vom Mittelmeer zum Persischen Golf*, 2 vols. (Berlin: Reimer, 1899/1900), 170.

106. See also Hanna, *Al-'ammiyya*, 212.

107. Ibid.

108. MAEN, Constantinople, Correspondance, Guillois to Montebello, 7 May 1890.

109. Quoted in Mazhar, "Al-thawra," 3; also appears in Hanna, *Al-'ammiyya*, 212.

110. MAEN, Constantinople, Correspondance, Guillois to Montebello, 7 May 1890.

111. Başbakanlık, Irade, Meclis-i Mahsus, 4607, telegram of *qa'immaqam* Ibrahim al-Atrash, received on 10 October 1889/28 Eylül 1305; MAEN, Constantinople, Correspondance, Guillois to Montebello, 21 October 1889.

112. On the reasons for this policy, see Schäbler, "State(s) Power and the Druzes," 342f. and *Aufstaende im Drusenbergland*, 165f.

113. See the map showing the land of the shaykhs. In a few cases reference was also made to the *'ammiyya*: in the village Umm al-Rumman, for example, the inhabitants who provided the figures reported that the father of Salman al-Atrash had still owned one-fourth of the village, but half of that had been taken from him "at the time of Mamduh Pasha"; MAEN, Beyrouth, 2381; village descriptions.

114. Oral history: Hamad Qarqut.

115. Hanna, *Al-'ammiyya*, 343.

116. Mentioned in Mu'dad Qarqut, "Awda'," 8.

117. MAEN, Constantinople, Guillois to Montebello, 29 October 1896; compare Amy Singer, *Palestinian Peasants and Ottoman Officials* (Cambridge: Cambridge University Press, 1994), 37.

118. On the maps, see note 67 above.

119. Compare Noel Maestracci's chapter on "Le régime foncier" in *La Syrie contemporaine: tout ce qu'il faut savoir sur les territoires placés sous mandat français* (Paris: Charles Lavauzelle, 1930), 127–34, for an ideal account of how things were to be done "by the book."

120. MAEN, Beyrouth, 2377, E. Achard, "Notes agricoles sur la Syrie," 24 January 1924.

121. "It is doubtful if a tenure more inimicable to good farming and development could have been devised by any community." Walpole, director of lands and surveys, quoted by Lars Wahlin, "Occurrence of Mushaʿ in Transjordan," *Geografiska Annaler* 70 B, no. 3 (1988): 375.

122. MAEN, Beyrouth, 389, E.-C. Achard, "Propriété rurale et condition du cultivateur en Syrie," 6 March 1925, 13; also MAEN, Beyrouth, 2377, Achard, Notes agricoles sur la Syrie, 24 January, 1922.

123. See Louis Cardon, "Le régime de la propriété foncière en Syrie et au Liban" (doctoral thesis, Paris, 1932), 175; see also Mohammed Sarrage, "La nécessité d'une réforme agraire en Syrie" (doctoral thesis, Toulouse, 1935), 35 f. For an overview of land laws, see ʿAbd Allah Hanna, "Al-qawanin al-nazima li-al-muzaraʿa, 1874–1958," *Dirasat tarikhiyya* 43/44 (1992): 247–60. For a list of decrees and laws relating to land in Lebanon, see Masʿud Dahir, *Al-judhur al-tarikhiyya li-al-masʿala al-ziraʿiyya al-lubnaniyya, 1900–1950* (Beirut: al-Jamiʿa al-Lubnaniyya, 1983).

124. MAEN, Beyrouth, 365/3, Reconnaissance des villages, village Tiller, nahie Tarin, caza Homs.

125. Ibid.

126. Ibid. For this village a detailed list of shareholders is given; the 2,000 hectares of Kafr Toum were held by 25 persons, 19 males and 6 females, in 7,012 shares. The biggest shareholder held 2,415 shares, the smallest 28; all shareholders were members of the Tayfur clan. The cultivators for the lands were recruited from the neighboring villages.

127. M. C. Duraffourd, *Notice sur le démembrement et l'aménagement des terres "Mouchaa" possédées dans l'indivision collective, extrait de l'Etude sur les villages communautaires existants en Syrie.* Copy at Institut français d'études arabes de Damas, Fonds Henri Laoust (n.p: Régie du cadastre des Etats de Syrie et du Liban, 1935), 1. Also MAEN, Beyrouth 872, Travaux d'amélioration foncière des terrains agricoles.

128. Doreen Warriner, *Land and Poverty in the Middle East* (London: Royal Institute of International Affairs, 1948), 21.

129. Ibid., 91.

130. For example the monthly report of August 1921 in MAEN, Beyrouth, 2377.

131. MAEN, Beyrouth, 870, Rapport relativ aux travaux du cadastre et d'amélioration foncière effectués en 1938; 871, Rapport, 1939.

132. MAEN, Beyrouth, 551, Directives politiques, Tarrit to de Martel, 7 May 1935.

133. MAEN, Beyrouth, 1560, Schoeffler to Weygand, 7 June 1923. None of the French officers would voluntarily serve in the Jabal, a fact of which Carbillet frequently reminded his superiors. Even his official letters betray his zeal: they are seldom without multiple exclamation points and underlinings, in particular with the words "indispensable" and "urgent." Letters in MAEN, Beyrouth 982.

134. Capitaine Carbillet, *Au Djebel Druse. Choses vues et vécues* (Paris: Editions Argo, 1929), 22.

135. MAEN, Beyrouth 982, Bulletin de Renseignements, 2 May 1924.

136. France, Ministère des affaires étrangères, *Rapport à la Société des Nations sur la situation de la Syrie et du Liban* (Paris: Imprimerie nationale, 1925), 17.

137. MAEN, Beyrouth 1638, Bulletin de renseignements no. 18, 16 February 1925.

138. Ibid., Bulletin de renseignements no. 23, 25 February 1925.

139. Birgit Schaebler, "From Moroccan Formula to Colonial Development Aid: French Rural Policies in Southern Syria," paper presented at the workshop on Rethinking French Colonial Rule in Morocco and Syria, Middle East Studies Association Conference, Providence, Rhode Island, 1996.

140. Ministère des affaires étrangères, *Rapport à la Société des Nations sur la situation de la Syrie et du Liban* (Paris: Imprimerie nationale, 1926–1939); Cardon, "Le régime de la propriété foncière," 178f.; Yussof Samara, "Agrarverhältnisse Syriens," dissertation, Munich, 1938, 29.

141. MAEN, Beyrouth 870, Rapport relatif aux travaux du cadastre et d'amélioration foncière effectués en 1936, 129.

142. This stipulation was part of a rebel proclamation in 1926; MAEN, Beyrouth, 1638, Bulletin de renseignements, December 1926, annexe.

143. For a fine attempt to reconstruct Palestine beyond the Arab-Israeli conflict, see Beshara Doumani, *Rediscovering Palestine: Merchants and Peasants in Jabal Nablus, 1700–1900* (Berkeley: University of California Press, 1995).

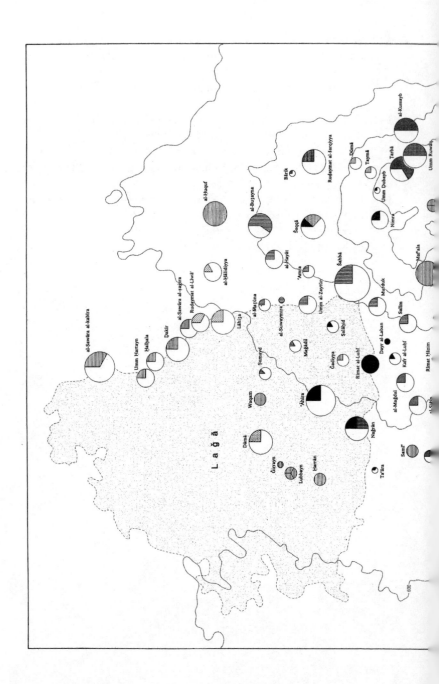

Landownership

first rank clans

Ḥalabī
ʿĀmir
Šalġīn
Qunṭār
ʿAzzām
Naṣr
Hunaydī
Abū Faḫr
Abū ʿAssāf
Qalʿānī
Saḥnāwī
Sallām
Naṣṣār
Darwīš
Kiwān
Aṭraš

pattern representing various smaller clans

rest of the lands, equally distributed among the other clans / families of the village

village lands

1–999 ha
1.000–1.999 ha
2.000–2.999 ha
3.000–4.999 ha
5.000–7.999 ha
8.000–12.000 ha

B. Schäbler 1994

al-Dibra
Tsʿīā
al-Ġūtba
Walġā
al-Ṣarhō
Sūʿrnā
Rufaydā
Sāʿr
al-Ḥarīsa
Bōsān
Sāla
Tīllīn
Abū Zarīq
al-Kafr
Maṣīd
al-Rahā
Sahwat al-Balāṭa
Hibrān
al-Afīna
Raṣṣāf
Karākir
ʿArā
al-Muġymir
Maydmikk
Sahwat al-Ḫidr
al-Qurayyā
al-Munaydra
ʿUrmān
Tall al-Lauz
Baham
al-Huwayyā
Qaysamā
Malah
Salbad
al-Mafqiq
Bakkā
Dibbīn
Umm al-Rummān
Ḥūt
ʿAzz
al-Ġāriyya
Ṣanntra
al-Muġayyir
Ḥirbat ʿAuwīd
al-ʿAnāt
Imtān

10 km

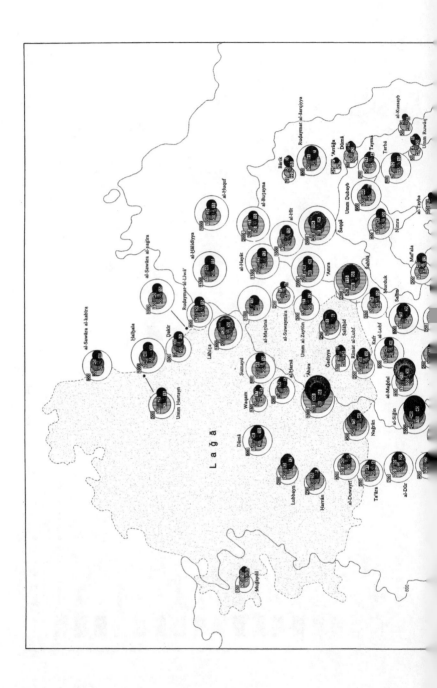

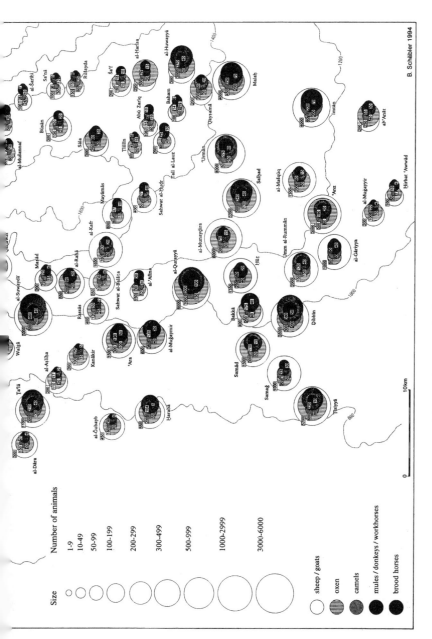

Livestock (in need of grazing land)

B. Schäbler 1994

Size   **Number of animals**

1-9
10-49
50-99
100-199
200-299
300-499
500-999
1000-2999
3000-6000

sheep / goats
oxen
camels
mules / donkeys / workhorses
brood horses

0   10 km

Bibliography

UNPUBLISHED MATERIAL

France

Ministère des affaires étrangères, Nantes. Beyrouth, 365/3, 389, 551, 870–872, 982, 1560, 1638, 2377, 2381; Beyrouth, Constantinople, Correspondance.

Ministère des affaires étrangères, Nantes, Fonds: Damas-Consulat, vols. 25, 29–30, 65; Alep-Consulat, vol. 27.

Ministère des affaires étrangères, Paris. Correspondance politique des consuls.

Germany

Politisches Archiv des Auswärtigen Amtes, Bonn.

Great Britain

Public Record Office, Colonial Office series 733.

Public Record Office, Foreign Office. 78/2259; 195/1264; series 371; 861/35, Aleppo.

Israel

Israel State Archives. RG 22, Land Registration and Land Settlement.

Jerusalem Sijill, vol. 35 #120.

Syria

Law Court Records, Damascus, Aleppo, Hamah

Turkey

Başakanlık Arşivi. İrade Meclis-i Masus, 2273/38, 4607; İrade-i Defter-i Hakani-2 MV 24225; Mühimme defteri #2, 134; #6, 59; #33, 315; Suriye Gelen-Giden, vols. 349–350; Şuraya-ı Devlet, 2273/38, 2884/ 31.

Tapu Tahrir Defter 16 (967/1560).

Topkapı Sarayı Arşivi: D-1511, D-3528/1, D-3642/23, D-4576, D-5262, D-961, E-7702, E-7816/8, E-7816/10, E-7816/1–11.

Türk ve İslam Eserleri Müzesi, document #2192.

United States

National Archives and Record Administration, Records of the Department of State, College Park, Md., 84/3247/7.

Theses and Dissertations

Brandt, Juergen. "Die Politik des französischen Imperialismus in Syrien und Libanon vom Ende des 1. Weltkriegs bis zum Vorabend des grossen Volksbefreiungskrieges." Diss. A, University of Leipzig, 1966.

Cardon, Louis. "Le régime de la propriété foncière en Syrie et au Liban." Doctoral thesis, Paris, 1932.

Fischbach, M. "State, Society, and Land in 'Ajlun (Northern TransJordan), 1850–1950." Ph.D. diss., Georgetown University, 1992.

Jorgens, Denise. "A Study of the Ottoman Land Code and Khedive Said's Law of 1858." Ph.D. diss., University of Chicago, 1995.

Qarqut, Mu'dad Hamad. "Awda' 'ala al-tarikh al-iqtisadi wa-al-ijtima'i li-muhafazat al-Suwayda' wa-al-wada'a al-zira'i al-rahin." Thesis submitted for diploma in agricultural planning and administration, under the supervision of Dr. 'Abd Allah Hanna, Damascus University, 1988.

Rogan, Eugene. "Incorporating the Periphery: The Ottoman Extension of Direct Rule over Southeastern Syria (Transjordan), 1867–1914." Ph.D. diss., Harvard University, 1991.

Samara, Yussof. "Agrarverhältnisse Syriens." Ph.D. diss., Munich, 1938.

Sarrage, Mohammed. "La nécessité d'une réforme agraire en Syrie." Doctoral thesis, University of Toulouse, 1935.

al-Zu'bi, M. S. "The Role of Agricultural Activity in the Household Economy: An Anthropological Case Study of Huwwara-Irbid" [in Arabic]. Master's thesis, Yarmouk University, Irbid, 1990.

Other

Fitzpatrick, Peter. "Consolations of the Law: Community and Deliberative Politics." Paper delivered at the workshop on Law and Deliberative Politics, Bielefeld, 26–27 February 1999.

Islamoglu-Inan, Huri. "Law, Property and State Power in the State Power in the Ottoman Empire." Unpublished manuscript.

Mazhar, Salah. "Al-thawra al-'ammiyya." Unpublished manuscript, al-Suwayda', 1972.

Owen, Roger. "The Role of *Musha'* (Co-ownership) in the Politico-Legal History of Mandatory Palestine." Paper prepared for the SSRC workshop on Law, Property, and State Power, Büyükada, 9–10 September 1992.

Schaebler, Birgit. "From Moroccan Formula to Colonial Development Aid: French Rural Policies in Southern Syria." Paper presented at the workshop on Rethinking French Colonial Rule in Morocco and Syria, Middle East Studies Association Conference, Providence, R.I., 1996.

PUBLISHED MATERIAL

Official

France

Ministère des affaires étrangères. *Rapport à la Société des Nations sur la situation de la Syrie et du Liban.* Paris: Imprimerie nationale, 1926–1939.

Great Britain

Cmd. 1540. *Palestine Disturbances in May 1921: Reports of the Commission of Inquiry with Correspondence in Relation Thereto. Presented to Parliament by Command of His Majesty, October 1921* [Haycraft Report]. London, 1921.

Cmd. 3530. *Report of the Commission on the Palestine Disturbances of August 1929* [Shaw Commission Report]. London, 1930.

Cmd. 3686. *Palestine: Report on Immigration, Land Settlement and Development* [Hope-Simpson Report]. London, 1930.

Cmd. 5479. *Palestine Royal Commission Report* [Peel Report]. London, 1937.

Colonial No. 133. *Palestine Royal Commission: Memoranda Prepared by the Government of Palestine.* London, 1937.

Colonial No. 134. *Palestine Royal Commission: Minutes of Evidence Heard by the Royal Commission at Public Sessions.* London, 1937.

Palestine

Government of Palestine. *A Survey of Palestine. Prepared in December 1945 and January 1946 for the Anglo-American Commission of Inquiry.* 2 vols. Jerusalem: Government Printer, 1946 and reprinted Washington D.C.: Institute for Palestine Studies, 1991.

Government of Palestine. Department of Development. *First Report on Agricultural Development and Land Settlement in Palestine,* by Lewis French, Director of Development. Jerusalem. 23 December 1931. [Letchworth, Herts.: Garden City Press, 1932?]

Government of Palestine. Department of Development. *Supplementary Report on Agricultural Development and Land Settlement in Palestine,* by Lewis French, Director of Development. Jerusalem: Government Printer, 1932.

Turkey

Salname Suriye. Vols. 8–18, 1293–1303 A.H.; 25, 1310–11 A.H.; 27, 1312–13 AH.

Books and Articles

Aberdam, Serge. *Aux origines du code rural, 1789–1900: Un siècle de débat.* Paris: Institut national de la recherche agronomique, 1982.

Abrams, Philip. "Notes on the Difficulty of Studying the State." *Journal of Historical Sociology* 1, no. 1 (March 1988): 58–89.

Abu al-Sha'r, Hind. *Irbid wa-jiwaruha (Nahiyat Bani 'Ubayd) 1850–1927.* Amman: Bank al-Amal, 1995.

Akgündüz, Ahmet. *Mukayeseli İslam ve Osmanlı Hukuku Külliyatı.* Diyarbakır: Dicle Universitesi Hukuk Fakultesi Yayınları, 1986.

Anderson, Perry. *Lineages of the Absolutist State.* London: New Left Review, 1976.

Aricanli, Tosun, and Mara Thomas. "Sidestepping Capitalism: On the Ottoman Road to Elsewhere." *Journal of Historical Sociology* 7, no. 1 (1994): 25–48.

Arnaud, André-Jean. *Essai d'analyse structurale du code civil français: la règle du jeu dans la paix bourgeoise.* Paris: Librairie générale de droit et de jurisprudence, 1973.

Arthurs, H. W. *Without the Law: Administrative Justice and Legal Pluralism in Nineteenth-Century England.* Toronto: University of Toronto Press, 1985.

Artin, Yacoub. *La Propriété foncière en Egypte.* Cairo: Imprimerie nationale du Boulaq, 1883.

Asad, Talal. *The Idea of an Anthropology of Islam.* Occasional Papers Series. Washington, D.C.: Center for Contemporary Arab Studies, Georgetown University, 1986.

———, ed. *Anthropology and the Colonial Encounter.* London: Ithaca Press, 1973.

al-'Asali, Kamil Jamil. *Watha'iq Maqdisiyya Tarikhiyya.* Amman: Matba'a al-Tawfiq, 1983.

Avineri, Shlomo. "Modernization and Arab Society." In *Israel, the Arabs and the Middle East,* edited by Irving Howe and Carl Gershman. New York: Quadrangle Books, 1972.

Baer, Gabriel. *Fellah and Townsman in the Middle East: Studies in Social History.* London: Frank Cass, 1982.

———. "Hikr." In *The Encyclopedia of Islam, New Edition. Supplement 1.* Leiden: Brill, 1982.

———. *A History of Landownership in Modern Egypt, 1800–1950.* London: Oxford University Press, 1962.

———. *Studies in the Social History of Modern Egypt.* Chicago: University of Chicago Press, 1969.

Bakhkhash, Na'um. *Akhbar Halab,* edited by Yusuf Qushaqji. Aleppo: Matba'a al-ihsan, 1985–1992.

Barakat, 'Ali. *Tatawwur al-milkiyya al-zira'iyya fi Misr wa-atharuhu 'ala al-haraka al-siyasiyya 1813–1914.* Cairo: Dar al-thaqafa aljadida, 1977.

Barkan, Ömer L. *Osmanlı İmparatorluğunda Zirai Ekonominin tabi olduğu Kurallar:* Burhaneddin Matbaasi, vol. 1, *Kanunlar.* Istanbul: Burhaneddin Matbaası, 1943.

———. *Türkiye'de Toprak Meselesi.* Istanbul: Gözlem Yayınları, 1980.

———. "Türk Toprak Hukuku Tarihinde Tanzimat ve 1247 (1858) Taribli Arazi Kanunnamesi." *Tanzimat 1.* Istanbul: Maarif Matbaasi, 1940.

Barkey, Karen. *Bandits and Bureaucrats.* Ithaca: Cornell University Press, 1994

Batatu, Hanna. *The Old Social Classes and the Revolutionary Movements of Iraq.* Princeton, N.J.: Princeton University Press, 1978.

Beik, William. *Absolutism and Society in Seventeenth-Century France: State Power and Provincial Aristocracy in Languedoc.* New York; Cambridge: Cambridge University Press, 1989.

Benda-Beckman, Franz von. *Property in Social Continuity.* The Hague: Martinus Nijhoff, 1979.

Bentham, Jeremy. *The Theory of Legislation,* edited by C. K. Ogden. London: Routledge and Kegan Paul, 1931.

Berktay, Halil. "Three Empires and the Societies They Governed: Iran, India and the Ottoman Empire." In *New Approaches to State and Peasant in Ottoman History,* edited by Halil Berktay and Suraiya Faroqhi. London: Frank Cass, 1992.

Bilici, Faruk, ed., *Le Waqf dans le monde musulman contemporain (XIXe–XXe siècles).* Istanbul: Institut français d'études anatoliennes, 1994.

Born, G. "(Im)materiality and Sociality: The Dynamics of Intellectual Property in a Computer Software Research Culture." *Social Anthropology* 14, no. 2 (June 1996): 101–16.

Bouron, Narcisse. *Les Druzes*. Paris: Berger-Levrault, 1930.

Burckhardt, John Lewis. *Travels in Syria and the Holy Land*. New York: AMS Press, 1983.

Carbillet, Capitaine. *Au Djebel Druse. Choses vues et vécues*. Paris: Editions Argo, 1929.

Cevdet Paşa, Ahmet. *Maruzat*, edited by Yusuf Hallaçoğlu. Turbe, Istanbul: Çağrı Yayınları, 1980.

————. *Tezakir*. Vol. 4, edited by Cavit Baysun. Ankara: Türk Tarih Kurumu Basımevi, 1986.

Chanock, Martin. "Paradigms, Policies, and Property: A Review of the Customary Law of Land Tenure." In *Law in Colonial Africa*, edited by Kristin Mann and Richard Roberts. London: James Currey, 1991.

Christelow, Alan. *Muslim Law Courts and the French Colonial State in Algeria*. Princeton, N.J.: Princeton University Press,1985.

Cin, Halil. *Osmanlı Toprak Düzeni ve Bu Düzenin Bozulması*. Istanbul: Boğaziçi Yayınları, 1985.

Cohen, Amnon, and Bernard Lewis. *Population and Revenue in the Towns of Palestine in the Sixteenth Century*. Princeton, N.J.: Princeton University Press, 1978.

Corrigan, Philip, and Derek Sayer. *The Great Arch: English State Formation as Cultural Revolution*. Oxford; New York: Blackwell, 1985.

————. "How the Law Rules." In *Law, State and Society*, edited by Bob Fryer et al. London: Croom Helm, 1981.

Cotterell, Roger. "Power, Property and the Law of Trusts: A Partial Agenda for Critical Legal Scholarship." In *Critical Legal Studies*, edited by Peter Fitzpatrick and Alan Hunt. Oxford: Basil Blackwell, 1987.

Cuno, Kenneth M. "The Origins of Private Ownership of Land in Egypt: A Reappraisal." *International Journal of Middle East Studies* 12 (1980): 245–75.

————. *The Pasha's Peasants: Land, Society, and Economy in Lower Egypt, 1740–1858*. Cambridge; New York: Cambridge University Press, 1992.

————. "Was the Land of Ottoman Egypt and Syria *Miri* or *Milk?* An Examination of Juridical Differences within the Hanafi School." *Studia Islamica* 81 (1995): 121–52.

Dahir, Mas'ud. *Al-judhur al-tarikhiyya li-al-mas'ala al-zira'iyya al-lubnaniyya, 1900–1950.* Beirut: al-Jami'a al-Lubnaniyya, 1983.

Deguilhem, Randi, ed. *Le Waqf dans l'espace islamique: outil de pouvoir socio-politique.* Damascus: Institut français de Damas, 1995.

Dirks, Nicholas. "From Little King to Landlord: Property, Law and the Gift under the Madras Permanent Settlement." *Comparative Studies in Society and History* 28 (1986): 307–33.

Donzelot, Jacques. *L'Invention du social.* Paris: Fayard, 1984.

Douin, Georges. *La Mission du Baron de Boislecomte. L'Egypte et la Syrie en 1833.* Cairo: Imprimerie de l'Institut français d'archéologie orientale du Caire pour la Société royale de géographie d'Egypte, 1927.

Doumani, Beshara. *Rediscovering Palestine: Merchants and Peasants in Jabal Nablus, 1700–1900.* Berkeley: University of California Press, 1995.

Drayton, Robert Harry, ed. *The Laws of Palestine.* London: Waterlow, 1934.

Duraffourd, C. M. *Notice sur le démembrement et l'aménagement des terres "Mouchaa" possédées dans l'indivision collective, extrait de l'Etude sur les villages communautaires existants en Syrie.* Copy at Institut français d'études arabes de Damas, Fonds Henri Laoust. N.p: Régie du cadastre des Etats de Syrie et du Liban, 1935.

Düzdağ, Ertugrul. *Şeyhülislam Ebussuud Efendi Fetvaleri.* Cemberlitas, Istanbul: Sule Yayınları, 1998.

Edelman, Bernard. *Ownership of the Image: Elements for a Marxist Theory of Law.* London: Routledge and Kegan Paul, 1979.

Eickelman, Dale F. *The Middle East: An Anthropological Approach.* Eaglewood Cliffs, N.J.: Prentice-Hall, 1981.

Eisenman, Robert H. *Islamic Law in Palestine and Israel: A History of the Survival of Tanzimat and Sharia in the British Mandate and the Jewish State.* Leiden: Brill, 1978.

Epstein, Eliyahou. "Le Hauran et ses habitants." *L'Asie française* 343 (September-October 1936): 244–54.

Ergüney, Hilmi. *Mecelle Külli Kaideleri.* Istanbul: Yenilik Basımevi, 1965.

Etzioni, Amitai. *Rights and the Common Good: The Communitarian Perspective.* New York: St. Martin's Press, 1995.

Farouk-Sluglett, Marion, and Peter Sluglett. "The Transformation of Land Tenure and Rural Social Structure in Central and Southern Iraq, c.1870–1958." *International Journal of Middle East Studies* 15 (1983): 491–505.

Faroqhi, Suraiya. "Agriculture and Rural Life in the Ottoman Empire (ca. 1500–1878): A Report on Scholarly Literature Published 1970–1985." *New Perspectives on Turkey* 1 (1987): 3–34.

———. *Pilgrims and Sultans: The Hajj under the Ottomans 1517–1683.* London: Tauris; New York: St. Martin's Press, 1994.

———. "Political Activity among Ottoman Taxpayers and the Problem of Sultanic Legitimation (1570–1650)." *Journal of the Economic and Social History of the Orient* 35 (1992): 1–39.

———. "Political Initiatives 'from the Bottom Up' in the Sixteenth and Seventeenth Century Ottoman Empire." In *Osmanistische Studien zur Wirtschafts- und Sozialgeschichte: In Memoriam Vanco Boskov*, edited by Hans Georg Majer. Wiesbaden: Harrassowitz, 1986.

———. "Political Tensions in the Anatolian Countryside Around 1600: An Attempt at Interpretation." In *Turkische Miszellen: Robert Anhegger: Festschrift, Armagani, Melanges,* edited by Jean-Louis Bacqué-Grammont et al. Istanbul: Editions Divit, 1987, 117–30.

———. "Towns, Agriculture and the State in Sixteenth-Century Ottoman Anatolia." *Journal of the Economic and Social History of the Orient* 33 (1990): 125–56.

Firestone, Ya'akov. "Crop-Sharing Economics in Mandatory Palestine." *Middle Eastern Studies* 11, no. 1 (1975): 3–23 (pt. 1) and no. 2 (1975): 175–94 (pt. 2).

———. "The Land-Equalizing Musha'-Village: A Reassessment." In *Ottoman Palestine 1800–1914: Studies in Economic and Social History,* edited by Gad G. Gilbar. Leiden: Brill, 1990.

———. "Production and Trade in an Islamic Context: *Sharika* Contracts in the Transitional Economy of Northern Samaria, 1853–1943." *International Journal of Middle East Studies* 6 (1975): 185–209 and 308–24.

Bibliography

Fischbach, M. "Al-Mukhayba Village: A Tale of Shaykhs, Efendis, Peasants, and Land in Transjordan." *Dirasat* 21, no. 1 (1994): 46–71.

Fisher, Stanley. *Ottoman Land Laws.* London: Oxford University Press, 1919.

Fleischer, Cornell. "The Lawgiver as Messiah: The Making of the Imperial Image in the Reign of Süleyman." In *Soliman le magnifique et son temps,* edited by Gilles Veinstein. Paris: La Documentation française, 1992, 159–77.

Foucault, Michel. *Michel Foucault: Beyond Structuralism and Hermeneutics,* edited by Hubert L. Dreyfus and Paul Rabinow. Chicago: University of Chicago Press, 1982.

———. "Omnes et Singulatim: Towards a Criticism, of 'Political Reason'." In *The Tanner Lectures on Human Values.* Vol. 1, edited by Sterling McMurrin. Salt Lake City: University of Utah Press, 1981, 225–54.

Frank, André Gunder. *Re-Orient: Global Economy in the Asian Age.* Berkeley: University of California Press, 1998.

Gatteschi, Domenico. *Real Property, Mortgage and Wakf According to Ottoman Law.* London: Wyman, 1884.

Genovese-Fox, Elizabeth. *The Origins of Physiocracy: Economic Revolution and Social Order in Eighteenth-Century France.* Ithaca: Cornell University Press, 1976.

Gentelle, Pierre. "Eléments pour une histoire des paysages et du peuplement du Djebel Hauran septentrional." In *Hauran I. Recherches archéologiques sur la Syrie du Sud à l'époque hellénistique et romaine,* edited by Jean-Marie Dentzer. 2 vols. Paris: Geuthner, 1985–86.

Gerber, Haim. *Ottoman Rule in Jerusalem, 1890–1914.* Berlin: Schwartz, 1985.

———. *The Social Origins of the Modern Middle East.* Boulder, Colo.: Lynne Rienner, 1987.

Goadby, Frederic M., and Moses J. Doukhan. *The Land Law of Palestine.* Tel Aviv: Shoshany's, 1935.

Gordon, Colin. "Governmental Rationality: An Introduction." In *The Foucault Effect: Studies in Governmentality,* edited by Graham

Burchell, Colin Gordon, and Peter Miller. London: Harvester Wheatsheaf, 1991.

Gran, Peter. *Islamic Roots of Capitalism: Egypt, 1760–1840.* Austin: University of Texas Press, 1979.

Guery, Alain. "Etat, classification sociale et compromis sous Louis XIV: la capitation de 1695." *Annales* 41, no. 5 (September–October 1986): 1041–60.

————. "Le roi dépensier: le don, le contraint et l'origine du système financier de la monarchie française de l'ancien régime." *Annales* 39, no. 6 (November-December 1984): 1241–69.

Guha, Ranajit. *A Rule of Property for Bengal: An Essay on the Idea of the Permanent Settlement.* Paris: Mouton, 1963.

Güran, Tevfik. "Osmanlı Imparatorluğunda Zirai Kredi Politikasının Gelişmesi, 1840–1910." In *Uluslararası Mithat Paşa Semineri: Bildiriler ve Tartışmalar.* Istanbul: Türk Tarih Kurumu Basımevi, 1984.

Habermas, Jurgen. *Between Facts and Norms: Contributions to a Discourse Theory of Law and Democracy.* Cambridge, Mass.: MIT Press, 1996.

————. *Legitimation Crisis.* Boston: Beacon Press, 1975.

————. *The Structural Transformation of the Public Sphere: An Inquiry into a Category of Bourgeois Society.* Cambridge, Mass.: MIT Press, 1989.

Hanna, 'Abd Allah. "Al-qawanin al-nazima li-al-muzara'a, 1874–1958." *Dirasat tarikhiyya* 43/44 (1992): 247–60.

————. *Al-'ammiyya wa-al-intifadat al-fallahiyya (1850–1918) fi Jabal Hawran.* Damascus: Al-ahali li-al tiba'a wa-al-nashr wa-al-tawzi, 1990.

Heffening, W. "Waqf." In *Shorter Encyclopedia of Islam.* Leiden: Brill, 1961, 624–28.

Heyd, Uriel. *Ottoman Documents on Palestine 1552–1615.* Oxford: Clarendon Press, 1960.

Hinnebusch, Raymond. *Party and Peasant in Syria: Rural Politics and Social Change under the Ba'th.* Cairo: American University, 1979.

Hinz, Walther. *Islamische Masse und Gewichte.* Leiden: Brill, 1970.

al-Hitta, Ahmad Ahmad. *Tarikh al-zira'a fi Misr fi ahd Muhammad 'Ali al-kabir.* [Cairo]: Dar al-ma'arif, 1950.

Huhn, Ingeborg. *Der Orientalist Johann Gottfried Wetzstein als preussischer Konsul in Damascus (1849–1861).* Berlin: Schwartz, 1989.

Hunayn, Jirjis. *Al-Atyan wa-al-dara'ib fi al-qutr al-Misri.* Bulaq, Egypt: al-Matba'a al-kubra al-amiriyya, 1904.

Hurewitz, J. C., ed. "Firmans Granted by the Sultans to the Viceroys of Egypt, 1841–73." In *Diplomacy in the Near and Middle East.* Princeton, N.J.: Van Nostrand, 1956.

Hütteroth, Wolf-Dieter. "Die Bedeutung kollektiver und individueller Landnahme für die Ausbildung von Streifen- und Blockfluren im Nahen Osten." In *Geographische Zeitschrift: Beitraege zur Genese der Siedlungs- und Agrarlandschaft in Europa.* Wiesbaden: Steiner, 1968.

Ibn 'Abidin, Muhammad Amin Ibn 'Umar. *Al-'uqud al-durriyya fi tanqih al-fatawa al-hamidiyya.* Bulaq, Dar al-tiba'a al-amira, 1854.

Imber, Colin. "The Ottoman Dynastic Myth." *Turcica* 19 (1987): 7–27.

Inalcik, Halil. "Adaletnameler." *Belgeler* 2, no. 3–4 (1965): 49–145.

———. "The Emergence of Big Farms, *Çiftliks:* State, Landlords and Tenants." In *Contributions à l'histoire économique et sociale de l'Empire ottoman,* edited by Jean-Louis Bacqué-Grammont and Paul Dumont. Louvain: Editions Peeters, 1983, 105–26.

———. "Islamization of Ottoman Laws on Land and Land Tax." In *Festgabe an Josef Matuz: Osmanik-Turkologie-Diplomatik,* edited by Christa Fragner and Klaus Schwarz with a foreword by Bert G. Fragner. Berlin: Schwarz, 1992.

———. "Sened-ı Ittifak ve Gülhane Hatt-ı Humayunu." *Belleten* 28 (1964): 603–90.

———. "Suleyman the Lawgiver and Ottoman Law." *Archivum Ottomanicum* 1 (1969): 105–38.

———. "Sultan Sülayman: The Man and the Statesman." In *Soliman le magnifique et son temps,* edited by Gilles Veinstein. Paris: La Documentation française, 1992, 89–103.

———. *Tanzimat ve Bulgar Meselesi.* Ankara: Türk Tarih Kurumu Basımevi, 1943.

———. "Turkish and Iranian Political Theories and Traditions in Kutadgu Bilig," and "State and Ideology under Sultan Suleyman I." In *The Middle East and the Balkans under the Ottoman Empire: Essays on Economy and Society.* Bloomington: Indiana University Press, 1993.

Inalcik, Halil, and Donald Quataert, eds. *An Economic and Social History of the Ottoman Empire, 1300–1914.* Cambridge; New York: Cambridge University Press, 1994.

Islamoglu-Inan, Huri. "Introduction" and "State and Peasants in the Ottoman Empire: A Study of Peasant Economy in North-Central Anatolia during the Sixteenth Century." In *The Ottoman Empire and the World Economy,* edited by Huri Islamoglu-Inan. Cambridge; New York: Cambridge University Press, 1987.

———. *Osmanlı İmparatorluğunda Devlet ve Köylü.* Istanbul: Iltesim Yayınları, 1991.

———. *State and Peasant in the Ottoman Empire: Agrarian Power Relations and Regional Economic Development in Ottoman Anatolia during the Sixteenth Century.* Leiden: Brill, 1994.

———. "Statistical Constitution of Property Rights on Land in the Nineteenth-Century Ottoman Empire: An Evaluation of Temettuat Registers." In *Constitution of Property Rights in Comparative Perspective,* edited by Huri Islamoglu. State University of New York, 2001.

Johansen, Baber. *The Islamic Law on Land Tax and Rent.* London: Croom Helm, 1988.

John, Michael. "The Politics of Legal Unity in Germany, 1870–1896." *Historical Journal* 28, no. 2 (1985): 341–56.

Jones, Eric L. *The European Miracle: Environments, Economics and Geopolitics in the History of Europe and Asia.* Cambridge: Cambridge University Press, 1981.

———. *Growth Recurring: Economic Change in World History.* Oxford: Clarendon; New York: Oxford University Press, 1988.

Kain, Roger J. P., and Elizabeth Baigent. *The Cadastral Map in the Service of the State: A History of Property Mapping.* Chicago: University of Chicago Press, 1992.

Kelley, D. R., and Bonnie G. Smith. "What Was Property? Legal Dimensions of the Social Question in France (1789–1848)." *Proceedings of the American Philosophical Society* 128, no. 3 (1984): 200–30.

Keyder, Çaglar, and Faruk Tabak, eds. *Landholding and Commercial Agriculture in the Middle East.* Albany: State University of New York, 1991.

Khalidi, Tarif. *Land Tenure and Social Transformation in the Middle East.* Beirut: American University of Beirut, 1984.

Khoury, Dina. *State and Provincial Society in the Ottoman Empire: Mosul, 1540–1834.* Cambridge: Cambridge University Press, 1997.

Kili, Suna, and Şeref Gözübüyük. *Türk Anayasa Metinleri.* Ankara: Ajans-Türk Matbaasi, 1957.

Klat, Paul. "Musha Holdings and Land Fragmentation in Syria." *Middle East Economic Papers* (1957): 12–23.

———. "The Origins of Land Ownership in Syria." *Middle East Economic Papers* (1958): 51–66.

Laqueur, Walter, ed. *The Israel-Arab Reader: A Documentary History of the Middle East Conflict.* Harmondsworth, U.K.: Penguin Books, 1969.

Latron, André. *La Vie rurale en Syrie et au Liban.* Beirut: Institut français de Damas, 1936.

Le Play, Frédéric. *Les Ouvriers de l'Orient.* Vol. 2 of *Les Ouvriers européens.* Tours: A Mame et fils, 1877.

Lewis, Norman. *Nomads and Settlers in Syria and Jordan, 1800–1980.* Cambridge: Cambridge University Press, 1987.

Locke, John. *Two Treaties of Government,* edited by Peter Laslett. Cambridge: Cambridge University Press, 1960.

Macpherson, C. B. "The Meaning of Property." In *Property: Mainstream and Critical Positions,* edited by C. B. Macpherson. Oxford: Blackwell, 1978.

Maestracci, Noel. *La Syrie contemporaine: tout ce qu'il faut savoir sur les territoires placés sous mandat français.* Paris: Charles Lavauzelle, 1930.

Maine, Sir Henry James Sumner. *Ancient Law.* London: John Murrray, 1920.

Mansur, As'ad. *Ta'rikh al-Nasira: min aqdam azmaniha ila ayyamina al-hadira.* Cairo: Matba'a al-hilal, 1934.

Marcus, Abraham. *The Middle East on the Eve of Modernity: Aleppo in the Eighteenth Century.* New York: Columbia University Press, 1989.

Mardin, Ebulula. *Medeni Hukuk Cephesinden Ahmet Cevdet Pasa.* Istanbul: Cumhuriyet Matbaası, 1946.

McChesney, R. D. *Waqf in Central Asia: Four Hundred Years in the History of a Muslim Shrine, 1480–1889.* Princeton, N.J.: Princeton University Press, 1991.

Meek, C. K. *Law and Authority in a Nigerian Tribe: A Study in Indirect Rule.* London: Oxford University Press, 1937.

Meinecke, Frederich. *Machiavellism: The Doctrine of Raison d'Etat and Its Place in Modern History.* London: Routledge and Kegan Paul, 1957.

Metcalf, Thomas. *The New Cambridge History of India, III.* Vol. 4, *Ideologies of the Raj.* Cambridge: Cambridge University Press, 1994.

Miller, Peter N. *Defining the Common Good.* Cambridge; New York: Cambridge University Press, 1994.

Mishaqa, Mikhayil. *Murder, Mayhem, Pillage and Plunder: The History of Lebanon in the Eighteenth and Nineteenth Centuries,* translated by Wheeler M. Thackston, Jr. Albany: State University of New York Press, 1988.

Mitchell, Timothy. "Making Space for the Nation State." In *Colonialism, Post-Colonialism and the Production of Space,* edited by D. Clayton and D. Gregory. Oxford: Blackwell, forthcoming.

———. "Society, Economy and the State Effect." In *State/Culture: State-Formation after the Cultural Turn,* edited by George Steinmetz. Ithaca, N.Y.: Cornell University Press, 1999.

Modarressi, Hossein. *Kharaj in Islamic Law.* London: Anchor, 1983.

Mundy, Martha. "La Propriété dite *musha'* en Syrie: une note analytique à propos les travaux de Ya'akov Firestone." *Revue du monde musulman et de la Méditerrannée* 79–80, nos. 1–2 (1996): 267–81.

———. "Qada' 'Ajlun in the Late Nineteenth Century: Interpreting a Region from the Ottoman Land Registers." *Levant* 28 (1996): 79–97.

———. "Shareholders and the State: Representing the Village in the Late Nineteenth-Century Land Registers of the Southern Hawran." In *The Syrian Land in the Eighteenth and Nineteenth Century,* Berliner Islamstudien, vol. 5, edited by Thomas Philipp. Stuttgart: Steiner, 1992.

———. "Village Land and Individual Title: Musha' and Ottoman Land Registration in the 'Ajlun District." In *Village, Steppe and State: The Social Origins of Modern Jordan,* edited by Eugene Rogan and Tariq Tell. London: British Academic Press, 1994.

Mundy, Martha, and Seteney Shami. Review of *Nomads and Settlers in Syria and Jordan, 1800–1980,* by Norman Lewis. *Journal of Peasant Studies* 16, no. 2 (1989): 292–4.

Mursi, Muhammad Kamil. *al-Milkiyya al-'aqariyya fi Misr watatawwuruhu al-tarikhi min ahd al-fara'ina hatta al-an.* Cairo: n.p., 1936.

al-Naqqash, Niqula, trans. *Min al-dustur al-jadid.* Beirut: al-Aba al-yasu'iyyin, 1873, 167–71.

Necipoğlu, Gülru. "The Süleymaniye Complex in Istanbul: An Interpretation." *Muqarnas* 3 (1985): 92–117.

Neocleous, Mark. *Administering Civil Society: Towards a Theory of State Power.* Houndmills, Basingstoke, U.K.: Macmillan Press; New York: St. Martin's Press, 1996.

North, Douglass C. *Structure and Change in Economic History.* New York: Norton, 1981.

Oestreich, Gerhard. *Neostoicism and the Early Modern State.* New York: Cambridge University Press, 1982.

Ongley, F., trans. *The Ottoman Land Code,* revised and annotated by Horace E. Miller. London: Clowes, 1892.

Oppenheim, Max Freiherr von. *Vom Mittelmeer zum Persischen Golf.* 2 vols. Berlin: Reimer, 1899/1900.

Ortaylı, Ilber. *Imparatorluğun En Uzun Yüzyılı.* Istanbul: Hil Yayınları, 1983.

Owen, Roger. *The Middle East in the World Economy.* London: Methuen, 1981.

Pamuk, Şevket. "Commodity Production for World-Markets and Relations of Production in Ottoman Agriculture, 1840–1913." In
Islamoglu-Inan, *The Ottoman Empire.*

Philips, Anne. *The Enigma of Colonialism: British Policy in West Africa.* London: James Currey, 1989.

Pottage, Alain. "The Cadastral Metaphor: Intersections of Property
and Topography." In *Statistical Constitution of Property Rights on
Land in Comparative Perspective,* edited by Huri Islamoglu. State
University of New York, 2001.

———. "The Originality of Registration." *Oxford Journal of Legal
Studies,* 15 (1995): 385–400.

Quataert, Donald. "Main Problems of the Economy during the
Tanzimat Period." In *150. Yılında Tanzimat,* edited by Hakkı
Dursun Yıldız. Ankara: Türk Tarih Kurumu, 1992.

Rafeq, Abdul-Karim. "City and Countryside in a Traditional Setting:
The Case of Damascus in the First Quarter of the Eighteenth Cen-
tury." In *The Syrian Land in the Eighteenth and Nineteenth Century.*
Berliner Islamstudien, vol. 5, edited by Thomas Philipp. Stuttgart:
Steiner, 1992, 312–23.

———. "Economic Relations between Damascus and the Dependent
Countryside, 1743–1771." In *The Islamic Middle East, 700–1900:
Studies in Economic and Social History,* edited by A. L. Udovitch.
Princeton, N.J.: Darwin Press, 1981, 653–85.

———. "Ghazza, dirasa 'umraniyya wa-ijtima'iyya wa-iqtisadiyya min
khilal al-watha'iq al-shar'iyya, 1273–1277 A.H./1857–1861 A.D." In
*Buhuth fi al-tarikh al-ijtima'i wa-al-iqtisadi li-bilad al-Sham fi al-'asr
al-hadith.* Damascus: n.p., 1985.

———. "The Impact of Europe on a Traditional Economy: The Case
of Damascus, 1840–1870." In *Economie et sociétés dans l'Empire
ottoman (fin du XVIIIe–début du XXe siècle),* edited by Jean-Louis
Bacqué-Grammont and Paul Dumont. Paris: CNRS, 1983, 411–32.

———. "New Light on the 1860 Riots in Ottoman Damascus." *Die
Welt des Islams* 28 (1988): 412–30.

Renner, Karl. *The Institutions of Private Law and Their Social Function.* London: Routledge and Kegan Paul, 1949.

Ridwan, Ridwan Muhammad. "Al-haraka al-'ammiyya." In *Al-
'ammiyya wa-al-intifadat al-fallahiyya (1850–1918) fi Jabal Hawran*

by 'Abd Allah Hanna. Damascus: Al-ahali li-al tiba'a wa-al-nashr wa-al-tawzi, 1990, 373–94.

Saltzman, Ariel. "An Ancien Regime Revisited: 'Privatization' and Political Economy in the Eighteenth-Century Ottoman Empire." *Politics and Society* 21, no. 4 (December 1993): 393–423.

Schäbler/Schaebler, Birgit. *Aufstände im Drusenbergland: Ethnizität und Integration einer ländlichen Gesellschaft Syriens vom Osmanischen Reich bis zur staatlichen Unabhängigkeit, 1850–1949.* Gotha: Perthes, 1996.

————. "Ulrich Jasper Seetzen (1767–1811): Jeveraner Patriot, aufgeklärter Kosmopolit und Orientreisender." In *Ulrich Jasper Seetzen (1767–1811): Leben und Werk. Die arabischen Lander und die Nahostforschung im napoleonischen Zeitalter. Vortrages des Kolloquiums vom 23. und 24. September in der Forschungs- und Landesbibliothek Gotha, Schloss Friedenstein.* Gotha: Forschungs- und Landesbibliothek, 1995.

————. "State(s) Power and the Druzes." In *The Syrian Land: Processes on Integration and Fragmentation in Bilad al-Sham from the Eighteenth to the Twentieth Centuries,* edited by Thomas Philipp and Birgit Schaebler. Stuttgart: Steiner, 1998.

————. "Von 'wilden Barbaren' zur 'Blüte der Zivilisation': Zur Transformation eines Konzeptes und zur Neubewertung des frünhen arabischen Nationalismus." In *Aneignung und Selbstbehauptung Antworten auf die europäische Expansion,* edited by Dietmar Rothermund. Munich: Oldenbourg, 1999.

Schacht, Joseph. *An Introduction to Islamic Law.* Oxford: Clarendon Press, 1964.

Schilcher, Linda Schatkowski. "The Grain Economy of Late Ottoman Syria and the Issue of Large-Scale Commercialization." In *Landholding and Commercial Agriculture in the Middle East,* edited by Çaglar Keyder and Faruk Tabak. Albany: State University of New York Press, 1991, 173–95.

————. "The Hawran Conflicts of the 1860s: A Chapter in the Rural History of Modern Syria." *International Journal of Middle East Studies* 13 (1981): 159–79.

————. "Violence in Rural Syria in the 1880s and 1890s: State Centralization, Rural Integration, and the World Market." In *Peasants and Politics in the Modern Middle East*, edited by Farhad Kazemi and John Waterbury. Miami: Florida International University Press, 1991, 50–84.

Schölch, Alexander. *Tahawwulat jadhriyya fi falastin: 1856–1882.* Amman: Matba'a al-jami'a al-Urduniyya, 1988. Arabic translation of *Palästina im Umbruch, 1856–1882: Untersuchungen zur wirtschaftlichen und sozio-politischen Entwicklung.* Stuttgart: Steiner, 1986.

Schumacher, Gottlieb. *Northern 'Ajlun: "Within the Decapolis."* London: Watt, 1890.

Seetzen, Ulrich Jasper. *Ulrich Jasper Seetzen's Reisen durch Syrien, Palästina, Phönicien, die Transjordan-Länder, Arabia Petraea und Unter-Ägypten*, edited by F. Kruse. Berlin: n.p., 1854–59.

Sewell, William. "Property, Labor and the Emergence of Socialism in France, 1789–1848." In *Consciousness and Class Experience in Nineteenth-Century Europe*, edited by John M. Merriman. New York: Holmes and Meier, 1979.

Seyitdanlıoğlu, Mehmet. *Tanzimat Devrinde Meclis-i Vala 1838–1868.* Ankara: Türk Tarih Kurumu Basımevi, 1994.

Shaw, Stanford J. "The Nineteenth-Century Ottoman Tax Reforms and Revenue System." *International Journal of Middle East Studies* 6 (1975): 421–59.

Shaw, Stanford J., and E. K. Shaw. *History of the Ottoman Empire and Modern Turkey.* Vol. 3, *Reform, Revolution and Republic: The Rise of Modern Turkey, 1808–1975.* New York: Cambridge University Press, 1977.

Singer, Amy. "The Mülknames of Hurrem Sultan's Waqf in Jerusalem." *Muqarnas* 14 (1997): 96–102.

———. *Palestinian Peasants and Ottoman Officials: Rural Administration around Sixteenth-Century Jerusalem.* Cambridge; New York: Cambridge University Press, 1994.

Stein, Kenneth W. *The Land Question in Palestine, 1917–1939.* Chapel Hill: University of North Carolina Press, 1984.

Stephan, F. H. "An Endowment Deed of Khasseki Sultan, Dated 24th May 1552." *Quarterly of the Department of Antiquities in Palestine* 10 (1944): 170–94.

Sugarman, David. "Law, Economy and the State in England, 1750–1914: Some Major Issues." In *Legality, Ideology and the State*, edited by David Sugarman. London: Academic Press, 1983.

al-Sughghayyir, Sa'id. *Banu Ma'ruf fi al-tarikh.* al-Qurayya, Syria: Zayn al-din, n.d.

Thompson, Edward P. "The Moral Economy of the English Crowd in the Eighteenth Century." *Past and Present* 50 (1971): 76–109.

———. *Whigs and Hunters: The Origin of the Black Act.* New York: Pantheon Books, 1975.

Thompson, Edward P., et al. *La guerrre du blé au XVIIIe siècle.* Paris: Les éditions de la passion, 1988.

Tribe, Keith. *Governing Economy: The Reformation of German Economic Discourse 1750–1840.* Cambridge: Cambridge University Press, 1988.

Tute, R. C. *The Ottoman Land Laws with a Commentary on the Ottoman Land Code of 7th Ramadan 1274.* Jerusalem: Greek Convent Press, 1927.

'Ubayd, Salama. *Al-thawra al-Suriyya al-kubra.* Beirut: Matbi' dar al-ghad, 1971.

Villeneuve, François. "L'Economie rurale et la vie des campagnes dans le Hauran antique." In *Hauran I. Recherches archéologiques sur la Syrie du Sud à l'époque hellénistique et romaine*, edited by Jean-Marie Dentzer. 2 vols. Paris: Geuthner, 1985–86.

Wahlin, Lars. "Occurrence of Musha' in Transjordan." *Geografiska Annaler* 70 B, no. 3 (1988): 375–79.

Walker, R. R. A. "The English Property Legislation of 1922–1926." *Journal of Comparative Legislation and International Law* 10, no. 4 (1928): 173–85.

"Waqfs and Other Institutions of Religious/Philanthropic Endowment in Comparative Perspective." *Journal of the Economic and Social History of the Orient* 38 (1995), special issue.

Warriner, Doreen. *Land and Poverty in the Middle East.* London: Royal Institute of International Affairs, 1948.

Washbrook, David. "Law, State and Agrarian Society in Colonial India." *Modern Asian Studies* 15, no. 3 (1981): 649–721.

Weulersse, Jacques. *Paysans de Syrie et du Proche Orient.* Paris: Gallimard, 1946.

Wirth, Eugen. *Syrien: Eine geographische Landeskunde.* Darmstadt: Wissenschaftliche Buchges, 1971.

Wittfogel, Karl. *Oriental Despotism.* New York: Vintage Books, 1981.

Yediyıldız, Bahaeddin. "Vakıf." In *Islam Ansiklopedisi* (19).

Yıldız, Hakkı Dursun, ed. *150. Yılında Tanzimat.* Ankara: Türk Tarih Kurumu, 1992

Young, George. *Corps de droit ottoman.* Oxford n.p., 1900–1906.

Contributors

Martin Bunton has been a Visiting Fellow at Harvard University and now teaches in the departments of history at Simon Fraser University and the University of Victoria. He is currently completing a book on the transformation of Palestinian property rights under British rule.

Huri Islamoglu teaches at Sabanci University, Istanbul. She is the author of *State and Peasant in the Ottoman Empire* (1994), editor of the *Ottoman Empire and the World Economy* (1987) and of *Constitutions of Property in Comparative Perspective* (2001). She is presently working on legal transformation as an aspect of modernity in the nineteenth-century Ottoman Empire, France, and China. She is also involved in research on regulatory practice and constitutions of the market in relation to the European Community and in post-socialist societies of eastern Europe.

Denise M. Jorgens received her doctorate from the Department of History at the University of Chicago in 1995. Her research has focused on a variety of topics in modern Middle East history. Currently, she is the Director of Programs and the International House at the University of Chicago.

Martha Mundy is a senior lecturer in anthropology at the London School of Economics. Her publications include *Domestic Government: Kinship, Community and Polity in North Yemen* (1995) and "The Family, Inheritance and Islam: A Re-examination of the Sociology of *fara'id* Law," in Aziz Al-Azmeh, ed., Islamic Law: *Social and Historical*

Contexts (1988). The article published in this volume forms part of a research project on "Property, Family and Administration: An Historical Anthropology of Islamic Jurisprudence and the Modern Ottoman State."

Roger Owen is the A. J. Meyer Professor of Middle East History at Harvard University. His books include *The Middle East in the World Economy* (revised, 1993) and *State, Power and Politics in the Making of the Modern Middle East* (revised, 2000).

Abdul-Karim Rafeq holds the William and Annie Bickers Professorship in Arab Middle Eastern Studies at the College of William and Mary. He was formerly Professor of Modern Arab History and chairman of the Department of History at the University of Damascus. He has written several books in Arabic, notably *The Arabs and the Ottomans 1516–1916* (second edition, 1993) and several articles in English on land tenure and the guilds in Ottoman Syria.

Birgit Schaebler has taught history and politics at the University of Erlangen-Nuremberg, Germany, and Duke University and is currently teaching history at Georgia College and State University. She published *Rebellions in the Druze Mountain: Ethnicity and Integration of a Rural Society in Syria from the End of the Ottoman Empire to Independence* (in German, 1996) and co-edited *The Syrian Land: Processes of Integration and Fragmentation in Bilad al-Sham from the Eighteenth to the Twentieth Century* (1998). Currently she is co-editing a volume on globalization and Middle Eastern societies, forthcoming with Syracuse University Press, and working on a cultural history of the colonial encounter between France and the Middle East.

Amy Singer is senior lecturer in Ottoman history in the Department of Middle Eastern and African History at Tel Aviv University. She published *Palestinian Peasants and Ottoman Officials* (1994) and her book, *Constructing Ottoman Beneficence: An Imperial Soup Kitchen in Jerusalem,* is in press at SUNY Press.

Index

HARVARD MIDDLE EASTERN MONOGRAPHS

1. *Syria: Development and Monetary Policy,* by Edmund Y. Asfour. 1959.

2. *The History of Modern Iran: An Interpretation,* by Joseph M. Upton. 1960.

3. *Contributions to Arabic Linguistics,* Charles A. Ferguson, Editor. 1960.

4. *Pan-Arabism and Labor,* by Willard A. Beling. 1960.

5. *The Industrialization of Iraq,* by Kathleen M. Langley. 1961.

6. *Buarij: Portrait of a Lebanese Muslim Village,* by Anne H. Fuller. 1961.

7. *Ottoman Egypt in the Eighteenth Century,* Stanford J. Shaw, Editor and Translator. 1962.

8. *Child Rearing in Lebanon,* by Edwin Terry Prothro. 1961.

9. *North Africa's French Legacy: 1954-1962,* by David C. Gordon. 1962.

10. *Communal Dialects in Baghdad,* by Haim Blanc. 1964.

11. *Ottoman Egypt in the Age of the French Revolution,* Translated with Introduction and Notes by Stanford J. Shaw. 1964.

12. *The Economy of Morocco: 1912-1962,* by Charles F. Stewart. 1964.

13. *The Economy of the Israeli Kibbutz,* by Eliyahu Kanovsky. 1966.

14. *The Syrian Social Nationalist Party: An Ideological Analysis,* by Labib Zuwiyya Yamak. 1966.

15. *The Practical Visions of Ya'qub Sanu',* by Irene L. Gendizier. 1966.

16. *The Surest Path: The Political Treatise of a Nineteenth-Century Muslim Statesman,* by Leon Carl Brown. 1967.

17. *High-Level Manpower in Economic Development: The Turkish Case,* by Richard D. Robinson. 1967.

18. *Rebirth of a Nation: The Origins and Rise of Moroccan Nationalism, 1912-1944,* by John P. Halsted. 1967.

19. *Women of Algeria: An Essay on Change,* by David C. Gordon. 1968.

20. *The Youth of Haouch El Harimi, A Lebanese Village,* by Judith R. Williams. 1968.

21. *The Problem of Diglossia in Arabic: A Comparative Study of Classical and Iraqi Arabic,* by Salih J. Al-Toma. 1969.

22. *The Seljuk Vezirate: A Study of Civil Administration,* by Carla L. Klausner. 1973.

23. and 24. *City in the Desert,* by Oleg Grabar, Renata Holod, James Knustad, and William Trousdale. 1978.

25. *Women's Autobiographies in Contemporary Iran,* Afsaneh Najmabadi, Editor. 1990.

26. *The Science of Mystic Lights,* by John Walbridge. 1992.

27. *Political Aspects of Islamic Philosophy: Essays in Honor of Muhsin S. Mahdi,* by Charles E. Butterworth. 1992.

28. *The Muslims of Bosnia-Herzegovina: Their Historic Development from the Middle Ages to the Dissolution of Yugoslavia,* Mark Pinson, Editor. 1994.

29. *Book of Gifts and Rarities: Kitāb al-Hadāyā wa al-Tuḥaf.* Ghāda al Hijjāwī al-Qaddūmī, Translator and Annotator. 1997.

30. *The Armenians of Iran: The Paradoxical Role of a Minority in a Dominant Culture: Articles and Documents.* Cosroe Chaqueri, Editor. 1998.

31. *In the Shadow of the Sultan: Culture, Power, and Politics in Morocco,* Rahma Bourqia and Susan Gilson Miller, editors. 1999.

32. *Hermeneutics and Honor: Negotiating Female "Public" Space in Islamic/ate Societies,* Asma Afsaruddin, editor, 1999.

33. *The Second Umayyad Caliphate: The Articulation of Caliphal Legitimacy in al-Andalus,* by Janina M. Safran. 2000.

34. *New Perspectives on Property and Land in the Middle East,* Roger Owen, editor. 2001.

Land was the major economic resource in the pre-modern Middle East. Questions of ownership, of access, of management, and of control occupied a central role in administration, in law, and in rural practice over many centuries. And changes in land regimes, such as those which took place in the nineteenth and early twentieth centuries were bound to have significant repercussions at all levels of society.

Nevertheless, the subject of land and property relations is still not well understood. It has also been bedeviled by a concentration on Islamic legal categories which often had little connection with property relations on the ground and by the assumption that the Middle East witnessed much the same passage from pre-modern to modern forms of property as is supposed to have taken place in Europe.

This study brings together contributions from six historians and one social anthropologist who have worked on the Middle Eastern land records and land ordinances themselves, from the 1850s to the 1930s. Their work not only challenges much of the conventional wisdom which still underpins historical thinking but also provides new and powerful insights into how the subject might be studied more fruitfully in the future.

CONTRIBUTORS INCLUDE

Martin Bunton, Huri Islamoglu, Denise Jorgens,
Martha Mundy, Abdul-Karim Rafeq,
Birgit Schaebler, Amy Singer

HARVARD CENTER FOR MIDDLE EASTERN STUDIES
CAMBRIDGE, MASSACHUSETTS 02138

ISBN 0-932885-26-8

9 780932 885265

90000

Cover design by Tim Jones
Cover art © Historical Picture Archive/Corbis